Statistics for Machir

Techniques for exploring supervised, unsupervised, and reinforcement learning models with Python and R

Pratap Dangeti

BIRMINGHAM - MUMBAI

Statistics for Machine Learning

First published: July 2017

Production reference: 1180717

Published by Packt Publishing Ltd.
Livery Place
35 Livery Street
Birmingham
B3 2PB, UK.
ISBN 978-1-78829-575-8

www.packtpub.com

Credits

Author
Pratap Dangeti

Reviewer
Manuel Amunategui

Commissioning Editor
Veena Pagare

Acquisition Editor
Aman Singh

Content Development Editor
Mayur Pawanikar

Technical Editor
Dinesh Pawar

Copy Editor
Safis Editing

Project Coordinator
Nidhi Joshi

Proofreader
Safis Editing

Indexer
Tejal Daruwale Soni

Graphics
Tania Dutta

Production Coordinator
Arvindkumar Gupta

About the Author

Pratap Dangeti develops machine learning and deep learning solutions for structured, image, and text data at TCS, analytics and insights, innovation lab in Bangalore. He has acquired a lot of experience in both analytics and data science. He received his master's degree from IIT Bombay in its industrial engineering and operations research program. He is an artificial intelligence enthusiast. When not working, he likes to read about next-gen technologies and innovative methodologies.

First and foremost, I would like to thank my mom, Lakshmi, for her support throughout my career and in writing this book. She has been my inspiration and motivation for continuing to improve my knowledge and helping me move ahead in my career. She is my strongest supporter, and I dedicate this book to her. I also thank my family and friends for their encouragement, without which it would not be possible to write this book.

I would like to thank my acquisition editor, Aman Singh, and content development editor, Mayur Pawanikar, who chose me to write this book and encouraged me constantly throughout the period of writing with their invaluable feedback and input.

About the Reviewer

Manuel Amunategui is vice president of data science at SpringML, a startup offering Google Cloud TensorFlow and Salesforce enterprise solutions. Prior to that, he worked as a quantitative developer on Wall Street for a large equity-options market-making firm and as a software developer at Microsoft. He holds master degrees in predictive analytics and international administration.

He is a data science advocate, blogger/vlogger (`amunategui.github.io`) and a trainer on Udemy and O'Reilly Media, and technical reviewer at Packt Publishing.

www.PacktPub.com

For support files and downloads related to your book, please visit www.PacktPub.com.

Did you know that Packt offers eBook versions of every book published, with PDF and ePub files available? You can upgrade to the eBook version at www.PacktPub.com and as a print book customer, you are entitled to a discount on the eBook copy. Get in touch with us at service@packtpub.com for more details.

At www.PacktPub.com, you can also read a collection of free technical articles, sign up for a range of free newsletters and receive exclusive discounts and offers on Packt books and eBooks.

https://www.packtpub.com/mapt

Get the most in-demand software skills with Mapt. Mapt gives you full access to all Packt books and video courses, as well as industry-leading tools to help you plan your personal development and advance your career.

Why subscribe?

- Fully searchable across every book published by Packt
- Copy and paste, print, and bookmark content
- On demand and accessible via a web browser

Customer Feedback

Thanks for purchasing this Packt book. At Packt, quality is at the heart of our editorial process. To help us improve, please leave us an honest review on this book's Amazon page at https://www.amazon.com/dp/1788295757.

If you'd like to join our team of regular reviewers, you can e-mail us at customerreviews@packtpub.com. We award our regular reviewers with free eBooks and videos in exchange for their valuable feedback. Help us be relentless in improving our products!

Table of Contents

Preface

Complex statistics in machine learning worry a lot of developers. Knowing statistics helps you build strong machine learning models that are optimized for a given problem statement. I believe that any machine learning practitioner should be proficient in statistics as well as in mathematics, so that they can speculate and solve any machine learning problem in an efficient manner. In this book, we will cover the fundamentals of statistics and machine learning, giving you a holistic view of the application of machine learning techniques for relevant problems. We will discuss the application of frequently used algorithms on various domain problems, using both Python and R programming. We will use libraries such as `scikit-learn`, `e1071`, `randomForest`, `c50`, `xgboost`, and so on. We will also go over the fundamentals of deep learning with the help of Keras software. Furthermore, we will have an overview of reinforcement learning with pure Python programming language.

The book is motivated by the following goals:

- To help newbies get up to speed with various fundamentals, whilst also allowing experienced professionals to refresh their knowledge on various concepts and to have more clarity when applying algorithms on their chosen data.
- To give a holistic view of both Python and R, this book will take you through various examples using both languages.
- To provide an introduction to new trends in machine learning, fundamentals of deep learning and reinforcement learning are covered with suitable examples to teach you state of the art techniques.

What this book covers

Chapter 1, *Journey from Statistics to Machine Learning*, introduces you to all the necessary fundamentals and basic building blocks of both statistics and machine learning. All fundamentals are explained with the support of both Python and R code examples across the chapter.

Chapter 2, *Parallelism of Statistics and Machine Learning*, compares the differences and draws parallels between statistical modeling and machine learning using linear regression and lasso/ridge regression examples.

Chapter 3, *Logistic Regression Versus Random Forest*, describes the comparison between logistic regression and random forest using a classification example, explaining the detailed steps in both modeling processes. By the end of this chapter, you will have a complete picture of both the streams of statistics and machine learning.

Chapter 4, *Tree-Based Machine Learning Models*, focuses on the various tree-based machine learning models used by industry practitioners, including decision trees, bagging, random forest, AdaBoost, gradient boosting, and XGBoost with the HR attrition example in both languages.

Chapter 5, *K-Nearest Neighbors and Naive Bayes*, illustrates simple methods of machine learning. K-nearest neighbors is explained using breast cancer data. The Naive Bayes model is explained with a message classification example using various NLP preprocessing techniques.

Chapter 6, *Support Vector Machines and Neural Networks*, describes the various functionalities involved in support vector machines and the usage of kernels. It then provides an introduction to neural networks. Fundamentals of deep learning are exhaustively covered in this chapter.

Chapter 7, *Recommendation Engines*, shows us how to find similar movies based on similar users, which is based on the user-user similarity matrix. In the second section, recommendations are made based on the movie-movies similarity matrix, in which similar movies are extracted using cosine similarity. And, finally, the collaborative filtering technique that considers both users and movies to determine recommendations, is applied, which is utilized alternating the least squares methodology.

Chapter 8, *Unsupervised Learning*, presents various techniques such as k-means clustering, principal component analysis, singular value decomposition, and deep learning based deep auto encoders. At the end is an explanation of why deep auto encoders are much more powerful than the conventional PCA techniques.

Chapter 9, *Reinforcement Learning*, provides exhaustive techniques that learn the optimal path to reach a goal over the episodic states, such as the Markov decision process, dynamic programming, Monte Carlo methods, and temporal difference learning. Finally, some use cases are provided for superb applications using machine learning and reinforcement learning.

What you need for this book

This book assumes that you know the basics of Python and R and how to install the libraries. It does not assume that you are already equipped with the knowledge of advanced statistics and mathematics, like linear algebra and so on.

The following versions of software are used throughout this book, but it should run fine with any more recent ones as well:

- Anaconda 3–4.3.1 (all python and its relevant packages are included in Anaconda, Python 3.6.1, NumPy 1.12.1, Pandas 0.19.2, and scikit-learn 0.18.1)
- R 3.4.0 and RStudio 1.0.143
- Theano 0.9.0
- Keras 2.0.2

Who this book is for

This book is intended for developers with little to no background in statistics who want to implement machine learning in their systems. Some programming knowledge in R or Python will be useful.

Conventions

In this book, you will find a number of text styles that distinguish between different kinds of information. Here are some examples of these styles and an explanation of their meaning. Code words in text, database table names, folder names, filenames, file extensions, pathnames, dummy URLs, user input, and Twitter handles are shown as follows: "The mode function was not implemented in the numpy package.". Any command-line input or output is written as follows:

```
>>> import numpy as np
>>> from scipy import stats
>>> data = np.array([4,5,1,2,7,2,6,9,3])
# Calculate Mean
>>> dt_mean = np.mean(data) ;
print ("Mean :",round(dt_mean,2))
```

New terms and important words are shown in bold.

 Warnings or important notes appear like this.

 Tips and tricks appear like this.

Reader feedback

Feedback from our readers is always welcome. Let us know what you thought about this book-what you liked or disliked. Reader feedback is important for us as it helps us to develop titles that you will really get the most out of. To send us general feedback, simply email feedback@packtpub.com, and mention the book's title in the subject of your message. If there is a topic that you have expertise in and you are interested in either writing or contributing to a book, see our author guide at www.packtpub.com/authors.

Customer support

Now that you are the proud owner of a Packt book, we have a number of things to help you to get the most from your purchase.

Downloading the example code

You can download the example code files for this book from your account at http://www.packtpub.com. If you purchased this book elsewhere, you can visit http://www.packtpub.com/support and register to have the files e-mailed directly to you. You can download the code files by following these steps:

1. Log in or register to our website using your e-mail address and password.
2. Hover the mouse pointer on the **SUPPORT** tab at the top.
3. Click on **Code Downloads & Errata**.
4. Enter the name of the book in the **Search** box.

5. Select the book for which you're looking to download the code files.
6. Choose from the drop-down menu where you purchased this book from.
7. Click on **Code Download**.

Once the file is downloaded, please make sure that you unzip or extract the folder using the latest version of:

- WinRAR / 7-Zip for Windows
- Zipeg / iZip / UnRarX for Mac
- 7-Zip / PeaZip for Linux

The code bundle for the book is also hosted on GitHub at `https://github.com/PacktPubl ishing/Statistics-for-Machine-Learning`. We also have other code bundles from our rich catalog of books and videos available at `https://github.com/PacktPublishing/`. Check them out!

Downloading the color images of this book

We also provide you with a PDF file that has color images of the screenshots/diagrams used in this book. The color images will help you better understand the changes in given outputs. You can download this file from `https://www.packtpub.com/sites/default/files/down loads/StatisticsforMachineLearning_ColorImages.pdf`.

Errata

Although we have taken care to ensure the accuracy of our content, mistakes do happen. If you find a mistake in one of our books-maybe a mistake in the text or the code-we would be grateful if you could report this to us. By doing so, you can save other readers from frustration and help us to improve subsequent versions of this book. If you find any errata, please report them by visiting `http://www.packtpub.com/submit-errata`, selecting your book, clicking on the **Errata Submission Form** link, and entering the details of your errata. Once your errata are verified, your submission will be accepted and the errata will be uploaded to our website or added to any list of existing errata under the Errata section of that title. To view the previously submitted errata, go to `https://www.packtpub.com/book s/content/support` and enter the name of the book in the search field. The required information will appear under the **Errata** section.

Piracy

Piracy of copyrighted material on the Internet is an ongoing problem across all media. At Packt, we take the protection of our copyright and licenses very seriously. If you come across any illegal copies of our works in any form on the Internet, please provide us with the location address or website name immediately. Please contact us at copyright@packtpub.com with a link to the suspected pirated material. We appreciate your help in protecting our authors and our ability to bring you valuable content.

Questions

If you have a problem with any aspects of this book, you can contact us at questions@packtpub.com, and we will do our best to address it.

1
Journey from Statistics to Machine Learning

In recent times, **machine learning** (**ML**) and data science have gained popularity like never before. This field is expected to grow exponentially in the coming years. First of all, what is machine learning? And why does someone need to take pains to understand the principles? Well, we have the answers for you. One simple example could be book recommendations in e-commerce websites when someone went to search for a particular book or any other product recommendations which were bought together to provide an idea to users which they might like. Sounds magic, right? In fact, utilizing machine learning, can achieve much more than this.

Machine learning is a branch of study in which a model can learn automatically from the experiences based on data without exclusively being modeled like in statistical models. Over a period and with more data, model predictions will become better.

In this first chapter, we will introduce the basic concepts which are necessary to understand both the statistical and machine learning terminology necessary to create a foundation for understanding the similarity between both the streams, who are either full-time statisticians or software engineers who do the implementation of machine learning but would like to understand the statistical workings behind the ML methods. We will quickly cover the fundamentals necessary for understanding the building blocks of models.

In this chapter, we will cover the following:

- Statistical terminology for model building and validation
- Machine learning terminology for model building and validation
- Machine learning model overview

Statistical terminology for model building and validation

Statistics is the branch of mathematics dealing with the collection, analysis, interpretation, presentation, and organization of numerical data.

Statistics are mainly classified into two subbranches:

- **Descriptive statistics**: These are used to summarize data, such as the mean, standard deviation for continuous data types (such as age), whereas frequency and percentage are useful for categorical data (such as gender).
- **Inferential statistics**: Many times, a collection of the entire data (also known as population in statistical methodology) is impossible, hence a subset of the data points is collected, also called a sample, and conclusions about the entire population will be drawn, which is known as inferential statistics. Inferences are drawn using hypothesis testing, the estimation of numerical characteristics, the correlation of relationships within data, and so on.

Statistical modeling is applying statistics on data to find underlying hidden relationships by analyzing the significance of the variables.

Machine learning

Machine learning is the branch of computer science that utilizes past experience to learn from and use its knowledge to make future decisions. Machine learning is at the intersection of computer science, engineering, and statistics. The goal of machine learning is to generalize a detectable pattern or to create an unknown rule from given examples. An overview of machine learning landscape is as follows:

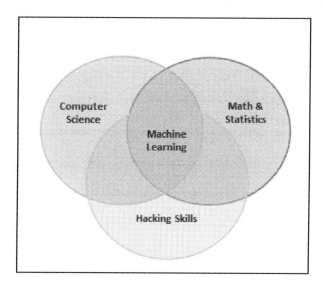

Machine learning is broadly classified into three categories but nonetheless, based on the situation, these categories can be combined to achieve the desired results for particular applications:

- **Supervised learning**: This is teaching machines to learn the relationship between other variables and a target variable, similar to the way in which a teacher provides feedback to students on their performance. The major segments within supervised learning are as follows:
    - Classification problem
    - Regression problem

- **Unsupervised learning**: In unsupervised learning, algorithms learn by themselves without any supervision or without any target variable provided. It is a question of finding hidden patterns and relations in the given data. The categories in unsupervised learning are as follows:
    - Dimensionality reduction
    - Clustering

- **Reinforcement learning**: This allows the machine or agent to learn its behavior based on feedback from the environment. In reinforcement learning, the agent takes a series of decisive actions without supervision and, in the end, a reward will be given, either +1 or -1. Based on the final payoff/reward, the agent reevaluates its paths. Reinforcement learning problems are closer to the artificial intelligence methodology rather than frequently used machine learning algorithms.

In some cases, we initially perform unsupervised learning to reduce the dimensions followed by supervised learning when the number of variables is very high. Similarly, in some artificial intelligence applications, supervised learning combined with reinforcement learning could be utilized for solving a problem; an example is self-driving cars in which, initially, images are converted to some numeric format using supervised learning and combined with driving actions (left, forward, right, and backward).

Major differences between statistical modeling and machine learning

Though there are inherent similarities between statistical modeling and machine learning methodologies, sometimes it is not obviously apparent for many practitioners. In the following table, we explain the differences succinctly to show the ways in which both streams are similar and the differences between them:

Statistical modeling	Machine learning
Formalization of relationships between variables in the form of mathematical equations.	Algorithm that can learn from the data without relying on rule-based programming.
Required to assume shape of the model curve prior to perform model fitting on the data (for example, linear, polynomial, and so on).	Does not need to assume underlying shape, as machine learning algorithms can learn complex patterns automatically based on the provided data.
Statistical model predicts the output with accuracy of 85 percent and having 90 percent confidence about it.	Machine learning just predicts the output with accuracy of 85 percent.
In statistical modeling, various diagnostics of parameters are performed, like p-value, and so on.	Machine learning models do not perform any statistical diagnostic significance tests.
Data will be split into 70 percent - 30 percent to create training and testing data. Model developed on training data and tested on testing data.	Data will be split into 50 percent - 25 percent - 25 percent to create training, validation, and testing data. Models developed on training and hyperparameters are tuned on validation data and finally get evaluated against test data.

Statistical models can be developed on a single dataset called training data, as diagnostics are performed at both overall accuracy and individual variable level.	Due to lack of diagnostics on variables, machine learning algorithms need to be trained on two datasets, called training and validation data, to ensure two-point validation.
Statistical modeling is mostly used for research purposes.	Machine learning is very apt for implementation in a production environment.
From the school of statistics and mathematics.	From the school of computer science.

Steps in machine learning model development and deployment

The development and deployment of machine learning models involves a series of steps that are almost similar to the statistical modeling process, in order to develop, validate, and implement machine learning models. The steps are as follows:

1. **Collection of data**: Data for machine learning is collected directly from structured source data, web scrapping, API, chat interaction, and so on, as machine learning can work on both structured and unstructured data (voice, image, and text).

2. **Data preparation and missing/outlier treatment**: Data is to be formatted as per the chosen machine learning algorithm; also, missing value treatment needs to be performed by replacing missing and outlier values with the mean/median, and so on.

3. **Data analysis and feature engineering**: Data needs to be analyzed in order to find any hidden patterns and relations between variables, and so on. Correct feature engineering with appropriate business knowledge will solve 70 percent of the problems. Also, in practice, 70 percent of the data scientist's time is spent on feature engineering tasks.

4. **Train algorithm on training and validation data**: Post feature engineering, data will be divided into three chunks (train, validation, and test data) rather than two (train and test) in statistical modeling. Machine learning are applied on training data and the hyperparameters of the model are tuned based on validation data to avoid overfitting.

5. **Test the algorithm on test data**: Once the model has shown a good enough performance on train and validation data, its performance will be checked against unseen test data. If the performance is still good enough, we can proceed to the next and final step.
6. **Deploy the algorithm**: Trained machine learning algorithms will be deployed on live streaming data to classify the outcomes. One example could be recommender systems implemented by e-commerce websites.

Statistical fundamentals and terminology for model building and validation

Statistics itself is a vast subject on which a complete book could be written; however, here the attempt is to focus on key concepts that are very much necessary with respect to the machine learning perspective. In this section, a few fundamentals are covered and the remaining concepts will be covered in later chapters wherever it is necessary to understand the statistical equivalents of machine learning.

Predictive analytics depends on one major assumption: that history repeats itself!

By fitting a predictive model on historical data after validating key measures, the same model will be utilized for predicting future events based on the same explanatory variables that were significant on past data.

The first movers of statistical model implementers were the banking and pharmaceutical industries; over a period, analytics expanded to other industries as well.

Statistical models are a class of mathematical models that are usually specified by mathematical equations that relate one or more variables to approximate reality. Assumptions embodied by statistical models describe a set of probability distributions, which distinguishes it from non-statistical, mathematical, or machine learning models

Statistical models always start with some underlying assumptions for which all the variables should hold, then the performance provided by the model is statistically significant. Hence, knowing the various bits and pieces involved in all building blocks provides a strong foundation for being a successful statistician.

In the following section, we have described various fundamentals with relevant codes:

- **Population**: This is the totality, the complete list of observations, or all the data points about the subject under study.

- **Sample**: A sample is a subset of a population, usually a small portion of the population that is being analyzed.

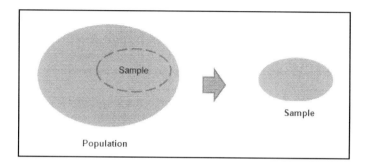

 Usually, it is expensive to perform an analysis on an entire population; hence, most statistical methods are about drawing conclusions about a population by analyzing a sample.

- **Parameter versus statistic**: Any measure that is calculated on the population is a parameter, whereas on a sample it is called a **statistic**.
- **Mean**: This is a simple arithmetic average, which is computed by taking the aggregated sum of values divided by a count of those values. The mean is sensitive to outliers in the data. An outlier is the value of a set or column that is highly deviant from the many other values in the same data; it usually has very high or low values.
- **Median**: This is the midpoint of the data, and is calculated by either arranging it in ascending or descending order. If there are N observations.
- **Mode**: This is the most repetitive data point in the data:

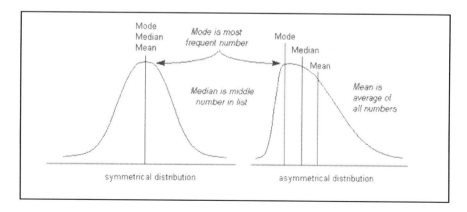

The Python code for the calculation of mean, median, and mode using a `numpy` array and the `stats` package is as follows:

```
>>> import numpy as np
>>> from scipy import stats

>>> data = np.array([4,5,1,2,7,2,6,9,3])

# Calculate Mean
>>> dt_mean = np.mean(data) ; print ("Mean :",round(dt_mean,2))

# Calculate Median
>>> dt_median = np.median(data) ; print ("Median :",dt_median)

# Calculate Mode
>>> dt_mode =  stats.mode(data); print ("Mode :",dt_mode[0][0])
```

The output of the preceding code is as follows:

```
Mean : 4.33333333333
Median : 4.0
Mode : 2
[Finished in 0.3s]
```

We have used a NumPy array instead of a basic list as the data structure; the reason behind using this is the `scikit-learn` package built on top of NumPy array in which all statistical models and machine learning algorithms have been built on NumPy array itself. The `mode` function is not implemented in the `numpy` package, hence we have used SciPy's `stats` package. SciPy is also built on top of NumPy arrays.

The R code for descriptive statistics (mean, median, and mode) is given as follows:

```
data <- c(4,5,1,2,7,2,6,9,3)
dt_mean = mean(data) ; print(round(dt_mean,2))
dt_median = median (data); print (dt_median)

func_mode <- function (input_dt) {
  unq <- unique(input_dt)
unq[which.max(tabulate(match(input_dt,unq)))]
}

dt_mode = func_mode (data); print (dt_mode)
```

We have used the default `stats` package for R; however, the `mode` function was not built-in, hence we have written custom code for calculating the mode.

- **Measure of variation**: Dispersion is the variation in the data, and measures the inconsistencies in the value of variables in the data. Dispersion actually provides an idea about the spread rather than central values.
- **Range**: This is the difference between the maximum and minimum of the value.
- **Variance**: This is the mean of squared deviations from the mean (xi = data points, μ = mean of the data, N = number of data points). The dimension of variance is the square of the actual values. The reason to use denominator $N-1$ for a sample instead of N in the population is due the degree of freedom. *1* degree of freedom lost in a sample by the time of calculating variance is due to extraction of substitution of sample:

$$population\ variance = \frac{1}{N}\sum_{i=1}^{N}(x_i - \mu)^2 \quad sample\ variance = \frac{1}{N-1}\sum_{i=1}^{N}(x_i - \mu)^2$$

- **Standard deviation**: This is the square root of variance. By applying the square root on variance, we measure the dispersion with respect to the original variable rather than square of the dimension:

$$population\ standard\ deviation\ (\sigma) = \sqrt{\frac{1}{N}\sum_{i=1}^{N}(x_i - \mu)^2} \quad sample\ standard\ deviation\ (s) = \sqrt{\frac{1}{N-1}\sum_{i=1}^{N}(x_i - \mu)^2}$$

- **Quantiles**: These are simply identical fragments of the data. Quantiles cover percentiles, deciles, quartiles, and so on. These measures are calculated after arranging the data in ascending order:
    - **Percentile**: This is nothing but the percentage of data points below the value of the original whole data. The median is the 50th percentile, as the number of data points below the median is about 50 percent of the data.
    - **Decile**: This is 10th percentile, which means the number of data points below the decile is 10 percent of the whole data.
    - **Quartile**: This is one-fourth of the data, and also is the 25th percentile. The first quartile is 25 percent of the data, the second quartile is 50 percent of the data, the third quartile is 75 percent of the data. The second quartile is also known as the median or 50th percentile or 5th decile.
    - **Interquartile range**: This is the difference between the third quartile and first quartile. It is effective in identifying outliers in data. The interquartile range describes the middle 50 percent of the data points.

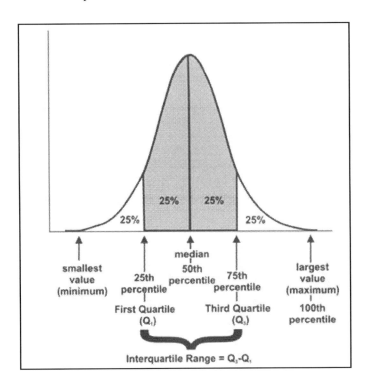

The Python code is as follows:

```
>>> from statistics import variance, stdev
>>> game_points =
np.array([35,56,43,59,63,79,35,41,64,43,93,60,77,24,82])

# Calculate Variance
>>> dt_var = variance(game_points) ; print ("Sample variance:",
round(dt_var,2))

# Calculate Standard Deviation
>>> dt_std = stdev(game_points) ; print ("Sample std.dev:",
round(dt_std,2))
# Calculate Range
>>> dt_rng = np.max(game_points,axis=0) -
np.min(game_points,axis=0) ; print ("Range:",dt_rng)

#Calculate percentiles
>>> print ("Quantiles:")
>>> for val in [20,80,100]:
>>>      dt_qntls = np.percentile(game_points,val)
>>>      print (str(val)+"%" ,dt_qntls)
# Calculate IQR
>>> q75, q25 = np.percentile(game_points, [75 ,25]); print ("Inter
quartile range:",q75-q25)
```

The output of the preceding code is as follows:

```
Sample variance: 400.64
Sample std.dev: 20.02
Range: 69
Quantiles:
20% 39.8
80% 77.4
100% 93.0
Inter quartile range: 28.5
[Finished in 0.2s]
```

The R code for dispersion (variance, standard deviation, range, quantiles, and IQR) is as follows:

```
game_points <- c(35,56,43,59,63,79,35,41,64,43,93,60,77,24,82)
dt_var = var(game_points); print(round(dt_var,2))
dt_std = sd(game_points); print(round(dt_std,2))
range_val<-function(x) return(diff(range(x)))
```

```
dt_range = range_val(game_points); print(dt_range)
dt_quantile = quantile(game_points,probs = c(0.2,0.8,1.0));
print(dt_quantile)
dt_iqr = IQR(game_points); print(dt_iqr)
```

- **Hypothesis testing**: This is the process of making inferences about the overall population by conducting some statistical tests on a sample. Null and alternate hypotheses are ways to validate whether an assumption is statistically significant or not.
- **P-value**: The probability of obtaining a test statistic result is at least as extreme as the one that was actually observed, assuming that the null hypothesis is true (usually in modeling, against each independent variable, a p-value less than 0.05 is considered significant and greater than 0.05 is considered insignificant; nonetheless, these values and definitions may change with respect to context).

The steps involved in hypothesis testing are as follows:

1. Assume a null hypothesis (usually no difference, no significance, and so on; a null hypothesis always tries to assume that there is no anomaly pattern and is always homogeneous, and so on).
2. Collect the sample.
3. Calculate test statistics from the sample in order to verify whether the hypothesis is statistically significant or not.
4. Decide either to accept or reject the null hypothesis based on the test statistic.

- **Example of hypothesis testing**: A chocolate manufacturer who is also your friend claims that all chocolates produced from his factory weigh at least 1,000 g and you have got a funny feeling that it might not be true; you both collected a sample of 30 chocolates and found that the average chocolate weight as 990 g with sample standard deviation as 12.5 g. Given the 0.05 significance level, can we reject the claim made by your friend?

The null hypothesis is that $\mu0 \geq 1000$ (all chocolates weigh more than 1,000 g).

Collected sample:

$$\bar{x} = 990, s = 12.5, n = 30$$

Calculate test statistic:

$$t = \frac{(\bar{x} - \mu_0)}{\left(\frac{s}{\sqrt{n}}\right)}$$

t = (990 - 1000) / (12.5/sqrt(30)) = - 4.3818

Critical t value from t tables = t0.05, 30 = 1.699 => - t0.05, 30 = -1.699

P-value = 7.03 e-05

Test statistic is *-4.3818*, which is less than the critical value of *-1.699*. Hence, we can reject the null hypothesis (your friend's claim) that the mean weight of a chocolate is above 1,000 g.

Also, another way of deciding the claim is by using the p-value. A p-value less than *0.05* means both claimed values and distribution mean values are significantly different, hence we can reject the null hypothesis:

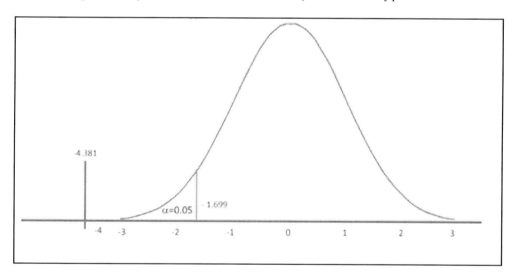

The Python code is as follows:

```
>>> from scipy import stats
>>> xbar = 990; mu0 = 1000; s = 12.5; n = 30

# Test Statistic
>>> t_smple  = (xbar-mu0)/(s/np.sqrt(float(n))); print ("Test
Statistic:",round(t_smple,2))

# Critical value from t-table
>>> alpha = 0.05
>>> t_alpha = stats.t.ppf(alpha,n-1); print ("Critical value
from t-table:",round(t_alpha,3))

#Lower tail p-value from t-table
>>> p_val = stats.t.sf(np.abs(t_smple), n-1); print ("Lower
tail p-value from t-table", p_val)
```

```
Test Statistic: -4.38
Critical value from t-table: -1.699
Lower tail p-value from t-table 7.03502572901e-05
[Finished in 0.3s]
```

The R code for T-distribution is as follows:

```
xbar = 990; mu0 = 1000; s = 12.5 ; n = 30
t_smple = (xbar - mu0)/(s/sqrt(n));print (round(t_smple,2))

alpha = 0.05
t_alpha = qt(alpha,df= n-1);print (round(t_alpha,3))

p_val = pt(t_smple,df = n-1);print (p_val)
```

- **Type I and II error**: Hypothesis testing is usually done on the samples rather than the entire population, due to the practical constraints of available resources to collect all the available data. However, performing inferences about the population from samples comes with its own costs, such as rejecting good results or accepting false results, not to mention separately, when increases in sample size lead to minimizing type I and II errors:

    - **Type I error**: Rejecting a null hypothesis when it is true
    - **Type II error**: Accepting a null hypothesis when it is false

- **Normal distribution**: This is very important in statistics because of the central limit theorem, which states that the population of all possible samples of size n from a population with mean μ and variance $\sigma 2$ approaches a normal distribution:

$$f(x) = \frac{1}{\sigma\sqrt{2\Pi}}\, e^{-\frac{(x-\mu)^2}{2\,\sigma^2}} \qquad X \sim N(\mu,\, \sigma^2)$$

Example: Assume that the test scores of an entrance exam fit a normal distribution. Furthermore, the mean test score is 52 and the standard deviation is 16.3. What is the percentage of students scoring 67 or more in the exam?

$$pr(X \geq 67) = pr\left(Z \geq \frac{(67-\mu)}{\sigma}\right) = 1 - pr\left(Z \leq \frac{(67-\mu)}{\sigma}\right)$$

$$= 1 - pr\left(Z \leq \frac{(67-52)}{16.3}\right) = 1 - 0.8212 = 0.1788$$

probability of students scoring more than 67 marks is $= 17.88\,\%$

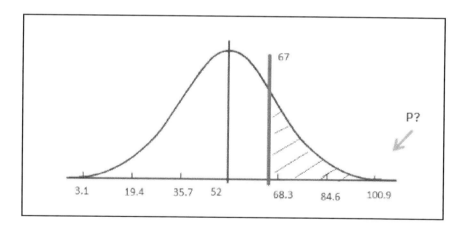

The Python code is as follows:

```
>>> from scipy import stats
>>> xbar = 67; mu0 = 52; s = 16.3

# Calculating z-score
>>> z = (67-52)/16.3

# Calculating probability under the curve
>>> p_val = 1- stats.norm.cdf(z)
>>> print ("Prob. to score more than 67 is
",round(p_val*100,2),"%")
```

```
Prob. to score more than 67 is  17.87 %
[Finished in 0.4s]
```

The R code for normal distribution is as follows:

```
xbar = 67; mu0 = 52; s = 16.3
pr = 1- pnorm(67, mean=52, sd=16.3)
print(paste("Prob. to score more than 67 is
",round(pr*100,2),"%"))
```

- **Chi-square**: This test of independence is one of the most basic and common hypothesis tests in the statistical analysis of categorical data. Given two categorical random variables X and Y, the chi-square test of independence determines whether or not there exists a statistical dependence between them.

  The test is usually performed by calculating $\chi2$ from the data and $\chi2$ with (m-1, n-1) degrees from the table. A decision is made as to whether both variables are independent based on the actual value and table value, whichever is higher:

$$\chi^2 = \sum_i \frac{(o_i - e_i)^2}{e_i} \qquad o_i = observed, e_i = expected$$

Example: In the following table, calculate whether the smoking habit has an impact on exercise behavior:

	Exercise: Frequent	Exercise: None	Exercise: Sometimes
Smoke: Heavy	7	1	3
Smoke: Never	87	18	84
Smoke: Occasional	12	3	4
Smoke: Regularly	9	1	7

The Python code is as follows:

```
>>> import pandas as pd
>>> from scipy import stats

>>> survey = pd.read_csv("survey.csv")

# Tabulating 2 variables with row & column variables
respectively
>>> survey_tab = pd.crosstab(survey.Smoke, survey.Exer, margins
= True)
```

While creating a table using the `crosstab` function, we will obtain both row and column totals fields extra. However, in order to create the observed table, we need to extract the variables part and ignore the totals:

```
# Creating observed table for analysis
>>> observed = survey_tab.ix[0:4,0:3]
```

The `chi2_contingency` function in the stats package uses the observed table and subsequently calculates its expected table, followed by calculating the p-value in order to check whether two variables are dependent or not. If *p-value < 0.05*, there is a strong dependency between two variables, whereas if *p-value > 0.05*, there is no dependency between the variables:

```
>>> contg = stats.chi2_contingency(observed= observed)
>>> p_value = round(contg[1],3)
>>> print ("P-value is: ",p_value)
```

```
P-value is:  0.483
[Finished in 0.6s]
```

The p-value is `0.483`, which means there is no dependency between the smoking habit and exercise behavior.

The R code for chi-square is as follows:

```
survey = read.csv("survey.csv",header=TRUE)
tbl = table(survey$Smoke,survey$Exer)
p_val = chisq.test(tbl)
```

- **ANOVA**: Analyzing variance tests the hypothesis that the means of two or more populations are equal. ANOVAs assess the importance of one or more factors by comparing the response variable means at the different factor levels. The null hypothesis states that all population means are equal while the alternative hypothesis states that at least one is different.

  Example: A fertilizer company developed three new types of universal fertilizers after research that can be utilized to grow any type of crop. In order to find out whether all three have a similar crop yield, they randomly chose six crop types in the study. In accordance with the randomized block design, each crop type will be tested with all three types of fertilizer separately. The following table represents the yield in g/m^2. At the 0.05 level of significance, test whether the mean yields for the three new types of fertilizers are all equal:

Fertilizer 1	Fertilizer 2	Fertilizer 3
62	54	48
62	56	62

90	58	92
42	36	96
84	72	92
64	34	80

The Python code is as follows:

```
>>> import pandas as pd
>>> from scipy import stats
>>> fetilizers = pd.read_csv("fetilizers.csv")
```

Calculating one-way ANOVA using the `stats` package:

```
>>> one_way_anova = stats.f_oneway(fetilizers["fertilizer1"],
fetilizers["fertilizer2"], fetilizers["fertilizer3"])

>>> print ("Statistic :", round(one_way_anova[0],2),", p-value
:",round(one_way_anova[1],3))
```

```
Statistic : 4.13 , p-value : 0.037
[Finished in 0.6s]
```

Result: The p-value did come as less than 0.05, hence we can reject the null hypothesis that the mean crop yields of the fertilizers are equal. Fertilizers make a significant difference to crops.

The R code for ANOVA is as follows:

```
fetilizers = read.csv("fetilizers.csv",header=TRUE)
r = c(t(as.matrix(fetilizers)))
f = c("fertilizer1","fertilizer2","fertilizer3")
k = 3; n = 6
tm = gl(k,1,n*k,factor(f))
blk = gl(n,k,k*n)
av = aov(r ~ tm + blk)
smry = summary(av)
```

- **Confusion matrix**: This is the matrix of the actual versus the predicted. This concept is better explained with the example of cancer prediction using the model:

	Predicted: Yes	Predicted: No
Actual: Yes	TP	FN
Actual: No	FP	TN

Some terms used in a confusion matrix are:

- **True positives (TPs)**: True positives are cases when we predict the disease as yes when the patient actually does have the disease.
- **True negatives (TNs)**: Cases when we predict the disease as no when the patient actually does not have the disease.
- **False positives (FPs)**: When we predict the disease as yes when the patient actually does not have the disease. FPs are also considered to be type I errors.
- **False negatives (FNs)**: When we predict the disease as no when the patient actually does have the disease. FNs are also considered to be type II errors.
- **Precision (P)**: When yes is predicted, how often is it correct?

$$(TP/TP+FP)$$

- **Recall (R)/sensitivity/true positive rate**: Among the actual yeses, what fraction was predicted as yes?

$$(TP/TP+FN)$$

- **F1 score (F1)**: This is the harmonic mean of the precision and recall. Multiplying the constant of *2* scales the score to *1* when both precision and recall are *1*:

$$F_1 = \frac{2}{\frac{1}{P} + \frac{1}{R}} \qquad \gg \qquad F_1 = \frac{2 * P * R}{P + R}$$

- **Specificity**: Among the actual nos, what fraction was predicted as no? Also equivalent to *1- false positive rate*:

(TN/TN+FP)

- **Area under curve (ROC)**: Receiver operating characteristic curve is used to plot between **true positive rate (TPR)** and **false positive rate (FPR)**, also known as a sensitivity and *1- specificity* graph:

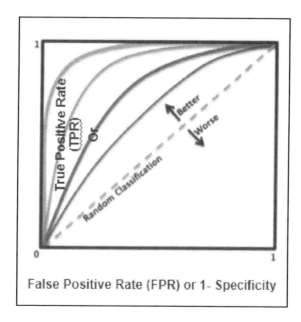

Area under curve is utilized for setting the threshold of cut-off probability to classify the predicted probability into various classes; we will be covering how this method works in upcoming chapters.

- **Observation and performance window**: In statistical modeling, the model tries to predict the event in advance rather than at the moment, so that some buffer time will exist to work on corrective actions. For example, a question from a credit card company would be, for example, what is the probability that a particular customer will default in the coming 12-month period? So that I can call him and offer any discounts or develop my collection strategies accordingly.

  In order to answer this question, a probability of default model (or behavioral scorecard in technical terms) needs to be developed by using independent variables from the past 24 months and a dependent variable from the next 12 months. After preparing data with X and Y variables, it will be split into 70 percent - 30 percent as train and test data randomly; this method is called **in-time validation** as both train and test samples are from the same time period:

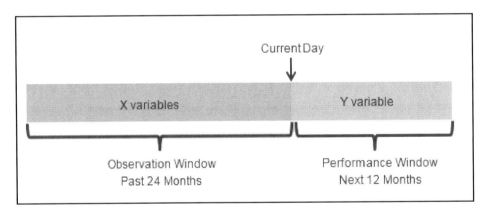

- **In-time and out-of-time validation**: In-time validation implies obtaining both a training and testing dataset from the same period of time, whereas out-of-time validation implies training and testing datasets drawn from different time periods. Usually, the model performs worse in out-of-time validation rather than in-time due to the obvious reason that the characteristics of the train and test datasets might differ.

- **R-squared (coefficient of determination)**: This is the measure of the percentage of the response variable variation that is explained by a model. It also a measure of how well the model minimizes error compared with just utilizing the mean as an estimate. In some extreme cases, R-squared can have a value less than zero also, which means the predicted values from the model perform worse than just taking the simple mean as a prediction for all the observations. We will study this parameter in detail in upcoming chapters:

$$\bar{y} = \frac{1}{n}\sum_{i=1}^{n} y_i \; ; \; SS_{tot} = \sum_i (y_i - \bar{y})^2 \; ; \; SS_{reg} = \sum_i (f_i - \bar{y})^2 \; ; \; SS_{res} = \sum_i (y_i - f_i)^2 = \sum_i e_i^2$$

$$R^2 \equiv 1 - \frac{SS_{res}}{SS_{tot}}$$

- **Adjusted R-squared**: The explanation of the adjusted R-squared statistic is almost the same as R-squared but it penalizes the R-squared value if extra variables without a strong correlation are included in the model:

$$R^2_{adjusted} = 1 - \frac{(1 - R^2)(n - 1)}{n - k - 1}$$

Here, $R2$ = sample R-squared value, n = sample size, k = number of predictors (or) variables.

Adjusted R-squared value is the key metric in evaluating the quality of linear regressions. Any linear regression model having the value of $R2\ adjusted >= 0.7$ is considered as a good enough model to implement.

Example: The R-squared value of a sample is *0.5*, with a sample size of *50* and the independent variables are *10* in number. Calculated adjusted R-squared:

$$R^2_{adjusted} = 1 - \frac{(1 - 0.5)(50 - 1)}{50 - 10 - 1} = 0.402$$

- **Maximum likelihood estimate (MLE)**: This is estimating the parameter values of a statistical model (logistic regression, to be precise) by finding the parameter values that maximize the likelihood of making the observations. We will cover this method in more depth in Chapter 3, *Logistic Regression Versus Random Forest*.

- **Akaike information criteria (AIC)**: This is used in logistic regression, which is similar to the principle of adjusted R-square for linear regression. It measures the relative quality of a model for a given set of data:

$$AIC = -2 * \ln(L) + 2 * k$$

Here, k = number of predictors or variables

The idea of AIC is to penalize the objective function if extra variables without strong predictive abilities are included in the model. This is a kind of regularization in logistic regression.

- **Entropy**: This comes from information theory and is the measure of impurity in the data. If the sample is completely homogeneous, the entropy is zero and if the sample is equally divided, it has an entropy of *1*. In decision trees, the predictor with the most heterogeneousness will be considered nearest to the root node to classify given data into classes in a greedy mode. We will cover this topic in more depth in `Chapter 4`, *Tree-Based Machine Learning Models*:

$$Entropy = -p_1 * log_2\, p_1 - \ ... - -p_n * log_2\, p_n$$

Here, n = number of classes. Entropy is maximal at the middle, with the value of *1* and minimal at the extremes as *0*. A low value of entropy is desirable as it will segregate classes better:

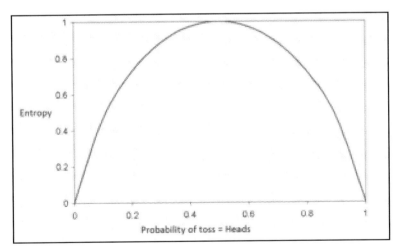

Example: Given two types of coin in which the first one is a fair one (*1/2* head and *1/2* tail probabilities) and the other is a biased one (*1/3* head and *2/3* tail probabilities), calculate the entropy for both and justify which one is better with respect to modeling:

$$Entropy\ of\ a\ Fair\ Coin = -\frac{1}{2} * log_2\frac{1}{2} - \frac{1}{2} * log_2\frac{1}{2} = 1\ bits$$

$$Entropy\ of\ a\ Biased\ Coin = -\frac{1}{3} * log_2\frac{1}{3} - \frac{2}{3} * log_2\frac{2}{3} = 0.9183\ bits$$

From both values, the decision tree algorithm chooses the biased coin rather than the fair coin as an observation splitter due to the fact the value of entropy is less.

- **Information gain**: This is the expected reduction in entropy caused by partitioning the examples according to a given attribute. The idea is to start with mixed classes and to keep partitioning until each node reaches its observations of the purest class. At every stage, the variable with maximum information gain is chosen in greedy fashion:

*Information gain = Entropy of parent - sum (weighted % * Entropy of child)*

Weighted % = Number of observations in particular child / sum (observations in all child nodes)

- **Gini**: Gini impurity is a measure of misclassification, which applies in a multiclass classifier context. Gini works almost the same as entropy, except Gini is faster to calculate:

$$Gini = 1 - \sum_i p_i^2$$

Here, i = number of classes. The similarity between Gini and entropy is shown as follows:

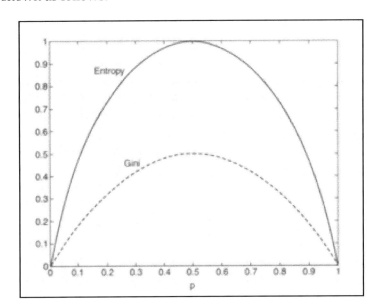

Bias versus variance trade-off

Every model has both bias and variance error components in addition to white noise. Bias and variance are inversely related to each other; while trying to reduce one component, the other component of the model will increase. The true art lies in creating a good fit by balancing both. The ideal model will have both low bias and low variance.

Errors from the bias component come from erroneous assumptions in the underlying learning algorithm. High bias can cause an algorithm to miss the relevant relations between features and target outputs; this phenomenon causes an underfitting problem.

On the other hand, errors from the variance component come from sensitivity to change in the fit of the model, even a small change in training data; high variance can cause an overfitting problem:

$$E\left(y_0 - \hat{f}(x_0)\right)^2 = Var\left(\hat{f}(x_0)\right) + \left[Bias(\hat{f}(x_0))\right]^2 + Var(\varepsilon)$$

An example of a high bias model is logistic or linear regression, in which the fit of the model is merely a straight line and may have a high error component due to the fact that a linear model could not approximate underlying data well.

An example of a high variance model is a decision tree, in which the model may create too much wiggly curve as a fit, in which even a small change in training data will cause a drastic change in the fit of the curve.

At the moment, state-of-the-art models are utilizing high variance models such as decision trees and performing ensemble on top of them to reduce the errors caused by high variance and at the same time not compromising on increases in errors due to the bias component. The best example of this category is random forest, in which many decision trees will be grown independently and ensemble in order to come up with the best fit; we will cover this in upcoming chapters:

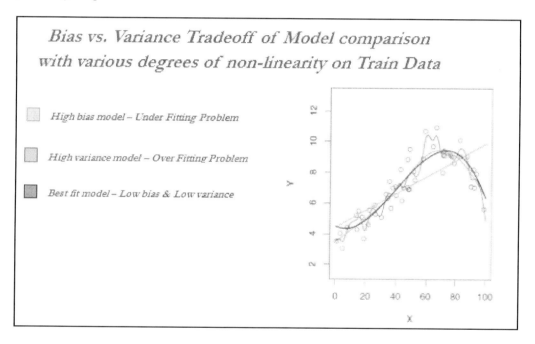

Train and test data

In practice, data usually will be split randomly 70-30 or 80-20 into train and test datasets respectively in statistical modeling, in which training data utilized for building the model and its effectiveness will be checked on test data:

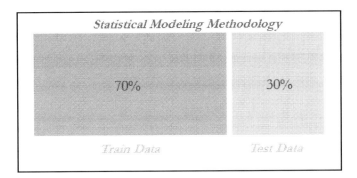

In the following code, we split the original data into train and test data by 70 percent - 30 percent. An important point to consider here is that we set the seed values for random numbers in order to repeat the random sampling every time we create the same observations in training and testing data. Repeatability is very much needed in order to reproduce the results:

```
# Train & Test split
>>> import pandas as pd
>>> from sklearn.model_selection import train_test_split

>>> original_data = pd.read_csv("mtcars.csv")
```

In the following code, train size is 0.7, which means 70 percent of the data should be split into the training dataset and the remaining 30% should be in the testing dataset. Random state is seed in this process of generating pseudo-random numbers, which makes the results reproducible by splitting the exact same observations while running every time:

```
>>> train_data,test_data = train_test_split(original_data,train_size =
0.7,random_state=42)
```

The R code for the train and test split for statistical modeling is as follows:

```
full_data = read.csv("mtcars.csv",header=TRUE)
set.seed(123)
numrow = nrow(full_data)
trnind = sample(1:numrow,size = as.integer(0.7*numrow))
train_data = full_data[trnind,]
test_data = full_data[-trnind,]
```

Machine learning terminology for model building and validation

There seems to be an analogy between statistical modeling and machine learning that we will cover in subsequent chapters in depth. However, a quick view has been provided as follows: in statistical modeling, linear regression with two independent variables is trying to fit the best plane with the least errors, whereas in machine learning independent variables have been converted into the square of error terms (squaring ensures the function will become convex, which enhances faster convergence and also ensures a global optimum) and optimized based on coefficient values rather than independent variables:

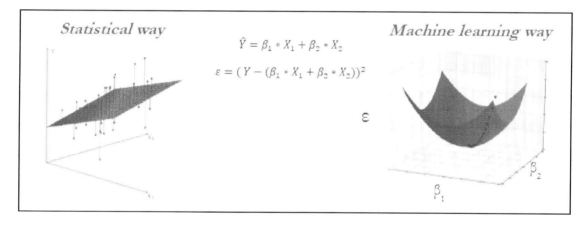

Machine learning utilizes optimization for tuning all the parameters of various algorithms. Hence, it is a good idea to know some basics about optimization.

Before stepping into gradient descent, the introduction of convex and non-convex functions is very helpful. Convex functions are functions in which a line drawn between any two random points on the function also lies within the function, whereas this isn't true for non-convex functions. It is important to know whether the function is convex or non-convex due to the fact that in convex functions, the local optimum is also the global optimum, whereas for non-convex functions, the local optimum does not guarantee the global optimum:

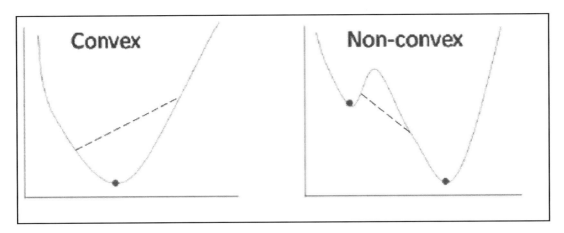

Does it seem like a tough problem? One turnaround could be to initiate a search process at different random locations; by doing so, it usually converges to the global optimum:

- Gradient descent: This is a way to minimize the objective function $J(\Theta)$ parameterized by the model's parameter $\Theta \, \varepsilon \, R^d$ by updating the parameters in the opposite direction to the gradient of the objective function with respect to the parameters. The learning rate determines the size of steps taken to reach the minimum.
- **Full batch gradient descent (all training observations considered in each and every iteration)**: In full batch gradient descent, all the observations are considered for each and every iteration; this methodology takes a lot of memory and will be slow as well. Also, in practice, we do not need to have all the observations to update the weights. Nonetheless, this method provides the best way of updating parameters with less noise at the expense of huge computation.
- **Stochastic gradient descent (one observation per iteration)**: This method updates weights by taking one observation at each stage of iteration. This method provides the quickest way of traversing weights; however, a lot of noise is involved while converging.

- **Mini batch gradient descent (about 30 training observations or more for each and every iteration)**: This is a trade-off between huge computational costs and a quick method of updating weights. In this method, at each iteration, about 30 observations will be selected at random and gradients calculated to update the model weights. Here, a question many can ask is, why the minimum 30 and not any other number? If we look into statistical basics, 30 observations required to be considering in order approximating sample as a population. However, even 40, 50, and so on will also do well in batch size selection. Nonetheless, a practitioner needs to change the batch size and verify the results, to determine at what value the model is producing the optimum results:

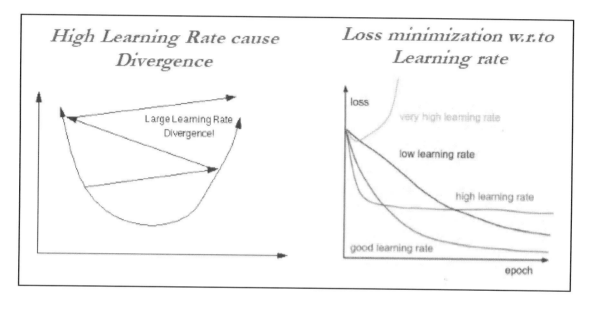

Linear regression versus gradient descent

In the following code, a comparison has been made between applying linear regression in a statistical way and gradient descent in a machine learning way on the same dataset:

```
>>> import numpy as np
>>> import pandas as pd
```

The following code describes reading data using a pandas DataFrame:

```
>>> train_data = pd.read_csv("mtcars.csv")
```

Converting DataFrame variables into NumPy arrays in order to process them in scikit learn packages, as scikit-learn is built on NumPy arrays itself, is shown next:

```
>>> X = np.array(train_data["hp"])   ; y = np.array(train_data["mpg"])
>>> X = X.reshape(32,1); y = y.reshape(32,1)
```

Importing linear regression from the scikit-learn package; this works on the least squares method:

```
>>> from sklearn.linear_model import LinearRegression
>>> model = LinearRegression(fit_intercept = True)
```

Fitting a linear regression model on the data and display intercept and coefficient of single variable (hp variable):

```
>>> model.fit(X,y)
>>> print ("Linear Regression Results" )
>>> print ("Intercept",model.intercept_[0] ,"Coefficient", model.coef_[0])
```

```
Linear Regression Results
Intercept 30.0988605396 Coefficient [-0.06822828]
Converged, iterations:   1144969
```

Now we will apply gradient descent from scratch; in future chapters, we can use the scikit-learn built-in modules rather than doing it from first principles. However, here, an illustration has been provided on the internal workings of the optimization method on which the whole machine learning has been built.

Defining the gradient descent function `gradient_descent` with the following:

- `x`: Independent variable.
- `y`: Dependent variable.
- `learn_rate`: Learning rate with which gradients are updated; too low causes slower convergence and too high causes overshooting of gradients.
- `batch_size`: Number of observations considered at each iteration for updating gradients; a high number causes a lower number of iterations and a lower number causes an erratic decrease in errors. Ideally, the batch size should be a minimum value of 30 due to statistical significance. However, various settings need to be tried to check which one is better.
- `max_iter`: Maximum number of iteration, beyond which the algorithm will get auto-terminated:

```
>>> def gradient_descent(x, y,learn_rate,
conv_threshold,batch_size, max_iter):
...      converged = False
...      iter = 0
...      m = batch_size
...      t0 = np.random.random(x.shape[1])
...      t1 = np.random.random(x.shape[1])
```

Mean square error calculation

Squaring of error has been performed to create the convex function, which has nice convergence properties:

```
...  MSE = (sum([(t0 + t1*x[i] - y[i])**2 for i in
range(m)])/ m)
```

The following code states, run the algorithm until it does not meet the convergence criteria:

```
...        while not converged:
...            grad0 = 1.0/m * sum([(t0 + t1*x[i] - y[i]) for i in range(m)])
...            grad1 = 1.0/m * sum([(t0 + t1*x[i] - y[i])*x[i] for i in
range(m)])
...            temp0 = t0 - learn_rate * grad0
...            temp1 = t1 - learn_rate * grad1
...            t0 = temp0
...            t1 = temp1
```

Calculate a new error with updated parameters, in order to check whether the new error changed more than the predefined convergence threshold value; otherwise, stop the iterations and return parameters:

```
...             MSE_New = (sum( [ (t0 + t1*x[i] - y[i])**2 for i in range(m)]
) / m)
...             if abs(MSE - MSE_New ) <= conv_threshold:
...                 print 'Converged, iterations: ', iter
...                 converged = True
...             MSE = MSE_New
...             iter += 1
...             if iter == max_iter:
...                 print 'Max interactions reached'
...                 converged = True
...             return t0,t1
```

The following code describes running the gradient descent function with defined values. Learn rate = 0.0003, convergence threshold = 1e-8, batch size = 32, maximum number of iteration = 1500000:

```
>>> if __name__ == '__main__':
...         Inter, Coeff = gradient_descent(x = X,y = y,learn_rate=0.00003 ,
conv_threshold = 1e-8, batch_size=32,max_iter=1500000)
...         print ('Gradient Descent Results')
...         print (('Intercept = %s Coefficient = %s') %(Inter, Coeff))
```

```
Gradient Descent Results
Intercept = [ 30.02495135] Coefficient = [-0.06781243]
[Finished in 0.1s]
```

The R code for linear regression versus gradient descent is as follows:

```
# Linear Regression
train_data = read.csv("mtcars.csv",header=TRUE)
model <- lm(mpg ~ hp, data = train_data)
print (coef(model))

# Gradient descent
gradDesc <- function(x, y, learn_rate, conv_threshold, batch_size,
max_iter) {
  m <- runif(1, 0, 1)
  c <- runif(1, 0, 1)
  ypred <- m * x + c
  MSE <- sum((y - ypred) ^ 2) / batch_size
  converged = F
  iterations = 0
```

```
while(converged == F) {
    m_new <- m - learn_rate * ((1 / batch_size) * (sum((ypred - y) * x)))
    c_new <- c - learn_rate * ((1 / batch_size) * (sum(ypred - y)))
    m <- m_new
    c <- c_new
    ypred <- m * x + c
    MSE_new <- sum((y - ypred) ^ 2) / batch_size
    if(MSE - MSE_new <= conv_threshold) {
        converged = T
        return(paste("Iterations:",iterations,"Optimal intercept:", c,
"Optimal slope:", m))
    }
    iterations = iterations + 1

    if(iterations > max_iter) {
        converged = T
        return(paste("Iterations:",iterations,"Optimal intercept:", c,
"Optimal slope:", m))
    }
    MSE = MSE_new
  }
}
gradDesc(x = train_data$hp,y =  train_data$mpg, learn_rate = 0.00003,
conv_threshold = 1e-8, batch_size = 32, max_iter = 1500000)
```

Machine learning losses

The loss function or cost function in machine learning is a function that maps the values of variables onto a real number intuitively representing some cost associated with the variable values. Optimization methods are applied to minimize the loss function by changing the parameter values, which is the central theme of machine learning.

Zero-one loss is $L0\text{-}1 = 1\ (m <= 0)$; in zero-one loss, value of loss is *0* for $m >= 0$ whereas *1* for $m < 0$. The difficult part with this loss is it is not differentiable, non-convex, and also NP-hard. Hence, in order to make optimization feasible and solvable, these losses are replaced by different surrogate losses for different problems.

Surrogate losses used for machine learning in place of zero-one loss are given as follows. The zero-one loss is not differentiable, hence approximated losses are being used instead:

- Squared loss (for regression)
- Hinge loss (SVM)
- Logistic/log loss (logistic regression)

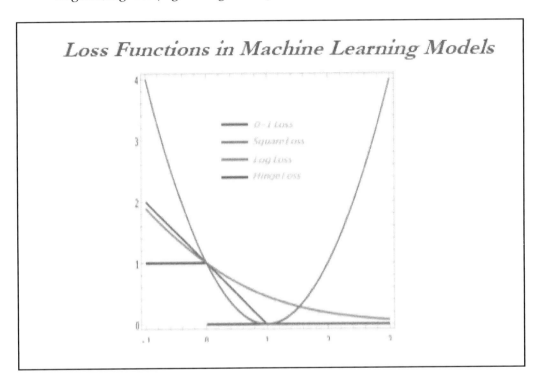

Some loss functions are as follows:

$$f_W(x) = sign(w.\phi(x))$$

$$Loss_{0-1}(x, y, w) = 1\left[f_W(x) \neq y \right] = 1\left[\underbrace{(w.\phi(x))y}_{\text{Margin}} \leq 0 \right]$$

$$Loss_{squared}(x, y, w) = \underbrace{\left(f_W(x) - y \right)^2}_{\text{Residual}}$$

$$Loss_{hinge}(x, y, w) = \max\left\{ 1 - (w.\phi(x))y, 0 \right\}$$

$$Loss_{logistic}(x, y, w) = \log\left(1 + e^{-(w.\phi(x))y} \right)$$

When to stop tuning machine learning models

When to stop tuning the hyperparameters in a machine learning model is a million-dollar question. This problem can be mostly solved by keeping tabs on training and testing errors. While increasing the complexity of a model, the following stages occur:

- **Stage 1**: Underfitting stage - high train and high test errors (or low train and low test accuracy)
- **Stage 2**: Good fit stage (ideal scenario) - low train and low test errors (or high train and high test accuracy)

- **Stage 3**: Overfitting stage - low train and high test errors (or high train and low test accuracy)

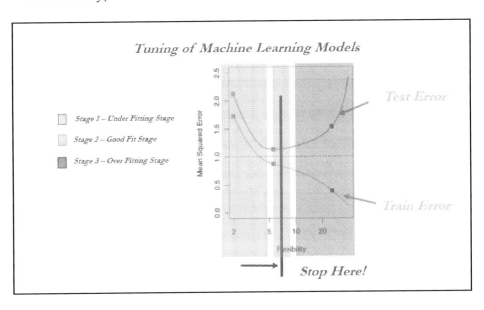

Train, validation, and test data

Cross-validation is not popular in the statistical modeling world for many reasons; statistical models are linear in nature and robust, and do not have a high variance/overfitting problem. Hence, the model fit will remain the same either on train or test data, which does not hold true in the machine learning world. Also, in statistical modeling, lots of tests are performed at the individual parameter level apart from aggregated metrics, whereas in machine learning we do not have visibility at the individual parameter level:

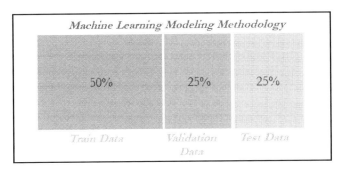

In the following code, both the R and Python implementation has been provided. If none of the percentages are provided, the default parameters are 50 percent for train data, 25 percent for validation data, and 25 percent for the remaining test data.

Python implementation has only one train and test split functionality, hence we have used it twice and also used the number of observations to split rather than the percentage (as shown in the previous train and test split example). Hence, a customized function is needed to split into three datasets:

```
>>> import pandas as pd
>>> from sklearn.model_selection import train_test_split
>>> original_data = pd.read_csv("mtcars.csv")
>>> def data_split(dat,trf = 0.5,vlf=0.25,tsf = 0.25):
...         nrows = dat.shape[0]
...         trnr = int(nrows*trf)
...         vlnr = int(nrows*vlf)
```

The following Python code splits the data into training and the remaining data. The remaining data will be further split into validation and test datasets:

```
...         tr_data,rmng = train_test_split(dat,train_size =
trnr,random_state=42)
...         vl_data, ts_data = train_test_split(rmng,train_size =
vlnr,random_state=45)
...         return (tr_data,vl_data,ts_data)
```

Implementation of the split function on the original data to create three datasets (by 50 percent, 25 percent, and 25 percent splits) is as follows:

```
>>> train_data, validation_data, test_data = data_split (original_data
,trf=0.5, vlf=0.25,tsf=0.25)
```

The R code for the train, validation, and test split is as follows:

```
# Train Validation & Test samples
trvaltest <- function(dat,prop = c(0.5,0.25,0.25)){
  nrw = nrow(dat)
  trnr = as.integer(nrw *prop[1])
  vlnr = as.integer(nrw*prop[2])
  set.seed(123)
  trni = sample(1:nrow(dat),trnr)
  trndata = dat[trni,]
  rmng = dat[-trni,]
  vlni = sample(1:nrow(rmng),vlnr)
  valdata = rmng[vlni,]
  tstdata = rmng[-vlni,]
  mylist = list("trn" = trndata,"val"= valdata,"tst" = tstdata)
```

```
        return(mylist)
}
outdata = trvaltest(mtcars,prop = c(0.5,0.25,0.25))
train_data = outdata$trn; valid_data = outdata$val; test_data = outdata$tst
```

Cross-validation

Cross-validation is another way of ensuring robustness in the model at the expense of computation. In the ordinary modeling methodology, a model is developed on train data and evaluated on test data. In some extreme cases, train and test might not have been homogeneously selected and some unseen extreme cases might appear in the test data, which will drag down the performance of the model.

On the other hand, in cross-validation methodology, data was divided into equal parts and training performed on all the other parts of the data except one part, on which performance will be evaluated. This process repeated as many parts user has chosen.

Example: In five-fold cross-validation, data will be divided into five parts, subsequently trained on four parts of the data, and tested on the one part of the data. This process will run five times, in order to cover all points in the data. Finally, the error calculated will be the average of all the errors:

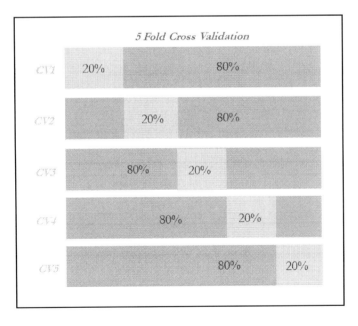

Grid search

Grid search in machine learning is a popular way to tune the hyperparameters of the model in order to find the best combination for determining the best fit:

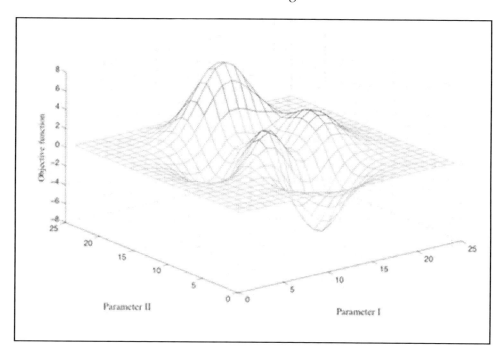

In the following code, implementation has been performed to determine whether a particular user will click an ad or not. Grid search has been implemented using a decision tree classifier for classification purposes. Tuning parameters are the depth of the tree, the minimum number of observations in terminal node, and the minimum number of observations required to perform the node split:

```
# Grid search
>>> import pandas as pd
>>> from sklearn.tree import DecisionTreeClassifier
>>> from sklearn.model_selection import train_test_split
>>> from sklearn.metrics import
classification_report,confusion_matrix,accuracy_score
>>> from sklearn.pipeline import Pipeline
>>> from sklearn.grid_search import GridSearchCV

>>> input_data = pd.read_csv("ad.csv",header=None)

>>> X_columns = set(input_data.columns.values)
```

```
>>> y = input_data[len(input_data.columns.values)-1]
>>> X_columns.remove(len(input_data.columns.values)-1)
>>> X = input_data[list(X_columns)]
```

Split the data into train and testing:

```
>>> X_train, X_test,y_train,y_test = train_test_split(X,y,train_size =
0.7,random_state=33)
```

Create a pipeline to create combinations of variables for the grid search:

```
>>> pipeline = Pipeline([
...          ('clf', DecisionTreeClassifier(criterion='entropy')) ])
```

Combinations to explore are given as parameters in Python dictionary format:

```
>>> parameters = {
...          'clf__max_depth': (50,100,150),
...          'clf__min_samples_split': (2, 3),
...          'clf__min_samples_leaf': (1, 2, 3)}
```

The `n_jobs` field is for selecting the number of cores in a computer; –1 means it uses all the cores in the computer. The scoring methodology is accuracy, in which many other options can be chosen, such as `precision`, `recall`, and `f1`:

```
>>> grid_search = GridSearchCV(pipeline, parameters, n_jobs=-1, verbose=1,
scoring='accuracy')
>>> grid_search.fit(X_train, y_train)
```

Predict using the best parameters of grid search:

```
>>> y_pred = grid_search.predict(X_test)
```

The output is as follows:

```
>>> print ('\n Best score: \n', grid_search.best_score_)
>>> print ('\n Best parameters set: \n')
>>> best_parameters = grid_search.best_estimator_.get_params()
>>> for param_name in sorted(parameters.keys()):
>>>     print ('\t%s: %r' % (param_name, best_parameters[param_name]))
>>> print ("\n Confusion Matrix on Test data
\n",confusion_matrix(y_test,y_pred))
>>> print ("\n Test Accuracy \n",accuracy_score(y_test,y_pred))
>>> print ("\nPrecision Recall f1 table \n",classification_report(y_test,
y_pred))
```

```
Fitting 3 folds for each of 18 candidates, totalling 54 fits
[Parallel(n_jobs=-1)]: Done   34 tasks       | elapsed:    7.0s
[Parallel(n_jobs=-1)]: Done   54 out of   54 | elapsed:    8.1s finished

Best score:
0.967320261438

Best parameters set:
        clf__max_depth: 150
        clf__min_samples_leaf: 1
        clf__min_samples_split: 3

Confusion Matrix on Test data
[[816  17]
 [ 19 132]]

Test Accuracy
0.963414634146

Precision Recall f1 table
precision   recall   f1-score    support
    0         0.98      0.98       0.98          833
    1         0.89      0.87       0.88          151
avg/total    0.96      0.96       0.96          984
[Finished in 0.1s]
```

The R code for grid searches on decision trees is as follows:

```
# Grid Search on Decision Trees
library(rpart)
input_data = read.csv("ad.csv",header=FALSE)
input_data$V1559 = as.factor(input_data$V1559)
set.seed(123)
numrow = nrow(input_data)
trnind = sample(1:numrow,size = as.integer(0.7*numrow))

train_data = input_data[trnind,];test_data = input_data[-trnind,]
minspset = c(2,3);minobset = c(1,2,3)
initacc = 0

for (minsp in minspset){
  for (minob in minobset){
    tr_fit = rpart(V1559 ~.,data = train_data,method = "class",minsplit =
minsp, minbucket = minob)
    tr_predt = predict(tr_fit,newdata = train_data,type = "class")
    tble = table(tr_predt,train_data$V1559)
    acc = (tble[1,1]+tble[2,2])/sum(tble)
    acc
```

```
      if (acc > initacc){
        tr_predtst = predict(tr_fit,newdata = test_data,type = "class")
        tblet = table(test_data$V1559,tr_predtst)
        acct = (tblet[1,1]+tblet[2,2])/sum(tblet)
        acct
        print(paste("Best Score"))
        print( paste("Train Accuracy ",round(acc,3),"Test
  Accuracy",round(acct,3)))
        print( paste(" Min split ",minsp," Min obs per node ",minob))
        print(paste("Confusion matrix on test data"))
        print(tblet)
        precsn_0 = (tblet[1,1])/(tblet[1,1]+tblet[2,1])
        precsn_1 = (tblet[2,2])/(tblet[1,2]+tblet[2,2])
        print(paste("Precision_0: ",round(precsn_0,3),"Precision_1:
  ",round(precsn_1,3)))
        rcall_0 = (tblet[1,1])/(tblet[1,1]+tblet[1,2])
        rcall_1 = (tblet[2,2])/(tblet[2,1]+tblet[2,2])
        print(paste("Recall_0: ",round(rcall_0,3),"Recall_1:
  ",round(rcall_1,3)))
        initacc = acc
      }
    }
  }
```

Machine learning model overview

Machine learning models are classified mainly into supervised, unsupervised, and reinforcement learning methods. We will be covering detailed discussions about each technique in later chapters; here is a very basic summary of them:

- **Supervised learning**: This is where an instructor provides feedback to a student on whether they have performed well in an examination or not. In which target variable do present and models do get tune to achieve it. Many machine learning methods fall in to this category:
    - Classification problems
    - Logistic regression
    - Lasso and ridge regression
    - Decision trees (classification trees)
    - Bagging classifier
    - Random forest classifier
    - Boosting classifier (adaboost, gradient boost, and xgboost)
    - SVM classifier

- Recommendation engine
- Regression problems
- Linear regression (lasso and ridge regression)
- Decision trees (regression trees)
- Bagging regressor
- Random forest regressor
- Boosting regressor - (adaboost, gradient boost, and xgboost)
- SVM regressor

- **Unsupervised learning**: Similar to the teacher-student analogy, in which the instructor does not present and provide feedback to the student and who needs to prepare on his/her own. Unsupervised learning does not have as many are in supervised learning:
  - **Principal component analysis (PCA)**
  - K-means clustering

- **Reinforcement learning**: This is the scenario in which multiple decisions need to be taken by an agent prior to reaching the target and it provides a reward, either +1 or -1, rather than notifying how well or how badly the agent performed across the path:
  - Markov decision process
  - Monte Carlo methods
  - Temporal difference learning

- **Logistic regression**: This is the problem in which outcomes are discrete classes rather than continuous values. For example, a customer will arrive or not, he will purchase the product or not, and so on. In statistical methodology, it uses the maximum likelihood method to calculate the parameter of individual variables. In contrast, in machine learning methodology, log loss will be minimized with respect to β coefficients (also known as weights). Logistic regression has a high bias and a low variance error.

- **Linear regression**: This is used for the prediction of continuous variables such as customer income and so on. It utilizes error minimization to fit the best possible line in statistical methodology. However, in machine learning methodology, squared loss will be minimized with respect to β coefficients. Linear regression also has a high bias and a low variance error.

- **Lasso and ridge regression**: This uses regularization to control overfitting issues by applying a penalty on coefficients. In ridge regression, a penalty is applied on the sum of squares of coefficients, whereas in lasso, a penalty is applied on the absolute values of the coefficients. The penalty can be tuned in order to change the dynamics of the model fit. Ridge regression tries to minimize the magnitude of coefficients, whereas lasso tries to eliminate them.

- **Decision trees**: Recursive binary splitting is applied to split the classes at each level to classify observations to their purest class. The classification error rate is simply the fraction of the training observations in that region that do not belong to the most common class. Decision trees have an overfitting problem due to their high variance in a way to fit; pruning is applied to reduce the overfitting problem by growing the tree completely. Decision trees have low a bias and a high variance error.

- **Bagging**: This is an ensemble technique applied on decision trees in order to minimize the variance error and at the same time not increase the error component due to bias. In bagging, various samples are selected with a subsample of observations and all variables (columns), subsequently fit individual decision trees independently on each sample and later ensemble the results by taking the maximum vote (in regression cases, the mean of outcomes calculated).

- **Random forest**: This is similar to bagging except for one difference. In bagging, all the variables/columns are selected for each sample, whereas in random forest a few subcolumns are selected. The reason behind the selection of a few variables rather than all was that during each independent tree sampled, significant variables always came first in the top layer of splitting which makes all the trees look more or less similar and defies the sole purpose of ensemble: that it works better on diversified and independent individual models rather than correlated individual models. Random forest has both low bias and variance errors.

- **Boosting**: This is a sequential algorithm that applies on weak classifiers such as a decision stump (a one-level decision tree or a tree with one root node and two terminal nodes) to create a strong classifier by ensembling the results. The algorithm starts with equal weights assigned to all the observations, followed by subsequent iterations where more focus was given to misclassified observations by increasing the weight of misclassified observations and decreasing the weight of properly classified observations. In the end, all the individual classifiers were combined to create a strong classifier. Boosting might have an overfitting problem, but by carefully tuning the parameters, we can obtain the best of the self machine learning model.

- **Support vector machines (SVMs)**: This maximizes the margin between classes by fitting the widest possible hyperplane between them. In the case of non-linearly separable classes, it uses kernels to move observations into higher-dimensional space and then separates them linearly with the hyperplane there.

- **Recommendation engine**: This utilizes a collaborative filtering algorithm to identify high-probability items to its respective users, who have not used it in the past, by considering the tastes of similar users who would be using that particular item. It uses the **alternating least squares (ALS)** methodology to solve this problem.

- **Principal component analysis (PCA)**: This is a dimensionality reduction technique in which principal components are calculated in place of the original variable. Principal components are determined where the variance in data is maximum; subsequently, the top *n* components will be taken by covering about 80 percent of variance and will be used in further modeling processes, or exploratory analysis will be performed as unsupervised learning.

- **K-means clustering**: This is an unsupervised algorithm that is mainly utilized for segmentation exercise. K-means clustering classifies the given data into *k* clusters in such a way that, within the cluster, variation is minimal and across the cluster, variation is maximal.

- **Markov decision process (MDP)**: In reinforcement learning, MDP is a mathematical framework for modeling decision-making of an agent in situations or environments where outcomes are partly random and partly under control. In this model, environment is modeled as a set of states and actions that can be performed by an agent to control the system's state. The objective is to control the system in such a way that the agent's total payoff is maximized.

- **Monte Carlo method**: Monte Carlo methods do not require complete knowledge of the environment, in contrast with MDP. Monte Carlo methods require only experience, which is obtained by sample sequences of states, actions, and rewards from actual or simulated interaction with the environment. Monte Carlo methods explore the space until the final outcome of a chosen sample sequences and update estimates accordingly.

- **Temporal difference learning**: This is a core theme in reinforcement learning. Temporal difference is a combination of both Monte Carlo and dynamic programming ideas. Similar to Monte Carlo, temporal difference methods can learn directly from raw experience without a model of the environment's dynamics. Like dynamic programming, temporal difference methods update estimates based in part on other learned estimates, without waiting for a final outcome. Temporal difference is the best of both worlds and is most commonly used in games such as AlphaGo and so on.

Summary

In this chapter, we have gained a high-level view of various basic building blocks and subcomponents involved in statistical modeling and machine learning, such as mean, variance, interquartile range, p-value, bias versus variance trade-off, AIC, Gini, area under the curve, and so on with respect to the statistics context, and cross-validation, gradient descent, and grid search concepts with respect to machine learning. We have explained all the concepts with the support of both Python and R code with various libraries such as `numpy`, `scipy`, `pandas`, and `scikit- learn`, and the `stats` model in Python and the basic `stats` package in R. In the next chapter, we will learn to draw parallels between statistical models and machine learning models with linear regression problems and ridge/lasso regression in machine learning using both Python and R code.

2
Parallelism of Statistics and Machine Learning

At first glance, machine learning seems to be distant from statistics. However, if we take a deeper look into them, we can draw parallels between both. In this chapter, we will deep dive into the details. Comparisons have been made between linear regression and lasso/ridge regression in order to provide a simple comparison between statistical modeling and machine learning. These are basic models in both worlds and are good to start with.

In this chapter, we will cover the following:

- Understanding of statistical parameters and diagnostics
- Compensating factors in machine learning models to equate statistical diagnostics
- Ridge and lasso regression
- Comparison of adjusted R-square with accuracy

Comparison between regression and machine learning models

Linear regression and machine learning models both try to solve the same problem in different ways. In the following simple example of a two-variable equation fitting the best possible plane, regression models try to fit the best possible hyperplane by minimizing the errors between the hyperplane and actual observations. However, in machine learning, the same problem has been converted into an optimization problem in which errors are modeled in squared form to minimize errors by altering the weights.

In statistical modeling, samples are drawn from the population and the model will be fitted on sampled data. However, in machine learning, even small numbers such as 30 observations would be good enough to update the weights at the end of each iteration; in a few cases, such as online learning, the model will be updated with even one observation:

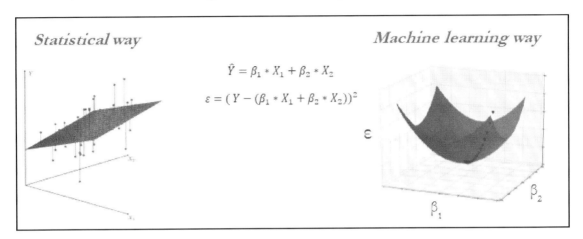

Machine learning models can be effectively parallelized and made to work on multiple machines in which model weights are broadcast across the machines, and so on. In the case of big data with Spark, these techniques are implemented.

Statistical models are parametric in nature, which means a model will have parameters on which diagnostics are performed to check the validity of the model. Whereas machine learning models are non-parametric, do not have any parameters, or curve assumptions; these models learn by themselves based on provided data and come up with complex and intricate functions rather than predefined function fitting.

Multi-collinearity checks are required to be performed in statistical modeling. Whereas, in machine learning space, weights automatically get adjusted to compensate the multi-collinearity problem. If we consider tree-based ensemble methods such as bagging, random forest, boosting, and so on, multi-collinearity does not even exist, as the underlying model is a decision tree, which does not have a multi-collinearity problem in the first place.

With the evolution of big data and distributed parallel computing, more complex models are producing state-of-the-art results which were impossible with past technology.

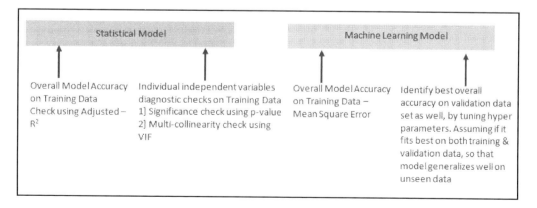

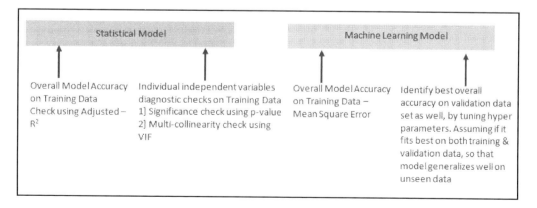

Compensating factors in machine learning models

Compensating factors in machine learning models to equate statistical diagnostics is explained with the example of a beam being supported by two supports. If one of the supports doesn't exist, the beam will eventually fall down by moving out of balance. A similar analogy is applied for comparing statistical modeling and machine learning methodologies here.

The two-point validation is performed on the statistical modeling methodology on training data using overall model accuracy and individual parameters significance test. Due to the fact that either linear or logistic regression has less variance by shape of the model itself, hence there would be very little chance of it working worse on unseen data. Hence, during deployment, these models do not incur too many deviated results.

However, in the machine learning space, models have a high degree of flexibility which can change from simple to highly complex. On top, statistical diagnostics on individual variables are not performed in machine learning. Hence, it is important to ensure the robustness to avoid overfitting of the models, which will ensure its usability during the implementation phase to ensure correct usage on unseen data.

As mentioned previously, in machine learning, data will be split into three parts (train data - 50 percent, validation data - 25 percent, testing data - 25 percent) rather than two parts in statistical methodology. Machine learning models should be developed on training data, and its hyperparameters should be tuned based on validation data to ensure the two-point validation equivalence; this way, the robustness of models is ensured without diagnostics performed at an individual variable level:

Before diving deep into comparisons between both streams, we will start understanding the fundamentals of each model individually. Let us start with linear regression! This model might sound trivial; however, knowing the linear regression working principles will create a foundation for more advanced statistical and machine learning models. Below are the assumptions of linear regression.

Assumptions of linear regression

Linear regression has the following assumptions, failing which the linear regression model does not hold true:

- The dependent variable should be a linear combination of independent variables
- No autocorrelation in error terms
- Errors should have zero mean and be normally distributed
- No or little multi-collinearity
- Error terms should be homoscedastic

These are explained in detail as follows:

- **The dependent variable should be a linear combination of independent variables**: Y should be a linear combination of X variables. Please note, in the following equation, $X2$ has raised to the power of 2, the equation is still holding the assumption of a linear combination of variables:

$$Y = A_0 + (\beta_1 * x_1) + (\beta_2 * x_2^2)$$

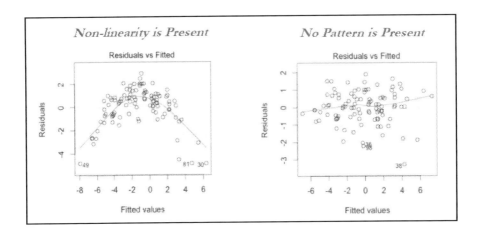

How to diagnose: Look into residual plots of residual versus independent variables. Also try to include polynomial terms and see any decrease in residual values, as polynomial terms may capture more signals from the data in case simple linear models do not capture them.

In the preceding sample graph, initially, linear regression was applied and the errors seem to have a pattern rather than being pure white noise; in this case, it is simply showing the presence of non-linearity. After increasing the power of the polynomial value, now the errors simply look like white noise.

- **No autocorrelation in error terms**: Presence of correlation in error terms penalized model accuracy.

    How to diagnose: Look for the Durbin-Watson test. Durbin-Watson's *d* tests the null hypothesis that the residuals are not linearly auto correlated. While *d* can lie between *0* and *4*, if *d ≈ 2* indicates no autocorrelation, *0<d<2* implies positive autocorrelation, and *2<d<4* indicates negative autocorrelation.

- **Error should have zero mean and be normally distributed**: Errors should have zero mean for the model to create an unbiased estimate. Plotting the errors will show the distribution of errors. Whereas, if error terms are not normally distributed, it implies confidence intervals will become too wide or narrow, which leads to difficulty in estimating coefficients based on minimization of least squares:

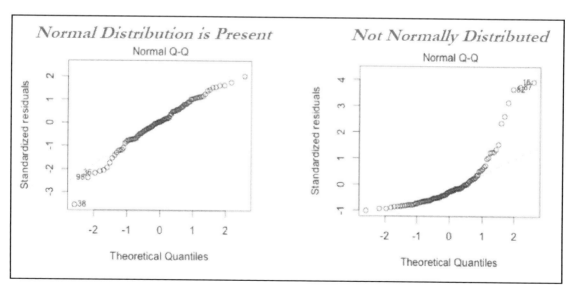

How to diagnose: Look into Q-Q plot and also tests such as Kolmogorov-Smirnov tests will be helpful. By looking into the above Q-Q plot, it is evident that the first chart shows errors are normally distributed, as the residuals do not seem to be deviating much compared with the diagonal-like line, whereas in the right-hand chart, it is clearly showing that errors are not normally distributed; in these scenarios, we need to reevaluate the variables by taking log transformations and so on to make residuals look as they do on the left-hand chart.

- **No or little multi-collinearity**: Multi-collinearity is the case in which independent variables are correlated with each other and this situation creates unstable models by inflating the magnitude of coefficients/estimates. It also becomes difficult to determine which variable is contributing to predict the response variable. *VIF* is calculated for each independent variable by calculating the R-squared value with respect to all the other independent variables and tries to eliminate which variable has the highest *VIF* value one by one:

$$VIF = \frac{1}{1 - R^2}$$

How to diagnose: Look into scatter plots, run correlation coefficient on all the variables of data. Calculate the **variance inflation factor (VIF)**. If *VIF <= 4* suggests no multi-collinearity, in banking scenarios, people use *VIF <= 2* also!

- **Errors should be homoscedastic**: Errors should have constant variance with respect to the independent variable, which leads to impractically wide or narrow confidence intervals for estimates, which degrades the model's performance. One reason for not holding homoscedasticity is due to the presence of outliers in the data, which drags the model fit toward them with higher weights:

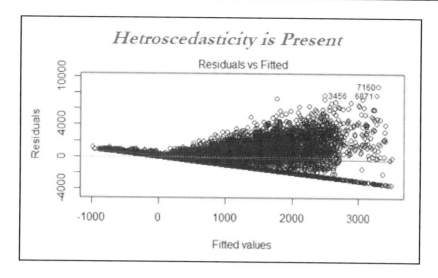

How to diagnose: Look into the residual versus dependent variables plot; if any pattern of cone or divergence does exist, it indicates the errors do not have constant variance, which impacts its predictions.

Steps applied in linear regression modeling

The following steps are applied in linear regression modeling in industry:

1. Missing value and outlier treatment
2. Correlation check of independent variables
3. Train and test random classification
4. Fit the model on train data
5. Evaluate model on test data

Example of simple linear regression from first principles

The entire chapter has been presented with the popular wine quality dataset which is openly available from the UCI machine learning repository at
https://archive.ics.uci.edu/ml/datasets/Wine+Quality.

Simple linear regression is a straightforward approach for predicting the dependent/response variable Y given the independent/predictor variable X. It assumes a linear relationship between X and Y:

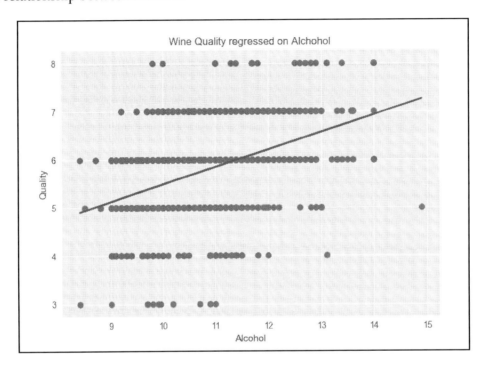

$\beta0$ and $\beta1$ are two unknown constants which are intercept and slope parameters respectively. Once we determine the constants, we can utilize them for the prediction of the dependent variable:

$$Y \approx \beta_0 + \beta_1 X ; \quad \hat{y} = \beta_0 + \beta_1 X$$

$$\hat{y}_i = \widehat{\beta_0} + \widehat{\beta_1} x_i \implies e_i = y_i - \hat{y}_i$$

$$RSS \ (Residual \ sum \ of \ squares) = e_1^2 + e_2^2 + \cdots + e_n^2$$

$$RSS = (y_1 - \widehat{\beta_0} - \widehat{\beta_1} x_1)^2 + (y_2 - \widehat{\beta_0} - \widehat{\beta_1} x_2)^2 + \cdots + (y_n - \widehat{\beta_0} - \widehat{\beta_1} x_n)^2$$

$$\widehat{\beta_1} = \frac{\sum_{i=1}^{n}(x_i - \bar{x})(y_i - \bar{y})}{\sum_{i=1}^{n}(x_i - \bar{x})^2} = \frac{cov(x, y)}{var(x)} \ ; \ \widehat{\beta_0} = \bar{y} - \widehat{\beta_1}\bar{x}$$

$$\bar{y} \equiv \frac{1}{n}\sum_{i=1}^{n} y_i \ ; \ \bar{x} \equiv \frac{1}{n}\sum_{i=1}^{n} x_i$$

Residuals are the differences between the *i*th observed response value and the *i*th response value that is predicted from the model. Residual sum of squares is shown. The least squares approach chooses estimates by minimizing errors.

In order to prove statistically that linear regression is significant, we have to perform hypothesis testing. Let's assume we start with the null hypothesis that there is no significant relationship between X and Y:

$$H_0: There\ is\ no\ relationship\ between\ X\ and\ Y$$

$$H_a: There\ is\ relationship\ between\ X\ and\ Y$$

$$H_0: \beta_1 = 0 \ ; \qquad H_a: \beta_1 \neq 0$$

Since, if *β1 = 0*, then the model shows no association between both variables (*Y = β0 + ε*), these are the null hypothesis assumptions; in order to prove this assumption right or wrong, we need to determine *β1* is sufficiently far from *0* (statistically significant in distance from *0* to be precise), that we can be confident that *β1* is nonzero and have a significant relationship between both variables. Now, the question is, how far is far enough from zero? It depends on the distribution of *β1*, which is its mean and standard error (similar to standard deviation). In some cases, if the standard error is small, even relatively small values may provide strong evidence that *β1 ≠ 0*, hence there is a relationship between X and Y. In contrast, if *SE(β1)* is large, then *β1* must be large in absolute value in order for us to reject the null hypothesis. We usually perform the following test to check how many standard deviations *β1* is away from the value *0*:

$$t = \frac{\widehat{\beta_1} - 0}{SE(\widehat{\beta_1})}$$

$$\bar{y} = \frac{1}{n}\sum_{i=1}^{n} y_i \ ; \ SS_{tot} = \sum_{i}(y_i - \bar{y})^2 \ ; \ SS_{reg} = \sum_{i}(f_i - \bar{y})^2 \ ; \ SS_{res} = \sum_{i}(y_i - f_i)^2 = \sum_{i} e_i^2$$

$$R^2 \equiv 1 - \frac{SS_{res}}{SS_{tot}}$$

With this t value, we calculate the probability of observing any value equal to $|t|$ or larger, assuming $\beta 1 = 0$; this probability is also known as the p-value. If *p-value < 0.05*, it signifies that $\beta 1$ is significantly far from *0*, hence we can reject the null hypothesis and agree that there exists a strong relationship, whereas if *p-value > 0.05*, we accept the null hypothesis and conclude that there is no significant relationship between both variables.

Once we have the coefficient values, we will try to predict the dependent value and check for the R-squared value; if the value is >= *0.7*, it means the model is good enough to deploy on unseen data, whereas if it is not such a good value (<*0.6*), we can conclude that this model is not good enough to deploy.

Example of simple linear regression using the wine quality data

In the wine quality data, the dependent variable (Y) is wine quality and the independent (X) variable we have chosen is alcohol content. We are testing here whether there is any significant relation between both, to check whether a change in alcohol percentage is the deciding factor in the quality of the wine:

```
>>> import pandas as pd
>>> from sklearn.model_selection import train_test_split
>>> from sklearn.metrics import r2_score

>>> wine_quality = pd.read_csv("winequality-red.csv",sep=';')
>>> wine_quality.rename(columns=lambda x: x.replace(" ", "_"),
inplace=True)
```

In the following step, the data is split into train and test using the 70 percent - 30 percent rule:

```
>>> x_train,x_test,y_train,y_test = train_test_split (wine_quality
['alcohol'], wine_quality["quality"],train_size = 0.7,random_state=42)
```

After splitting a single variable out of the DataFrame, it becomes a pandas series, hence we need to convert it back into a pandas DataFrame again:

```
>>> x_train = pd.DataFrame(x_train);x_test = pd.DataFrame(x_test)
>>> y_train = pd.DataFrame(y_train);y_test = pd.DataFrame(y_test)
```

The following function is for calculating the mean from the columns of the DataFrame. The mean was calculated for both `alcohol` (independent) and the `quality` (dependent) variables:

```
>>> def mean(values):
...         return round(sum(values)/float(len(values)),2)
>>> alcohol_mean = mean(x_train['alcohol'])
>>> quality_mean = mean(y_train['quality'])
```

Variance and covariance is indeed needed for calculating the coefficients of the regression model:

```
>>> alcohol_variance = round(sum((x_train['alcohol'] - alcohol_mean)**2),2)
>>> quality_variance = round(sum((y_train['quality'] - quality_mean)**2),2)

>>> covariance = round(sum((x_train['alcohol'] - alcohol_mean) *
(y_train['quality'] - quality_mean )),2)
>>> b1 = covariance/alcohol_variance
>>> b0 = quality_mean - b1*alcohol_mean
>>> print ("\n\nIntercept (B0):",round(b0,4),"Co-efficient
(B1):",round(b1,4))
```

After computing coefficients, it is necessary to predict the `quality` variable, which will test the quality of fit using R-squared value:

```
>>> y_test["y_pred"] = pd.DataFrame(b0+b1*x_test['alcohol'])
>>> R_sqrd = 1- ( sum((y_test['quality']-y_test['y_pred'])**2) /
sum((y_test['quality'] - mean(y_test['quality']))**2 ))
>>> print ("Test R-squared value",round(R_sqrd,4))
```

```
Intercept (B0): 1.6918 Co-efficient (B1): 0.377
Test R-squared value: 0.185
```

From the test R-squared value, we can conclude that there is no strong relationship between `quality` and `alcohol` variables in the wine data, as R-squared is less than *0.7*.

Simple regression fit using first principles is described in the following R code:

```r
wine_quality = read.csv("winequality-red.csv",header=TRUE,sep =
";",check.names = FALSE)
names(wine_quality) <- gsub(" ", "_", names(wine_quality))

set.seed(123)
numrow = nrow(wine_quality)
trnind = sample(1:numrow,size = as.integer(0.7*numrow))
train_data = wine_quality[trnind,]
test_data = wine_quality[-trnind,]

x_train = train_data$alcohol;y_train = train_data$quality
x_test = test_data$alcohol; y_test = test_data$quality

x_mean = mean(x_train); y_mean = mean(y_train)
x_var = sum((x_train - x_mean)**2) ; y_var = sum((y_train-y_mean)**2)
covariance = sum((x_train-x_mean)*(y_train-y_mean))

b1 = covariance/x_var
b0 = y_mean - b1*x_mean

pred_y = b0+b1*x_test

R2 <- 1 - (sum((y_test-pred_y )^2)/sum((y_test-mean(y_test))^2))
print(paste("Test Adjusted R-squared :",round(R2,4)))
```

Example of multilinear regression - step-by-step methodology of model building

In this section, we actually show the approach followed by industry experts while modeling using linear regression with sample wine data. The `statmodels.api` package has been used for multiple linear regression demonstration purposes instead of scikit-learn, due to the fact that the former provides diagnostics on variables, whereas the latter only provides final accuracy, and so on:

```python
>>> import numpy as np
>>> import pandas as pd
>>> import statsmodels.api as sm
>>> import matplotlib.pyplot as plt
>>> import seaborn as sns
>>> from sklearn.model_selection import train_test_split
```

```
>>> from sklearn.metrics import r2_score

>>> wine_quality = pd.read_csv("winequality-red.csv",sep=';')
# Step for converting white space in columns to _ value for better handling
>>> wine_quality.rename(columns=lambda x: x.replace(" ", "_"),
inplace=True)
>>> eda_colnms = [ 'volatile_acidity',  'chlorides', 'sulphates',
'alcohol','quality']
# Plots - pair plots
>>> sns.set(style='whitegrid',context = 'notebook')
```

Pair plots for sample five variables are shown as follows; however, we encourage you to try various combinations to check various relationships visually between the various other variables:

```
>>> sns.pairplot(wine_quality[eda_colnms],size = 2.5,x_vars= eda_colnms,
y_vars= eda_colnms)
>>> plt.show()
```

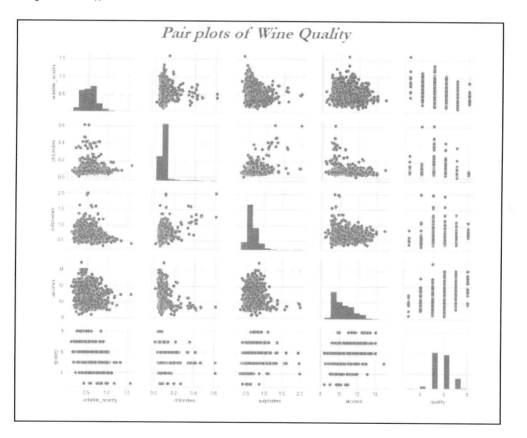

In addition to visual plots, correlation coefficients are calculated to show the level of correlation in numeric terminology; these charts are used to drop variables in the initial stage, if there are many of them to start with:

```
>>> # Correlation coefficients
>>> corr_mat = np.corrcoef(wine_quality[eda_colnms].values.T)
>>> sns.set(font_scale=1)
>>> full_mat = sns.heatmap(corr_mat, cbar=True, annot=True, square=True,
fmt='.2f',annot_kws={'size': 15}, yticklabels=eda_colnms,
xticklabels=eda_colnms)
>>> plt.show()
```

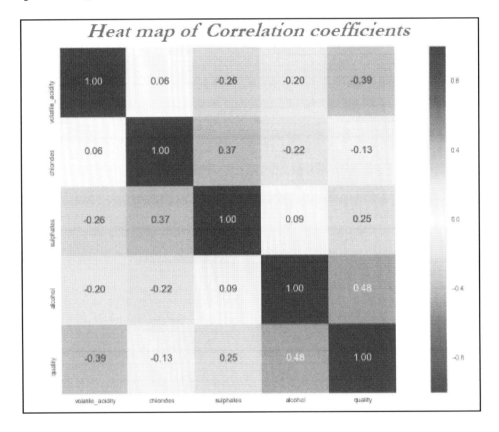

Backward and forward selection

There are various methods to add or remove variables to determine the best possible model.

In the backward method, iterations start with considering all the variables and we will remove variables one by one until all the prescribed statistics are met (such as no insignificance and multi-collinearity, and so on). Finally, the overall statistic will be checked, such as if R-squared value is > *0.7* , it is considered a good model, else reject it. In industry, practitioners mainly prefer to work on backward methods.

In the case of forward, we will start with no variables and keep on adding significant variables until the overall model's fit improves.

In the following method, we have used the backward selection method, starting with all the 11 independent variables and removing them one by one from analysis after each iteration (insignificant and multi-collinear variable):

```
>>> colnms = ['fixed_acidity', 'volatile_acidity', 'citric_acid',
'residual_sugar', 'chlorides', 'free_sulfur_dioxide',
'total_sulfur_dioxide', 'density', 'pH', 'sulphates', 'alcohol']

>>> pdx = wine_quality[colnms]
>>> pdy = wine_quality["quality"]
```

Create the train and test data by randomly performing the data split. The `random_state` (random seed) is used for reproducible results:

```
>>> x_train,x_test,y_train,y_test = train_test_split(pdx, pdy, train_size =
0.7, random_state = 42)
```

In the following code, adding `constant` means creating an intercept variable. If we do not create an intercept, the coefficients will change accordingly:

```
>>> x_train_new = sm.add_constant(x_train)
>>> x_test_new = sm.add_constant(x_test)
>>> full_mod = sm.OLS(y_train,x_train_new)
```

The following code creates a model summary including R-squared, adjusted R-squared, and the p-value of independent variables:

```
>>> full_res = full_mod.fit()
>>> print ("\n \n",full_res.summary())
```

The following code calculated VIF for all individual variables from first principles. Here we are calculating the R-squared value for each variable and converting it into a VIF value:

```
>>> print ("\nVariance Inflation Factor")
>>> cnames = x_train.columns
>>> for i in np.arange(0,len(cnames)):
...       xvars = list(cnames)
...       yvar = xvars.pop(i)
...       mod = sm.OLS(x_train[yvar],sm.add_constant( x_train_new[xvars]))
...       res = mod.fit()
...       vif = 1/(1-res.rsquared)
...       print (yvar,round(vif,3))
```

The preceding code generates the following output, from which we can start thinking about tuning the multilinear regression model.

Iteration 1:

```
                         OLS Regression Results
==============================================================================
Dep. Variable:              quality   R-squared:                       0.361
Model:                          OLS   Adj. R-squared:                  0.355
Method:               Least Squares   F-statistic:                     56.90
Date:              Sun, 02 Apr 2017   Prob (F-statistic):           8.34e-100
Time:                      11:26:48   Log-Likelihood:                 -1103.5
No. Observations:              1119   AIC:                             2231.
Df Residuals:                  1107   BIC:                             2291.
Df Model:                        11
Covariance Type:          nonrobust
==============================================================================
                        coef    std err          t      P>|t|      [95.0% Conf. Int.]
------------------------------------------------------------------------------
const                17.9626     25.237      0.712      0.477     -31.555     67.480
fixed_acidity         0.0235      0.031      0.769      0.442      -0.036      0.083
volatile_acidity     -1.0996      0.145     -7.599      0.000      -1.384     -0.816
citric_acid          -0.2479      0.177     -1.402      0.161      -0.595      0.099
residual_sugar        0.0077      0.018      0.429      0.668      -0.028      0.043
chlorides            -1.6736      0.500     -3.344      0.001      -2.656     -0.692
free_sulfur_dioxide   0.0046      0.003      1.706      0.088      -0.001      0.010
total_sulfur_dioxide -0.0033      0.001     -3.723      0.000      -0.005     -0.002
density             -14.2396     25.750     -0.553      0.580     -64.763     36.284
pH                   -0.3192      0.227     -1.404      0.161      -0.766      0.127
sulphates             0.8128      0.135      6.007      0.000       0.547      1.078
alcohol               0.2920      0.032      9.268      0.000       0.230      0.354
==============================================================================
Omnibus:                     29.060   Durbin-Watson:                   2.001
Prob(Omnibus):                0.000   Jarque-Bera (JB):               50.192
Skew:                        -0.193   Prob(JB):                     1.26e-11
Kurtosis:                     3.963   Cond. No.                     1.13e+05
==============================================================================
```

The key metrics to focus on while tuning the model are AIC, adjusted R-squared, individual variable's $P>|t|$, and VIF values (shown as follows). Any model would be considered as good to go having the following thumb rule criteria:

- **AIC**: No absolute value is significant. It is a relative measure, the lower the better.
- **Adjusted R-squared**: It is ≥ 0.7.
- **Individual variable's p-value (P>|t|)**: It is ≤ 0.05.
- **Individual variable's VIF**: It is ≤ 5 (in the banking industry, at some places, people use ≤ 2 as well).

```
Variance Inflation Factor
fixed_acidity 7.189
volatile_acidity 1.824
citric_acid 3.139
residual_sugar 1.742
chlorides 1.463
free_sulfur_dioxide 1.973
total_sulfur_dioxide 2.205
density 5.902
pH 3.224
sulphates 1.428
alcohol 2.93
```

By looking into the preceding results, `residual_sugar` has highest the p-value of `0.668` and `fixed_acidity` has the highest VIF value of `7.189`. In this situation, always first remove the most insignificant variable, as insignificance is a more serious problem than multi-collinearity, though both should be removed while reaching the final model.

Run the preceding code after removing the `residual_sugar` variable from the columns list; we get the following result from iteration 2:

- **AIC**: Merely reduced from 2231 to 2229.
- **Adjusted R-squared**: Value did not change from 0.355.
- **Individual variable's p-value (P>|t|)**: Density is still coming in as most insignificant with a value of 0.713.
- **Individual variable's VIF**: The `fixed_acidity` has the $VIF \geq 5$. However, the `density` variable needs to be removed first, as priority is given to insignificance.

Iteration 2:

```
                          OLS Regression Results
===========================================================================
Dep. Variable:              quality   R-squared:                     0.361
Model:                          OLS   Adj. R-squared:                0.355
Method:               Least Squares   F-statistic:                   62.62
Date:              Sun, 02 Apr 2017   Prob (F-statistic):         1.12e-100
Time:                      11:38:31   Log-Likelihood:               -1103.6
No. Observations:              1119   AIC:                           2229.
Df Residuals:                  1108   BIC:                           2284.
Df Model:                        10
Covariance Type:            nonrobust
===========================================================================
                        coef    std err          t      P>|t|    [95.0% Conf. Int.]
---------------------------------------------------------------------------
const                11.3324     19.948      0.568      0.570    -27.807     50.472
fixed_acidity         0.0175      0.027      0.645      0.519     -0.036      0.071
volatile_acidity     -1.0997      0.145     -7.602      0.000     -1.384     -0.816
citric_acid          -0.2417      0.176     -1.372      0.170     -0.587      0.104
density              -7.4762     20.356     -0.367      0.713    -47.416     32.464
chlorides            -1.6752      0.500     -3.349      0.001     -2.657     -0.694
free_sulfur_dioxide   0.0047      0.003      1.775      0.076     -0.000      0.010
total_sulfur_dioxide -0.0033      0.001     -3.718      0.000     -0.005     -0.002
pH                   -0.3524      0.214     -1.648      0.100     -0.772      0.067
sulphates             0.8010      0.132      6.049      0.000      0.541      1.061
alcohol               0.2988      0.027     11.010      0.000      0.246      0.352
===========================================================================
Omnibus:                     27.765    Durbin-Watson:                 2.000
Prob(Omnibus):                0.000    Jarque-Bera (JB):             47.597
Skew:                        -0.185    Prob(JB):                   4.62e-11
Kurtosis:                     3.940    Cond. No.                   8.92e+04
===========================================================================
```

```
Variance Inflation Factor
fixed_acidity 5.707
volatile_acidity 1.824
citric_acid 3.118
density 3.691
chlorides 1.463
free_sulfur_dioxide 1.942
total_sulfur_dioxide 2.204
pH 2.852
sulphates 1.368
alcohol 2.176
```

Based on iteration 2, we need to remove the density variable and rerun the exercise until no violation of p-value and VIF happens. We did skip the intermediate steps to save space; however, you are encouraged to manually do the step-by-step process of removing variables one by one.

The model could not be improved further after iteration 5, as it satisfies all the p-value and VIF criteria. The results are presented here.

Iteration 5:

```
                          OLS Regression Results
==============================================================================
Dep. Variable:                quality   R-squared:                       0.360
Model:                            OLS   Adj. R-squared:                  0.356
Method:                 Least Squares   F-statistic:                     89.21
Date:                Sun, 02 Apr 2017   Prob (F-statistic):          4.31e-103
Time:                        11:46:12   Log-Likelihood:                -1104.7
No. Observations:                1119   AIC:                             2225.
Df Residuals:                    1111   BIC:                             2266.
Df Model:                           7
Covariance Type:            nonrobust
==============================================================================
                        coef    std err          t      P>|t|      [95.0% Conf. Int.]
------------------------------------------------------------------------------
const                 3.9210      0.486      8.074      0.000       2.968      4.874
volatile_acidity     -0.9941      0.119     -8.327      0.000      -1.228     -0.760
chlorides            -1.8800      0.474     -3.963      0.000      -2.811     -0.949
free_sulfur_dioxide   0.0054      0.003      2.075      0.038       0.000      0.010
total_sulfur_dioxide -0.0036      0.001     -4.395      0.000      -0.005     -0.002
pH                   -0.3469      0.141     -2.465      0.014      -0.623     -0.071
sulphates             0.7872      0.130      6.049      0.000       0.532      1.043
alcohol               0.2987      0.020     14.672      0.000       0.259      0.339
==============================================================================
Omnibus:                       27.862   Durbin-Watson:                   1.998
Prob(Omnibus):                  0.000   Jarque-Bera (JB):               47.326
Skew:                          -0.189   Prob(JB):                     5.29e-11
Kurtosis:                       3.934   Cond. No.                     1.71e+03
==============================================================================
```

```
Variance Inflation Factor
volatile_acidity 1.243
chlorides 1.317
free_sulfur_dioxide 1.878
total_sulfur_dioxide 1.956
pH 1.236
sulphates 1.322
alcohol 1.225
```

In this example, we have got the final results after iteration 5:

- **AIC**: Reduced from 2231 from iteration 1 to 2225 in iteration 5.
- **Adjusted R-squared**: Value changed to 0.356, which is a slight improvement but not worth enough!
- **Individual variable's p-value (P>|t|)**: None of the variables are insignificant; all values are less than 0.05.
- **Individual variable's VIF**: All variables are less than five. Hence, we do not need to remove any further variable based on VIF value.

We have got the answer that no strong relationship between the dependent and independent variables exists. However, we can still predict based on the testing data and calculate R-square to reconfirm.

 If a predictive model shows as strong relationship, the prediction step is a must-have utilize model in the deployment stage. Hence, we are predicting and evaluating the R-squared value here.

The following code steps utilize the model to predict on testing data:

```
>>> # Prediction of data
>>> y_pred = full_res.predict(x_test_new)
>>> y_pred_df = pd.DataFrame(y_pred)
>>> y_pred_df.columns = ['y_pred']

>>> pred_data = pd.DataFrame(y_pred_df['y_pred'])
>>> y_test_new = pd.DataFrame(y_test)
>>> y_test_new.reset_index(inplace=True)
>>> pred_data['y_test'] = pd.DataFrame(y_test_new['quality'])
```

For R-square calculation, the scikit-learn package `sklean.metrics` module is utilized:

```
>>> # R-square calculation
>>> rsqd = r2_score(y_test_new['quality'].tolist(),
y_pred_df['y_pred'].tolist())
>>> print ("\nTest R-squared value:",round(rsqd,4))
```

```
Test R-squared value: 0.3519
```

The adjusted R-square value for test data appears as 0.3519, whereas the training R-square is 0.356. From the final results, we can conclude that the relationship between the independent variable and dependent variable (quality) is not able to be established with linear regression methodology.

The R code for linear regression on the wine data is as follows:

```
library(usdm)
# Linear Regression
wine_quality = read.csv("winequality-red.csv",header=TRUE,sep =
";",check.names = FALSE)
names(wine_quality) <- gsub(" ", "_", names(wine_quality))

set.seed(123)
numrow = nrow(wine_quality)
trnind = sample(1:numrow,size = as.integer(0.7*numrow))
train_data = wine_quality[trnind,]
test_data = wine_quality[-trnind,]
xvars = c("volatile_acidity","chlorides","free_sulfur_dioxide",
          "total_sulfur_dioxide","pH","sulphates","alcohol")
yvar = "quality"
frmla = paste(yvar,"~",paste(xvars,collapse = "+"))
lr_fit = lm(as.formula(frmla),data = train_data)
print(summary(lr_fit))
#VIF calculation
wine_v2 = train_data[,xvars]
print(vif(wine_v2))
#Test prediction
pred_y = predict(lr_fit,newdata = test_data)
R2 <- 1 - (sum((test_data[,yvar]-pred_y )^2)/sum((test_data[,yvar]-
mean(test_data[,yvar]))^2))
print(paste("Test Adjusted R-squared :",R2))
```

Machine learning models - ridge and lasso regression

In linear regression, only the **residual sum of squares** (RSS) is minimized, whereas in ridge and lasso regression, a penalty is applied (also known as **shrinkage penalty**) on coefficient values to regularize the coefficients with the tuning parameter λ.

When $\lambda=0$, the penalty has no impact, ridge/lasso produces the same result as linear regression, whereas $\lambda \to \infty$ will bring coefficients to zero:

$$RSS\,(\beta) = \sum_{i=1}^{n} \left(y_i - \beta_0 - \sum_{j=1}^{p} \beta_j x_{ij} \right)^2$$

$$Objective\ function\ to\ minimize\ in\ Ridge\ Regression\ =\ RSS(\beta) + \lambda \sum_{j=1}^{p} \beta_j^2$$

$$Objective\ function\ to\ minimize\ in\ Lasso\ Regression\ =\ RSS(\beta) + \lambda \sum_{j=1}^{p} |\beta_j|$$

Before we go deeper into ridge and lasso, it is worth understanding some concepts on Lagrangian multipliers. One can show the preceding objective function in the following format, where the objective is just RSS subjected to cost constraint (s) of budget. For every value of λ, there is an s such that will provide the equivalent equations, as shown for the overall objective function with a penalty factor:

$$Lasso \to minimize\ \{RSS(\beta)\}\quad s.to.\ \sum_{j=1}^{p} |\beta_j| \leq s$$

$$Ridge \to minimize\ \{RSS(\beta)\}\quad s.to.\ \sum_{j=1}^{p} \beta_j^2 \leq s$$

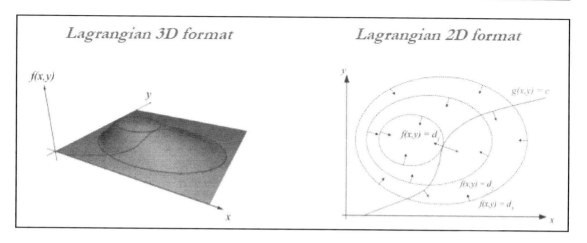

Ridge regression works well in situations where the least squares estimates have high variance. Ridge regression has computational advantages over best subset selection, which requires 2P models. In contrast, for any fixed value of λ, ridge regression only fits a single model and the model-fitting procedure can be performed very quickly.

One disadvantage of ridge regression is it will include all the predictors and shrinks the weights according to their importance, but it does not set the values exactly to zero in order to eliminate unnecessary predictors from models; this issue is overcome in lasso regression. Given a situation where the number of predictors is significantly large, using ridge may provide accuracy, but it includes all the variables, which is not desired in a compact representation of the model; this issue is not present in lasso, as it will set the weights of unnecessary variables to zero.

Models generated from lasso are very much like subset selection, hence they are much easier to interpret than those produced by ridge regression.

Example of ridge regression machine learning

Ridge regression is a machine learning model in which we do not perform any statistical diagnostics on the independent variables and just utilize the model to fit on test data and check the accuracy of the fit. Here, we have used the `scikit-learn` package:

```
>>> from sklearn.linear_model import Ridge

>>> wine_quality = pd.read_csv("winequality-red.csv",sep=';')
>>> wine_quality.rename(columns=lambda x: x.replace(" ", "_"),
inplace=True)
```

```
>>> all_colnms = ['fixed_acidity', 'volatile_acidity', 'citric_acid',
'residual_sugar', 'chlorides', 'free_sulfur_dioxide',
'total_sulfur_dioxide', 'density', 'pH', 'sulphates', 'alcohol']

>>> pdx = wine_quality[all_colnms]
>>> pdy = wine_quality["quality"]

>>> x_train,x_test,y_train,y_test = train_test_split(pdx,pdy,train_size =
0.7,random_state=42)
```

A simple version of a grid search from scratch is described as follows, in which various values of `alphas` are to be tested in a grid search to test the model's fitness:

```
>>> alphas = [1e-4,1e-3,1e-2,0.1,0.5,1.0,5.0,10.0]
```

Initial values of R-squared are set to 0 in order to keep track of its updated value and to print whenever the new value is greater than the existing value:

```
>>> initrsq = 0

>>> print ("\nRidge Regression: Best Parameters\n")
>>> for alph in alphas:
...        ridge_reg = Ridge(alpha=alph)
...        ridge_reg.fit(x_train,y_train)    0
...        tr_rsqrd = ridge_reg.score(x_train,y_train)
...        ts_rsqrd = ridge_reg.score(x_test,y_test)
```

The following code always keeps track of the test R-squared value and prints if the new value is greater than the existing best value:

```
>>>       if ts_rsqrd > initrsq:
...            print ("Lambda: ",alph,"Train R-Squared
value:",round(tr_rsqrd,5),"Test R-squared value:",round(ts_rsqrd,5))
...            initrsq = ts_rsqrd
```

This is shown in the following screenshot:

```
Ridge Regression: Best Parameters

Lambda:  0.0001 Train R-Squared value: 0.3612 Test R-squared value: 0.35135
```

Also, please note that the test R-squared value generated from ridge regression is similar to the value obtained from multiple linear regression (0.3519), but with no stress on the diagnostics of variables, and so on. Hence, machine learning models are relatively compact and can be utilized for learning automatically without manual intervention to retrain the model; this is one of the biggest advantages of using ML models for deployment purposes.

The R code for ridge regression on the wine quality data is as follows:

```
# Ridge regression
library(glmnet)

wine_quality = read.csv("winequality-red.csv",header=TRUE,sep =
";",check.names = FALSE)
names(wine_quality) <- gsub(" ", "_", names(wine_quality))

set.seed(123)
numrow = nrow(wine_quality)
trnind = sample(1:numrow,size = as.integer(0.7*numrow))
train_data = wine_quality[trnind,]; test_data = wine_quality[-trnind,]

xvars =
c("fixed_acidity","volatile_acidity","citric_acid","residual_sugar","chlori
des","free_sulfur_dioxide",
"total_sulfur_dioxide","density","pH","sulphates","alcohol")
yvar = "quality"

x_train = as.matrix(train_data[,xvars]);y_train = as.double (as.matrix
(train_data[,yvar]))
x_test = as.matrix(test_data[,xvars])

print(paste("Ridge Regression"))
lambdas = c(1e-4,1e-3,1e-2,0.1,0.5,1.0,5.0,10.0)
initrsq = 0
for (lmbd in lambdas){
  ridge_fit = glmnet(x_train,y_train,alpha = 0,lambda = lmbd)
  pred_y = predict(ridge_fit,x_test)
  R2 <- 1 - (sum((test_data[,yvar]-pred_y )^2)/sum((test_data[,yvar]-
mean(test_data[,yvar]))^2))
  if (R2 > initrsq){
    print(paste("Lambda:",lmbd,"Test Adjusted R-squared :",round(R2,4)))
    initrsq = R2
  }
}
```

Example of lasso regression machine learning model

Lasso regression is a close cousin of ridge regression, in which absolute values of coefficients are minimized rather than the square of values. By doing so, we eliminate some insignificant variables, which are a very much compacted representation similar to OLS methods.

The following implementation is similar to ridge regression apart from penalty application on mod/absolute value of coefficients:

```
>>> from sklearn.linear_model import Lasso

>>> alphas = [1e-4,1e-3,1e-2,0.1,0.5,1.0,5.0,10.0]
>>> initrsq = 0
>>> print ("\nLasso Regression: Best Parameters\n")

>>> for alph in alphas:
...       lasso_reg = Lasso(alpha=alph)
...       lasso_reg.fit(x_train,y_train)
...       tr_rsqrd = lasso_reg.score(x_train,y_train)
...       ts_rsqrd = lasso_reg.score(x_test,y_test)

...       if ts_rsqrd > initrsq:
...           print ("Lambda: ",alph,"Train R-Squared
value:",round(tr_rsqrd,5),"Test R-squared value:",round(ts_rsqrd,5))
...               initrsq = ts_rsqrd
```

This is shown in the following screenshot:

```
Lasso Regression: Best Parameters

Lambda:  0.0001 Train R-Squared value: 0.36101 Test R-squared value: 0.35057
```

```
>>> ridge_reg = Ridge(alpha=0.001)
>>> ridge_reg.fit(x_train,y_train)
>>> print ("\nRidge Regression coefficient values of Alpha = 0.001\n")
>>> for i in range(11):
...       print (all_colnms[i],": ",ridge_reg.coef_[i])

>>> lasso_reg = Lasso(alpha=0.001)
>>> lasso_reg.fit(x_train,y_train)
>>> print ("\nLasso Regression coefficient values of Alpha = 0.001\n")
>>> for i in range(11):
...       print (all_colnms[i],": ",lasso_reg.coef_[i])
```

The following results show the coefficient values of both methods; the coefficient of density has been set to 0 in lasso regression, whereas the density value is -5.5672 in ridge regression; also, none of the coefficients in ridge regression are zero values:

```
Ridge Regression coeficcient values of Alpha = 0.001

fixed_acidity :  0.015506587508
volatile_acidity :  -1.10509823549
citric_acid :  -0.248798655324
residual_sugar :  0.00401889539284
chlorides :  -1.68438396209
free_sulfur_dioxide :  0.00463690171096
total_sulfur_dioxide :  -0.00328376790411
density :  -5.5672717468
pH :  -0.362480017204
sulphates :  0.800919122803
alcohol :  0.299918244295
```

```
Lasso Regression coeficcient values of Alpha = 0.001

fixed_acidity :  0.0141495463691
volatile_acidity :  -1.09062360905
citric_acid :  -0.185295150047
residual_sugar :  -0.000136610246787
chlorides :  -1.05877579704
free_sulfur_dioxide :  0.00483164817515
total_sulfur_dioxide :  -0.00326722885596
density :  -0.0
pH :  -0.256901925871
sulphates :  0.694487540316
alcohol :  0.307756149124
```

The R code for lasso regression on the wine quality data is as follows:

```
# Above Data processing steps are same as Ridge Regression, only below
section of the code do change

# Lasso Regression
print(paste("Lasso Regression"))
lambdas = c(1e-4,1e-3,1e-2,0.1,0.5,1.0,5.0,10.0)
initrsq = 0
for (lmbd in lambdas){
  lasso_fit = glmnet(x_train,y_train,alpha = 1,lambda = lmbd)
  pred_y = predict(lasso_fit,x_test)
  R2 <- 1 - (sum((test_data[,yvar]-pred_y )^2)/sum((test_data[,yvar]-
mean(test_data[,yvar]))^2))
  if (R2 > initrsq){
    print(paste("Lambda:",lmbd,"Test Adjusted R-squared :",round(R2,4)))
    initrsq = R2
  }
}
```

Regularization parameters in linear regression and ridge/lasso regression

Adjusted R-squared in linear regression always penalizes, adding extra variables with less significance is one type of regularizing the data in linear regression, but it will adjust to the unique fit of the model. Whereas, in machine learning, many parameters are adjusted to regularize the overfitting problem. In the example of lasso/ridge regression penalty parameter (λ) adjusted to regularization, there are infinite values that can be applied to regularize the model in infinite ways:

$$R^2_{adjusted} = 1 - \frac{(1 - R^2)(n - 1)}{n - k - 1}$$

$$Ridge\ Regression = RSS(\beta) + \lambda \sum_{j=1}^{p} \beta_j^2$$

Overall, there are many similarities between the statistical way and machine learning way of predicting the pattern.

Summary

In this chapter, you have learned the comparison of statistical models with machine learning models applied on regression problems. The multiple linear regression methodology has been illustrated with a step-by-step iterative process using the `statsmodel` package by removing insignificant and multi-collinear variables. Whereas, in machine learning models, removal of variables does not need to be removed and weights get adjusted automatically, but have parameters which can be tuned to fine-tune the model fit, as machine learning models learn by themselves based on data rather than exclusively being modeled by removing variables manually. Though we got almost the same accuracy results between linear regression and lasso/ridge regression methodologies, by using highly powerful machine learning models such as random forest, we can achieve much better uplift in model accuracy than conventional statistical models. In the next chapter, we will be covering a classification example with logistic regression and a highly powerful machine learning model, such as random forest, in detail.

3
Logistic Regression Versus Random Forest

In this chapter, we will be making a comparison between logistic regression and random forest, with a classification example of German credit data. Logistic regression is a very popularly utilized technique in the credit and risk industry for checking the probability of default problems. Major challenges nowadays being faced by credit and risk departments with regulators are due to the black box nature of machine learning models, which is slowing down the usage of advanced models in this space. However, by drawing comparisons of logistic regression with random forest, some turnarounds could be possible; here we will discuss the variable importance chart and its parallels to the p-value of logistic regression, also we should not forget the major fact that significant variables remain significant in any of the models on a fair ground, though some change in variable significance always exists between any two models.

Maximum likelihood estimation

Logistic regression works on the principle of maximum likelihood estimation; here, we will explain in detail what it is in principle so that we can cover some more fundamentals of logistic regression in the following sections. Maximum likelihood estimation is a method of estimating the parameters of a model given observations, by finding the parameter values that maximize the likelihood of making the observations, this means finding parameters that maximize the probability p of event 1 and $(1-p)$ of non-event 0, as you know:

$$probability\ (event + non\text{-}event) = 1$$

Example: Sample *(0, 1, 0, 0, 1, 0)* is drawn from binomial distribution. What is the maximum likelihood estimate of μ?

Solution: Given the fact that for binomial distribution $P(X=1) = \mu$ and $P(X=0) = 1- \mu$ where μ is the parameter:

$$Likelihood \ of \ \mu = L(\mu)$$
$$= P(x = 0) * P(x = 1) * P(x = 0) * P(x = 0) * P(x = 1) * P(x = 0)$$
$$= (1 - \mu) * \mu * (1 - \mu) * (1 - \mu) * \mu * (1 - \mu)$$
$$L(\mu) = (1 - \mu)^4 \mu^2$$

Here, *log* is applied to both sides of the equation for mathematical convenience; also, maximizing likelihood is the same as the maximizing log of likelihood:

$$\log(L(\mu)) = \log((1 - \mu)^4 \mu^2)$$
$$\log(L(\mu)) = 4 * \log(1 - \mu) + 2 * \log(\mu)$$

Determining the maximum value of μ by equating derivative to zero:

$$\frac{\partial}{\partial\mu} \log(L(\mu)) = 0$$
$$\Rightarrow 4 * \frac{1}{1 - \mu} * (-1) + 2 * \frac{1}{\mu} = 0$$
$$-4 * \mu + 2 * (1 - \mu) = 0$$
$$\mu = \frac{1}{3}$$

However, we need to do double differentiation to determine the saddle point obtained from equating derivative to zero is maximum or minimum. If the μ value is maximum; double differentiation of *log(L(μ))* should be a negative value:

$$\frac{\partial^2}{\partial\mu^2} \log(L(\mu)) = -4 * \frac{1}{(1 - \mu)^2} - \frac{2}{\mu^2}$$

Even without substitution of μ value in double differentiation, we can determine that it is a negative value, as denominator values are squared and it has a negative sign against both terms. Nonetheless, we are substituting and the value is:

$$\frac{\partial^2}{\partial\mu^2} \log(L(\mu)) = -4 * \frac{1}{\left(1 - \frac{1}{3}\right)^2} - \frac{2}{\left(\frac{1}{3}\right)^2} = -9 - 18 = -27$$

Hence it has been proven that at value $\mu = 1/3$, it is maximizing the likelihood. If we substitute the value in the log likelihood function, we will obtain:

$$L(\mu) = \left(1 - \frac{1}{3}\right)^4 \frac{1^2}{3} = 0.021948$$
$$\ln\left(L(\mu)\right) = \ln(0.021948) = -3.819$$
$$-2 \ln\left(L(\mu)\right) = -2 * -3.819 = 7.63$$

The reason behind calculating *-2*ln(L)* is to replicate the metric calculated in proper logistic regression. In fact:

$$AIC = -2*ln(L) + 2*k$$

So, logistic regression tries to find the parameters by maximizing the likelihood with respect to individual parameters. But one small difference is, in logistic regression, Bernoulli distribution will be utilized rather than binomial. To be precise, Bernoulli is just a special case of the binomial, as the primary outcome is only two categories from which all the trails are made.

Logistic regression – introduction and advantages

Logistic regression applies maximum likelihood estimation after transforming the dependent variable into a *logit* variable (natural log of the odds of the dependent variable occurring or not) with respect to independent variables. In this way, logistic regression estimates the probability of a certain event occurring. In the following equation, *log* of odds changes linearly as a function of explanatory variables:

$$log(odds) = \log \left(\frac{p}{1 - p}\right) = \beta_0 + \beta_1 * X_1 + \beta_2 * X_2 + \cdots + \beta_n * X_n$$

One can simply ask, why odds, *log(odds)* and not probability? In fact, this is interviewers favorite question in analytics interviews.

The reason is as follows:

$$Range of Proability = [0,1]$$

$$Range of Odds = [0, +\infty] as Odds = \frac{Probability}{1 - Probability}$$

$$Range of \log(odds) = [-\infty, +\infty]$$

By converting probability to *log(odds)*, we have expanded the range from [0, 1] to [- ∞, +∞]. By fitting model on probability we will encounter a restricted range problem, and also by applying log transformation, we cover-up the non-linearity involved and we can just fit with a linear combination of variables.

One more question one ask is what will happen if someone fit the linear regression on a 0-1 problem rather than on logistic regression?

A brief explanation is provided with the following image:

- Error terms will tend to be large at the middle values of X (independent variable) and small at the extreme values, which is the violation of linear regression assumptions that errors should have zero mean and should be normally distributed
- Generates nonsensical predictions of greater than *1* and less than *0* at end values of X
- The **ordinary least squares (OLS)** estimates are inefficient and standard errors are biased
- High error variance in the middle values of X and low variance at ends

All the preceding issues are solved by using logistic regression.

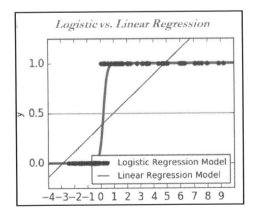

Terminology involved in logistic regression

Logistic regression is favorite ground for many interviewers to test the depth of an analyst with respect to their statistical acumen. It has been said that, even if someone understands 1,000 concepts in logistic regression, there would always be a question 1,001 from an interviewer. Hence, it would really be worth building knowledge on logistic regression from its fundamentals in order to create a solid foundation:

- **Information value (IV)**: This is very useful in the preliminary filtering of variables prior to including them in the model. IV is mainly used by industry for eliminating major variables in the first step prior to fitting the model, as the number of variables present in the final model would be about 10. Hence, initial processing is needed to reduce variables from 400+ in number or so.

$$Information\ Value = \ln\left(\frac{\%good}{\%bad}\right) * (\%good - \%bad)$$

$$Weight\ Of\ Evidence = \ln\left(\frac{\%good}{\%bad}\right)$$

Information Value	Predictive Power
<0.02	Useless for prediction
0.02 to 0.1	Weak predictor
0.1 to 0.3	Medium predictor
0.3 to 0.5	Strong predictor
> 0.5	Suspicious or too good predictor

- **Example**: In the following table, continuous variable (price) has been broken down into deciles (10 bins) based on price range and the counted number of events and non-events in that bin, and the information value has been calculated for all the segments and added together. We got the total value as *0.0356*, meaning it is a weak predictor to classify events.

Range	Bin Number	Events	Non Events	%of Events [E] (Events/Total Events)	% of Non-Events [NE] (Non Events/Total Non Events)	[E] -[NE]	WOE = ln(E/NE)	IV = WOE * (E-NE)
0-50	1	40	394	5%	5%	0.003	0.062	0.0002
51-100	2	68	900	9%	12%	-0.024	-0.234	0.0056
101-150	3	78	984	10%	13%	-0.021	-0.186	0.0040
151-200	4	102	1194	14%	15%	-0.016	-0.111	0.0018
201-250	5	108	1218	15%	16%	-0.011	-0.074	0.0008
251-300	6	110	1164	15%	15%	-0.001	-0.010	0.0000
301-350	7	82	772	11%	10%	0.011	0.107	0.0012
351-400	8	46	330	6%	4%	0.019	0.379	0.0074
401-450	9	42	368	6%	5%	0.009	0.179	0.0017
>451	10	68	470	9%	6%	0.031	0.416	0.0129
	Total	744	7794				I.V.Total	0.0356

- **Akaike information criteria (AIC)**: This measures the relative quality of a statistical model for a given set of data. It is a trade-off between bias versus variance. During a comparison between two models, the model with less AIC is preferred over higher value.

  If we closely observe the below equation, *k* parameter (the number of variables included in the model) is penalizing the overfitting phenomena of the model. This means that we can artificially prove the training accuracy of the model by incorporating more not so significant variables in the model; by doing so, we may get better accuracy on training data, but on testing data, accuracy will decrease. This phenomenon could be some sort of regularization in logistic regression:

$$AIC = -2*ln(L) + 2*k$$

L = Maximum value of Likelihood (log transformation applied for mathematical convenience)

k = Number of variables in the model

- **Receiver operating characteristic (ROC) curve**: This is a graphical plot that illustrates the performance of a binary classifier as its discriminant threshold is varied. The curve is created by plotting **true positive rate (TPR)** against **false positive rate (FPR)** at various threshold values.

  A simple way to understand the utility of the ROC curve is that, if we keep the threshold value (threshold is a real value between *0* and *1*, used to convert the predicted probability of output into class, as logistic regression predicts the probability) very low, we will put most of the predicted observations under the positive category, even when some of them should be placed under the negative category. On the other hand, keeping the threshold at a very high level penalizes the positive category, but the negative category will improve. Ideally, the threshold should be set in a way that trade-offs value between both categories and produces higher overall accuracy:

Optimum threshold = Threshold where maximum (sensitivity + specificity) is possible

  Before we jump into the nitty-gritty, we will visualize the confusion matrix to understand the various following formulas:

	Predicted: YES	Predicted: NO
Actual: YES	TP (True Positive)	FN (False Negative)
Actual: NO	FP (False Positive)	TN (True Negative)

$$Accuracy = \frac{TP + TN}{TP + FP + TN + FN}$$

$$Precision = \frac{TP}{TP + FP}$$

$$Recall\ (Sensitivity\ or\ TPR) = \frac{TP}{TP + FN}$$

$$f1\ score = \frac{2 * Precision * Recall}{Precision + Recall}$$

$$FPR\ (1 - Specificity) = \frac{FP}{FP + TN}$$

$$Specificity\ (TNR) = \frac{TN}{FP + TN}$$

The ROC curve will look as follows:

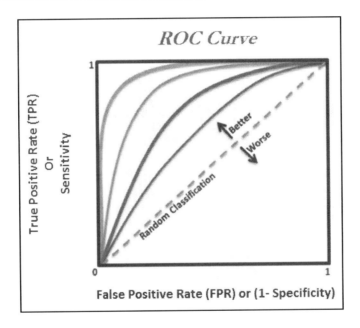

- **Rank ordering**: After sorting observations in descending order by predicted probabilities, deciles are created (10 equal bins with 10 percent of total observations in each bin). By adding up the number of events in each decile, we will get aggregated events for each decile and this number should be in decreasing order, else it will be in serious violation of logistic regression methodology.

  One way to think about why rank ordering is important? It will be very useful when we set the cut-off points at the top three to four deciles to send marketing campaigns where the segments have a higher chance of responding to the campaign. If rank order does not hold for the model, even after selecting the top three to four deciles, there will be a significant chunk left out below the cut-off point, which is dangerous.

- **Concordance/c-statistic**: This is a measure of quality of fit for a binary outcome in a logistic regression model. It is a proportion of pairs in which the predicted event probability is higher for the actual event than non-event.

- **Example**: In the following table, both actual and predicted values are shown with a sample of seven rows. Actual is the true category, either default or not; whereas predicted is predicted probabilities from the logistic regression model. Calculate the concordance value.

Actual	Predicted
1	0.92
0	0.34
0	0.12
1	0.4
1	0.64
0	0.82
1	0.84

For calculating concordance, we need to split the table into two (each table with actual values as *1* and *0*) and apply the Cartesian product of each row from both tables to form pairs:

Actual	Predicted
1	0.92
1	0.4
1	0.64
1	0.84

Actual	Predicted
0	0.34
0	0.12
0	0.82

In the following table, the complete Cartesian product has been calculated and has classified the pair as a concordant pair whenever the predicted probability for *1* category is higher than the predicted probability for *0* category. If it is the other way around, then the pair has been classified as a discordant pair. In special cases, if both probabilities are the same, those pairs will be classified as tied instead.

Actual	Predicted	Actual	Predicted	Concordant pair	Discordant pair
1	0.92	0	0.34	✓	
1	0.92	0	0.12	✓	
1	0.92	0	0.82	✓	
1	0.4	0	0.34	✓	
1	0.4	0	0.12	✓	
1	0.4	0	0.82		✓
1	0.64	0	0.34	✓	
1	0.64	0	0.12	✓	
1	0.64	0	0.82		✓
1	0.84	0	0.34	✓	
1	0.84	0	0.12	✓	
1	0.84	0	0.82	✓	

$$\% \text{ concordant pairs} = \frac{\text{Number of Concordant pairs}}{\text{Total pairs}} = \frac{10}{12} = 83.3\%$$

$$\% \text{ discordant pairs} = \frac{\text{Number of Discordant pairs}}{\text{Total pairs}} = \frac{2}{12} = 16.67\%$$

$$\% \text{ tied pairs} = \frac{\text{Number of Tied pairs}}{\text{Total pairs}} = \frac{0}{12} = 0\%$$

$$c \text{ statistic or } c \text{ index} = 0.5 + \frac{(\%\text{Concordant pairs} - \%\text{Discordant pairs})}{2}$$
$$= 0.5 + \frac{(0.833 - 0.1667)}{2} = 0.83315 = 83.315\%$$

$$Somers'D = (\% \text{ Concordant pairs} - \% \text{ Discordant pairs}) = (0.833 - 0.1667)$$
$$= 0.663$$

- **C-statistic**: This is 0.83315 percent or 83.315 percent, and any value greater than 0.7 percent or 70 percent is considered a good model to use for practical purposes.
- **Divergence**: The distance between the average score of default accounts and the average score of non-default accounts. The greater the distance, the more effective the scoring system is at segregating good and bad observations.
- **K-S statistic**: This is the maximum distance between two population distributions. It helps with discriminating default accounts from non-default accounts.

- **Population stability index (PSI)**: This is the metric used to check that drift in the current population on which the credit scoring model will be used is the same as the population with respective to development time:
  - *PSI <= 0.1*: This states no change in characteristics of the current population with respect to the development population
  - *0.1 < PSI <= 0.25*: This signifies some change has taken place and warns for attention, but can still be used
  - *PSI >0.25*: This indicates a large shift in the score distribution of the current population compared with development time

Applying steps in logistic regression modeling

The following steps are applied in linear regression modeling in industry:

1. Exclusion criteria and good-bad definition finalization
2. Initial data preparation and univariate analysis
3. Derived/dummy variable creation
4. Fine classing and coarse classing
5. Fitting the logistic model on the training data
6. Evaluating the model on test data

Example of logistic regression using German credit data

Open source German credit data has been utilized from the UCI machine learning repository to model logistic regression: `https://archive.ics.uci.edu/ml/datasets/Statlog+(German+Credit+Data)`.

```
>>> import os
>>> os.chdir("D:\\Book writing\\Codes\\Chapter 3")

>>> import numpy as np
>>> import pandas as pd

>>> from sklearn.model_selection import train_test_split
>>> from sklearn.metrics import accuracy_score,classification_report

>>> credit_data = pd.read_csv("credit_data.csv")
```

The following code describes the top five rows of the data:

```
>>> print (credit_data.head())
```

Status_of_existing_ checking_account	Duration_ in_month	Credit_history	Purpose	Credit_amount	Savings_Account	Present_Employment _since	Installment_rate _in_percentage_ of_disposable_in come	Personal_statu s_and_sex	Other_debtors	Present_resi dence_since	Property
A11	6	A34	A43	1169	A65	A75	4	A93	A101	4	A121
A12	48	A32	A43	5951	A61	A73	2	A92	A101	2	A121
A14	12	A34	A46	2096	A61	A74	2	A93	A101	3	A121
A11	42	A32	A42	7882	A61	A74	2	A93	A103	4	A122
A11	24	A33	A40	4870	A61	A73	3	A93	A101	4	A124

Property	Age_in_years	Other_installment _plans	Housing	Number_of_existing_c redits_at_this_bank	Job	Number_of_People_being_liable _to_provide_maintenance_for	Telephone	Foreign_worker	class
A121	67	A143	A152	2	A173	1	A192	A201	1
A121	22	A143	A152	1	A173	1	A191	A201	2
A121	49	A143	A152	1	A172	2	A191	A201	1
A122	45	A143	A153	1	A173	2	A191	A201	1
A124	53	A143	A153	2	A173	2	A191	A201	2

Altogether, we have 20 explanatory variables with one dependent variable called `class`. The value of `class` variable 2 indicates default and 1 describes non-default. In order to model as 0-1 problem, we have removed the value by 1 in the following code:

```
>>> credit_data['class'] = credit_data['class']-1
```

In order to know the predictive ability of each variable with respect to the independent variable, here we have done an information value calculation. In the following code, both categorical and continuous variables have been taken into consideration.

If the datatype is `object`, this means it is a categorical variable and any other variable such as `int64` and so on, will be treated as continuous and will be binned into 10 equal parts (also known as deciles) accordingly.

```
>>> def IV_calc(data,var):
...     if data[var].dtypes == "object":
...       dataf = data.groupby([var])['class'].agg(['count','sum'])
...           dataf.columns = ["Total","bad"]
...           dataf["good"] = dataf["Total"] – dataf["bad"]
...           dataf["bad_per"] = dataf["bad"]/dataf["bad"].sum()
...           dataf["good_per"] = dataf["good"]/dataf["good"].sum()
...           dataf["I_V"] = (dataf["good_per"] – dataf["bad_per"]) *
np.log(dataf["good_per"]/dataf["bad_per"])
...           return dataf
...     else:
...           data['bin_var'] = pd.qcut(data[var].rank(method='first'),10)
```

```
...         dataf = data.groupby(['bin_var'])['class'].agg(['count','sum'])
...         dataf.columns = ["Total","bad"]
...         dataf["good"] = dataf["Total"] - dataf["bad"]
...         dataf["bad_per"] = dataf["bad"]/dataf["bad"].sum()
...         dataf["good_per"] = dataf["good"]/dataf["good"].sum()
...         dataf["I_V"] = (dataf["good_per"] - dataf["bad_per"]) *
np.log(dataf["good_per"]/dataf["bad_per"])
...         return dataf
```

Information value has been calculated for `Credit_history` (categorical) and `Duration_in_month` (continuous) for illustration purposes. The overall IV obtained for `Credit_history` is 0.29, which illustrates medium predictive power and `Duration_in_month` as 0.34, which is a strong predictor.

```
>>> print ("\n\nCredit History - Information Value\n")
>>> print (IV_calc(credit_data,'Credit_history'))
```

Credit_History- Information Value					
	Total	bad	good	bad_per	good_per	I_V
A30	46	27	19	0.091525	0.026685	0.079915
A31	44	26	18	0.088136	0.025281	0.078495
A32	533	161	372	0.545763	0.522472	0.001016
A33	90	32	58	0.108475	0.081461	0.007737
A34	294	49	245	0.166102	0.344101	0.129643
					Total_IV	0.296806

```
>>> print ("\n\nCredit History - Duration in month\n")
>>> print (IV_calc(credit_data,'Duration_in_month'))
```

Duration_in_Months- Information Value						
	Total	bad	good	bad_per	good_per	I_V
[1,101.6]	101	10	91	0.033898	0.127809	0.124636
(101.6,202.2]	101	16	85	0.054237	0.119382	0.051397
(202.2,302.8]	100	25	75	0.084746	0.105337	0.004479
(302.8,403.4]	101	29	72	0.098305	0.101124	0.00008
(403.4,504]	101	21	80	0.071186	0.11236	0.018791
(504,604.6]	100	38	62	0.128814	0.087079	0.016341
(604.6,705.2]	101	30	71	0.101695	0.099719	0.000039
(705.2,805.8]	100	32	68	0.108475	0.095506	0.001651
(805.8,906.4]	101	45	56	0.152542	0.078652	0.048946
(906.4,1007]	101	49	52	0.166102	0.073034	0.076472
					Total_IV	0.342832

However, in real scenarios, initial data sometimes has around 500 variables or even more. In that case it is difficult to run the code individually for each variable separately. The following code has been developed for automating the calculation of the total information value for all the discrete and continuous variables in one single go!

```
>>> discrete_columns = ['Status_of_existing_checking_account',
'Credit_history', 'Purpose', 'Savings_Account','Present_Employment_since',
'Personal_status_and_sex',
'Other_debtors','Property','Other_installment_plans', 'Housing', 'Job',
'Telephone', 'Foreign_worker']

>>> continuous_columns = ['Duration_in_month', 'Credit_amount',
'Installment_rate_in_percentage_of_disposable_income',
'Present_residence_since',
'Age_in_years','Number_of_existing_credits_at_this_bank',
'Number_of_People_being_liable_to_provide_maintenance_for']

>>> total_columns = discrete_columns + continuous_columns
# List of IV values
>>> Iv_list = []
>>> for col in total_columns:
...     assigned_data = IV_calc(data = credit_data,var = col)
...     iv_val = round(assigned_data["I_V"].sum(),3)
...     dt_type = credit_data[col].dtypes
...     Iv_list.append((iv_val,col,dt_type))

>>> Iv_list = sorted(Iv_list,reverse = True)

>>> for i in range(len(Iv_list)):
...     print (Iv_list[i][0],",",Iv_list[i][1],",type =",Iv_list[i][2])
```

In the following output, all the variables with an information value are shown in descending order. After the information value, variable name, and the type of the variable have also been shown. If the type is `object`, this means that it is a categorical variable; similarly, if type is `int64` this means it is a 64-bit integer value. We will be considering the top 15 variables for the next stage of analysis.

```
Information Value by descending order

0.655 , Status_of_existing_checking_account ,type = object
0.343 , Duration_in_month ,type = int64
0.297 , Credit_history ,type = object
0.165 , Savings_Account ,type = object
0.165 , Age_in_years ,type = int64
0.15 , Credit_amount ,type = int64
0.145 , Purpose ,type = object
0.13 , Property ,type = object
0.112 , Present_Employment_since ,type = object
0.087 , Personal_status_and_sex ,type = object
0.076 , Number_of_existing_credits_at_this_bank ,type = int64
0.07 , Installment_rate_in_percentage_of_disposable_income ,type = int64
0.066 , Foreign_worker ,type = object
0.062 , Other_installment_plans ,type = object
0.055 , Other_debtors ,type = object
0.053 , Present_residence_since ,type = int64
0.05 , Housing ,type = object
0.046 , Job ,type = object
0.035 , Number_of_People_being_liable_to_provide_maintenance_for ,type = int64
0.0 , Telephone ,type = object
```

After retaining the top 15 variables, we have the following variables in the discrete and continuous categories. Subsequently, we will do dummy variable coding for the discrete variables and use continuous as it is.

```
>>> dummy_stseca =
pd.get_dummies(credit_data['Status_of_existing_checking_account'],
prefix='status_exs_accnt')
>>> dummy_ch = pd.get_dummies(credit_data['Credit_history'],
prefix='cred_hist')
>>> dummy_purpose = pd.get_dummies(credit_data['Purpose'],
prefix='purpose')
>>> dummy_savacc = pd.get_dummies(credit_data['Savings_Account'],
prefix='sav_acc')
>>> dummy_presc = pd.get_dummies(credit_data['Present_Employment_since'],
prefix='pre_emp_snc')
```

```
>>> dummy_perssx = pd.get_dummies(credit_data['Personal_status_and_sex'],
prefix='per_stat_sx')
>>> dummy_property = pd.get_dummies(credit_data['Property'],
prefix='property')
>>> dummy_othinstpln =
pd.get_dummies(credit_data['Other_installment_plans'],
prefix='oth_inst_pln')
>>> dummy_forgnwrkr = pd.get_dummies(credit_data['Foreign_worker'],
prefix='forgn_wrkr')
>>> dummy_othdts = pd.get_dummies(credit_data['Other_debtors'],
prefix='oth_debtors')

>>> continuous_columns = ['Duration_in_month', 'Credit_amount',
'Installment_rate_in_percentage_of_disposable_income', 'Age_in_years',
'Number_of_existing_credits_at_this_bank' ]

>>> credit_continuous = credit_data[continuous_columns]
>>> credit_data_new = pd.concat([dummy_stseca,dummy_ch,
dummy_purpose,dummy_savacc, dummy_presc,dummy_perssx, dummy_property,
dummy_othinstpln,dummy_othdts,
dummy_forgnwrkr,credit_continuous,credit_data['class']],axis=1)
```

Data has been evenly split between train and test at a 70-30 ratio, `random_state` is `42` used as a seed for pseudo random number generation in order to create reproducible results when run multiple users by multiple times.

```
>>> x_train,x_test,y_train,y_test = train_test_split(
credit_data_new.drop(['class'] ,axis=1),credit_data_new['class'],train_size
= 0.7,random_state=42)

>>> y_train = pd.DataFrame(y_train)
>>> y_test = pd.DataFrame(y_test)
```

While generating dummy variables using the `pd.get_dummies()` function, the number of dummy being produced is equal to the number of classes in it. However, the number of dummies variables created will be less in one number compared the with number of classes in a variable is good enough (if all the other remaining variable are `0`, this will represent the one extra class) to represent in this setting. For example, if the class of sample variable *decision response* can take any of the three values (*yes*, *no*, and *can't say*), this can be represented with two dummy variables (*d1, d2*) for representing all the settings.

- If *d1 =1* and *d2 = 0*, we can assign category *yes*
- If *d1=0* and *d2 = 1*, we can assign category *no*
- If *d1 = 0* and *d2 = 0*, we can assign category *can't say*

In this way, using two dummy variables we have represented all three categories. Similarly, we can represent *N* category of variables with *N-1* dummy variables.

In fact, having the same number of dummy variables will produce NAN values in output due to the redundancy it creates. Hence, we are here removing one extra category column from all the categorical variables for which dummies have been created:

```
>>> remove_cols_extra_dummy = ['status_exs_accnt_A11', 'cred_hist_A30',
'purpose_A40', 'sav_acc_A61','pre_emp_snc_A71','per_stat_sx_A91',
'oth_debtors_A101','property_A121', 'oth_inst_pln_A141','forgn_wrkr_A201']
```

Here, we have created the extra list for removing insignificant variables step by step iteratively while working on backward elimination methodology; after the end of each iteration, we will keep adding the most insignificant and multi-collinear variable to `remove_cols_insig` list, so that those variables are removed while training the model.

```
>>> remove_cols_insig = []
>>> remove_cols = list(set(remove_cols_extra_dummy+remove_cols_insig))
```

Now for the most important step of the model, the application of `Logit` function, n variables, and creating summary:

```
>>> import statsmodels.api as sm
>>> logistic_model = sm.Logit(y_train, sm.add_constant(x_train.drop(
remove_cols, axis=1))).fit()
>>> print (logistic_model.summary())
```

Summary code generates the following output, among which the most insignificant variable is `purpose_A46`, with a p-value of `0.937`:

```
Optimization terminated successfully.
        Current function value: 0.439329
        Iterations 7
                    Logit Regression Results
==============================================================================
Dep. Variable:                  class   No. Observations:                 704
Model:                          Logit   Df Residuals:                     663
Method:                           MLE   Df Model:                          40
Date:                Wed, 12 Apr 2017   Pseudo R-squ.:                 0.2686
Time:                        06:41:35   Log-Likelihood:               -309.29
converged:                       True   LL-Null:                      -422.87
                                        LLR p-value:                 5.196e-28
==============================================================================
                                                       coef    std err          z      P>|z|      [95.0% Conf. Int.]
------------------------------------------------------------------------------
const                                                1.2218      1.064      1.148      0.251     -0.864      3.308
status_exs_accnt_A12                                 -0.2309      0.260     -0.888      0.375     -0.741      0.279
status_exs_accnt_A13                                 -1.4723      0.466     -3.161      0.002     -2.385     -0.559
status_exs_accnt_A14                                 -1.7335      0.289     -5.999      0.000     -2.300     -1.167
cred_hist_A31                                         0.8636      0.658      1.313      0.189     -0.426      2.153
cred_hist_A32                                        -0.5329      0.467     -1.140      0.254     -1.449      0.383
cred_hist_A33                                        -0.7443      0.532     -1.398      0.162     -1.787      0.299
cred_hist_A34                                        -1.5604      0.489     -3.189      0.001     -2.520     -0.601
purpose_A41                                          -1.6520      0.468     -3.532      0.000     -2.569     -0.735
purpose_A410                                         -1.2060      0.846     -1.425      0.154     -2.865      0.453
purpose_A42                                          -0.9504      0.331     -2.867      0.004     -1.600     -0.301
purpose_A43                                          -0.7821      0.299     -2.615      0.009     -1.368     -0.196
purpose_A44                                          -0.6901      0.980     -0.704      0.481     -2.610      1.230
purpose_A45                                          -0.4104      0.607     -0.676      0.499     -1.600      0.780
purpose_A46                                           0.0366      0.465      0.079      0.937     -0.875      0.948
purpose_A48                                          -1.7829      0.999     -1.785      0.074     -3.741      0.175
purpose_A49                                          -0.7105      0.408     -1.740      0.082     -1.511      0.090
sav_acc_A62                                          -0.7680      0.360     -2.132      0.033     -1.474     -0.062
sav_acc_A63                                          -0.2615      0.486     -0.538      0.590     -1.214      0.691
sav_acc_A64                                          -0.8680      0.566     -1.533      0.125     -1.978      0.242
sav_acc_A65                                          -0.7004      0.325     -2.157      0.031     -1.337     -0.064
pre_emp_snc_A72                                      -0.4988      0.474     -1.052      0.293     -1.428      0.431
pre_emp_snc_A73                                      -0.5957      0.429     -1.389      0.165     -1.436      0.245
pre_emp_snc_A74                                      -0.9484      0.486     -1.950      0.051     -1.902      0.005
pre_emp_snc_A75                                      -0.6107      0.445     -1.372      0.170     -1.483      0.262
per_stat_sx_A92                                      -0.9690      0.471     -2.058      0.040     -1.892     -0.046
per_stat_sx_A93                                      -1.6427      0.467     -3.515      0.000     -2.559     -0.727
per_stat_sx_A94                                      -1.2197      0.562     -2.170      0.030     -2.321     -0.118
property_A122                                         0.5686      0.319      1.784      0.074     -0.056      1.193
property_A123                                         0.2314      0.281      0.825      0.410     -0.319      0.781
property_A124                                         0.8290      0.379      2.186      0.029      0.086      1.572
oth_inst_pln_A142                                     0.6717      0.527      1.274      0.202     -0.361      1.705
oth_inst_pln_A143                                    -0.2197      0.291     -0.754      0.451     -0.790      0.351
oth_debtors_A102                                      1.0078      0.496      2.032      0.042      0.036      1.980
oth_debtors_A103                                     -0.7974      0.481     -1.658      0.097     -1.740      0.145
forgn_wrkr_A202                                      -1.6571      0.876     -1.891      0.059     -3.375      0.060
Duration_in_month                                    0.0215      0.011      1.997      0.046      0.000      0.043
Credit_amount                                        0.0001   5.17e-05      2.114      0.034   7.98e-06      0.000
Installment_rate_in_percentage_of_disposable_income  0.4154      0.112      3.705      0.000      0.196      0.635
Age_in_years                                         -0.0217      0.011     -2.070      0.038     -0.042     -0.001
Number_of_existing_credits_at_this_bank              0.3664      0.217      1.687      0.092     -0.059      0.792
==============================================================================
```

Also, VIF values are calculated to check multi-collinearity, although insignificant variables need to be removed prior to the removal of multi-collinear variables with *VIF > 5*. From the following results, `Per_stat_sx_A93` is coming in as the most multi-collinear variable with a VIF of `6.177`:

```
>>> print ("\nVariance Inflation Factor")
>>> cnames = x_train.drop(remove_cols,axis=1).columns
>>> for i in np.arange(0,len(cnames)):
...     xvars = list(cnames)
...     yvar = xvars.pop(i)
...     mod = sm.OLS(x_train.drop(remove_cols,axis=1)[yvar], sm.add_constant(
x_train.drop (remove_cols,axis=1)[xvars]))
...     res = mod.fit()
...     vif = 1/(1-res.rsquared)
...     print (yvar,round(vif,3))
```

```
Variance Inflation Factor
status_exs_accnt_A12 1.739
status_exs_accnt_A13 1.258
status_exs_accnt_A14 1.85
cred_hist_A31 2.092
cred_hist_A32 7.036
cred_hist_A33 2.648
cred_hist_A34 6.043
purpose_A41 1.434
purpose_A410 1.189
purpose_A42 1.624
purpose_A43 1.876
purpose_A44 1.091
purpose_A45 1.158
purpose_A46 1.279
purpose_A48 1.172
purpose_A49 1.619
sav_acc_A62 1.152
sav_acc_A63 1.14
sav_acc_A64 1.096
sav_acc_A65 1.173
pre_emp_snc_A72 3.555
pre_emp_snc_A73 5.026
pre_emp_snc_A74 3.583
pre_emp_snc_A75 4.43
per_stat_sx_A92 5.619
per_stat_sx_A93 6.177
per_stat_sx_A94 2.903
property_A122 1.558
property_A123 1.661
property_A124 1.928
oth_inst_pln_A142 1.369
oth_inst_pln_A143 1.427
oth_debtors_A102 1.141
oth_debtors_A103 1.171
forgn_wrkr_A202 1.159
Duration_in_month 2.013
Credit_amount 2.474
Installment_rate_in_percentage_of_disposable_income 1.404
Age_in_years 1.444
Number_of_existing_credits_at_this_bank 1.574
```

We also check how good the classifier is at trying to predict the results, for which we will run the c-statistic value, which calculates the proportion of concordant pairs out of the total pairs. The higher the value is the better, but at minimum it should have 0.7 for deploying the model in a production environment. The following code describes the various steps involved in the calculation of c-statistic from first principles:

```
>>> y_pred = pd.DataFrame (logistic_model. predict(sm.add_constant
(x_train.drop (remove_cols,axis=1))))
>>> y_pred.columns = ["probs"]
>>> both = pd.concat([y_train,y_pred],axis=1)
```

Zeros is the data split from the actual and predicted table with the condition applied on zero as an actual class. Whereas, ones is the split with the condition applied on one as an actual class.

```
>>> zeros = both[['class','probs']][both['class']==0]
>>> ones = both[['class','probs']][both['class']==1]

>>> def df_crossjoin(df1, df2, **kwargs):
...     df1['_tmpkey'] = 1
...     df2['_tmpkey'] = 1
...     res = pd.merge(df1, df2, on='_tmpkey', **kwargs).drop('_tmpkey',
axis=1)
...     res.index = pd.MultiIndex.from_product((df1.index, df2.index))
...     df1.drop('_tmpkey', axis=1, inplace=True)
...     df2.drop('_tmpkey', axis=1, inplace=True)
...     return res
```

In the following step, we are producing Cartesian products for both one and zero data to calculate concordant and discordant pairs:

```
>>> joined_data = df_crossjoin(ones,zeros)
```

A pair is concordant if the probability against the 1 class is higher than the 0 class and discordant if the probability against the 1 class is less than the 0 class. If both probabilities are same, we put them in the tied pair category. The higher the number of concordant pairs is, the better the model is!

```
>>> joined_data['concordant_pair'] = 0
>>> joined_data.loc[joined_data['probs_x'] > joined_data['probs_y'],
'concordant_pair'] =1
>>> joined_data['discordant_pair'] = 0
>>> joined_data.loc[joined_data['probs_x'] < joined_data['probs_y'],
'discordant_pair'] =1
>>> joined_data['tied_pair'] = 0
>>> joined_data.loc[joined_data['probs_x'] ==
joined_data['probs_y'],'tied_pair'] =1
```

```
>>> p_conc = (sum(joined_data['concordant_pair'])*1.0 )/
(joined_data.shape[0])
>>> p_disc = (sum(joined_data['discordant_pair'])*1.0 )/
(joined_data.shape[0])

>>> c_statistic = 0.5 + (p_conc - p_disc)/2.0
>>> print ("\nC-statistic:",round(c_statistic,4))
```

```
C-statistic: 0.8388
```

The `c-statistic` obtained is `0.8388`, which is greater than the 0.7 needed to be considered as a good model.

We will always keep a tab on how c-statistic and log-likelihood (AIC) is changing (here it is -309.29) while removing various variables one by one in order to justify when to stop.

Prior to removing insignificant variable `purpose_A46`, it is important to check its VIF and `Per_stat_sx_A93` variable's p-value. There might some situations in which we need to take both metrics into consideration and do trade-offs as well.

However, the following table is the clear result that we need to remove `pupose_A46` variable:

Variable	p-value	VIF
purpose_A46	0.937	1.279
Per_stat_sx_A93	0.000	6.177

After we remove the `purpose_A46` variable, we need to reiterate the process until no insignificant and multi-collinear variables exist. However, we need to keep a tab on how AIC and c-statistic values are changing. In the following code, we have shown the order of variables removed one by one, however we encourage users to do this hands-on to validate the results independently:

```
>>> remove_cols_insig = ['purpose_A46', 'purpose_A45', 'purpose_A44',
'sav_acc_A63', ... 'oth_inst_pln_A143','property_A123',
'status_exs_accnt_A12', 'pre_emp_snc_A72', ...
'pre_emp_snc_A75','pre_emp_snc_A73', 'cred_hist_A32', 'cred_hist_A33', ...
'purpose_A410','pre_emp_snc_A74','purpose_A49', 'purpose_A48',
'property_A122', ... 'per_stat_sx_A92','forgn_wrkr_A202','per_stat_sx_A94',
'purpose_A42', ...
'oth_debtors_A102','Age_in_years','sav_acc_A64','sav_acc_A62',
'sav_acc_A65', ... 'oth_debtors_A103']
```

Finally, after eliminating the insignificant and multi-collinear variables, the following final results are obtained:

- Log-Likelihood: -334.35
- c-statistic: 0.8035

If we compare these with initial values, *log*-likelihood minimized from -309.29 to -334.35, which is a the good sign and c-statistic also decreased slightly from 0.8388 to 0.8035. But still, the model is holding good with a much lower number of variables. Removing extra variables without impacting model performance much will create efficiency during the implementation of the model as well!

```
Optimization terminated successfully.
        Current function value: 0.474931
        Iterations 6
                    Logit Regression Results
==============================================================================
Dep. Variable:                 class   No. Observations:                  704
Model:                         Logit   Df Residuals:                      690
Method:                          MLE   Df Model:                           13
Date:               Thu, 13 Apr 2017   Pseudo R-squ.:                  0.2093
Time:                       06:53:27   Log-Likelihood:                -334.35
converged:                      True   LL-Null:                       -422.87
                                       LLR p-value:                 6.813e-31
==============================================================================
                                          coef    std err          z      P>|z|      [95.0% Conf. Int.]
------------------------------------------------------------------------------
const                                  -2.1782      0.458     -4.753      0.000      -3.077      -1.280
status_exs_accnt_A13                   -1.1011      0.421     -2.616      0.009      -1.926      -0.276
status_exs_accnt_A14                   -1.5561      0.232     -6.710      0.000      -2.011      -1.102
cred_hist_A31                           0.9028      0.445      2.029      0.042       0.031       1.775
cred_hist_A34                          -0.9717      0.268     -3.631      0.000      -1.496      -0.447
purpose_A41                            -1.3009      0.415     -3.132      0.002      -2.115      -0.487
purpose_A43                            -0.5359      0.225     -2.378      0.017      -0.978      -0.094
per_stat_sx_A93                        -0.7401      0.206     -3.598      0.000      -1.143      -0.337
property_A124                           0.7233      0.267      2.706      0.007       0.199       1.247
oth_inst_pln_A142                       1.1535      0.440      2.619      0.009       0.290       2.017
Duration_in_month                       0.0185      0.010      1.903      0.057      -0.001       0.038
Credit_amount                           0.0001   4.8e-05      2.232      0.026    1.31e-05       0.000
Installment_rate_in_percentage_of_disposable_income  0.3783  0.103  3.658  0.000  0.176  0.581
Number_of_existing_credits_at_this_bank  0.3876      0.190      2.044      0.041       0.016       0.759
==============================================================================

Variance Inflation Factor
status_exs_accnt_A13 1.076
status_exs_accnt_A14 1.131
cred_hist_A31 1.052
cred_hist_A34 1.352
purpose_A41 1.106
purpose_A43 1.117
per_stat_sx_A93 1.103
property_A124 1.192
oth_inst_pln_A142 1.023
Duration_in_month 1.816
Credit_amount 2.258
Installment_rate_in_percentage_of_disposable_income 1.306
Number_of_existing_credits_at_this_bank 1.341

C-statistic: 0.8035
```

The ROC curve has been plotted against TPR versus FPR in the following chart, and also the area under the curve has been described which has a value of *0.80*.

```
>>> import matplotlib.pyplot as plt
>>> from sklearn import metrics
>>> from sklearn.metrics import auc
>>> fpr, tpr, thresholds = metrics.roc_curve(both['class'],both['probs'],
pos_label=1)

>>> roc_auc = auc(fpr,tpr)
>>> plt.figure()
>>> lw = 2
>>> plt.plot(fpr, tpr, color='darkorange', lw=lw, label='ROC curve (area =
%0.2f)' % roc_auc)
>>> plt.plot([0, 1], [0, 1], color='navy', lw=lw, linestyle='--')
>>> plt.xlim([0.0, 1.0])
>>> plt.ylim([0.0, 1.05])
>>> plt.xlabel('False Positive Rate (1-Specificity)')
>>> plt.ylabel('True Positive Rate')
>>> plt.title('ROC Curve - German Credit Data')
>>> plt.legend(loc="lower right")
>>> plt.show()
```

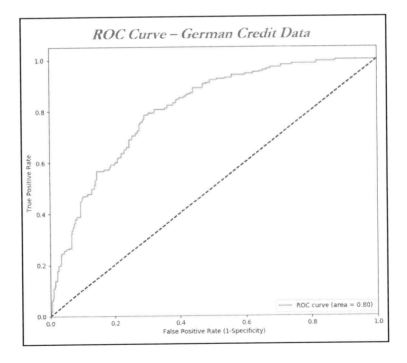

Once we have found the best situation from the training dataset, the next and final task is to predict the category from the probability to default value. There are many ways to set the threshold value to convert predicted probability into an actual class. In the following code, we have done a simple grid search to determine the best probability threshold cut-off. Nonetheless, even sensitivity and specificity curves could be utilized for this task.

```
>>> for i in list(np.arange(0,1,0.1)):
...     both["y_pred"] = 0
...     both.loc[both["probs"] > i, 'y_pred'] = 1
...     print ("Threshold",i,"Train Accuracy:",
round(accuracy_score(both['class'], both['y_pred']),4))
```

```
Threshold 0.0 Train Accuracy: 0.2884
Threshold 0.1 Train Accuracy: 0.527
Threshold 0.2 Train Accuracy: 0.6634
Threshold 0.3 Train Accuracy: 0.7273
Threshold 0.4 Train Accuracy: 0.7457
Threshold 0.5 Train Accuracy: 0.7713
Threshold 0.6 Train Accuracy: 0.75
Threshold 0.7 Train Accuracy: 0.7386
Threshold 0.8 Train Accuracy: 0.7244
Threshold 0.9 Train Accuracy: 0.7131
```

From the preceding results, we find that, at threshold 0.5 value we can see the maximum accuracy of 0.7713. Hence, we set the threshold at 0.5 for classifying test data as well:

```
>>> both["y_pred"] = 0
>>> both.loc[both["probs"] > 0.5, 'y_pred'] = 1
>>> print ("\nTrain Confusion Matrix\n\n", pd.crosstab(both['class'],
both['y_pred'], ... rownames = ["Actuall"],colnames = ["Predicted"]))
>>> print ("\nTrain
Accuracy:",round(accuracy_score(both['class'],both['y_pred']),4))
```

Results are discussed next. After setting the threshold to 0.5 and the classified predicted probabilities into 0 or 1 classes, the Confusion matrix has been calculated by taking actual values in rows and predicted values in columns, which shows accuracy of 0.7713 or 77.13 percent:

```
Train Confusion Matrix

Predicted    0    1
Actuall
0          453   48
1          113   90

Train Accuracy: 0.7713
```

Now, a threshold of 0.5 will be applied on test data to verify whether the model is consistent across various data sets with the following code:

```
>>> y_pred_test = pd.DataFrame( logistic_model.predict( sm.add_constant(
... x_test.drop(remove_cols,axis=1)))))
>>> y_pred_test.columns = ["probs"]
>>> both_test = pd.concat([y_test,y_pred_test],axis=1)
>>> both_test["y_pred"] = 0
>>> both_test.loc[both_test["probs"] > 0.5, 'y_pred'] = 1
>>> print ("\nTest Confusion Matrix\n\n", pd.crosstab( both_test['class'],
... both_test['y_pred'],rownames = ["Actuall"],colnames = ["Predicted"]))
>>> print ("\nTest Accuracy:", round(accuracy_score( both_test['class'],
... both_test['y_pred']),4))
```

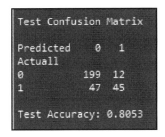

```
Test Confusion Matrix

Predicted     0    1
Actuall
0            199   12
1            47    45

Test Accuracy: 0.8053
```

From the results of the test data, accuracy obtained is 0.8053 or 80.53 percent; our logistic regression classifier is classifying default versus non-default very powerfully!

R code for logistic regression is as follows:

```
# Variable Importance
library(mctest)
library(dummies)
library(Information)
library(pROC)
credit_data = read.csv("credit_data.csv")
credit_data$class = credit_data$class-1

# I.V Calculation
IV <- create_infotables(data=credit_data, y="class", parallel=FALSE)
for (i in 1:length(colnames(credit_data))-1){
  seca = IV[[1]][i][1]
  sum(seca[[1]][5])
print(paste(colnames(credit_data)[i],",IV_Value:",round(sum(seca[[1]][5]),4
)))
}

# Dummy variables creation
dummy_stseca
```

```r
=data.frame(dummy(credit_data$Status_of_existing_checking_account))
dummy_ch = data.frame(dummy(credit_data$Credit_history))
dummy_purpose = data.frame(dummy(credit_data$Purpose))
dummy_savacc = data.frame(dummy(credit_data$Savings_Account)) dummy_presc =
data.frame(dummy(credit_data$Present_Employment_since)) dummy_perssx =
data.frame(dummy(credit_data$Personal_status_and_sex)) dummy_othdts =
data.frame(dummy(credit_data$Other_debtors)) dummy_property =
data.frame(dummy(credit_data$Property)) dummy_othinstpln =
data.frame(dummy(credit_data$Other_installment_plans))
dummy_forgnwrkr = data.frame(dummy(credit_data$Foreign_worker))

# Cleaning the variables name from . to _
colClean <- function(x){ colnames(x) <- gsub("\\.", "_", colnames(x)); x }
dummy_stseca = colClean(dummy_stseca) ;dummy_ch = colClean(dummy_ch)
dummy_purpose = colClean(dummy_purpose); dummy_savacc=
colClean(dummy_savacc)
dummy_presc= colClean(dummy_presc);dummy_perssx= colClean(dummy_perssx);
dummy_othdts= colClean(dummy_othdts);dummy_property=
colClean(dummy_property);
dummy_othinstpln= colClean(dummy_othinstpln);dummy_forgnwrkr=
colClean(dummy_forgnwrkr);

continuous_columns = c('Duration_in_month',
'Credit_amount','Installment_rate_in_percentage_of_disposable_income',
'Age_in_years','Number_of_existing_credits_at_this_bank')
credit_continuous = credit_data[,continuous_columns]
credit_data_new =
cbind(dummy_stseca,dummy_ch,dummy_purpose,dummy_savacc,dummy_presc,dummy_pe
rssx,
dummy_othdts,dummy_property,dummy_othinstpln,dummy_forgnwrkr,credit_continu
ous,credit_data$class)
colnames(credit_data_new)[51] <- "class"

# Setting seed for repeatability of results of train & test split
set.seed(123)
numrow = nrow(credit_data_new)
trnind = sample(1:numrow,size = as.integer(0.7*numrow))
train_data = credit_data_new[trnind,]
test_data = credit_data_new[-trnind,]

remove_cols_extra_dummy =
c("Status_of_existing_checking_account_A11","Credit_history_A30",
"Purpose_A40", "Savings_Account_A61", "Present_Employment_since_A71",
"Personal_status_and_sex_A91" "Other_debtors_A101", "Property_A121",
"Other_installment_plans_A141", "Foreign_worker_A201")

# Removing insignificant variables one by one
remove_cols_insig =
```

```
c("Purpose_A46","Purpose_A45","Purpose_A44","Savings_Account_A63",
"Other_installment_plans_A143", "Property_A123",
"Status_of_existing_checking_account_A12", "Present_Employment_since_A72",
"Present_Employment_since_A75",
"Present_Employment_since_A73","Credit_history_A32","Credit_history_A33",
"Purpose_A40","Present_Employment_since_A74","Purpose_A49","Purpose_A48",
"Property_A122","Personal_status_and_sex_A92","Foreign_worker_A202",
"Personal_status_and_sex_A94","Purpose_A42","Other_debtors_A102",
"Age_in_years","Savings_Account_A64","Savings_Account_A62",
"Savings_Account_A65", "Other_debtors_A103")
remove_cols = c(remove_cols_extra_dummy,remove_cols_insig)
glm_fit = glm(class ~.,family = "binomial",data =
train_data[,!(names(train_data) %in% remove_cols)])

# Significance check - p_value summary(glm_fit)

# Multi collinearity check - VIF
remove_cols_vif = c(remove_cols,"class")
vif_table = imcdiag(train_data[,!(names(train_data) %in%
remove_cols_vif)],train_data$class,detr=0.001, conf=0.99)
vif_table

# Predicting probabilities
 train_data$glm_probs = predict(glm_fit,newdata = train_data,type =
"response")
test_data$glm_probs = predict(glm_fit,newdata = test_data,type =
"response")

# Area under
ROC ROC1 <- roc(as.factor(train_data$class),train_data$glm_probs)
plot(ROC1, col = "blue")
print(paste("Area under the curve",round(auc(ROC1),4)))

# Actual prediction based on threshold tuning
threshold_vals = c(0.1,0.2,0.3,0.4,0.5,0.6,0.7,0.8,0.9)
for (thld in threshold_vals){
  train_data$glm_pred = 0
  train_data$glm_pred[train_data$glm_probs>thld]=1
  tble = table(train_data$glm_pred,train_data$class)
  acc = (tble[1,1]+tble[2,2])/sum(tble)
  print(paste("Threshold",thld,"Train accuracy",round(acc,4)))
}

# Best threshold from above search is 0.5 with accuracy as 0.7841
best_threshold = 0.5

# Train confusion matrix & accuracy
train_data$glm_pred = 0
```

```
train_data$glm_pred[train_data$glm_probs>best_threshold]=1
tble = table(train_data$glm_pred,train_data$class)
acc = (tble[1,1]+tble[2,2])/sum(tble)
print(paste("Confusion Matrix - Train Data"))
 print(tble) print(paste("Train accuracy",round(acc,4)))

# Test confusion matrix & accuracy
test_data$glm_pred = 0
test_data$glm_pred[test_data$glm_probs>best_threshold]=1
tble_test = table(test_data$glm_pred,test_data$class)
acc_test = (tble_test[1,1]+tble_test[2,2])/sum(tble_test)
print(paste("Confusion Matrix - Test Data")) print(tble_test)
print(paste("Test accuracy",round(acc_test,4)))
```

Random forest

The **random forest** (**RF**) is a very powerful technique which is used frequently in the data science field for solving various problems across industries, as well as a silver bullet for winning competitions like Kaggle. We will cover various concepts from the basics to in depth in the next chapter; here we are restricted to the bare necessities. Random forest is an ensemble of decision trees, as we know, logistic regression has very high bias and low variance technique; on the other hand, decision trees have high variance and low bias, which makes decision trees unstable. By averaging decision trees, we will minimize the variance component the of model, which makes approximate nearest to an ideal model.

RF focuses on sampling both observations and variables of training data to develop independent decision trees and take majority voting for classification and averaging for regression problems respectively. In contrast, bagging samples only observations at random and selects all columns that have the deficiency of representing significant variables at root for all decision trees. This way makes trees that are dependent on each other, for which accuracy will be penalized.

The following are a few rules of thumb when selecting sub-samples from observations using random forest. Nonetheless, any of the parameters can be tuned to improve results further! Each tree is developed on sampled data drawn from training data and fitted as shown

About 2/3 of observations in training data for each individual tree

Select columns sqrt(p) -> For classification problem if p is total columns in training data

p/3 -> for regression problem if p is number of columns

In the following diagram, two samples were shown with blue and pink colors, where, in the bagging scenario, a few observations and all columns are selected. Whereas, in random forest, a few observations and columns are selected to create uncorrelated individual trees.

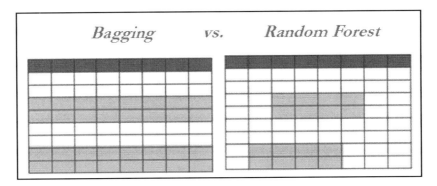

In the following diagram, a sample idea shows how RF classifier works. Each tree has grown separately, and the depth of each tree varies as per the selected sample, but in the end, voting is performed to determine the final class.

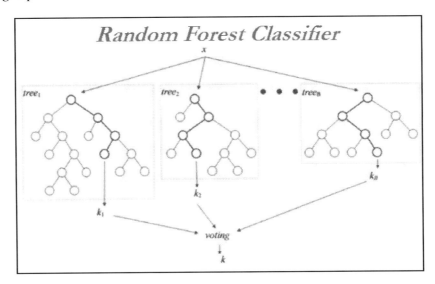

Due to the ensemble of decision trees, RF suffered interpretability and could not determine the significance of each variable; only variable importance could be provided instead. In the following graph, a sample of variable performance has been provided, consisting of a mean decrease in *Gini*:

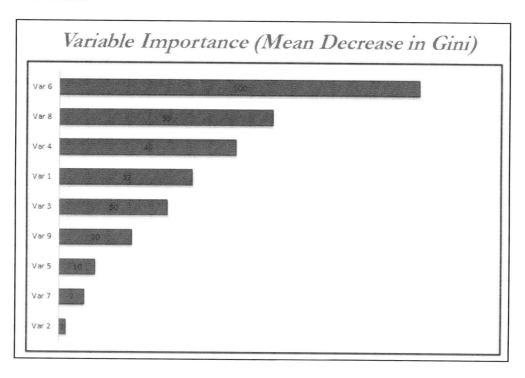

Example of random forest using German credit data

The same German credit data is being utilized to illustrate the random forest model in order to provide an apple to apple comparison. A very significant difference anyone can observe compared with logistic regression is that effort applied on data preprocessing drastically decreases. The following differences are worth a mention:

- In RF, we have not removed variables one by one from analysis based on significance and VIF values, as significance tests are not applicable for ML models. However five-fold cross validation has been performed on training data to ensure the model's robustness.

- We have removed one extra dummy variable in the logistic regression procedure, whereas in RF we have not removed the extra dummy variable from the analysis, as the latter automatically takes care of multi-collinearity. In fact, the underlying single model on which ensemble has been built is a decision tree, for which multi-collinearity is not a problem at all. We will cover decision trees in depth in the next chapter.
- Random forest requires much less human effort and intervention to train the model than logistic regression. This way of working makes ML models a favorite for software engineers to deploy them with much ease. Also, ML models can learn based on data automatically without much hassle.

Random forest applied on German credit data:

```
>>> import pandas as pd
>>> from sklearn.ensemble import RandomForestClassifier

>>> credit_data = pd.read_csv("credit_data.csv")
>>> credit_data['class'] = credit_data['class']-1
```

The creation of dummy variables step is similar to the logistic regression preprocessing step:

```
>>> dummy_stseca =
pd.get_dummies(credit_data['Status_of_existing_checking_account'],
prefix='status_exs_accnt')
>>> dummy_ch = pd.get_dummies(credit_data['Credit_history'],
prefix='cred_hist')
>>> dummy_purpose = pd.get_dummies(credit_data['Purpose'],
prefix='purpose')
>>> dummy_savacc = pd.get_dummies(credit_data['Savings_Account'],
prefix='sav_acc')
>>> dummy_presc = pd.get_dummies(credit_data['Present_Employment_since'],
prefix='pre_emp_snc')
>>> dummy_perssx = pd.get_dummies(credit_data['Personal_status_and_sex'],
prefix='per_stat_sx')
>>> dummy_othdts = pd.get_dummies(credit_data['Other_debtors'],
prefix='oth_debtors')
>>> dummy_property = pd.get_dummies(credit_data['Property'],
prefix='property')
>>> dummy_othinstpln =
pd.get_dummies(credit_data['Other_installment_plans'],
prefix='oth_inst_pln')
>>> dummy_housing = pd.get_dummies(credit_data['Housing'],
prefix='housing')
>>> dummy_job = pd.get_dummies(credit_data['Job'], prefix='job')
>>> dummy_telephn = pd.get_dummies(credit_data['Telephone'],
```

```
prefix='telephn')
>>> dummy_forgnwrkr = pd.get_dummies(credit_data['Foreign_worker'],
prefix='forgn_wrkr')

>>> continuous_columns = ['Duration_in_month', 'Credit_amount',
'Installment_rate_in_percentage_of_disposable_income',
'Present_residence_since','Age_in_years','Number_of_existing_credits_at_thi
s_bank',
'Number_of_People_being_liable_to_provide_maintenance_for']

>>> credit_continuous = credit_data[continuous_columns]
```

In the following variables combination step, we have not removed the one extra dummy variable out of all the categorical variables. All dummy variables created for `status_of_existing_checking_account` variable have been used in random forest, rather than the one column that is removed in logistic regression, due to the representative nature of the variable with respect to all the other variables.

```
>>> credit_data_new = pd.concat([dummy_stseca, dummy_ch,dummy_purpose,
dummy_savacc,dummy_presc,dummy_perssx,dummy_othdts, dummy_property,
dummy_othinstpln,dummy_housing,dummy_job, dummy_telephn, dummy_forgnwrkr,
credit_continuous,credit_data['class']],axis=1)
```

In the following example, data has been split 70-30. The reason is due to the fact that we would be performing five-fold cross-validation in grid search during training, which produces a similar effect of splitting the data into 50-25-25 of train, validation, and test datasets respectively.

```
>>> x_train,x_test,y_train,y_test = train_test_split( credit_data_new.drop(
['class'],axis=1),credit_data_new['class'],train_size =
0.7,random_state=42)
```

The random forest ML model is applied with assumed hyperparameter values, as follows:

- Number of trees is `1000`
- Criterion of slitting is `gini`
- Maximum depth each decision tree can grow is `100`
- Minimum observations required at each not to be eligible for splitting is `3`
- Minimum number of observations in tree node should be `2`

However, optimum parameter values needs to be tuned using grid search:

```
>>> rf_fit = RandomForestClassifier( n_estimators=1000, criterion="gini",
max_depth=100, min_samples_split=3,min_samples_leaf=2)
>>> rf_fit.fit(x_train,y_train)

>>> print ("\nRandom Forest -Train Confusion Matrix\n\n",
pd.crosstab(y_train, rf_fit.predict( x_train),rownames =
["Actuall"],colnames = ["Predicted"]))
>>> print ("\n Random Forest - Train accuracy",round(accuracy_score(
y_train, rf_fit.predict(x_train)),3))

>>> print ("\nRandom Forest - Test Confusion
Matrix\n\n",pd.crosstab(y_test, rf_fit.predict(x_test),rownames =
["Actuall"],colnames = ["Predicted"]))
>>> print ("\nRandom Forest - Test accuracy",round(accuracy_score(y_test,
rf_fit.predict(x_test)),3))
```

```
Random Forest - Train Confusion Matrix

Predicted    0    1
Actuall
0          501    0
1           18  185

Random Forest - Train accuracy 0.974


Random Forest - Test Confusion Matrix

Predicted    0    1
Actuall
0          210    1
1           43   49

Random Forest - Test accuracy 0.855
```

From observing the above results, the test accuracy produced from random forest is 0.855, which is much higher than the test accuracy of 0.8053 from logistic regression results, even after the careful tuning and removing insignificant and multi-collinear variables. This entire phenomenon boils down to the core theme of bias versus variance trade-off. Linear models are very robust and do not have enough variance to fit non-linearity in data, however, with ensemble techniques, we can minimize the variance error from a conventional decision tree, which produces the result with minimum errors from both bias and variance components.

The accuracy of the random forest can be further optimized by using the grid search method to obtain the optimum hyperparameters, for which accuracy could be much higher than the randomly chosen hyperparameters. In the next section, we will be covering the grid search method in detail.

Grid search on random forest

Grid search has been performed by changing various hyperparameters with the following settings. However, readers are encouraged to try other parameters to explore further in this space.

- Number of trees is (1000, 2000, 3000)
- Maximum depth is (100, 200, 300)
- Minimum samples per split are (2, 3)
- Minimum samples in leaf node are (1, 2)

Import `Pipeline` as follows:

```
>>> from sklearn.pipeline import Pipeline
>>> from sklearn.model_selection import train_test_split,GridSearchCV
```

The `Pipeline` function creates the combinations which will be applied one by one sequentially to determine the best possible combination:

```
>>> pipeline = Pipeline([
('clf',RandomForestClassifier(criterion='gini'))])
>>> parameters = {
...        'clf__n_estimators':(1000,2000,3000),
...        'clf__max_depth':(100,200,300),
...        'clf__min_samples_split':(2,3),
...        'clf__min_samples_leaf':(1,2)  }
```

In the following, grid search utilizes cross-validation of five to ensure robustness in the model, which is the ML way of creating two-point validation of the model:

```
>>> grid_search = GridSearchCV(pipeline,parameters,n_jobs=-1,  cv=5,
verbose=1, ... scoring='accuracy')
>>> grid_search.fit(x_train,y_train)

>>> print ('Best Training score: %0.3f' % grid_search.best_score_)
>>> print ('Best parameters set:')
>>> best_parameters = grid_search.best_estimator_.get_params()
>>> for param_name in sorted(parameters.keys()):
...     print ('\t%s: %r' % (param_name, best_parameters[param_name]))
```

```
>>> predictions = grid_search.predict(x_test)

>>> print ("Testing accuracy:",round(accuracy_score(y_test,
predictions),4))
>>> print ("\nComplete report of Testing
data\n",classification_report(y_test, ... predictions))

>>> print ("\n\nRandom Forest Grid Search- Test Confusion Matrix\n\n",
pd.crosstab(y_test, predictions,rownames = ["Actuall"],colnames =
["Predicted"]))
```

```
Fitting 5 folds for each of 36 candidates, totalling 180 fits
[Parallel(n_jobs=-1)]: Done   34 tasks       | elapsed:    47.7s
[Parallel(n_jobs=-1)]: Done  180 out of 180  | elapsed:   4.0min finished
Best Training score: 0.820
Best parameters set:
        clf__max_depth: 300
        clf__min_samples_leaf: 1
        clf__min_samples_split: 3
        clf__n_estimators: 1000
Testing accuracy: 0.8911

Complete report of Testing data
            precision    recall  f1-score   support

        0        0.87      1.00      0.93       211
        1        0.98      0.65      0.78        92

avg / total      0.90      0.89      0.88       303
```

```
Random Forest Grid Search- Test Confusion Matrix

Predicted    0    1
Actuall
0           210    1
1            32   60
```

From the result of grid search, it is apparent that best test accuracy is 0.8911 or 89.11 percent, which is about a 10 percent uplift from the logistic regression model. By predicting 10 percent better accuracy, losses incurred due to sanctioning loans to bad customers will be greatly decreased.

In a simple random forest model, train accuracy is 97.4 percent, but test accuracy is comparatively lower at 85.5 percent; whereas, in grid search methodology, train accuracy is 82 percent, but test accuracy is 89.11 percent. This highlights the issue of overfitting by building a model on single data compared with a five-fold cross validation methodology used in grid search. Hence, it is advisable to perform cross-validation to avoid over-fitting problems and ensure robustness in machine learning models.

Finally, If we compare the confusion matrix of logistic regression with random forest, false positives are greatly minimized.

- Logistic regression—43 actual default customers have been predicted as non-default category
- Random forest with grid search—32 actual default customers have been predicted as non-default category

Losses incurred by these extra 11 customers will be eliminated using machine learning models in the credit industry, which is a life saver for avoiding huge losses by giving credit to unworthy customers!

The R code for random forest with grid search on German credit data is as follows:

```
# Random Forest
library(randomForest)
library(e1071)
credit_data = read.csv("credit_data.csv")
credit_data$class = credit_data$class-1
credit_data$class = as.factor(credit_data$class)

set.seed(123)
numrow = nrow(credit_data)
trnind = sample(1:numrow,size = as.integer(0.7*numrow))
train_data = credit_data[trnind,]
test_data = credit_data[-trnind,]

rf_fit = randomForest(class~.,data = train_data, mtry=4, maxnodes=
2000,ntree=1000,nodesize = 2)
rf_pred = predict(rf_fit,data = train_data,type = "response")
rf_predt = predict(rf_fit,newdata = test_data,type ="response")

tble = table(train_data$class,rf_pred)
tblet = table(test_data$class,rf_predt)

acc = (tble[1,1]+tble[2,2])/sum(tble)
acct = (tblet[1,1]+tblet[2,2])/sum(tblet)
print(paste("Train acc",round(acc,4),"Test acc",round(acct,4)))
```

```
# Grid Search
rf_grid = tune(randomForest,class~.,data = train_data,ranges = list( mtry =
c(4,5),
  maxnodes = c(700,1000),
  ntree = c(1000,2000,3000),
  nodesize = c(1,2)
),
tunecontrol = tune.control(cross = 5)
)
summary(rf_grid)
best_model = rf_grid$best.model
summary(best_model)

 y_pred_train = predict(best_model,data = train_data)
train_conf_mat = table(train_data$class,y_pred_train)
print(paste("Train Confusion Matrix - Grid Search:")) print(train_conf_mat)
train_acc = (train_conf_mat[1,1]+ train_conf_mat[2,2])/sum(train_conf_mat)
print(paste("Train_accuracy-Grid Search:",round(train_acc,4)))

y_pred_test = predict(best_model,newdata = test_data)
test_conf_mat = table(test_data$class,y_pred_test)
print(paste("Test Confusion Matrix - Grid Search:")) print(test_conf_mat)

test_acc = (test_conf_mat[1,1]+ test_conf_mat[2,2]) /sum(test_conf_mat)
print(paste("Test_accuracy-Grid Search:",round(test_acc,4)))
```

Variable importance plot

Variable importance plot provides a list of the most significant variables in descending order by a mean decrease in Gini. The top variables contribute more to the model than the bottom ones and also have high predictive power in classifying default and non-default customers.

Surprisingly, grid search does not have variable importance functionality in Python scikit-learn, hence we are using the best parameters from grid search and plotting the variable importance graph with simple random forest `scikit-learn` function. Whereas, in R programming, we have that provision, hence R code would be compact here:

```
>>> import matplotlib.pyplot as plt
>>> rf_fit = RandomForestClassifier(n_estimators=1000, criterion="gini",
max_depth=300, min_samples_split=3,min_samples_leaf=1)
>>> rf_fit.fit(x_train,y_train)
>>> importances = rf_fit.feature_importances_
>>> std = np.std([tree.feature_importances_ for tree in
rf_fit.estimators_], axis=0)
```

```
>>> indices = np.argsort(importances)[::-1]

>>> colnames = list(x_train.columns)
# Print the feature ranking
>>> print("\nFeature ranking:\n")
>>> for f in range(x_train.shape[1]):
...     print ("Feature", indices[f], ",", colnames[indices[f]],
round(importances [indices[f]],4))

>>> plt.figure()
>>> plt.bar(range(x_train.shape[1]), importances[indices], color="r", yerr=
std[indices],   align="center")
>>> plt.xticks(range(x_train.shape[1]), indices)
>>> plt.xlim([-1, x_train.shape[1]])
>>> plt.show()
```

R code for variable importance random forest is as follows:

```
# Variable Importance
vari = varImpPlot(best_model)
print(paste("Variable Importance - Table"))
print(vari)
```

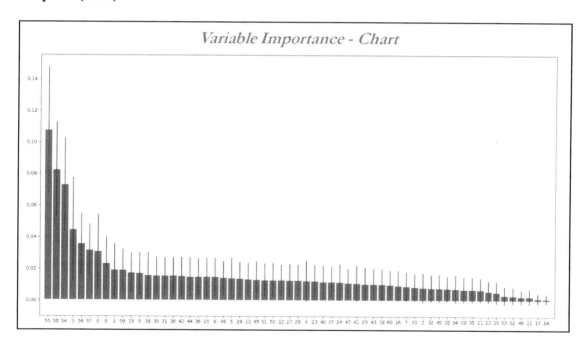

Variable Importance - Chart

Due to the presence of many variables, it is difficult to represent the variables, names on the graph, hence the same is presented as follows. The `Credit_amount` stands at first in predicting variables with a mean decrease in Gini of `0.1075`, subsequently followed by other variables:

```
Feature ranking:

Feature 55 , Credit_amount 0.1075
Feature 58 , Age_in_years 0.0826                                    Feature 4 , cred_hist_A30 0.0123
Feature 54 , Duration_in_month 0.0729                               Feature 23 , sav_acc_A65 0.0122
Feature 3 , status_exs_accnt_A14 0.0446                             Feature 40 , oth_inst_pln_A141 0.0115
Feature 56 , Installment_rate_in_percentage_of_disposable_income 0.0355   Feature 37 , property_A122 0.0115
Feature 57 , Present_residence_since 0.0315                         Feature 24 , pre_emp_snc_A71 0.0114
Feature 0 , status_exs_accnt_A11 0.0307                             Feature 47 , job_A172 0.0109
Feature 8 , cred_hist_A34 0.0231                                    Feature 41 , oth_inst_pln_A142 0.0108
Feature 1 , status_exs_accnt_A12 0.0191                             Feature 29 , per_stat_sx_A91 0.0103
Feature 59 , Number_of_existing_credits_at_this_bank 0.0191         Feature 43 , housing_A151 0.0103
Feature 19 , sav_acc_A61 0.0172                                     Feature 18 , purpose_A49 0.01
Feature 9 , purpose_A40 0.017                                       Feature 60 , Number_of_People_being_liable_to_provide_maintenance_for 0.0099
Feature 39 , property_A124 0.0157                                   Feature 16 , purpose_A46 0.0093
Feature 30 , per_stat_sx_A92 0.0155                                 Feature 7 , cred_hist_A33 0.009
Feature 31 , per_stat_sx_A93 0.0155                                 Feature 33 , oth_debtors_A101 0.0084
Feature 38 , property_A123 0.0155                                   Feature 2 , status_exs_accnt_A13 0.008
Feature 42 , oth_inst_pln_A143 0.0152                               Feature 32 , per_stat_sx_A94 0.0078
Feature 44 , housing_A152 0.0149                                    Feature 45 , housing_A153 0.0077
Feature 36 , property_A121 0.0149                                   Feature 10 , purpose_A41 0.0076
Feature 25 , pre_emp_snc_A72 0.0147                                 Feature 34 , oth_debtors_A102 0.0074
Feature 6 , cred_hist_A32 0.0147                                    Feature 20 , sav_acc_A62 0.007
Feature 48 , job_A173 0.014                                         Feature 35 , oth_debtors_A103 0.0069
Feature 5 , cred_hist_A31 0.0139                                    Feature 21 , sav_acc_A63 0.0067
Feature 26 , pre_emp_snc_A73 0.0137                                 Feature 22 , sav_acc_A64 0.0057
Feature 13 , purpose_A43 0.0131                                     Feature 15 , purpose_A45 0.005
Feature 49 , job_A174 0.0131                                        Feature 53 , forgn_wrkr_A202 0.0033
Feature 51 , telephn_A192 0.0128                                    Feature 52 , forgn_wrkr_A201 0.0031
Feature 50 , telephn_A191 0.0127                                    Feature 46 , job_A171 0.0024
Feature 12 , purpose_A42 0.0127                                     Feature 11 , purpose_A410 0.0023
Feature 27 , pre_emp_snc_A74 0.0127                                 Feature 17 , purpose_A48 0.0013
Feature 28 , pre_emp_snc_A75 0.0126                                 Feature 14 , purpose_A44 0.001
Feature 4 , cred_hist_A30 0.0123
```

Comparison of logistic regression with random forest

One major issue facing the credit risk industry from regulators is due to the black box nature of machine learning models. This section focuses upon drawing parallels between logistic regression and random forest models to create transparency for random forest, so that it will be less intimidating for regulators while approving implementation of machine learning models. Last but not least, readers will also be educated on the comparison of statistical models with machine learning models.

In the following table, both models explanatory variables have been put in descending order based on the importance of them towards the model contribution. In the logistic regression model, it is the p-value (minimum is a better predictor), and for random forest it is the mean decrease in Gini (maximum is a better predictor). Many of the variables are very much matching in importance like, `status_exs_accnt_A14`, `credit_hist_A34`, `Installment_rate_in_percentage_of_disposable_income`, `property_A_24`, `Credit_amount`, `Duration_in_month`, and so on.

Logistic Regression - Summary				Variable Importance - Random Forest		
Variable	**Co-efficient**	**p-value**	**Feature Number**	**Variable Name**		**Mean Decrese in Gini**
const	-2.1782	0	55	Credit_amount		0.1075
status_exs_accnt_A14	-1.5561	0	58	Age_in_years		0.0826
cred_hist_A34	-0.9717	0	54	Duration_in_month		0.0729
per_stat_sx_A93	-0.7401	0	3	status_exs_accnt_A14		0.0446
Installment_rate_in_percentage_of_disposable_income	0.3783	0	56	Installment_rate_in_percentage_of_disposable_income		0.0355
purpose_A41	-1.3009	0.002	57	Present_residence_since		0.0315
property_A124	0.7233	0.007	0	status_exs_accnt_A11		0.0307
status_exs_accnt_A13	-1.1011	0.009	8	cred_hist_A34		0.0231
oth_inst_pln_A142	1.1535	0.009	1	status_exs_accnt_A12		0.0191
purpose_A43	-0.5359	0.017	59	Number_of_existing_credits_at_this_bank		0.0191
Credit_amount	0.0001	0.026	19	sav_acc_A61		0.0172
Number_of_existing_credits_at_this_bank	0.3876	0.041	9	purpose_A40		0.017
cred_hist_A31	0.9028	0.042	39	property_A124		0.0157
Duration_in_month	0.0185	0.057	30	per_stat_sx_A92		0.0155
			31	per_stat_sx_A93		0.0155
			38	property_A123		0.0155
			42	oth_inst_pln_A143		0.0152
			44	housing_A152		0.0149
			36	property_A121		0.0149
			25	pre_emp_snc_A72		0.0147
			6	cred_hist_A32		0.0147
			48	job_A173		0.014
			5	cred_hist_A31		0.0139
			26	pre_emp_snc_A73		0.0137
			13	purpose_A43		0.0131
			49	job_A174		0.0131
			51	telephn_A192		0.0128
			50	telephn_A191		0.0127
			12	purpose_A42		0.0127
			27	pre_emp_snc_A74		0.0127
			28	pre_emp_snc_A75		0.0126
			4	cred_hist_A30		0.0123
			23	sav_acc_A65		0.0122
			40	oth_inst_pln_A141		0.0115

One major underlying fact which readers should not ignore is that important variables remain important in any of the models, whether it is statistical or machine learning. But by carefully comparing this way, a credit and risk department can provide an explanation to regulators and convince them about the implementation of machine learning models.

Summary

In this chapter, you have learned the working principles of logistic regression and its step-by-step solving methodology by iteratively removing insignificant and multi-collinear variables to find the best fit by constantly checking AIC and concordance values to determine the best model in a statistical way. Subsequently we looked at machine learning model and random forest being applied to calculate the test accuracy. It was found that, by carefully tuning the hyperparameters of random forest using grid search, we were able to uplift the results by 10 percent in terms of test accuracy from 80 percent from logistic regression to 90 percent from random forest.

In the next chapter, we will be covering complete tree based models such as decision trees, random forest, boosted trees, ensemble of models, and so on to further improve accuracy!

4
Tree-Based Machine Learning Models

he goal of tree-based methods is to segment the feature space into a number of simple rectangular regions, to subsequently make a prediction for a given observation based on either mean or mode (mean for regression and mode for classification, to be precise) of the training observations in the region to which it belongs. Unlike most other classifiers, models produced by decision trees are easy to interpret. In this chapter, we will be covering the following decision tree-based models on HR data examples for predicting whether a given employee will leave the organization in the near future or not. In this chapter, we will learn the following topics:

- Decision trees - simple model and model with class weight tuning
- Bagging (bootstrap aggregation)
- Random Ffrest - basic random forest and application of grid search on hypyerparameter tuning
- Boosting (AdaBoost, gradient boost, extreme gradient boost - XGBoost)
- Ensemble of ensembles (with heterogeneous and homogeneous models)

Introducing decision tree classifiers

Decision tree classifiers produce rules in simple English sentences, which can easily be interpreted and presented to senior management without any editing. Decision trees can be applied to either classification or regression problems. Based on features in data, decision tree models learn a series of questions to infer the class labels of samples.

In the following figure, simple recursive decision rules have been asked by a programmer himself to do relevant actions. The actions would be based on the provided answers for each question, whether yes or no.

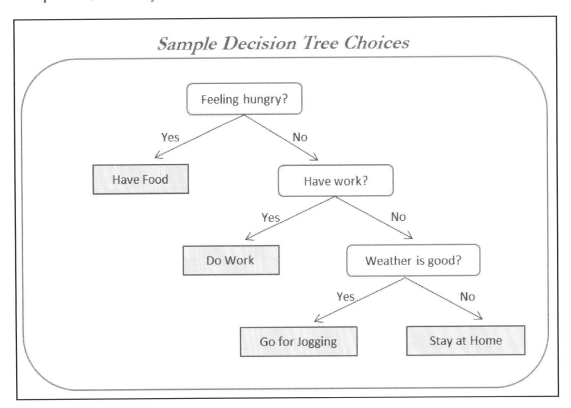

Terminology used in decision trees

Decision Trees do not have much machinery as compared with logistic regression. Here we have a few metrics to study. We will majorly focus on impurity measures; decision trees split variables recursively based on set impurity criteria until they reach some stopping criteria (minimum observations per terminal node, minimum observations for split at any node, and so on):

- **Entropy:** Entropy came from information theory and is the measure of impurity in data. If the sample is completely homogeneous, the entropy is zero, and if the sample is equally divided, it has entropy of one. In decision trees, the predictor with most heterogeneousness will be considered nearest to the root node to classify the given data into classes in a greedy mode. We will cover this topic in more depth in this chapter:

$$Entropy = -p_1 * log_2 \, p_1 \, - \, ... - -p_n * log_2 \, p_n$$

  Where n = number of classes. Entropy is maximum in the middle, with a value of *1* and minimum at the extremes with a value of *0*. The low value of entropy is desirable, as it will segregate classes better.

- **Information Gain:** Information gain is the expected reduction in entropy caused by partitioning the examples according to a given attribute. The idea is to start with mixed classes and to continue partitioning until each node reaches its observations of purest class. At every stage, the variable with maximum information gain is chosen in a greedy fashion.

  *Information Gain = Entropy of Parent - sum (weighted % * Entropy of Child)*

  Weighted % = Number of observations in particular child/sum (observations in all child nodes)

- **Gini:** Gini impurity is a measure of misclassification, which applies in a multi-class classifier context. Gini works similar to entropy, except Gini is quicker to calculate:

$$Gini = 1 - \sum_i p_i^2$$

Where i = *Number of classes*. The similarity between Gini and entropy is shown in the following figure:

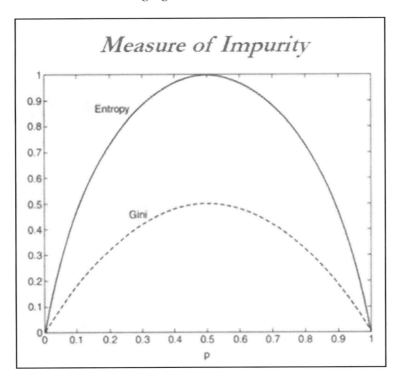

Decision tree working methodology from first principles

In the following example, the response variable has only two classes: whether to play tennis or not. But the following table has been compiled based on various conditions recorded on various days. Now, our task is to find out which output the variables are resulting in most significantly: YES or NO.

1. This example comes under the Classification tree:

Day	Outlook	Temperature	Humidity	Wind	Play tennis
D1	Sunny	Hot	High	Weak	No
D2	Sunny	Hot	High	Strong	No

D3	Overcast	Hot	High	Weak	Yes
D4	Rain	Mild	High	Weak	Yes
D5	Rain	Cool	Normal	Weak	Yes
D6	Rain	Cool	Normal	Strong	No
D7	Overcast	Cool	Normal	Strong	Yes
D8	Sunny	Mild	High	Weak	No
D9	Sunny	Cool	Normal	Weak	Yes
D10	Rain	Mild	Normal	Weak	Yes
D11	Sunny	Mild	Normal	Strong	Yes
D12	Overcast	Mild	High	Strong	Yes
D13	Overcast	Hot	Normal	Weak	Yes
D14	Rain	Mild	High	Strong	No

2. Taking the Humidity variable as an example to classify the Play Tennis field:
   - **CHAID:** Humidity has two categories and our expected values should be evenly distributed in order to calculate how distinguishing the variable is:

Humidity category	Play tennis		Expected		Difference	
	No	Yes	No	Yes	No	Yes
High	4	3	2.5	4.5	1.5	-1.5
Normal	1	6	2.5	4.5	-1.5	1.5
	5	9	5	9		

Calculating x^2 (Chi-square) value:

$$= \Sigma \frac{(O-E)^2}{E} \; = \; \frac{(1.5)^2}{2.5} + \frac{(-1.5)^2}{4.5} + \frac{(-1.5)^2}{2.5} + \frac{(1.5)^2}{4.5} = 2.8$$

Calculating degrees of freedom = (r-1) * (c-1)

Where r = number of row components/number of variable categories, C = number of response variables.

Here, there are two row categories (High and Normal) and two column categories (No and Yes).

Hence = *(2-1) * (2-1) = 1*

p-value for Chi-square 2.8 with 1 d.f = 0.0942

p-value can be obtained with the following Excel formulae: = *CHIDIST (2.8, 1) = 0.0942*

In a similar way, we will calculate the *p-value* for all variables and select the best variable with a low p-value.

- **ENTROPY**:

Entropy = - Σ p * $\log_2$ p

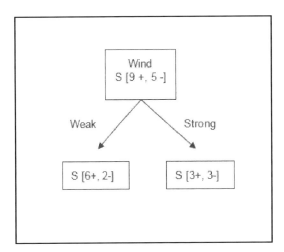

$$Entropy = -\left(\frac{9}{14}\right) * Log_2\left(\frac{9}{14}\right) - \left(\frac{5}{14}\right) * Log_2\left(\frac{5}{14}\right)$$

$$= 0.4097 + 0.5305 = 0.9402$$

$$Log_2\left(\frac{9}{14}\right) = Log\ (9/14)\ /\ Log\ 2 = -0.6374$$

$$Entropy_{High} = -\left(\frac{3}{7}\right) * Log_2\left(\frac{3}{7}\right) - \left(\frac{4}{7}\right) * Log_2\left(\frac{4}{7}\right)$$
$$= 0.523 + 0.4613 = 0.9851$$

$$Entropy_{Normal} = -\left(\frac{1}{7}\right) * Log_2\left(\frac{1}{7}\right) - \left(\frac{6}{7}\right) * Log_2\left(\frac{6}{7}\right)$$
$$= 0.4010 + 0.1906 = 0.5916$$

$$Information\ gain = Total\ Entropy - \left(\frac{7}{14}\right) * Entropy_{High} - \left(\frac{7}{14}\right) * Entropy_{Normal}$$
$$= 0.9402 - \left(\frac{7}{14}\right) * 0.9851 - \left(\frac{7}{14}\right) * 0.5916 = 0.1518$$

In a similar way, we will calculate *information gain* for all variables and select the best variable with the *highest information gain*.

- **GINI**:

$Gini = 1 - \Sigma p^2$

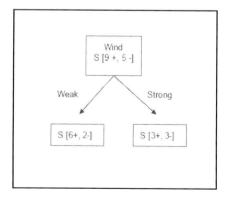

$$\text{Gini} = 1 - \left(\frac{9}{14}\right)^2 - \left(\frac{5}{14}\right)^2 = 0.459$$

$$\text{Gini}_{\text{Normal}} = 1 - \left(\frac{1}{7}\right)^2 - \left(\frac{6}{7}\right)^2 = 0.2448$$

$$\text{Expected Gini} = \left(\frac{7}{14}\right) * 0.489 + \left(\frac{7}{14}\right) * 0.2448 = 0.3669$$

In a similar way, we will calculate *Expected Gini* for all variables and select the best with the *lowest expected value*.

For the purpose of a better understanding, we will also do similar calculations for the Wind variable:

- **CHAID:** Wind has two categories and our expected values should be evenly distributed in order to calculate how distinguishing the variable is:

	Play tennis		Expected		Difference	
	No	Yes	No	Yes	No	Yes
Weak	2	6	2.5	4.5	-0.5	1.5
Strong	3	3	2.5	4.5	0.5	-1.5
	5	9	5	9		

$$= \frac{(-0.5)^2}{2.5} + \frac{(1.5)^2}{4.5} + \frac{(0.5)^2}{2.5} + \frac{(-1.5)^2}{4.5} = 1.2$$

$$\text{p-value} = 0.2733$$

- **ENTROPY:**

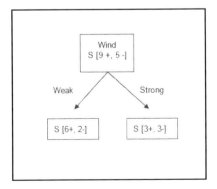

$$Entropy_{Weak} = -\left(\frac{6}{8}\right) * Log_2\left(\frac{6}{8}\right) - \left(\frac{2}{8}\right) * Log_2\left(\frac{2}{8}\right)$$

$$= 0.3112 + 0.5 = 0.8112$$

$$Entropy_{Strong} = -\left(\frac{3}{6}\right) * Log_2\left(\frac{3}{6}\right) - \left(\frac{3}{6}\right) * Log_2\left(\frac{3}{6}\right) = 0.5 + 0.5 = 1$$

$$Information\ gain = Total\ Entropy - \left(\frac{8}{14}\right) * Entropy_{Weak} - \left(\frac{6}{14}\right) * Entropy_{Strong}$$

$$= 0.9402 - \left(\frac{8}{14}\right) * 0.8112 - \left(\frac{6}{14}\right) * 1 = 0.0482$$

- **GINI**:

$$Gini_{Weak} = 1 - \left(\frac{6}{8}\right)^2 - \left(\frac{2}{8}\right)^2 = 0.375$$

$$Gini_{Strong} = 1 - \left(\frac{3}{6}\right)^2 - \left(\frac{3}{6}\right)^2 = 0.5$$

$$Expected\ Gini = \left(\frac{8}{14}\right) * 0.375 + \left(\frac{6}{14}\right) * 0.5 = 0.4285$$

Now we will compare both variables for all three metrics so that we can understand them better.

Variables	CHAID (p-value)	Entropy information gain	Gini expected value
Humidity	0.0942	0.1518	0.3669
Wind	0.2733	0.0482	0.4285
Better	Low value	High value	Low value

For all three calculations, Humidity is proven to be a better classifier than Wind. Hence, we can confirm that all methods convey a similar story.

Comparison between logistic regression and decision trees

Before we dive into the coding details of decision trees, here, we will quickly compare the differences between logistic regression and decision trees, so that we will know which model is better and in what way.

Logistic regression	Decision trees
Logistic regression model looks like an equation between independent variables with respect to its dependent variable.	Tree classifiers produce rules in simple English sentences, which can be easily explained to senior management.
Logistic regression is a parametric model, in which the model is defined by having parameters multiplied by independent variables to predict the dependent variable.	Decision Trees are a non-parametric model, in which no pre-assumed parameter exists. Implicitly performs variable screening or feature selection.
Assumptions are made on response (or dependent) variable, with binomial or Bernoulli distribution.	No assumptions are made on the underlying distribution of the data.
Shape of the model is predefined (logistic curve).	Shape of the model is not predefined; model fits in best possible classification based on the data instead.
Provides very good results when independent variables are continuous in nature, and also linearity holds true.	Provides best results when most of the variables are categorical in nature.
Difficult to find complex interactions among variables (non-linear relationships between variables).	Non-linear relationships between parameters do not affect tree performance. Often uncover complex interactions. Trees can handle numerical data with highly skewed or multi-modal, as well as categorical predictors with either ordinal or non-ordinal structure.
Outliers and missing values deteriorate the performance of logistic regression.	Outliners and missing values are dealt with grace in decision trees.

Comparison of error components across various styles of models

Errors need to be evaluated in order to measure the effectiveness of the model in order to improve the model's performance further by tuning various knobs. Error components consist of a bias component, variance component, and pure white noise:

$$E(y_0 - \hat{f}(x_0))^2 = Var\left(\hat{f}(x_0)\right) + [Bias\left(\hat{f}(x_0)\right)]^2 + Var(\varepsilon)$$

Out of the following three regions:

- The first region has high bias and low variance error components. In this region, models are very robust in nature, such as linear regression or logistic regression.
- Whereas the third region has high variance and low bias error components, in this region models are very wiggly and vary greatly in nature, similar to decision trees, but due to the great amount of variability in the nature of their shape, these models tend to overfit on training data and produce less accuracy on test data.
- Last but not least, the middle region, also called the second region, is the ideal sweet spot, in which both bias and variance components are moderate, causing it to create the lowest total errors.

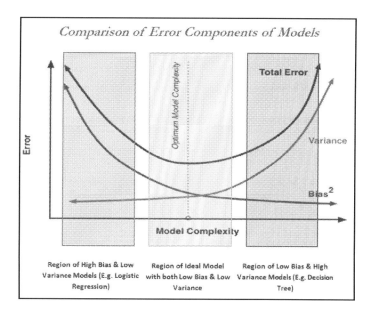

Remedial actions to push the model towards the ideal region

Models with either high bias or high variance error components do not produce the ideal fit. Hence, some makeovers are required to do so. In the following diagram, the various methods applied are shown in detail. In the case of linear regression, there would be a high bias component, meaning the model is not flexible enough to fit some non-linearities in data. One turnaround is to break the single line into small linear pieces and fit them into the region by constraining them at knots, also called **Linear Spline**. Whereas decision trees have a high variance problem, meaning even a slight change in *X* values leads to large changes in its corresponding *Y* values, this issue can be resolved by performing an ensemble of the decision trees:

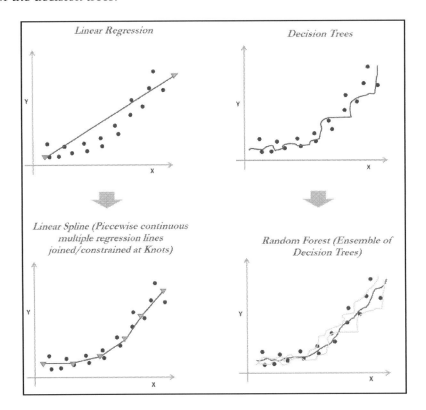

In practice, implementing splines would be a difficult and not so popular method, due to the involvement of the many equations a practitioner has to keep tabs on, in addition to checking the linearity assumption and other diagnostic KPIs (p-values, AIC, multi-collinearity, and so on) of each separate equation. Instead, performing ensemble on decision trees is most popular in the data science community, similar to bagging, random forest, and boosting, which we will be covering in depth in later parts of this chapter. Ensemble techniques tackle variance problems by aggregating the results from highly variable individual classifiers such as decision trees.

HR attrition data example

In this section, we will be using IBM Watson's HR Attrition data (the data has been utilized in the book after taking prior permission from the data administrator) shared in Kaggle datasets under open source license agreement `https://www.kaggle.com/pavansubhasht/ibm-hr-analytics-attrition-dataset` to predict whether employees would attrite or not based on independent explanatory variables:

```
>>> import pandas as pd
>>> hrattr_data = pd.read_csv("WA_Fn-UseC_-HR-Employee-Attrition.csv")

>>> print (hrattr_data.head())
```

There are about 1470 observations and 35 variables in this data, the top five rows are shown here for a quick glance of the variables:

RelationshipSatisfaction	StandardHours	StockOptionLevel	TotalWorkingYears	TrainingTimesLastYear	WorkLifeBalance	YearsAtCompany	YearsInCurrentRole	YearsSinceLastPromotion	YearsWithCurrManager
1	80	0	8	0	1	6	4	0	5
4	80	1	10	3	3	10	7	1	7
2	80	0	7	3	3	0	0	0	0
3	80	0	8	3	3	8	7	3	0
4	80	1	6	3	3	2	2	2	2

HourlyRate	JobInvolvement	JobLevel	JobRole	JobSatisfaction	MaritalStatus	MonthlyIncome	MonthlyRate	NumCompaniesWorked	Over18	OverTime	PercentSalaryHike	PerformanceRating
94	3	2	Sales Executive	4	Single	5993	19479	8	Y	Yes	11	3
61	2	2	Research Scientist	2	Married	5130	24907	1	Y	No	23	4
92	2	1	Laboratory Technician	3	Single	2090	2396	6	Y	Yes	15	3
56	3	1	Research Scientist	3	Married	2909	23159	1	Y	Yes	11	3
40	3	1	Laboratory Technician	2	Married	3468	16632	9	Y	No	12	3

Age	Attrition	BusinessTravel	DailyRate	Department	DistanceFromHome	Education	EducationField	EmployeeCount	EmployeeNumber	EnvironmentSatisfaction	Gender
41	Yes	Travel_Rarely	1102	Sales	1	2	Life Sciences	1	1	2	Female
49	No	Travel_Frequently	279	Research & Development	8	1	Life Sciences	1	2	3	Male
37	Yes	Travel_Rarely	1373	Research & Development	2	2	Other	1	4	4	Male
33	No	Travel_Frequently	1392	Research & Development	3	4	Life Sciences	1	5	4	Female
27	No	Travel_Rarely	591	Research & Development	2	1	Medical	1	7	1	Male

The following code is used to convert Yes or No categories into 1 and 0 for modeling purposes, as scikit-learn does not fit the model on character/categorical variables directly, hence dummy coding is required to be performed for utilizing the variables in models:

```
>>> hrattr_data['Attrition_ind'] = 0
>>> hrattr_data.loc[hrattr_data['Attrition'] =='Yes', 'Attrition_ind'] = 1
```

Dummy variables are created for all seven categorical variables (shown here in alphabetical order), which are Business Travel, Department, Education Field, Gender, Job Role, Marital Status, and Overtime. We have ignored four variables from the analysis, as they do not change across the observations, which are Employee count, Employee number, Over18, and Standard Hours:

```
>>> dummy_busnstrvl = pd.get_dummies(hrattr_data['BusinessTravel'],
prefix='busns_trvl')
>>> dummy_dept = pd.get_dummies(hrattr_data['Department'], prefix='dept')
>>> dummy_edufield = pd.get_dummies(hrattr_data['EducationField'],
prefix='edufield')
>>> dummy_gender = pd.get_dummies(hrattr_data['Gender'], prefix='gend')
>>> dummy_jobrole = pd.get_dummies(hrattr_data['JobRole'],
prefix='jobrole')
>>> dummy_maritstat = pd.get_dummies(hrattr_data['MaritalStatus'],
prefix='maritalstat')
>>> dummy_overtime = pd.get_dummies(hrattr_data['OverTime'],
prefix='overtime')
```

Continuous variables are separated and will be combined with the created dummy variables later:

```
>>> continuous_columns = ['Age','DailyRate','DistanceFromHome',
'Education',
'EnvironmentSatisfaction','HourlyRate','JobInvolvement','JobLevel','JobSati
sfaction', 'MonthlyIncome', 'MonthlyRate',
'NumCompaniesWorked','PercentSalaryHike',  'PerformanceRating',
'RelationshipSatisfaction','StockOptionLevel', 'TotalWorkingYears',
'TrainingTimesLastYear','WorkLifeBalance', 'YearsAtCompany',
'YearsInCurrentRole', 'YearsSinceLastPromotion','YearsWithCurrManager']

>>> hrattr_continuous = hrattr_data[continuous_columns]
```

In the following step, both derived dummy variables from categorical variables and straight continuous variables are combined:

```
>>> hrattr_data_new = pd.concat([dummy_busnstrvl, dummy_dept,
dummy_edufield, dummy_gender, dummy_jobrole, dummy_maritstat,
dummy_overtime, hrattr_continuous, hrattr_data['Attrition_ind']],axis=1)
```

Here, we have not removed one extra derived dummy variable for each categorical variable due to the reason that multi-collinearity does not create a problem in decision trees as it does in either logistic or linear regression, hence we can simply utilize all the derived variables in the rest of the chapter, as all the models utilize decision trees as an underlying model, even after performing ensembles of it.

Once basic data has been prepared, it needs to be split by 70-30 for training and testing purposes:

```
# Train and Test split
>>> from sklearn.model_selection import train_test_split
>>> x_train,x_test,y_train,y_test = train_test_split( hrattr_data_new.drop
(['Attrition_ind'], axis=1),hrattr_data_new['Attrition_ind'],   train_size
= 0.7, random_state=42)
```

R Code for Data Preprocessing on HR Attrition Data:

```
hrattr_data = read.csv("WA_Fn-UseC_-HR-Employee-Attrition.csv")
str(hrattr_data);summary(hrattr_data)
hrattr_data$Attrition_ind = 0;
hrattr_data$Attrition_ind[   hrattr_data$Attrition=="Yes"]=1
hrattr_data$Attrition_ind=   as.factor(hrattr_data$Attrition_ind)
remove_cols = c("EmployeeCount","EmployeeNumber","Over18",
"StandardHours","Attrition")
hrattr_data_new =   hrattr_data[,!(names(hrattr_data) %in% remove_cols)]
set.seed(123)
numrow = nrow(hrattr_data_new)
trnind = sample(1:numrow,size =   as.integer(0.7*numrow))
train_data =   hrattr_data_new[trnind,]
test_data = hrattr_data_new[-trnind,]
# Code for calculating   precision, recall for 0 and 1 categories and # at
overall level which   will be used in all the classifiers in # later
sections
frac_trzero =    (table(train_data$Attrition_ind)[[1]])/nrow(train_data)
frac_trone =    (table(train_data$Attrition_ind)[[2]])/nrow(train_data)
frac_tszero =    (table(test_data$Attrition_ind)[[1]])/nrow(test_data)
frac_tsone = (table(test_data$Attrition_ind)[[2]])/nrow(test_data)
prec_zero <-    function(act,pred){   tble = table(act,pred)
return( round(    tble[1,1]/(tble[1,1]+tble[2,1]),4))}
```

```
prec_one <-    function(act,pred){ tble = table(act,pred)
return( round(    tble[2,2]/(tble[2,2]+tble[1,2]),4))}
recl_zero <-    function(act,pred){tble = table(act,pred)
return( round(    tble[1,1]/(tble[1,1]+tble[1,2]),4))}
recl_one <-    function(act,pred){ tble = table(act,pred)
return( round(    tble[2,2]/(tble[2,2]+tble[2,1]),4))}
accrcy <-    function(act,pred){ tble = table(act,pred)
return(    round((tble[1,1]+tble[2,2])/sum(tble),4))}
```

Decision tree classifier

The DecisionTtreeClassifier from scikit-learn has been utilized for modeling purposes, which is available in the tree submodule:

```
# Decision Tree Classifier
>>> from sklearn.tree import DecisionTreeClassifier
```

The parameters selected for the DT classifier are in the following code with splitting criterion as Gini, Maximum depth as 5, minimum number of observations required for qualifying split is 2, and the minimum samples that should be present in the terminal node is 1:

```
>>> dt_fit = DecisionTreeClassifier(criterion="gini",
max_depth=5,min_samples_split=2,  min_samples_leaf=1,random_state=42)
>>> dt_fit.fit(x_train,y_train)

>>> print ("\nDecision Tree - Train Confusion  Matrix\n\n",
pd.crosstab(y_train, dt_fit.predict(x_train),rownames =
["Actuall"],colnames = ["Predicted"]))
>>> from sklearn.metrics import accuracy_score, classification_report
>>> print ("\nDecision Tree - Train accuracy\n\n",round(accuracy_score
(y_train, dt_fit.predict(x_train)),3))
>>> print ("\nDecision Tree - Train Classification Report\n",
classification_report(y_train, dt_fit.predict(x_train)))

>>> print ("\n\nDecision Tree - Test Confusion
Matrix\n\n",pd.crosstab(y_test, dt_fit.predict(x_test),rownames =
["Actuall"],colnames = ["Predicted"]))
>>> print ("\nDecision Tree - Test accuracy",round(accuracy_score(y_test,
dt_fit.predict(x_test)),3))
>>> print ("\nDecision Tree - Test Classification Report\n",
classification_report( y_test, dt_fit.predict(x_test)))
```

```
Decision Tree - Train Confusion Matrix

Predicted    0    1
Actuall
0           844    9
1            98   78

Decision Tree - Train accuracy: 0.896

Decision Tree - Train Classification Report
            precision    recall  f1-score   support

         0       0.90      0.99      0.94       853
         1       0.90      0.44      0.59       176

avg / total       0.90      0.90      0.88      1029


Decision Tree - Test Confusion Matrix

Predicted    0    1
Actuall
0           361   19
1            49   12

Decision Tree - Test accuracy: 0.846

Decision Tree - Test Classification Report
            precision    recall  f1-score   support

         0       0.88      0.95      0.91       380
         1       0.39      0.20      0.26        61

avg / total       0.81      0.85      0.82       441
```

By carefully observing the results, we can infer that, even though the test accuracy is high (84.6%), the precision and recall of one category (*Attrition = Yes*) is low (*precision = 0.39* and *recall = 0.20*). This could be a serious issue when management tries to use this model to provide some extra benefits proactively to the employees with a high chance of attrition prior to actual attrition, as this model is unable to identify the real employees who will be leaving. Hence, we need to look for other modifications; one way is to control the model by using class weights. By utilizing class weights, we can increase the importance of a particular class at the cost of an increase in other errors.

For example, by increasing class weight to category *1*, we can identify more employees with the characteristics of actual attrition, but by doing so, we will mark some of the non-potential churner employees as potential attriters (which should be acceptable).

Another classical example of the important use of class weights is, in banking scenarios. When giving loans, it is better to reject some good applications than accepting bad loans. Hence, even in this case, it is a better idea to use higher weightage to defaulters over non-defaulters:

R Code for Decision Tree Classifier Applied on HR Attrition Data:

```
# Decision Trees using C5.0    package
library(C50)
dtree_fit = C5.0(train_data[-31],train_data$Attrition_ind,costs    =
NULL,control = C5.0Control(minCases = 1))
summary(dtree_fit)
tr_y_pred = predict(dtree_fit,    train_data,type = "class")
ts_y_pred =    predict(dtree_fit,test_data,type = "class")
tr_y_act =    train_data$Attrition_ind;ts_y_act = test_data$Attrition_ind
tr_tble =    table(tr_y_act,tr_y_pred)
print(paste("Train    Confusion Matrix"))
print(tr_tble)
tr_acc =    accrcy(tr_y_act,tr_y_pred)
trprec_zero =    prec_zero(tr_y_act,tr_y_pred);
trrecl_zero =    recl_zero(tr_y_act,tr_y_pred)
trprec_one =    prec_one(tr_y_act,tr_y_pred);
trrecl_one =    recl_one(tr_y_act,tr_y_pred)
trprec_ovll = trprec_zero *frac_trzero    + trprec_one*frac_trone
trrecl_ovll = trrecl_zero    *frac_trzero + trrecl_one*frac_trone
print(paste("Decision Tree    Train accuracy:",tr_acc))
print(paste("Decision Tree    - Train Classification Report"))
print(paste("Zero_Precision",trprec_zero,"Zero_Recall",trrecl_zero))
print(paste("One_Precision",trprec_one,"One_Recall",trrecl_one))
print(paste("Overall_Precision",round(trprec_ovll,4),"Overall_Recall",
round(trrecl_ovll,4)))
ts_tble =    table(ts_y_act,ts_y_pred)
print(paste("Test    Confusion Matrix"))
print(ts_tble)
ts_acc =    accrcy(ts_y_act,ts_y_pred)
tsprec_zero =    prec_zero(ts_y_act,ts_y_pred); tsrecl_zero =
recl_zero(ts_y_act,ts_y_pred)
tsprec_one =    prec_one(ts_y_act,ts_y_pred); tsrecl_one =
recl_one(ts_y_act,ts_y_pred)
tsprec_ovll = tsprec_zero *frac_tszero    + tsprec_one*frac_tsone
tsrecl_ovll = tsrecl_zero    *frac_tszero + tsrecl_one*frac_tsone
print(paste("Decision Tree    Test accuracy:",ts_acc))
print(paste("Decision Tree    - Test Classification Report"))
print(paste("Zero_Precision",tsprec_zero,"Zero_Recall",tsrecl_zero))
print(paste("One_Precision",tsprec_one,"One_Recall",tsrecl_one))
print(paste("Overall_Precision",round(tsprec_ovll,4),
"Overall_Recall",round(tsrecl_ovll,4)))
```

Tuning class weights in decision tree classifier

In the following code, class weights are tuned to see the performance change in decision trees with the same parameters. A dummy DataFrame is created to save all the results of various precision-recall details of combinations:

```
>>> dummyarray = np.empty((6,10))
>>> dt_wttune = pd.DataFrame(dummyarray)
```

Metrics to be considered for capture are weight for zero and one category (for example, if the weight for zero category given is 0.2, then automatically, weight for the one should be 0.8, as total weight should be equal to 1), training and testing accuracy, precision for zero category, one category, and overall. Similarly, recall for zero category, one category, and overall are also calculated:

```
>>> dt_wttune.columns = ["zero_wght","one_wght","tr_accuracy",
"tst_accuracy", "prec_zero","prec_one", "prec_ovll",
"recl_zero","recl_one","recl_ovll"]
```

Weights for the zero category are verified from 0.01 to 0.5, as we know we do not want to explore cases where the zero category will be given higher weightage than one category:

```
>>> zero_clwghts = [0.01,0.1,0.2,0.3,0.4,0.5]

>>> for i in range(len(zero_clwghts)):
...     clwght = {0:zero_clwghts[i],1:1.0-zero_clwghts[i]}
...     dt_fit = DecisionTreeClassifier(criterion="gini",  max_depth=5,
... min_samples_split=2, min_samples_leaf=1,random_state=42,class_weight =
clwght)
...     dt_fit.fit(x_train,y_train)
...     dt_wttune.loc[i, 'zero_wght'] = clwght[0]
...     dt_wttune.loc[i, 'one_wght'] = clwght[1]
...     dt_wttune.loc[i, 'tr_accuracy'] = round(accuracy_score(y_train,
dt_fit.predict( x_train)),3)
...     dt_wttune.loc[i, 'tst_accuracy'] =
round(accuracy_score(y_test,dt_fit.predict( x_test)),3)
...     clf_sp =
classification_report(y_test,dt_fit.predict(x_test)).split()
...     dt_wttune.loc[i, 'prec_zero'] = float(clf_sp[5])
...     dt_wttune.loc[i, 'prec_one'] = float(clf_sp[10])
...     dt_wttune.loc[i, 'prec_ovll'] = float(clf_sp[17])
...     dt_wttune.loc[i, 'recl_zero'] = float(clf_sp[6])
...     dt_wttune.loc[i, 'recl_one'] = float(clf_sp[11])
...     dt_wttune.loc[i, 'recl_ovll'] = float(clf_sp[18])
...     print ("\nClass Weights",clwght,"Train
```

```
accuracy:",round(accuracy_score( y_train,dt_fit.predict(x_train)),3),"Test
accuracy:",round(accuracy_score(y_test, dt_fit.predict(x_test)),3))
...     print ("Test Confusion
Matrix\n\n",pd.crosstab(y_test,dt_fit.predict( x_test),rownames =
["Actuall"],colnames = ["Predicted"]))
```

```
Class Weights {0: 0.01, 1: 0.99} Train accuracy: 0.342 Test accuracy: 0.272
Test Confusion Matrix


Predicted  0   1
Actuall
0          65  315
1          6   55


Class Weights {0: 0.1, 1: 0.9} Train accuracy: 0.806 Test accuracy: 0.732
Test Confusion Matrix


Predicted   0   1
Actuall
0           282 98
1           20  41


Class Weights {0: 0.2, 1: 0.8} Train accuracy: 0.871 Test accuracy: 0.83
Test Confusion Matrix


Predicted   0   1
Actuall
0           341 39
1           36  25


Class Weights {0: 0.3, 1: 0.7} Train accuracy: 0.881 Test accuracy: 0.839
Test Confusion Matrix


Predicted   0   1
Actuall
0           345 35
1           36  25


Class Weights {0: 0.4, 1: 0.6} Train accuracy: 0.894 Test accuracy: 0.832
Test Confusion Matrix


Predicted   0   1
Actuall
0           346 34
1           40  21


Class Weights {0: 0.5, 1: 0.5} Train accuracy: 0.896 Test accuracy: 0.846
Test Confusion Matrix


Predicted   0   1
Actuall
0           361 19
1           49  12
```

From the preceding screenshot, we can seen that at class weight values of 0.3 (for zero) and 0.7 (for one) it is identifying a higher number of attriters (25 out of 61) without compromising test accuracy 83.9% using decision trees methodology:

R Code for Decision Tree Classifier with class weights Applied on HR Attrition Data:

```
#Decision Trees using C5.0    package - Error Costs
library(C50)
class_zero_wgt =    c(0.01,0.1,0.2,0.3,0.4,0.5)
for (cwt in class_zero_wgt){
  cwtz = cwt
  cwto = 1-cwtz
  cstvr = cwto/cwtz
  error_cost <- matrix(c(0,    1, cstvr, 0), nrow = 2)
  dtree_fit = C5.0(train_data[-31],train_data$Attrition_ind,
  costs = error_cost,control = C5.0Control(  minCases =   1))
  summary(dtree_fit)
  tr_y_pred =    predict(dtree_fit, train_data,type = "class")
  ts_y_pred =    predict(dtree_fit,test_data,type = "class")
  tr_y_act =    train_data$Attrition_ind;
  ts_y_act =    test_data$Attrition_ind
  tr_acc =    accrcy(tr_y_act,tr_y_pred)
  ts_acc =    accrcy(ts_y_act,ts_y_pred)
  print(paste("Class    weights","{0:",cwtz,"1:",cwto,"}",
              "Decision    Tree Train accuracy:",tr_acc,
              "Decision    Tree Test accuracy:",ts_acc))
  ts_tble =    table(ts_y_act,ts_y_pred)
  print(paste("Test    Confusion Matrix"))
  print(ts_tble)
}
```

Bagging classifier

As we have discussed already, decision trees suffer from high variance, which means if we split the training data into two random parts separately and fit two decision trees for each sample, the rules obtained would be very different. Whereas low variance and high bias models, such as linear or logistic regression, will produce similar results across both samples. Bagging refers to bootstrap aggregation (repeated sampling with replacement and perform aggregation of results to be precise), which is a general purpose methodology to reduce the variance of models. In this case, they are decision trees.

Aggregation reduces the variance, for example, when we have n independent observations $x_1, x_2, ..., x_n$ each with variance σ^2 and the variance of the mean x of the observations is given by σ^2/n, which illustrates by averaging a set of observations that it reduces variance. Here, we are reducing variance by taking many samples from training data (also known as bootstrapping), building a separate decision tree on each sample separately, averaging the predictions for regression, and calculating mode for classification problems in order to obtain a single low-variance model that will have both low bias and low variance:

$$Predictions\ from\ each\ decision\ tree\ classifier\quad \hat{f}_1(x), \hat{f}_2(x), ...\ \hat{f}_B(x)$$

$$\hat{f_{avg}}(x) = \frac{1}{B} \sum_{b=1}^{B} \hat{f}_b(x)$$

In a bagging procedure, rows are sampled while selecting all the columns/variables (whereas, in random forest, both rows and columns would be sampled, which we will cover in the next section) and fitting individual trees for each sample. In the following diagram, two colors (pink and blue) represent two samples, and for each sample, a few rows are sampled, but all the columns (variables) are selected every time. One issue that exists due to the selection of all columns is that most of the trees will describe the same story, in which the most important variable will appear initially in the split, and this repeats in all the trees, which will not produce de-correlated trees, so we may not get better performance when applying variance reduction. This issue will be avoided in random forest (we will cover this in the next section of the chapter), in which we will sample both rows and columns as well:

Bootstrap Aggregation (Bagging)

In the following code, the same HR data has been used to fit the bagging classifier in order to compare the results apple to apple with respect to decision trees:

```
# Bagging Classifier
>>> from sklearn.tree import DecisionTreeClassifier
>>> from sklearn.ensemble import BaggingClassifier
```

The base classifier used here is Decision Trees with the same parameter setting that we used in the decision tree example:

```
>>> dt_fit = DecisionTreeClassifier(criterion="gini",
max_depth=5,min_samples_split=2,
min_samples_leaf=1,random_state=42,class_weight = {0:0.3,1:0.7})
```

Parameters used in bagging are, `n_estimators` to represent the number of individual decision trees used as 5,000, maximum samples and features selected are 0.67 and 1.0 respectively, which means it will select 2/3rd of observations for each tree and all the features. For further details, please refer to the scikit-learn manual http://scikit-learn.o rg/stable/modules/generated/sklearn.ensemble.BaggingClassifier.html:

```
>>> bag_fit = BaggingClassifier(base_estimator= dt_fit,n_estimators=5000,
max_samples=0.67,
...                  max_features=1.0,bootstrap=True,
...                  bootstrap_features=False, n_jobs=-1,random_state=42)

>>> bag_fit.fit(x_train, y_train)

>>> print ("\nBagging - Train Confusion Matrix\n\n",pd.crosstab(y_train,
bag_fit.predict(x_train),rownames = ["Actuall"],colnames = ["Predicted"]))
>>> print ("\nBagging- Train accuracy",round(accuracy_score(y_train,
bag_fit.predict(x_train)),3))
>>> print ("\nBagging  - Train Classification
Report\n",classification_report(y_train, bag_fit.predict(x_train)))

>>> print ("\n\nBagging - Test Confusion Matrix\n\n",pd.crosstab(y_test,
bag_fit.predict(x_test),rownames = ["Actuall"],colnames = ["Predicted"]))
>>> print ("\nBagging - Test accuracy",round(accuracy_score(y_test,
bag_fit.predict(x_test)),3))
>>> print ("\nBagging - Test Classification
Report\n",classification_report(y_test, bag_fit.predict(x_test)))
```

```
Bagging - Train Confusion Matrix

Predicted   0    1
Actuall
0          846    7
1           72  104

Bagging- Train accuracy 0.923

Bagging  - Train Classification Report
             precision   recall  f1-score   support

         0      0.92      0.99      0.96       853
         1      0.94      0.59      0.72       176

avg / total      0.92      0.92      0.92      1029



Bagging - Test Confusion Matrix

Predicted   0    1
Actuall
0          372    8
1           48   13

Bagging - Test accuracy 0.873

Bagging - Test Classification Report
             precision   recall  f1-score   support

         0      0.89      0.98      0.93       380
         1      0.62      0.21      0.32        61

avg / total      0.85      0.87      0.85       441
```

After analyzing the results from bagging, the test accuracy obtained was 87.3%, whereas for decision tree it was 84.6%. Comparing the number of actual attrited employees identified, there were 13 in bagging, whereas in decision tree there were 12, but the number of 0 classified as 1 significantly reduced to 8 compared with 19 in DT. Overall, bagging improves performance over the single tree:

R Code for Bagging Classifier Applied on HR Attrition Data:

```
# Bagging Classifier - using   Random forest package but all variables
selected
library(randomForest)
set.seed(43)
rf_fit = randomForest(Attrition_ind~.,data   = train_data,mtry=30,maxnodes=
64,classwt = c(0.3,0.7), ntree=5000,nodesize =   1)
tr_y_pred = predict(rf_fit,data   = train_data,type = "response")
```

```
ts_y_pred =    predict(rf_fit,newdata = test_data,type = "response")
tr_y_act = train_data$Attrition_ind;ts_y_act    = test_data$Attrition_ind
tr_tble =    table(tr_y_act,tr_y_pred)
print(paste("Train   Confusion Matrix"))
print(tr_tble)
tr_acc =    accrcy(tr_y_act,tr_y_pred)
trprec_zero =    prec_zero(tr_y_act,tr_y_pred); trrecl_zero =
recl_zero(tr_y_act,tr_y_pred)
trprec_one =    prec_one(tr_y_act,tr_y_pred);
trrecl_one =    recl_one(tr_y_act,tr_y_pred)
trprec_ovll = trprec_zero   *frac_trzero + trprec_one*frac_trone
trrecl_ovll = trrecl_zero   *frac_trzero + trrecl_one*frac_trone
print(paste("Random Forest   Train accuracy:",tr_acc))
print(paste("Random Forest   - Train Classification Report"))
print(paste("Zero_Precision",trprec_zero,"Zero_Recall",trrecl_zero))
print(paste("One_Precision",trprec_one,"One_Recall",trrecl_one))
print(paste("Overall_Precision",round(trprec_ovll,4),"Overall_Recall",
round(trrecl_ovll,4)))
ts_tble =    table(ts_y_act,ts_y_pred)
print(paste("Test   Confusion Matrix"))
print(ts_tble)
ts_acc =    accrcy(ts_y_act,ts_y_pred)
tsprec_zero =    prec_zero(ts_y_act,ts_y_pred); tsrecl_zero =
recl_zero(ts_y_act,ts_y_pred)
tsprec_one =    prec_one(ts_y_act,ts_y_pred);
tsrecl_one =    recl_one(ts_y_act,ts_y_pred)
tsprec_ovll = tsprec_zero   *frac_tszero + tsprec_one*frac_tsone
tsrecl_ovll = tsrecl_zero   *frac_tszero + tsrecl_one*frac_tsone
print(paste("Random Forest   Test accuracy:",ts_acc))
print(paste("Random Forest   - Test Classification Report"))
print(paste("Zero_Precision",tsprec_zero,"Zero_Recall",tsrecl_zero))
print(paste("One_Precision",tsprec_one,"One_Recall",tsrecl_one))
print(paste("Overall_Precision",round(tsprec_ovll,4),"Overall_Recall",
round(tsrecl_ovll,4)))
```

Random forest classifier

Random forests provide an improvement over bagging by doing a small tweak that utilizes de-correlated trees. In bagging, we build a number of decision trees on bootstrapped samples from training data, but the one big drawback with the bagging technique is that it selects all the variables. By doing so, in each decision tree, order of candidate/variable chosen to split remains more or less the same for all the individual trees, which look correlated with each other. Variance reduction on correlated individual entities does not work effectively while aggregating them.

In random forest, during bootstrapping (repeated sampling with replacement), samples were drawn from training data; not just simply the second and third observations randomly selected, similar to bagging, but it also selects the few predictors/columns out of all predictors (m predictors out of total p predictors).

The thumb rule for variable selection of m variables out of total variables p, is $m = sqrt(p)$ for classification and $m = p/3$ for regression problems randomly to avoid correlation among the individual trees. By doing so, significant improvement in accuracies can be achieved. This ability of RF makes it one of the favorite algorithms used by the data science community, as a winning recipe across various competitions or even for solving practical problems in various industries.

In the following diagram, different colors represent different bootstrap samples. In the first sample, the 1st, 3rd, 4th, and 7th columns are selected, whereas in the second bootstrap sample, the 2nd, 3rd, 4th, and 5th columns are selected respectively. In this way, any columns can be selected at random, whether they are adjacent to each other or not. Though the thumb rules of *sqrt (p)* or *p/3* are given, readers are encouraged to tune the number of predictors to be selected:

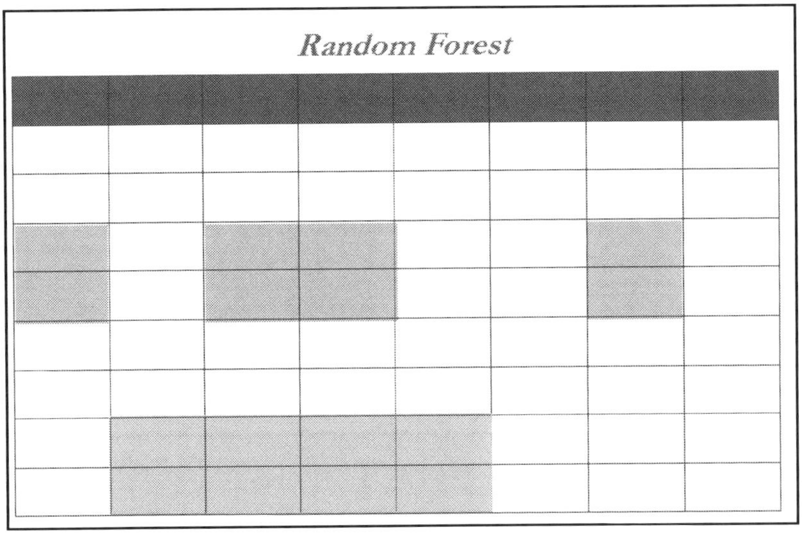

The sample plot shows the impact of a test error change while changing the parameters selected, and it is apparent that a *m = sqrt(p)* scenario gives better performance on test data compared with *m =p* (we can call this scenario bagging):

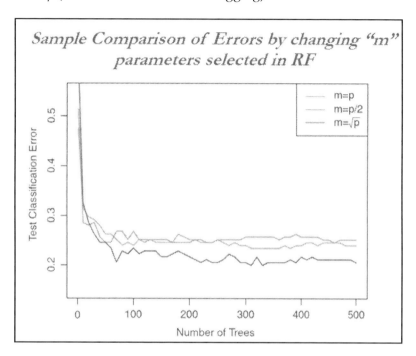

Random forest classifier has been utilized from the `scikit-learn` package here for illustration purposes:

```
# Random Forest Classifier
>>> from sklearn.ensemble import RandomForestClassifier
```

The parameters used in random forest are: `n_estimators` representing the number of individual decision trees used is 5000, maximum features selected are *auto,* which means it will select *sqrt(p)* for classification and *p/3* for regression automatically. Here is the straightforward classification problem though. Minimum samples per leaf provides the minimum number of observations required in the terminal node:

```
>>> rf_fit = RandomForestClassifier(n_estimators=5000,criterion="gini",
max_depth=5,
min_samples_split=2,bootstrap=True,max_features='auto',random_state=42,
min_samples_leaf=1,class_weight = {0:0.3,1:0.7})
>>> rf_fit.fit(x_train,y_train)

>>> print ("\nRandom Forest - Train Confusion
```

```
Matrix\n\n",pd.crosstab(y_train, rf_fit.predict(x_train),rownames =
["Actuall"],colnames = ["Predicted"]))
>>> print ("\nRandom Forest - Train accuracy",round(accuracy_score(y_train,
rf_fit.predict(x_train)),3))
>>> print ("\nRandom Forest  - Train Classification
Report\n",classification_report( y_train, rf_fit.predict(x_train)))

>>> print ("\n\nRandom Forest - Test Confusion
Matrix\n\n",pd.crosstab(y_test, rf_fit.predict(x_test),rownames =
["Actuall"],colnames = ["Predicted"]))
>>> print ("\nRandom Forest - Test accuracy",round(accuracy_score(y_test,
rf_fit.predict(x_test)),3))
>>> print ("\nRandom Forest - Test Classification
Report\n",classification_report( y_test, rf_fit.predict(x_test)))
```

```
Random Forest - Train Confusion Matrix

Predicted    0    1
Actuall
0          841   12
1           76  100

Random Forest - Train accuracy 0.914

Random Forest  - Train Classification Report
             precision    recall  f1-score   support

          0       0.92      0.99      0.95       853
          1       0.89      0.57      0.69       176

avg / total       0.91      0.91      0.91      1029



Random Forest - Test Confusion Matrix

Predicted    0    1
Actuall
0          373    7
1           47   14

Random Forest - Test accuracy 0.878

Random Forest - Test Classification Report
             precision    recall  f1-score   support

          0       0.89      0.98      0.93       380
          1       0.67      0.23      0.34        61

avg / total       0.86      0.88      0.85       441
```

Random forest classifier produced 87.8% test accuracy compared with bagging 87.3%, and also identifies 14 actually attrited employees in contrast with bagging, for which 13 attrited employees have been identified:

```
# Plot of Variable importance by mean decrease in gini
>>> model_ranks =
pd.Series(rf_fit.feature_importances_,index=x_train.columns,
name='Importance').sort_values(ascending=False, inplace=False)
>>> model_ranks.index.name = 'Variables'
>>> top_features =
model_ranks.iloc[:31].sort_values(ascending=True,inplace=False)
>>> import matplotlib.pyplot as plt
>>> plt.figure(figsize=(20,10))
>>> ax = top_features.plot(kind='barh')
>>> _ = ax.set_title("Variable Importance Plot")
>>> _ = ax.set_xlabel('Mean decrease in Variance')
>>> _ = ax.set_yticklabels(top_features.index, fontsize=13)
```

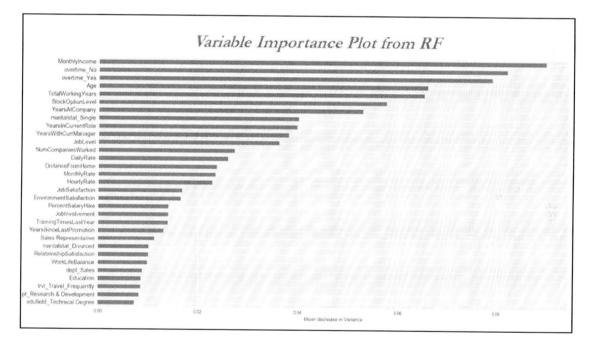

From the variable importance plot, it seems that the monthly income variable seems to be most significant, followed by overtime, total working years, stock option levels, years at company, and so on. This provides us with some insight into what are major contributing factors that determine whether the employee will remain with the company or leave the organization:

R Code for Random Forest Classifier Applied on HR Attrition Data:

```r
# Random Forest
library(randomForest)
set.seed(43)
rf_fit =    randomForest(Attrition_ind~.,data = train_data,mtry=6, maxnodes=
64,classwt =   c(0.3,0.7),ntree=5000,nodesize = 1)
tr_y_pred = predict(rf_fit,data    = train_data,type = "response")
ts_y_pred =    predict(rf_fit,newdata = test_data,type = "response")
tr_y_act =    train_data$Attrition_ind;ts_y_act = test_data$Attrition_ind
tr_tble =    table(tr_y_act,tr_y_pred)
print(paste("Train   Confusion Matrix"))
print(tr_tble)
tr_acc =    accrcy(tr_y_act,tr_y_pred)
trprec_zero = prec_zero(tr_y_act,tr_y_pred);    trrecl_zero =
recl_zero(tr_y_act,tr_y_pred)
trprec_one =    prec_one(tr_y_act,tr_y_pred); trrecl_one =
recl_one(tr_y_act,tr_y_pred)
trprec_ovll = trprec_zero    *frac_trzero + trprec_one*frac_trone
trrecl_ovll = trrecl_zero    *frac_trzero + trrecl_one*frac_trone
print(paste("Random Forest   Train accuracy:",tr_acc))
print(paste("Random Forest    – Train Classification Report"))
print(paste("Zero_Precision",trprec_zero,"Zero_Recall",trrecl_zero))
print(paste("One_Precision",trprec_one,"One_Recall",trrecl_one))
print(paste("Overall_Precision",round(trprec_ovll,4),"Overall_Recall",round
(trrecl_ovll,4)))
ts_tble =    table(ts_y_act,ts_y_pred)
print(paste("Test    Confusion Matrix"))
print(ts_tble)
ts_acc =    accrcy(ts_y_act,ts_y_pred)
tsprec_zero = prec_zero(ts_y_act,ts_y_pred);    tsrecl_zero =
recl_zero(ts_y_act,ts_y_pred)
tsprec_one =    prec_one(ts_y_act,ts_y_pred); tsrecl_one =
recl_one(ts_y_act,ts_y_pred)
tsprec_ovll = tsprec_zero    *frac_tszero + tsprec_one*frac_tsone
tsrecl_ovll = tsrecl_zero    *frac_tszero + tsrecl_one*frac_tsone
print(paste("Random Forest    Test accuracy:",ts_acc))
print(paste("Random Forest    – Test Classification Report"))
print(paste("Zero_Precision",tsprec_zero,"Zero_Recall",tsrecl_zero))
print(paste("One_Precision",tsprec_one,"One_Recall",tsrecl_one))
print(paste("Overall_Precision",round(tsprec_ovll,4),"Overall_Recall",round
(tsrecl_ovll,4)))
```

Random forest classifier - grid search

Tuning parameters in a machine learning model plays a critical role. Here, we are showing a grid search example on how to tune a random forest model:

```
# Random Forest Classifier - Grid Search
>>> from sklearn.pipeline import Pipeline
>>> from sklearn.model_selection import train_test_split,GridSearchCV

>>> pipeline = Pipeline([
('clf',RandomForestClassifier(criterion='gini',class_weight =
{0:0.3,1:0.7}))])
```

Tuning parameters are similar to random forest parameters apart from verifying all the combinations using the pipeline function. The number of combinations to be evaluated will be *(3 x 3 x 2 x 2) *5 =36*5 = 180* combinations. Here 5 is used in the end, due to the cross validation of five-fold:

```
>>> parameters = {
...          'clf__n_estimators':(2000,3000,5000),
...          'clf__max_depth':(5,15,30),
...          'clf__min_samples_split':(2,3),
...          'clf__min_samples_leaf':(1,2)   }

>>> grid_search =
GridSearchCV(pipeline,parameters,n_jobs=-1,cv=5,verbose=1,
scoring='accuracy')
>>> grid_search.fit(x_train,y_train)

>>> print ('Best Training score: %0.3f' % grid_search.best_score_)
>>> print ('Best parameters set:')
>>> best_parameters = grid_search.best_estimator_.get_params()
>>> for param_name in sorted(parameters.keys()):
...     print ('\t%s: %r' % (param_name, best_parameters[param_name]))

>>> predictions = grid_search.predict(x_test)

>>> print ("Testing accuracy:",round(accuracy_score(y_test,
predictions),4))
>>> print ("\nComplete report of Testing
data\n",classification_report(y_test, predictions))

>>> print ("\n\nRandom Forest Grid Search- Test Confusion
Matrix\n\n",pd.crosstab( y_test, predictions,rownames =
["Actuall"],colnames = ["Predicted"]))
```

```
Fitting 5 folds for each of 36 candidates, totalling 180 fits
[Parallel(n_jobs=-1)]: Done  34 tasks    | elapsed:  1.3min
[Parallel(n_jobs=-1)]: Done 180 out of 180 | elapsed:  7.1min finished
Best Training score: 0.867
Best parameters set:
        clf__max_depth: 5
        clf__min_samples_leaf: 2
        clf__min_samples_split: 2
        clf__n_estimators: 3000
Testing accuracy: 0.8753

Complete report of Testing data
            precision    recall  f1-score   support

        0       0.89       0.98      0.93       380
        1       0.64       0.23      0.34        61

avg / total     0.85       0.88      0.85       441


Random Forest Grid Search- Test Confusion Matrix

Predicted    0   1
Actuall
0          372   8
1           47  14
```

In the preceding results, grid search seems to not provide much advantage compared with the already explored random forest result. But, practically, most of the times, it will provide better and more robust results compared with a simple exploration of models. However, by carefully evaluating many different combinations, it will eventually discover the best parameters combination:

R Code for random forest classifier with grid search applied on HR attrition data:

```
# Grid Search - Random Forest
library(e1071)
library(randomForest)
rf_grid =   tune(randomForest,Attrition_ind~.,data = train_data,classwt =
c(0.3,0.7),ranges = list( mtry = c(5,6),
  maxnodes = c(32,64), ntree =   c(3000,5000), nodesize = c(1,2)
),
tunecontrol =   tune.control(cross = 5) )
print(paste("Best   parameter from Grid Search"))
print(summary(rf_grid))
```

```
best_model = rf_grid$best.model
tr_y_pred=predict(best_model,data    = train_data,type ="response")
ts_y_pred=predict(best_model,newdata    = test_data,type= "response")
tr_y_act =    train_data$Attrition_ind;
ts_y_act= test_data$Attrition_ind
tr_tble =    table(tr_y_act,tr_y_pred)
print(paste("Random Forest    Grid search Train Confusion Matrix"))
print(tr_tble)
tr_acc =    accrcy(tr_y_act,tr_y_pred)
trprec_zero =    prec_zero(tr_y_act,tr_y_pred); trrecl_zero =
recl_zero(tr_y_act,tr_y_pred)
trprec_one =    prec_one(tr_y_act,tr_y_pred); trrecl_one =
recl_one(tr_y_act,tr_y_pred)
trprec_ovll = trprec_zero    *frac_trzero + trprec_one*frac_trone
trrecl_ovll = trrecl_zero    *frac_trzero + trrecl_one*frac_trone
print(paste("Random Forest    Grid Search Train accuracy:",tr_acc))
print(paste("Random Forest    Grid Search – Train Classification Report"))
print(paste("Zero_Precision",trprec_zero,"Zero_Recall",trrecl_zero))
print(paste("One_Precision",trprec_one,"One_Recall",trrecl_one))
print(paste("Overall_Precision",round(trprec_ovll,4),"Overall_Recall",round
(trrecl_ovll,4)))
ts_tble =    table(ts_y_act,ts_y_pred)
print(paste("Random Forest    Grid search Test Confusion Matrix"))
print(ts_tble)
ts_acc =    accrcy(ts_y_act,ts_y_pred)
tsprec_zero =    prec_zero(ts_y_act,ts_y_pred); tsrecl_zero =
recl_zero(ts_y_act,ts_y_pred)
tsprec_one =    prec_one(ts_y_act,ts_y_pred); tsrecl_one =
recl_one(ts_y_act,ts_y_pred)
tsprec_ovll = tsprec_zero    *frac_tszero + tsprec_one*frac_tsone
tsrecl_ovll = tsrecl_zero    *frac_tszero + tsrecl_one*frac_tsone
print(paste("Random Forest    Grid Search Test accuracy:",ts_acc))
print(paste("Random Forest    Grid Search – Test Classification Report"))
print(paste("Zero_Precision",tsprec_zero,"Zero_Recall",tsrecl_zero))
print(paste("One_Precision",tsprec_one,"One_Recall",tsrecl_one))
print(paste("Overall_Precision",round(tsprec_ovll,4),"Overall_Recall",round
(tsrecl_ovll,4)))
```

AdaBoost classifier

Boosting is another state-of-the art model that is being used by many data scientists to win so many competitions. In this section, we will be covering the **AdaBoost** algorithm, followed by **gradient boost** and **extreme gradient boost** (**XGBoost**). Boosting is a general approach that can be applied to many statistical models. However, in this book, we will be discussing the application of boosting in the context of decision trees. In bagging, we have taken multiple samples from the training data and then combined the results of individual trees to create a single predictive model; this method runs in parallel, as each bootstrap sample does not depend on others. Boosting works in a sequential manner and does not involve bootstrap sampling; instead, each tree is fitted on a modified version of an original dataset and finally added up to create a strong classifier:

$$H(x) = \sum_t \rho_t h_t(x)$$

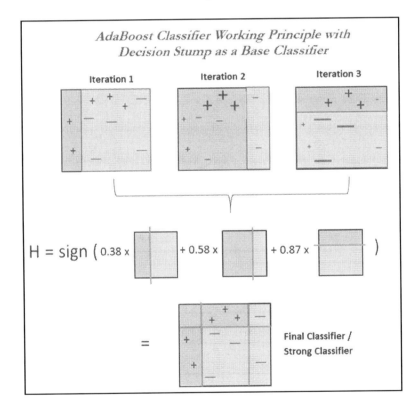

The preceding figure is the sample methodology on how AdaBoost works. We will cover step-by-step procedures in detail in the following algorithm description. Initially, a simple classifier has been fitted on the data (also called a decision stump, which splits the data into just two regions) and whatever the classes correctly classified will be given less weightage in the next iteration (iteration 2) and higher weightage for misclassified classes (observer + blue icons), and again another decision stump/weak classifier will be fitted on the data and will change the weights again for the next iteration (iteration 3, here check the - symbols for which weight has been increased). Once it finishes the iterations, these are combined with weights (weights automatically calculated for each classifier at each iteration based on error rate) to come up with a strong classifier, which predicts the classes with surprising accuracy.

Algorithm for AdaBoost consists of the following steps:

1. Initialize the observation weights $w_i = 1/N$, $i=1, 2, \ldots, N$. Where $N = $ *Number of observations.*

2. For $m = 1$ to M:
   - Fit a classifier $Gm(x)$ to the training data using weights w_i
   - Compute:

$$err_m = \frac{\sum_{i=1}^{N} w_i I(y_i \neq G_m(x_i))}{\sum_{i=1}^{N} w_i}$$

   - Compute:

$$\alpha_m = \log \left(\frac{1-err_m}{err_m}\right)$$

   - Set:

$$w_i < - w_i * \exp\left[\alpha_m * I\left(y_i \neq G_m(x_i)\right)\right], i = 1,2, \ldots, N$$

3. Output:

$$G(x) = sign\left[\sum_{m=1}^{M} \alpha_m G_m(x)\right]$$

All the observations are given equal weight.

In bagging and random forest algorithms, we deal with the columns of the data; whereas, in boosting, we adjust the weights of each observation and don't elect a few columns.

We fit a classifier on the data and evaluate overall errors. The error used for calculating weight should be given for that classifier in the final additive model (α) evaluation. The intuitive sense is that the higher weight will be given for the model with fewer errors. Finally, weights for each observation will be updated. Here, weight will be increased for incorrectly classified observations in order to give more focus to the next iterations, and weights will be reduced for correctly classified observations.

All the weak classifiers are combined with their respective weights to form a strong classifier. In the following figure, a quick idea is shared on how weights changed in the last iteration compared with the initial iteration:

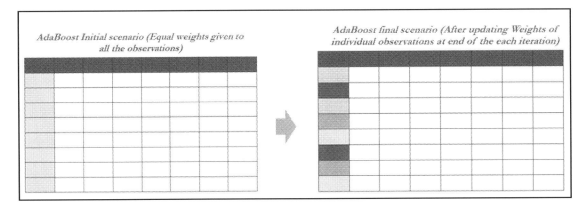

```
# Adaboost Classifier
>>> from sklearn.tree import DecisionTreeClassifier
>>> from sklearn.ensemble import AdaBoostClassifier
```

Decision stump is used as a base classifier for AdaBoost. If we observe the following code, the depth of the tree remains as 1, which has decision taking ability only once (also considered a weak classifier):

```
>>> dtree = DecisionTreeClassifier(criterion='gini',max_depth=1)
```

In AdaBoost, decision stump has been used as a base estimator to fit on whole datasets and then fits additional copies of the classifier on the same dataset up to 5000 times. The learning rate shrinks the contribution of each classifer by 0.05. There is a trade-off between learning rate and the number of estimators. By carefully choosing a low learning rate and a long number of estimators, one can converge optimum very much, however at the expense of computing power:

```
>>>adabst_fit = AdaBoostClassifier(base_estimator=
dtree,n_estimators=5000,learning_rate=0.05,random_state=42)

>>>adabst_fit.fit(x_train, y_train)
>>>print ("\nAdaBoost - Train Confusion Matrix\n\n", pd.crosstab(y_train,
adabst_fit.predict(x_train), rownames = ["Actuall"],colnames =
["Predicted"]))
>>>print ("\nAdaBoost - Train
accuracy",round(accuracy_score(y_train,adabst_fit.predict(x_train)), 3))
>>>print ("\nAdaBoost  - Train Classification
Report\n",classification_report(y_train,adabst_fit.predict(x_train)))
```

```
AdaBoost - Train Confusion Matrix

Predicted    0    1
Actuall
0          844    9
1           55  121

AdaBoost  - Train accuracy 0.938

AdaBoost  - Train Classification Report
             precision    recall  f1-score   support

          0       0.94      0.99      0.96       853
          1       0.93      0.69      0.79       176

avg / total       0.94      0.94      0.93      1029



AdaBoost  - Test Confusion Matrix

Predicted    0   1
Actuall
0          360  20
1           38  23

AdaBoost  - Test accuracy 0.868

AdaBoost - Test Classification Report
             precision    recall  f1-score   support

          0       0.90      0.95      0.93       380
          1       0.53      0.38      0.44        61

avg / total       0.85      0.87      0.86       441
```

The result of the AdaBoost seems to be much better than the known best random forest classifiers in terms of the recall of 1 value. Though there is a slight decrease in accuracy to 86.8% compared with the best accuracy of 87.8%, the number of 1's predicted is 23 from the RF, which is 14 with some expense of increase in 0's, but it really made good progress in terms of identifying actual attriters:

R Code for AdaBoost classifier applied on HR attrition data:

```
# Adaboost classifier using  C5.0 with trails included for boosting
library(C50)
class_zero_wgt = 0.3
class_one_wgt = 1-class_zero_wgt
cstvr =   class_one_wgt/class_zero_wgt
error_cost <- matrix(c(0, 1,   cstvr, 0), nrow = 2)
# Fitting Adaboost model
ada_fit = C5.0(train_data[-31],train_data$Attrition_ind,costs   =
error_cost, trails = 5000,control = C5.0Control(minCases = 1))
summary(ada_fit)
tr_y_pred = predict(ada_fit,   train_data,type = "class")
ts_y_pred =   predict(ada_fit,test_data,type = "class")
tr_y_act =   train_data$Attrition_ind;ts_y_act = test_data$Attrition_ind
tr_tble = table(tr_y_act,tr_y_pred)
print(paste("AdaBoost -   Train Confusion Matrix"))
print(tr_tble)
tr_acc =   accrcy(tr_y_act,tr_y_pred)
trprec_zero =   prec_zero(tr_y_act,tr_y_pred); trrecl_zero =
recl_zero(tr_y_act,tr_y_pred)
trprec_one =   prec_one(tr_y_act,tr_y_pred); trrecl_one =
recl_one(tr_y_act,tr_y_pred)
trprec_ovll = trprec_zero   *frac_trzero + trprec_one*frac_trone
trrecl_ovll = trrecl_zero   *frac_trzero + trrecl_one*frac_trone
print(paste("AdaBoost   Train accuracy:",tr_acc))
print(paste("AdaBoost -   Train Classification Report"))
print(paste("Zero_Precision",trprec_zero,"Zero_Recall",trrecl_zero))
print(paste("One_Precision",trprec_one,"One_Recall",trrecl_one))
print(paste("Overall_Precision",round(trprec_ovll,4),"Overall_Recall",round
(trrecl_ovll,4)))
ts_tble =   table(ts_y_act,ts_y_pred)
print(paste("AdaBoost -   Test Confusion Matrix"))
print(ts_tble)
ts_acc =   accrcy(ts_y_act,ts_y_pred)
tsprec_zero =   prec_zero(ts_y_act,ts_y_pred); tsrecl_zero =
recl_zero(ts_y_act,ts_y_pred)
tsprec_one =   prec_one(ts_y_act,ts_y_pred); tsrecl_one =
recl_one(ts_y_act,ts_y_pred)
tsprec_ovll = tsprec_zero   *frac_tszero + tsprec_one*frac_tsone
tsrecl_ovll = tsrecl_zero   *frac_tszero + tsrecl_one*frac_tsone
```

```
print(paste("AdaBoost Test    accuracy:",ts_acc))
print(paste("AdaBoost -    Test Classification Report"))
print(paste("Zero_Precision",tsprec_zero,"Zero_Recall",tsrecl_zero))
print(paste("One_Precision",tsprec_one,"One_Recall",tsrecl_one))
print(paste("Overall_Precision",round(tsprec_ovll,4),"Overall_Recall",round
(tsrecl_ovll,4)))
```

Gradient boosting classifier

Gradient boosting is one of the competition-winning algorithms that work on the principle of boosting weak learners iteratively by shifting focus towards problematic observations that were difficult to predict in previous iterations and performing an ensemble of weak learners, typically decision trees. It builds the model in a stage-wise fashion like other boosting methods do, but it generalizes them by allowing optimization of an arbitrary differentiable loss function.

Let's start understanding Gradient Boosting with a simple example, as GB challenges many data scientists in terms of understanding the working principle:

1. Initially, we fit the model on observations producing 75% accuracy and the remaining unexplained variance is captured in the *error* term:

$$Y = F(x) + error$$

2. Then we will fit another model on the error term to pull the extra explanatory component and add it to the original model, which should improve the overall accuracy:

$$error = G(x) + error2$$

3. Now, the model is providing 80% accuracy and the equation looks as follows:

$$Y = F(x) + G(x) + error2$$

4. We continue this method one more time to fit a model on the **error2** component to extract a further explanatory component:

$$error2 = H(x) + error3$$

5. Now, model accuracy is further improved to 85% and the final model equation looks as follows:

$$Y = F(x) + G(x) + H(x) + error3$$

6. Here, if we use weighted average (higher importance given to better models that predict results with greater accuracy than others) rather than simple addition, it will improve the results further. In fact, this is what the gradient boosting algorithm does!

$$Y = \alpha * F(x) + \beta * G(x) + \gamma * H(x) + error4$$

 After incorporating weights, the name of the error changed from **error3** to **error4**, as both errors may not be exactly the same. If we find better weights, we will probably get accuracy of 90% instead of simple addition, where we have only got 85%.

Gradient boosting involves three elements:

- **Loss function to be optimized:** Loss function depends on the type of problem being solved. In the case of regression problems, mean squared error is used, and in classification problems, logarithmic loss will be used. In boosting, at each stage, unexplained loss from prior iterations will be optimized rather than starting from scratch.

- **Weak learner to make predictions:** Decision trees are used as a weak learner in gradient boosting.

- **Additive model to add weak learners to minimize the loss function:** Trees are added one at a time and existing trees in the model are not changed. The gradient descent procedure is used to minimize the loss when adding trees.

The algorithm for Gradient boosting consists of the following steps:

1. Initialize:

$$f_0(x) = argmin_\gamma \sum_{i=1}^{N} L(y_i, \gamma)$$

2. For *m* = *1* to M:
   - a) For *i* = *1, 2, ..., N* compute:

$$r_{im} = -\left[\frac{\partial L\left(y_i, f(x_i)\right)}{\partial f(x_i)} \right]_{f=f_{m-1}}$$

   - b) Fit a regression tree to the targets r_{im} giving terminal regions R_{jm}, j = 1, 2, ..., J_m,
   - c) For j = 1, 2, ..., J_m, compute:

$$\gamma_{jm} = \arg\min_{\gamma} \sum_{x_i \in R_{jm}} L(y_i, f_{m-1}(x_i) + \gamma)$$

   - d) Update:

$$f_m(x) = f_{m-1}(x) + \sum_{j=1}^{J_m} \gamma_{jm} I(x \in R_{jm})$$

3. Output:

$$\hat{f}(x) = f_M(x)$$

Initializes the constant optimal constant model, which is just a single terminal node that will be utilized as a starting point to tune it further in next steps. (*2a*), calculates the residuals/errors by comparing actual outcome with predicted results, followed by (*2b* and *2c*) in which the next decision tree will be fitted on error terms to bring in more explanatory power to the model, and in (*2d*) add the extra component to the model at last iteration. Finally, ensemble all weak learners to create a strong learner.

Comparison between AdaBoosting versus gradient boosting

After understanding both AdaBoost and gradient boost, readers may be curious to see the differences in detail. Here, we are presenting exactly that to quench your thirst!

AdaBoost	GradientBoost
Both AdaBoost and Gradient Boost use a base weak learner and they try to boost the performance of a weak learner by iteratively shifting the focus towards problematic observations that were difficult to predict. At the end, a strong learner is formed by addition (or weighted addition) of the weak learners.	
In AdaBoost, shift is done by up-weighting observations that were misclassified before.	Gradient boost identifies difficult observations by large residuals computed in the previous iterations.
In AdaBoost "shortcomings" are identified by high-weight data points.	In Gradientboost "shortcomings" are identified by gradients.
Exponential loss of AdaBoost gives more weights for those samples fitted worse.	Gradient boost further dissect error components to bring in more explanation.
AdaBoost is considered as a special case of Gradient boost in terms of loss function, in which exponential losses.	Concepts of gradients are more general in nature.

The gradient boosting classifier from the scikit-learn package has been used for computation here:

```
# Gradientboost Classifier
>>> from sklearn.ensemble import GradientBoostingClassifier
```

Parameters used in the gradient boosting algorithms are as follows. Deviance has been used for loss, as the problem we are trying to solve is 0/1 binary classification. The learning rate has been chosen as 0.05, number of trees to build is 5000 trees, minimum sample per leaf/terminal node is 1, and minimum samples needed in a bucket for qualification for splitting is 2:

```
>>> gbc_fit = GradientBoostingClassifier (loss='deviance',
learning_rate=0.05, n_estimators=5000, min_samples_split=2,
min_samples_leaf=1, max_depth=1, random_state=42 )

>>> gbc_fit.fit(x_train,y_train)
>>> print ("\nGradient Boost - Train Confusion
Matrix\n\n",pd.crosstab(y_train, gbc_fit.predict(x_train),rownames =
["Actuall"],colnames = ["Predicted"]))
>>> print ("\nGradient Boost - Train
```

```
accuracy",round(accuracy_score(y_train, gbc_fit.predict(x_train)),3))
>>> print ("\nGradient Boost - Train Classification
Report\n",classification_report( y_train, gbc_fit.predict(x_train)))

>>> print ("\n\nGradient Boost - Test Confusion
Matrix\n\n",pd.crosstab(y_test, gbc_fit.predict(x_test),rownames =
["Actuall"],colnames = ["Predicted"]))
>>> print ("\nGradient Boost - Test accuracy",round(accuracy_score(y_test,
gbc_fit.predict(x_test)),3)) >>> print ("\nGradient Boost - Test
Classification Report\n",classification_report( y_test,
gbc_fit.predict(x_test)))
```

```
Ensemble of Models - Test Confusion Matrix

Predicted    0   1
Actuall
0          367  13
1           42  19

Ensemble of Models - Test accuracy 0.875

Ensemble of Models - Test Classification Report
             precision    recall  f1-score   support

          0       0.90      0.97      0.93       380
          1       0.59      0.31      0.41        61

avg / total       0.86      0.88      0.86       441
```

If we analyze the results, Gradient boosting has given better results than AdaBoost with the highest possible test accuracy of 87.5% with most 1's captured as 24, compared with AdaBoost with which the test accuracy obtained was 86.8%. Hence, it has been proven that it is no wonder why every data scientist tries to use this algorithm to win competitions!

The R code for gradient boosting classifier applied on HR attrition data:

```
# Gradient boosting
library(gbm)

library(caret)
set.seed(43)
# Giving weights to all the observations in a way that total #weights will
be euqal 1
model_weights <- ifelse(train_data$Attrition_ind == "0",
        (1/table(train_data$Attrition_ind)[1]) * 0.3,
           (1/table(train_data$Attrition_ind)[2]) * 0.7)
# Setting parameters for GBM
grid <- expand.grid(n.trees = 5000, interaction.depth = 1, shrinkage = .04,
n.minobsinnode = 1)
# Fitting the GBM model
gbm_fit <- train(Attrition_ind ~ ., data = train_data, method = "gbm",
weights = model_weights,
                  tuneGrid=grid,verbose = FALSE)
# To print variable importance plot
summary(gbm_fit)

tr_y_pred = predict(gbm_fit, train_data,type = "raw")
ts_y_pred = predict(gbm_fit,test_data,type = "raw")
tr_y_act = train_data$Attrition_ind;ts_y_act = test_data$Attrition_ind

tr_tble = table(tr_y_act,tr_y_pred)
print(paste("Gradient Boosting - Train Confusion Matrix"))
print(tr_tble)

tr_acc = accrcy(tr_y_act,tr_y_pred)
trprec_zero = prec_zero(tr_y_act,tr_y_pred); trrecl_zero =
recl_zero(tr_y_act,tr_y_pred)
trprec_one = prec_one(tr_y_act,tr_y_pred); trrecl_one =
recl_one(tr_y_act,tr_y_pred)

trprec_ovll = trprec_zero *frac_trzero + trprec_one*frac_trone
trrecl_ovll = trrecl_zero *frac_trzero + trrecl_one*frac_trone

print(paste("Gradient Boosting Train accuracy:",tr_acc))
print(paste("Gradient Boosting - Train Classification Report"))
print(paste("Zero_Precision",trprec_zero,"Zero_Recall",trrecl_zero))
print(paste("One_Precision",trprec_one,"One_Recall",trrecl_one))
print(paste("Overall_Precision",round(trprec_ovll,4),"Overall_Recall",round
(trrecl_ovll,4)))


ts_tble = table(ts_y_act,ts_y_pred)
```

```
print(paste("Gradient Boosting - Test Confusion Matrix"))
print(ts_tble)
ts_acc = accrcy(ts_y_act,ts_y_pred)
tsprec_zero = prec_zero(ts_y_act,ts_y_pred); tsrecl_zero =
recl_zero(ts_y_act,ts_y_pred)
tsprec_one = prec_one(ts_y_act,ts_y_pred); tsrecl_one =
recl_one(ts_y_act,ts_y_pred)
tsprec_ovll = tsprec_zero *frac_tszero + tsprec_one*frac_tsone
tsrecl_ovll = tsrecl_zero *frac_tszero + tsrecl_one*frac_tsone
print(paste("Gradient Boosting Test accuracy:",ts_acc))
print(paste("Gradient Boosting - Test Classification Report"))
print(paste("Zero_Precision",tsprec_zero,"Zero_Recall",tsrecl_zero))
print(paste("One_Precision",tsprec_one,"One_Recall",tsrecl_one))
print(paste("Overall_Precision",round(tsprec_ovll,4),"Overall_Recall",round
(tsrecl_ovll,4)))


# Use the following code for performing cross validation on data - At the
moment commented though
#fitControl <- trainControl(method = "repeatedcv", number = 4, repeats = 4)
# gbmFit1 <- train(Attrition_ind ~ ., data = train_data,
method = # "gbm", trControl = fitControl,tuneGrid=grid,verbose = FALSE)
```

Extreme gradient boosting - XGBoost classifier

XGBoost is the new algorithm developed in 2014 by *Tianqi Chen* based on the Gradient boosting principles. It has created a storm in the data science community since its inception. XGBoost has been developed with both deep consideration in terms of system optimization and principles in machine learning. The goal of the library is to push the extremes of the computation limits of machines to provide scalable, portable, and accurate results:

```
# Xgboost Classifier
>>> import xgboost as xgb
>>> xgb_fit = xgb.XGBClassifier(max_depth=2, n_estimators=5000,
learning_rate=0.05)
>>> xgb_fit.fit(x_train, y_train)

>>> print ("\nXGBoost - Train Confusion Matrix\n\n",pd.crosstab(y_train,
xgb_fit.predict(x_train),rownames = ["Actuall"],colnames = ["Predicted"]))
>>> print ("\nXGBoost - Train accuracy",round(accuracy_score(y_train,
xgb_fit.predict(x_train)),3))
>>> print ("\nXGBoost  - Train Classification
Report\n",classification_report(y_train, xgb_fit.predict(x_train)))
>>> print ("\n\nXGBoost - Test Confusion Matrix\n\n",pd.crosstab(y_test,
```

```
xgb_fit.predict(x_test),rownames = ["Actuall"],colnames = ["Predicted"]))
>>> print ("\nXGBoost - Test accuracy",round(accuracy_score(y_test,
xgb_fit.predict(x_test)),3))
>>> print ("\nXGBoost - Test Classification
Report\n",classification_report(y_test, xgb_fit.predict(x_test)))
```

```
XGBoost - Train Confusion Matrix

Predicted    0    1
Actuall
0          853    0
1            0  176

XGBoost - Train accuracy 1.0

XGBoost  - Train Classification Report
              precision    recall  f1-score   support

          0       1.00      1.00      1.00       853
          1       1.00      1.00      1.00       176

avg / total       1.00      1.00      1.00      1029



XGBoost - Test Confusion Matrix

Predicted    0    1
Actuall
0          361   19
1           38   23

XGBoost - Test accuracy 0.871

XGBoost - Test Classification Report
              precision    recall  f1-score   support

          0       0.90      0.95      0.93       380
          1       0.55      0.38      0.45        61

avg / total       0.86      0.87      0.86       441
```

The results obtained from **XGBoost** are almost similar to gradient boosting. The test accuracy obtained was 87.1%, whereas boosting got 87.5%, and also the number of 1's identified is 23 compared with 24 in gradient boosting. The greatest advantage of XGBoost over Gradient boost is in terms of performance and the options available to control model tune. By changing a few of them, makes XGBoost even beat gradient boost as well!

The R code for xtreme gradient boosting (XGBoost) classifier applied on HR attrition data:

```
# Xgboost Classifier
library(xgboost); library(caret)

hrattr_data = read.csv("WA_Fn-UseC_-HR-Employee-Attrition.csv")
str(hrattr_data); summary(hrattr_data)
# Target variable creation
hrattr_data$Attrition_ind = 0;
hrattr_data$Attrition_ind[hrattr_data$Attrition=="Yes"]=1

# Columns to be removed due to no change in its value across observations
remove_cols =
c("EmployeeCount","EmployeeNumber","Over18","StandardHours","Attrition")
hrattr_data_new = hrattr_data[,!(names(hrattr_data) %in% remove_cols)]

# List of  variables with continuous values
continuous_columns = c('Age','DailyRate', 'DistanceFromHome', 'Education',
'EnvironmentSatisfaction', 'HourlyRate', 'JobInvolvement', 'JobLevel',
'JobSatisfaction','MonthlyIncome', 'MonthlyRate', 'NumCompaniesWorked',
'PercentSalaryHike', 'PerformanceRating', 'RelationshipSatisfaction',
'StockOptionLevel', 'TotalWorkingYears',  'TrainingTimesLastYear',
'WorkLifeBalance', 'YearsAtCompany', 'YearsInCurrentRole',
'YearsSinceLastPromotion', 'YearsWithCurrManager')

# list of categorical variables
ohe_feats = c('BusinessTravel', 'Department',
'EducationField','Gender','JobRole', 'MaritalStatus', 'OverTime')

# one-hot-encoding categorical features
dummies <- dummyVars(~ BusinessTravel+Department+
EducationField+Gender+JobRole+MaritalStatus+OverTime, data =
hrattr_data_new)
df_all_ohe <- as.data.frame(predict(dummies, newdata = hrattr_data_new))

# Cleaning column names and replace . with _

colClean <- function(x){ colnames(x) <- gsub("\\.", "_", colnames(x)); x }
df_all_ohe = colClean(df_all_ohe)

hrattr_data_new$Attrition_ind = as.integer(hrattr_data_new$Attrition_ind)
```

```
# Combining both continuous and dummy variables from categories
hrattr_data_v3 = cbind(df_all_ohe,hrattr_data_new [,(names(hrattr_data_new)
%in% continuous_columns)], hrattr_data_new$Attrition_ind)

names(hrattr_data_v3)[52] = "Attrition_ind"

# Train and Test split based on 70% and 30%
set.seed(123)
numrow = nrow(hrattr_data_v3)
trnind = sample(1:numrow,size = as.integer(0.7*numrow))
train_data = hrattr_data_v3[trnind,]
test_data = hrattr_data_v3[-trnind,]

# Custom functions for calculation of Precision and Recall
frac_trzero = (table(train_data$Attrition_ind)[[1]])/nrow(train_data)
frac_trone = (table(train_data$Attrition_ind)[[2]])/nrow(train_data)

frac_tszero = (table(test_data$Attrition_ind)[[1]])/nrow(test_data)
frac_tsone = (table(test_data$Attrition_ind)[[2]])/nrow(test_data)
prec_zero <- function(act,pred){  tble = table(act,pred)
return( round( tble[1,1]/(tble[1,1]+tble[2,1]),4)  ) }

prec_one <- function(act,pred){ tble = table(act,pred)
return( round( tble[2,2]/(tble[2,2]+tble[1,2]),4)   ) }

recl_zero <- function(act,pred){tble = table(act,pred)
return( round( tble[1,1]/(tble[1,1]+tble[1,2]),4)   ) }

recl_one <- function(act,pred){ tble = table(act,pred)
return( round( tble[2,2]/(tble[2,2]+tble[2,1]),4)  ) }

accrcy <- function(act,pred){ tble = table(act,pred)
return( round((tble[1,1]+tble[2,2])/sum(tble),4)) }

y = train_data$Attrition_ind

# XGBoost Classifier Training
xgb <- xgboost(data = data.matrix(train_data[,-52]),label = y,eta =
0.04,max_depth = 2, nround=5000, subsample = 0.5, colsample_bytree = 0.5,
seed = 1, eval_metric = "logloss", objective = "binary:logistic",nthread =
3)

# XGBoost value prediction on train and test data
tr_y_pred_prob <- predict(xgb, data.matrix(train_data[,-52]))
tr_y_pred <- as.numeric(tr_y_pred_prob > 0.5)
ts_y_pred_prob <- predict(xgb, data.matrix(test_data[,-52]))
ts_y_pred <- as.numeric(ts_y_pred_prob > 0.5)
tr_y_act = train_data$Attrition_ind;ts_y_act = test_data$Attrition_ind
```

```
tr_tble = table(tr_y_act,tr_y_pred)

# XGBoost Metric predictions on Train Data
print(paste("Xgboost - Train Confusion Matrix"))
print(tr_tble)
tr_acc = accrcy(tr_y_act,tr_y_pred)
trprec_zero = prec_zero(tr_y_act,tr_y_pred); trrecl_zero =
recl_zero(tr_y_act,tr_y_pred)
trprec_one = prec_one(tr_y_act,tr_y_pred); trrecl_one =
recl_one(tr_y_act,tr_y_pred)
trprec_ovll = trprec_zero *frac_trzero + trprec_one*frac_trone
trrecl_ovll = trrecl_zero *frac_trzero + trrecl_one*frac_trone

print(paste("Xgboost Train accuracy:",tr_acc))
print(paste("Xgboost - Train Classification Report"))
print(paste("Zero_Precision",trprec_zero,"Zero_Recall",trrecl_zero))
print(paste("One_Precision",trprec_one,"One_Recall",trrecl_one))
print(paste("Overall_Precision",round(trprec_ovll,4),"Overall_Recall",round
(trrecl_ovll,4)))

# XGBoost Metric predictions on Test Data
ts_tble = table(ts_y_act,ts_y_pred)
print(paste("Xgboost - Test Confusion Matrix"))
print(ts_tble)
ts_acc = accrcy(ts_y_act,ts_y_pred)
tsprec_zero = prec_zero(ts_y_act,ts_y_pred); tsrecl_zero =
recl_zero(ts_y_act,ts_y_pred)
tsprec_one = prec_one(ts_y_act,ts_y_pred); tsrecl_one =
recl_one(ts_y_act,ts_y_pred)
tsprec_ovll = tsprec_zero *frac_tszero + tsprec_one*frac_tsone
tsrecl_ovll = tsrecl_zero *frac_tszero + tsrecl_one*frac_tsone

print(paste("Xgboost Test accuracy:",ts_acc))
print(paste("Xgboost - Test Classification Report"))
print(paste("Zero_Precision",tsprec_zero,"Zero_Recall",tsrecl_zero))
print(paste("One_Precision",tsprec_one,"One_Recall",tsrecl_one))
print(paste("Overall_Precision",round(tsprec_ovll,4),"Overall_Recall",round
(tsrecl_ovll,4)))
```

Ensemble of ensembles - model stacking

Ensemble of ensembles or model stacking is a method to combine different classifiers into a meta-classifier that has a better generalization performance than each individual classifier in isolation. It is always advisable to take opinions from many people when you are in doubt, when dealing with problems in your personal life too! There are two ways to perform ensembles on models:

- **Ensemble with different types of classifiers:** In this methodology, different types of classifiers (for example, logistic regression, decision trees, random forest, and so on) are fitted on the same training data and results are combined based on either majority voting or average, based on if it is classification or regression problems.
- **Ensemble with a single type of classifiers, but built separately on various bootstrap samples:** In this methodology, bootstrap samples are drawn from training data and, each time, separate models will be fitted (individual models could be decision trees, random forest, and so on) on the drawn sample, and all these results are combined at the end to create an ensemble. This method suits dealing with highly flexible models where variance reduction still improves performance.

Ensemble of ensembles with different types of classifiers

As briefly mentioned in the preceding section, different classifiers will be applied on the same training data and the results ensembled either taking majority voting or applying another classifier (also known as a meta-classifier) fitted on results obtained from individual classifiers. This means, for meta-classifier X, variables would be model outputs and Y variable would be an actual 0/1 result. By doing this, we will obtain the weightage that should be given for each classifier and those weights will be applied accordingly to classify unseen observations. All three methods of application of ensemble of ensembles are shown here:

- **Majority voting or average:** In this method, a simple mode function (classification problem) is applied to select the category with the major number of appearances out of individual classifiers. Whereas, for regression problems, an average will be calculated to compare against actual values.

- **Method of application of meta-classifiers on outcomes:** Predict actual outcome either 0 or 1 from individual classifiers and apply a meta-classifier on top of 0's and 1's. A small problem with this type of approach is that the meta-classifier will be a bit brittle and rigid. I mean 0's and 1's just gives the result, rather than providing exact sensibility (such as probability).

- **Method of application of meta-classifiers on probabilities:** In this method, probabilities are obtained from individual classifiers instead of 0's and 1's. Applying meta-classifier on probabilities makes this method a bit more flexible than the first method. Though users can experiment with both methods to see which one performs better. After all, machine learning is all about exploration and trial and error methodologies.

In the following diagram, the complete flow of model stacking has been described with various stages:

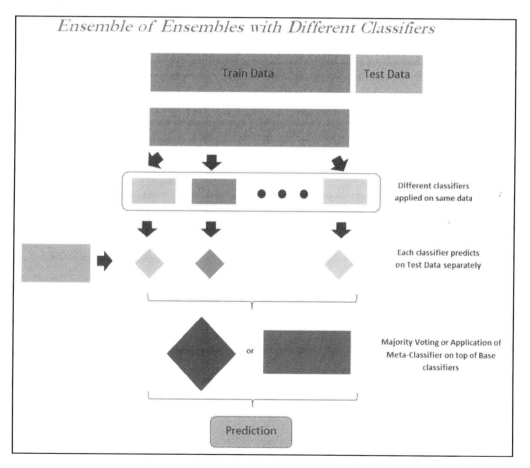

Steps in following ensemble with multiple classifiers example:

- Four classifiers have been used separately on training data (logistic regression, decision tree, random forest, and AdaBoost)
- Probabilities have been determined for all four classifiers, however, only the probability for category 1 has been utilized in meta-classifier due to the reason that the probability of class 0 + probability of class 1 = 1, hence only one probability is good enough to represent, or else multi-collinearity issues appearing
- Logistic regression has been used as a meta-classifier to model the relationship between four probabilities (obtained from each individual classifier) with respect to a final 0/1 outcome
- Coefficients have been calculated for all four variables used in meta-classifier and applied on new data for calculating the final aggregated probability for classifying observations into the respective categories:

```
#Ensemble of Ensembles - by fitting various classifiers
>>> clwght = {0:0.3,1:0.7}

# Classifier 1 - Logistic Regression
>>> from sklearn.linear_model import LogisticRegression
>>> clf1_logreg_fit =
LogisticRegression(fit_intercept=True,class_weight=clwght)
>>> clf1_logreg_fit.fit(x_train,y_train)

>>> print ("\nLogistic Regression for Ensemble - Train Confusion
Matrix\n\n",pd.crosstab( y_train, clf1_logreg_fit.predict(x_train),rownames
= ["Actuall"],colnames = ["Predicted"]))
>>> print ("\nLogistic Regression for Ensemble - Train accuracy",round(
accuracy_score(y_train,clf1_logreg_fit.predict(x_train)),3))
>>> print ("\nLogistic Regression for Ensemble - Train Classification
Report\n", classification_report(y_train,clf1_logreg_fit.predict(x_train)))
>>> print ("\n\nLogistic Regression for Ensemble - Test Confusion
Matrix\n\n",pd.crosstab( y_test,clf1_logreg_fit.predict(x_test),rownames =
["Actuall"],colnames = ["Predicted"]))     >
>> print ("\nLogistic Regression for Ensemble - Test accuracy",round(
accuracy_score(y_test,clf1_logreg_fit.predict(x_test)),3))
>>> print ("\nLogistic Regression for Ensemble - Test Classification
Report\n", classification_report( y_test,clf1_logreg_fit.predict(x_test)))

# Classifier 2 - Decision Tree
>>> from sklearn.tree import DecisionTreeClassifier
>>> clf2_dt_fit = DecisionTreeClassifier(criterion="gini", max_depth=5,
min_samples_split=2, min_samples_leaf=1, random_state=42,
class_weight=clwght)
```

```
>>> clf2_dt_fit.fit(x_train,y_train)

>>> print ("\nDecision Tree for Ensemble - Train Confusion
Matrix\n\n",pd.crosstab( y_train, clf2_dt_fit.predict(x_train),rownames =
["Actuall"],colnames = ["Predicted"]))
>>> print ("\nDecision Tree for Ensemble - Train accuracy",
round(accuracy_score( y_train,clf2_dt_fit.predict(x_train)),3))
>>> print ("\nDecision Tree for Ensemble - Train Classification Report\n",
classification_report(y_train,clf2_dt_fit.predict(x_train)))
>>> print ("\n\nDecision Tree for Ensemble - Test Confusion Matrix\n\n",
pd.crosstab(y_test, clf2_dt_fit.predict(x_test),rownames =
["Actuall"],colnames = ["Predicted"]))
>>> print ("\nDecision Tree for Ensemble - Test
accuracy",round(accuracy_score(y_test, clf2_dt_fit.predict(x_test)),3))

>>> print ("\nDecision Tree for Ensemble - Test Classification Report\n",
classification_report(y_test, clf2_dt_fit.predict(x_test)))


# Classifier 3 - Random Forest
>>> from sklearn.ensemble import RandomForestClassifier
>>> clf3_rf_fit = RandomForestClassifier(n_estimators=10000,
criterion="gini", max_depth=6,
min_samples_split=2,min_samples_leaf=1,class_weight = clwght)
>>> clf3_rf_fit.fit(x_train,y_train)

>>> print ("\nRandom Forest for Ensemble - Train Confusion Matrix\n\n",
pd.crosstab(y_train, clf3_rf_fit.predict(x_train),rownames =
["Actuall"],colnames = ["Predicted"]))
>>> print ("\nRandom Forest for Ensemble - Train
accuracy",round(accuracy_score( y_train,clf3_rf_fit.predict(x_train)),3))
>>> print ("\nRandom Forest for Ensemble - Train Classification Report\n",
classification_report(y_train,clf3_rf_fit.predict(x_train)))

>>> print ("\n\nRandom Forest for Ensemble - Test Confusion
Matrix\n\n",pd.crosstab( y_test, clf3_rf_fit.predict(x_test),rownames =
["Actuall"],colnames = ["Predicted"]))
>>> print ("\nRandom Forest for Ensemble - Test
accuracy",round(accuracy_score( y_test,clf3_rf_fit.predict(x_test)),3))
>>> print ("\nRandom Forest for Ensemble - Test Classification Report\n",
classification_report(y_test,clf3_rf_fit.predict(x_test)))


# Classifier 4 - Adaboost classifier
>>> from sklearn.ensemble import AdaBoostClassifier
>>> clf4_dtree =
DecisionTreeClassifier(criterion='gini',max_depth=1,class_weight = clwght)
>>> clf4_adabst_fit = AdaBoostClassifier(base_estimator= clf4_dtree,
                n_estimators=5000,learning_rate=0.05,random_state=42)
>>> clf4_adabst_fit.fit(x_train, y_train)
```

```
>>> print ("\nAdaBoost for Ensemble  - Train Confusion
Matrix\n\n",pd.crosstab(y_train, clf4_adabst_fit.predict(x_train),rownames
= ["Actuall"],colnames = ["Predicted"]))
>>> print ("\nAdaBoost for Ensemble  - Train
accuracy",round(accuracy_score(y_train,
clf4_adabst_fit.predict(x_train)),3))
>>> print ("\nAdaBoost for Ensemble  - Train Classification Report\n",
classification_report(y_train,clf4_adabst_fit.predict(x_train)))
>>> print ("\n\nAdaBoost for Ensemble  - Test Confusion Matrix\n\n",
pd.crosstab(y_test, clf4_adabst_fit.predict(x_test),rownames =
["Actuall"],colnames = ["Predicted"]))
>>> print ("\nAdaBoost for Ensemble  - Test
accuracy",round(accuracy_score(y_test, clf4_adabst_fit.predict(x_test)),3))
>>> print ("\nAdaBoost for Ensemble  - Test Classification Report\n",
classification_report(y_test, clf4_adabst_fit.predict(x_test)))
```

In the following step, we perform an ensemble of classifiers:

```
>> ensemble = pd.DataFrame()
```

In the following step, we take probabilities only for category 1, as it gives intuitive sense for high probability and indicates the value towards higher class 1. But this should not stop someone if they really want to fit probabilities on a 0 class instead. In that case, low probability values are preferred for category 1, which gives us a little bit of a headache!

```
>>> ensemble["log_output_one"] =
pd.DataFrame(clf1_logreg_fit.predict_proba( x_train))[1]
>>> ensemble["dtr_output_one"] =
pd.DataFrame(clf2_dt_fit.predict_proba(x_train))[1]
>>> ensemble["rf_output_one"] =
pd.DataFrame(clf3_rf_fit.predict_proba(x_train))[1]
>>> ensemble["adb_output_one"] =
pd.DataFrame(clf4_adabst_fit.predict_proba( x_train))[1]
>>> ensemble = pd.concat([ensemble,pd.DataFrame(y_train).reset_index(drop =
True )],axis=1)

# Fitting meta-classifier
>>> meta_logit_fit =  LogisticRegression(fit_intercept=False)
>>> meta_logit_fit.fit(ensemble[['log_output_one', 'dtr_output_one',
'rf_output_one', 'adb_output_one']],ensemble['Attrition_ind'])
>>> coefs =  meta_logit_fit.coef_
>>> ensemble_test = pd.DataFrame()
>>> ensemble_test["log_output_one"] =
pd.DataFrame(clf1_logreg_fit.predict_proba( x_test))[1]
>>> ensemble_test["dtr_output_one"] =
pd.DataFrame(clf2_dt_fit.predict_proba( x_test))[1]
>>> ensemble_test["rf_output_one"] =
pd.DataFrame(clf3_rf_fit.predict_proba( x_test))[1]
```

```
>>> ensemble_test["adb_output_one"] =
pd.DataFrame(clf4_adabst_fit.predict_proba( x_test))[1]
>>> coefs =  meta_logit_fit.coef_
>>> ensemble_test = pd.DataFrame()
>>> ensemble_test["log_output_one"] =
pd.DataFrame(clf1_logreg_fit.predict_proba( x_test))[1]
>>> ensemble_test["dtr_output_one"] =
pd.DataFrame(clf2_dt_fit.predict_proba( x_test))[1]
>>> ensemble_test["rf_output_one"] =
pd.DataFrame(clf3_rf_fit.predict_proba( x_test))[1]
>>> ensemble_test["adb_output_one"] =
pd.DataFrame(clf4_adabst_fit.predict_proba( x_test))[1]
>>> print ("\n\nEnsemble of Models - Test Confusion
Matrix\n\n",pd.crosstab(
ensemble_test['Attrition_ind'],ensemble_test['all_one'],rownames =
["Actuall"], colnames = ["Predicted"]))
>>> print ("\nEnsemble of Models - Test accuracy",round(accuracy_score
(ensemble_test['Attrition_ind'],ensemble_test['all_one']),3))
>>> print ("\nEnsemble of Models - Test Classification Report\n",
classification_report( ensemble_test['Attrition_ind'],
ensemble_test['all_one']))
```

```
Ensemble of Models - Test Confusion Matrix

Predicted    0   1
Actuall
0          367  13
1           42  19

Ensemble of Models - Test accuracy 0.875

Ensemble of Models - Test Classification Report
             precision   recall  f1-score   support

          0      0.90     0.97      0.93       380
          1      0.59     0.31      0.41        61

avg / total      0.86     0.88      0.86       441
```

Though code prints **Train**, **Test accuracies**, **Confusion Matrix**, and **Classification Reports**, we have not shown them here due to space constraints. Users are advised to run and check the results on their computers. Test accuracy came as *87.5%*, which is the highest value (the same as gradient boosting results). However, by careful tuning, ensembles do give much better results based on adding better models and removing models with low weights:

```
>>> coefs = meta_logit_fit.coef_
>>> print ("Co-efficients for LR, DT, RF and AB are:",coefs)
```

```
Co-efficients for LR, DT, RF & AB are: [[ 0.89396453  1.10803139  6.58847747 -8.25118547]]
```

It seems that, surprisingly, AdaBoost is dragging down performance of the ensemble. A tip is to either change the parameters used in AdaBoost and rerun the entire exercise, or remove the AdaBoost classifier from the ensemble and rerun the ensemble step to see if there is any improvement in ensemble test accuracy, precision, and recall values:

R Code for Ensemble of Ensembles with different Classifiers Applied on HR Attrition Data:

```
# Ensemble of Ensembles with different type of Classifiers setwd
("D:\\Book writing\\Codes\\Chapter 4")

hrattr_data = read.csv("WA_Fn-UseC_-HR-Employee-Attrition.csv")
str(hrattr_data)
summary(hrattr_data)

hrattr_data$Attrition_ind = 0;
hrattr_data$Attrition_ind[hrattr_data$Attrition=="Yes"]=1
hrattr_data$Attrition_ind = as.factor(hrattr_data$Attrition_ind)

remove_cols = c ("EmployeeCount","EmployeeNumber","Over18",
"StandardHours","Attrition")
hrattr_data_new = hrattr_data[,!(names(hrattr_data) %in% remove_cols)]

set.seed(123)
numrow = nrow(hrattr_data_new)
trnind = sample(1:numrow,size = as.integer(0.7*numrow))
train_data = hrattr_data_new[trnind,]
test_data = hrattr_data_new[-trnind,]

# Ensemble of Ensembles with different type of Classifiers
train_data$Attrition_ind = as.factor(train_data$Attrition_ind)

# Classifier 1 - Logistic Regression
glm_fit = glm(Attrition_ind ~.,family = "binomial",data = train_data)
glm_probs = predict(glm_fit,newdata = train_data,type = "response")

# Classifier 2 - Decision Tree classifier
library(C50)
dtree_fit = C5.0(train_data[-31],train_data$Attrition_ind,
          control = C5.0Control(minCases = 1))
dtree_probs = predict(dtree_fit,newdata = train_data,type = "prob")[,2]

# Classifier 3 - Random Forest
library(randomForest)
rf_fit = randomForest(Attrition_ind~., data = train_data,mtry=6,maxnodes=
64,ntree=5000,nodesize = 1)
rf_probs = predict(rf_fit,newdata = train_data,type = "prob")[,2]

# Classifier 4 - Adaboost
```

```
ada_fit = C5.0(train_data[-31],train_data$Attrition_ind,trails =
5000,control = C5.0Control(minCases = 1))
ada_probs = predict(ada_fit,newdata = train_data,type = "prob")[,2]


# Ensemble of Models
ensemble = data.frame(glm_probs,dtree_probs,rf_probs,ada_probs)
ensemble = cbind(ensemble,train_data$Attrition_ind)
names(ensemble)[5] = "Attrition_ind"
rownames(ensemble) <- 1:nrow(ensemble)


# Meta-classifier on top of individual classifiers
meta_clf = glm(Attrition_ind~.,data = ensemble,family = "binomial")
meta_probs = predict(meta_clf, ensemble,type = "response")


ensemble$pred_class = 0
ensemble$pred_class[meta_probs>0.5]=1


# Train confusion and accuracy metrics
tr_y_pred = ensemble$pred_class
tr_y_act = train_data$Attrition_ind;ts_y_act = test_data$Attrition_ind
tr_tble = table(tr_y_act,tr_y_pred)
print(paste("Ensemble - Train Confusion Matrix"))
print(tr_tble)


tr_acc = accrcy(tr_y_act,tr_y_pred)
print(paste("Ensemble Train accuracy:",tr_acc))


# Now verifying on test data
glm_probs = predict(glm_fit,newdata = test_data,type = "response")
dtree_probs = predict(dtree_fit,newdata = test_data,type = "prob")[,2]
rf_probs = predict(rf_fit,newdata = test_data,type = "prob")[,2]
ada_probs = predict(ada_fit,newdata = test_data,type = "prob")[,2]


ensemble_test = data.frame(glm_probs,dtree_probs,rf_probs,ada_probs)
ensemble_test = cbind(ensemble_test,test_data$Attrition_ind)
names(ensemble_test)[5] = "Attrition_ind"


rownames(ensemble_test) <- 1:nrow(ensemble_test)
meta_test_probs = predict(meta_clf,newdata = ensemble_test,type =
"response")
ensemble_test$pred_class = 0
ensemble_test$pred_class[meta_test_probs>0.5]=1


# Test confusion and accuracy metrics
ts_y_pred = ensemble_test$pred_class
ts_tble = table(ts_y_act,ts_y_pred)
print(paste("Ensemble - Test Confusion Matrix"))
print(ts_tble)
```

```
ts_acc = accrcy(ts_y_act,ts_y_pred)
print(paste("Ensemble Test accuracy:",ts_acc))
```

Ensemble of ensembles with bootstrap samples using a single type of classifier

In this methodology, bootstrap samples are drawn from training data and, each time, separate models will be fitted (individual models could be decision trees, random forest, and so on) on the drawn sample, and all these results are combined at the end to create an ensemble. This method suits dealing with highly flexible models where variance reduction will still improve performance:

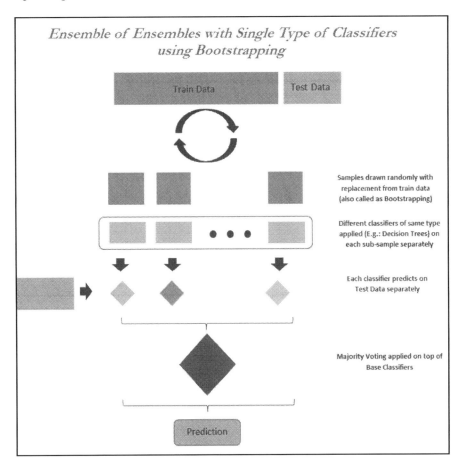

In the following example, AdaBoost is used as a base classifier and the results of individual AdaBoost models are combined using the bagging classifier to generate final outcomes. Nonetheless, each AdaBoost is made up of decision trees with a depth of 1 (decision stumps). Here, we would like to show that classifier inside classifier inside classifier is possible (sounds like the Inception movie though!):

```
# Ensemble of Ensembles - by applying bagging on simple classifier
>>> from sklearn.tree import DecisionTreeClassifier
>>> from sklearn.ensemble import BaggingClassifier
>>> from sklearn.ensemble import AdaBoostClassifier
>>> clwght = {0:0.3,1:0.7}
```

The following is the base classifier (decision stump) used in the AdaBoost classifier:

```
>>> eoe_dtree =
DecisionTreeClassifier(criterion='gini',max_depth=1,class_weight = clwght)
```

Each AdaBoost classifier consists of 500 decision trees with a learning rate of 0.05:

```
>>> eoe_adabst_fit = AdaBoostClassifier(base_estimator= eoe_dtree,
n_estimators=500,learning_rate=0.05,random_state=42)
>>> eoe_adabst_fit.fit(x_train, y_train)

>>> print ("\nAdaBoost - Train Confusion Matrix\n\n",pd.crosstab(y_train,
eoe_adabst_fit.predict(x_train),rownames = ["Actuall"],colnames =
["Predicted"]))
>>> print ("\nAdaBoost - Train accuracy",round(accuracy_score(y_train,
eoe_adabst_fit.predict(x_train)),3))
>>> print ("\nAdaBoost - Train Classification
Report\n",classification_report(y_train, eoe_adabst_fit.predict(x_train)))

>>> print ("\n\nAdaBoost - Test Confusion Matrix\n\n",pd.crosstab(y_test,
eoe_adabst_fit.predict(x_test),rownames = ["Actuall"],colnames =
["Predicted"]))
>>> print ("\nAdaBoost - Test accuracy",round(accuracy_score(y_test,
eoe_adabst_fit.predict(x_test)),3))
>>> print ("\nAdaBoost - Test Classification
Report\n",classification_report(y_test, eoe_adabst_fit.predict(x_test)))
```

The bagging classifier consists of 50 AdaBoost classifiers to ensemble the ensembles:

```
>>> bag_fit = BaggingClassifier(base_estimator=
eoe_adabst_fit,n_estimators=50,
max_samples=1.0,max_features=1.0, bootstrap=True,
bootstrap_features=False,n_jobs=-1,random_state=42)
>>> bag_fit.fit(x_train, y_train)
>>> print ("\nEnsemble of AdaBoost - Train Confusion
Matrix\n\n",pd.crosstab( y_train,bag_fit.predict(x_train),rownames =
```

```
["Actuall"],colnames = ["Predicted"]))
>>> print ("\nEnsemble of AdaBoost - Train
accuracy",round(accuracy_score(y_train, bag_fit.predict(x_train)),3))
>>> print ("\nEnsemble of AdaBoost - Train Classification Report\n",
classification_report( y_train,bag_fit.predict(x_train)))

>>> print ("\n\nEnsemble of AdaBoost - Test Confusion
Matrix\n\n",pd.crosstab(y_test, bag_fit.predict(x_test),rownames =
["Actuall"],colnames = ["Predicted"]))
>>> print ("\nEnsemble of AdaBoost - Test
accuracy",round(accuracy_score(y_test,bag_fit.predict(x_test)),3))
>>> print ("\nEnsemble of AdaBoost - Test Classification Report\n",
classification_report(y_test,bag_fit.predict(x_test)))
```

```
Ensemble of AdaBoost - Train Confusion Matrix

Predicted    0    1
Actuall
0          824   29
1           69  107

Ensemble of AdaBoost - Train accuracy 0.905

Ensemble of AdaBoost  - Train Classification Report
              precision    recall  f1-score   support

          0       0.92      0.97      0.94       853
          1       0.79      0.61      0.69       176

avg / total       0.90      0.90      0.90      1029



Ensemble of AdaBoost - Test Confusion Matrix

Predicted    0    1
Actuall
0          359   21
1           36   25

Ensemble of AdaBoost - Test accuracy 0.871

Ensemble of AdaBoost - Test Classification Report
              precision    recall  f1-score   support

          0       0.91      0.94      0.93       380
          1       0.54      0.41      0.47        61

avg / total       0.86      0.87      0.86       441
```

The results of the ensemble on AdaBoost have shown some improvements, in which the test accuracy obtained is 87.1%, which is almost to that of gradient boosting at 87.5%, which is the best value we have seen so far. However, the number of 1's identified is 25 here, which is greater than Gradient Boosting. Hence, it has been proven that an ensemble of ensembles does work! Unfortunately, these types of functions are not available in R software, hence we are not writing the equivalent R-code here.

Summary

In this chapter, you have learned the complete details about tree-based models, which are currently the most used in the industry, including individual decision trees with grid search and an ensemble of trees such as bagging, random forest, boosting (including AdaBoost, gradient boost and XGBoost), and finally, ensemble of ensembles, also known as model stacking, for further improving accuracy by reducing variance errors by aggregating results further. In model stacking, you have learned how to determine the weights for each model, so that decisions can be made as to which model to keep in the final results to obtain the best possible accuracy.

In the next chapter, you will be learning k-nearest neighbors and Naive Bayes, which are less computationally intensive than tree-based models. The Naive Bayes model will be explained with an NLP use case. In fact, Naive Bayes and SVM are often used where variables (number of dimensions) are very high in number to classify.

5
K-Nearest Neighbors and Naive Bayes

In the previous chapter, we have learned about computationally intensive methods. In contrast, this chapter discusses the simple methods to balance it out! We will be covering the two techniques, called **k-nearest neighbors** (**KNN**)and Naive Bayes here. Before touching on KNN, we explained the issue with the curse of dimensionality with a simulated example. Subsequently, breast cancer medical examples have been utilized to predict whether the cancer is malignant or benign using KNN. In the final section of the chapter, Naive Bayes has been explained with spam/ham classification, which also involves the application of the **natural language processing** (**NLP**) techniques consisting of the following basic preprocessing and modeling steps:

- Punctuation removal
- Word tokenization and lowercase conversion
- Stopwords removal
- Stemming
- Lemmatization with POS tagging
- Conversion of words into TF-IDF to create numerical representation of words
- Application of the Naive Bayes model on TF-IDF vectors to predict if the message is either spam or ham on both train and test data

K-nearest neighbors

K-nearest neighbors is a non-parametric machine learning model in which the model memorizes the training observation for classifying the unseen test data. It can also be called instance-based learning. This model is often termed as lazy learning, as it does not learn anything during the training phase like regression, random forest, and so on. Instead it starts working only during the testing/evaluation phase to compare the given test observations with nearest training observations, which will take significant time in comparing each test data point. Hence, this technique is not efficient on big data; also, performance does deteriorate when the number of variables is high due to the **curse of dimensionality**.

KNN voter example

KNN is explained better with the following short example. Objective is to predict the party for which voter will vote based on their neighborhood, precisely geolocation (latitude and longitude). Here we assume that we can identify the potential voter to which political party they would be voting based on majority voters did voted for that particular party in that vicinity, so that they have high probability to vote for the majority party. However, tuning the k-value (number to consider, among which majority should be counted) is the million-dollar question (as same as any machine learning algorithm):

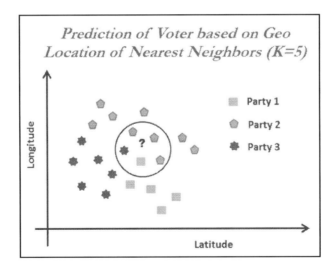

In the preceding diagram, we can see that the voter of the study will vote for **Party 2**. As within the vicinity, one neighbor has voted for **Party 1** and the other voter voted for **Party 3**. But three voters voted for **Party 2**. In fact, by this way KNN solves any given classification problem. Regression problems are solved by taking mean of its neighbors within the given circle or vicinity or k-value.

Curse of dimensionality

KNN completely depends on distance. Hence, it is worth studying about the curse of dimensionality to understand when KNN deteriorates its predictive power with the increase in number of variables required for prediction. This is an obvious fact that high-dimensional spaces are vast. Points in high-dimensional spaces tend to be dispersing from each other more compared with the points in low-dimensional space. Though there are many ways to check the curve of dimensionality, here we are using uniform random values between zero and one generated for 1D, 2D, and 3D space to validate this hypothesis.

In the following lines of codes, mean distance between 1,000 observations have been calculated with the change in dimensions. It is apparent that with the increase in dimensions, distance between points increases logarithmically, which gives us the hint that we need to have exponential increase in data points with increase in dimensions in order to make machine learning algorithms work correctly:

```
>>> import numpy as np
>>> import pandas as pd

# KNN Curse of Dimensionality
>>> import random,math
```

The following code generates random numbers between zero and one from uniform distribution with the given dimension, which is equivalent of length of array or list:

```
>>> def random_point_gen(dimension):
...     return [random.random() for _ in range(dimension)]
```

The following function calculates root mean sum of squares of Euclidean distances (2-norm) between points by taking the difference between points and sum the squares and finally takes square root of total distance:

```
>>> def distance(v,w):
...     vec_sub = [v_i-w_i for v_i,w_i in zip(v,w)]
...     sum_of_sqrs = sum(v_i*v_i for v_i in vec_sub)
...     return math.sqrt(sum_of_sqrs)
```

Both dimension and number of pairs are utilized for calculating the distances with the following code:

```
>>> def random_distances_comparison(dimension,number_pairs):
...     return
[distance(random_point_gen(dimension),random_point_gen(dimension))
        for _ in range(number_pairs)]

>>> def mean(x):
...     return sum(x) / len(x)
```

Experiment has been done by changing dimensions from 1 to 201 with the increase of 5 dimensions to check the increase in distance:

```
>>> dimensions = range(1, 201, 5)
```

Both minimum and average distances have been calculated to check, however, both illustrate the similar story:

```
>>> avg_distances = []
>>> min_distances = []

>>> dummyarray = np.empty((20,4))
>>> dist_vals = pd.DataFrame(dummyarray)
>>> dist_vals.columns =
["Dimension","Min_Distance","Avg_Distance","Min/Avg_Distance"]

>>> random.seed(34)
>>> i = 0
>>> for dims in dimensions:
...     distances = random_distances_comparison(dims, 1000)
...     avg_distances.append(mean(distances))
...     min_distances.append(min(distances))
...     dist_vals.loc[i,"Dimension"] = dims
...     dist_vals.loc[i,"Min_Distance"] = min(distances)
...     dist_vals.loc[i,"Avg_Distance"] = mean(distances)
...     dist_vals.loc[i,"Min/Avg_Distance"] =
min(distances)/mean(distances)
...     print(dims, min(distances), mean(distances), min(distances)*1.0 /
mean( distances))
...     i = i+1

# Plotting Average distances for Various Dimensions
>>> import matplotlib.pyplot as plt
>>> plt.figure()
>>> plt.xlabel('Dimensions')
>>> plt.ylabel('Avg. Distance')
>>> plt.plot(dist_vals["Dimension"],dist_vals["Avg_Distance"])
```

```
>>> plt.legend(loc='best')

>>> plt.show()
```

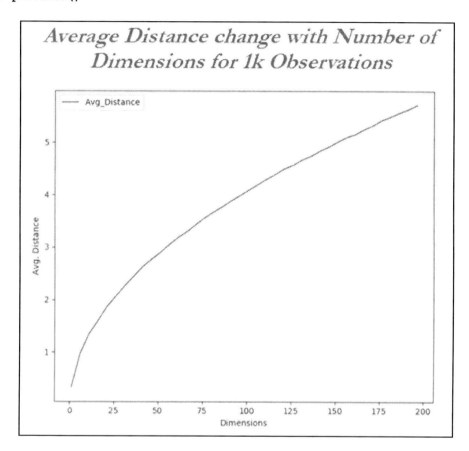

 From the preceding graph, it is proved that with the increase in dimensions, mean distance increases logarithmically. Hence the higher the dimensions, the more data is needed to overcome the curse of dimensionality!

Curse of dimensionality with 1D, 2D, and 3D example

A quick analysis has been done to see how distance 60 random points are expanding with the increase in dimensionality. Initially random points are drawn for one-dimension:

```
# 1-Dimension Plot
>>> import numpy as np
>>> import pandas as pd
>>> import matplotlib.pyplot as plt

>>> one_d_data = np.random.rand(60,1)
>>> one_d_data_df = pd.DataFrame(one_d_data)
>>> one_d_data_df.columns = ["1D_Data"]
>>> one_d_data_df["height"] = 1

>>> plt.figure()
>>> plt.scatter(one_d_data_df['1D_Data'],one_d_data_df["height"])
>>> plt.yticks([])
>>> plt.xlabel("1-D points")
>>> plt.show()
```

If we observe the following graph, all 60 data points are very nearby in one-dimension:

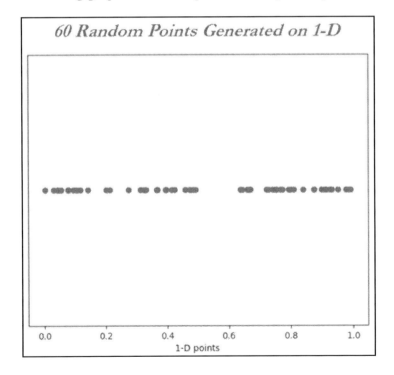

Here we are repeating the same experiment in a 2D space, by taking 60 random numbers with x and y co-ordinate space and plotted them visually:

```
# 2- Dimensions Plot
>>> two_d_data = np.random.rand(60,2)
>>> two_d_data_df = pd.DataFrame(two_d_data)
>>> two_d_data_df.columns = ["x_axis","y_axis"]

>>> plt.figure()
>>> plt.scatter(two_d_data_df['x_axis'],two_d_data_df["y_axis"])
>>> plt.xlabel("x_axis");plt.ylabel("y_axis")
>>> plt.show()
```

By observing the 2D graph we can see that more gaps have been appearing for the same 60 data points:

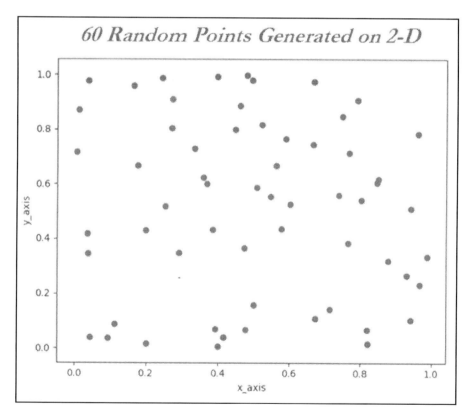

Finally, 60 data points are drawn for 3D space. We can see the further increase in spaces, which is very apparent. This has proven to us visually by now that with the increase in dimensions, it creates lot of space, which makes a classifier weak to detect the signal:

```
# 3- Dimensions Plot
>>> three_d_data = np.random.rand(60,3)
>>> three_d_data_df = pd.DataFrame(three_d_data)
>>> three_d_data_df.columns = ["x_axis","y_axis","z_axis"]

>>> from mpl_toolkits.mplot3d import Axes3D
>>> fig = plt.figure()
>>> ax = fig.add_subplot(111, projection='3d')
>>>
ax.scatter(three_d_data_df['x_axis'],three_d_data_df["y_axis"],three_d_data
_df ["z_axis"])
>>> plt.show()
```

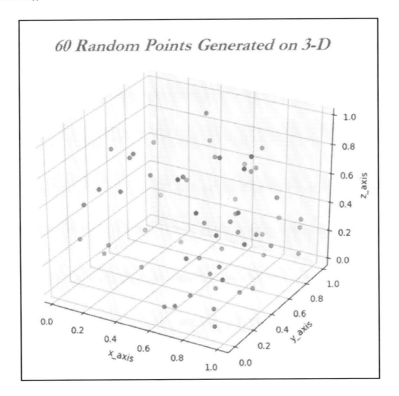

KNN classifier with breast cancer Wisconsin data example

Breast cancer data has been utilized from the UCI machine learning repository `http://archive.ics.uci.edu/ml/datasets/Breast+Cancer+Wisconsin+%28Diagnostic%29` for illustration purposes. Here the task is to find whether the cancer is malignant or benign based on various collected features such as clump thickness and so on using the KNN classifier:

```
# KNN Classifier - Breast Cancer
>>> import numpy as np
>>> import pandas as pd
>>> from sklearn.metrics import accuracy_score,classification_report
>>> breast_cancer = pd.read_csv("Breast_Cancer_Wisconsin.csv")
```

The following are the first few rows to show how the data looks like. The `Class` value has class 2 and 4. Value 2 and 4 represent benign and malignant class, respectively. Whereas all the other variables do vary between value 1 and 10, which are very much categorical in nature:

ID_Number	Clump_Thickness	Unif_Cell_Size	Unif_Cell_Shape	Marg_Adhesion	Single_Epith_Cell_Size	Bare_Nuclei	Bland_Chromatin	Normal_Nucleoli	Mitoses	Class
1000025	5	1	1	1	2	1	3	1	1	2
1002945	5	4	4	5	7	10	3	2	1	2
1015425	3	1	1	1	2	2	3	1	1	2
1016277	6	8	8	1	3	4	3	7	1	2
1017023	4	1	1	3	2	1	3	1	1	2

Only the `Bare_Nuclei` variable has some missing values, here we are replacing them with the most frequent value (category value 1) in the following code:

```
>>> breast_cancer['Bare_Nuclei'] =
breast_cancer['Bare_Nuclei'].replace('?', np.NAN)
>>> breast_cancer['Bare_Nuclei'] =
breast_cancer['Bare_Nuclei'].fillna(breast_cancer[
'Bare_Nuclei'].value_counts().index[0])
```

Use the following code to convert the classes to a 0 and 1 indicator for using in the classifier:

```
>>> breast_cancer['Cancer_Ind'] = 0
>>> breast_cancer.loc[breast_cancer['Class']==4,'Cancer_Ind'] = 1
```

In the following code, we are dropping non-value added variables from analysis:

```
>>> x_vars = breast_cancer.drop(['ID_Number','Class','Cancer_Ind'],axis=1)
>>> y_var = breast_cancer['Cancer_Ind']
>>> from sklearn.preprocessing import StandardScaler
>>> x_vars_stdscle = StandardScaler().fit_transform(x_vars.values)
>>> from sklearn.model_selection import train_test_split
```

As KNN is very sensitive to distances, here we are standardizing all the columns before applying algorithms:

```
>>> x_vars_stdscle_df = pd.DataFrame(x_vars_stdscle, index=x_vars.index,
columns=x_vars.columns)
>>> x_train,x_test,y_train,y_test =
train_test_split(x_vars_stdscle_df,y_var, train_size = 0.7,random_state=42)
```

KNN classifier is being applied with neighbor value of 3 and p value indicates it is 2-norm, also known as Euclidean distance for computing classes:

```
>>> from sklearn.neighbors import KNeighborsClassifier
>>> knn_fit = KNeighborsClassifier(n_neighbors=3,p=2,metric='minkowski')
>>> knn_fit.fit(x_train,y_train)

>>> print ("\nK-Nearest Neighbors - Train Confusion
Matrix\n\n",pd.crosstab(y_train, knn_fit.predict(x_train),rownames =
["Actuall"],colnames = ["Predicted"]) )
>>> print ("\nK-Nearest Neighbors - Train
accuracy:",round(accuracy_score(y_train, knn_fit.predict(x_train)),3))
>>> print ("\nK-Nearest Neighbors - Train Classification Report\n",
classification_report( y_train,knn_fit.predict(x_train)))

>>> print ("\n\nK-Nearest Neighbors - Test Confusion
Matrix\n\n",pd.crosstab(y_test, knn_fit.predict(x_test),rownames =
["Actuall"],colnames = ["Predicted"]))
>>> print ("\nK-Nearest Neighbors - Test accuracy:",round(accuracy_score(
y_test,knn_fit.predict(x_test)),3))
>>> print ("\nK-Nearest Neighbors - Test Classification Report\n",
classification_report(y_test,knn_fit.predict(x_test)))
```

```
K-Nearest Neighbors - Train Confusion Matrix

 Predicted     0    1
Actuall
0           309    6
1             4  170

K-Nearest Neighbors - Train accuracy: 0.98

K-Nearest Neighbors - Train Classification Report
              precision    recall   f1-score    support

         0       0.99       0.98      0.98         315
         1       0.97       0.98      0.97         174

avg / total       0.98       0.98      0.98         489


K-Nearest Neighbors - Test Confusion Matrix

 Predicted     0    1
Actuall
0           141    2
1             3   64

K-Nearest Neighbors - Test accuracy: 0.976

K-Nearest Neighbors - Test Classification Report
              precision    recall   f1-score    support

         0       0.98       0.99      0.98         143
         1       0.97       0.96      0.96          67

avg / total       0.98       0.98      0.98         210
```

From the results, it is appearing that KNN is working very well in classifying malignant and benign classes well, obtaining test accuracy of 97.6 percent with 96 percent of recall on malignant class. The only deficiency of KNN classifier would be, it is computationally intensive during test phase, as each test observation will be compared with all the available observations in train data, which practically KNN does not learn a thing from training data. Hence, we are also calling it a lazy classifier!

The R code for KNN classifier is as follows:

```
# KNN Classifier
setwd("D:\\Book writing\\Codes\\Chapter 5")
breast_cancer = read.csv("Breast_Cancer_Wisconsin.csv")

# Column Bare_Nuclei have some missing values with "?" in place, we are
replacing with median values
# As Bare_Nuclei is discrete variable
breast_cancer$Bare_Nuclei = as.character(breast_cancer$Bare_Nuclei)
breast_cancer$Bare_Nuclei[breast_cancer$Bare_Nuclei=="?"] =
median(breast_cancer$Bare_Nuclei,na.rm = TRUE)
breast_cancer$Bare_Nuclei = as.integer(breast_cancer$Bare_Nuclei)
# Classes are 2 & 4 for benign & malignant respectively, we # have
converted #
to zero-one problem, as it is easy to convert to work # around with models
breast_cancer$Cancer_Ind = 0
breast_cancer$Cancer_Ind[breast_cancer$Class==4]=1
breast_cancer$Cancer_Ind = as.factor( breast_cancer$Cancer_Ind)

# We have removed unique id number from modeling as unique # numbers does
not provide value in modeling
# In addition, original class variable also will be removed # as the same
has been replaced with derived variable

remove_cols = c("ID_Number","Class")
breast_cancer_new = breast_cancer[,!(names(breast_cancer) %in%
remove_cols)]

# Setting seed value for producing repetitive results
# 70-30 split has been made on the data

set.seed(123)
numrow = nrow(breast_cancer_new)
trnind = sample(1:numrow,size = as.integer(0.7*numrow))
train_data = breast_cancer_new[trnind,]
test_data = breast_cancer_new[-trnind,]

# Following is classical code for computing accuracy, # precision & recall

frac_trzero = (table(train_data$Cancer_Ind)[[1]])/nrow(train_data)
frac_trone = (table(train_data$Cancer_Ind)[[2]])/nrow(train_data)

frac_tszero = (table(test_data$Cancer_Ind)[[1]])/nrow(test_data)
frac_tsone = (table(test_data$Cancer_Ind)[[2]])/nrow(test_data)

prec_zero <- function(act,pred){ tble = table(act,pred)
return( round( tble[1,1]/(tble[1,1]+tble[2,1]),4) ) }
```

```
prec_one <- function(act,pred){ tble = table(act,pred)
return( round( tble[2,2]/(tble[2,2]+tble[1,2]),4) ) }

recl_zero <- function(act,pred){tble = table(act,pred)
return( round( tble[1,1]/(tble[1,1]+tble[1,2]),4) ) }

recl_one <- function(act,pred){ tble = table(act,pred)
return( round( tble[2,2]/(tble[2,2]+tble[2,1]),4) ) }

accrcy <- function(act,pred){ tble = table(act,pred)
return( round((tble[1,1]+tble[2,2])/sum(tble),4)) }

# Importing Class package in which KNN function do present library(class)

# Choosing sample k-value as 3 & apply on train & test data # respectively

k_value = 3
tr_y_pred = knn(train_data,train_data,train_data$Cancer_Ind,k=k_value)
ts_y_pred = knn(train_data,test_data,train_data$Cancer_Ind,k=k_value)

# Calculating confusion matrix, accuracy, precision & # recall on train
data

tr_y_act = train_data$Cancer_Ind;ts_y_act = test_data$Cancer_Ind
tr_tble = table(tr_y_act,tr_y_pred)
print(paste("Train Confusion Matrix"))
print(tr_tble)

tr_acc = accrcy(tr_y_act,tr_y_pred)
trprec_zero = prec_zero(tr_y_act,tr_y_pred); trrecl_zero =
recl_zero(tr_y_act,tr_y_pred)
trprec_one = prec_one(tr_y_act,tr_y_pred); trrecl_one =
recl_one(tr_y_act,tr_y_pred)
trprec_ovll = trprec_zero *frac_trzero + trprec_one*frac_trone
trrecl_ovll = trrecl_zero *frac_trzero + trrecl_one*frac_trone

print(paste("KNN Train accuracy:",tr_acc))
print(paste("KNN - Train Classification Report"))
print(paste("Zero_Precision",trprec_zero,"Zero_Recall",trrecl_zero))
print(paste("One_Precision",trprec_one,"One_Recall",trrecl_one))
print(paste("Overall_Precision",round(trprec_ovll,4),"Overall_Recall",round
(trrecl_ovll,4)))

# Calculating confusion matrix, accuracy, precision & # recall on test data

ts_tble = table(ts_y_act, ts_y_pred)
print(paste("Test Confusion Matrix"))
print(ts_tble)
```

```
ts_acc = accrcy(ts_y_act,ts_y_pred)
tsprec_zero = prec_zero(ts_y_act,ts_y_pred); tsrecl_zero =
recl_zero(ts_y_act,ts_y_pred)
tsprec_one = prec_one(ts_y_act,ts_y_pred); tsrecl_one =
recl_one(ts_y_act,ts_y_pred)

tsprec_ovll = tsprec_zero *frac_tszero + tsprec_one*frac_tsone
tsrecl_ovll = tsrecl_zero *frac_tszero + tsrecl_one*frac_tsone

print(paste("KNN Test accuracy:",ts_acc))
print(paste("KNN - Test Classification Report"))
print(paste("Zero_Precision",tsprec_zero,"Zero_Recall",tsrecl_zero))
print(paste("One_Precision",tsprec_one,"One_Recall",tsrecl_one))
print(paste("Overall_Precision",round(tsprec_ovll,4),"Overall_Recall",round
(tsrecl_ovll,4)))
```

Tuning of k-value in KNN classifier

In the previous section, we just checked with only the k-value of three. Actually, in any machine learning algorithm, we need to tune the knobs to check where the better performance can be obtained. In the case of KNN, the only tuning parameter is k-value. Hence, in the following code, we are determining the best k-value with grid search:

```
# Tuning of K- value for Train & Test data
>>> dummyarray = np.empty((5,3))
>>> k_valchart = pd.DataFrame(dummyarray)
>>> k_valchart.columns = ["K_value","Train_acc","Test_acc"]

>>> k_vals = [1,2,3,4,5]

>>> for i in range(len(k_vals)):
...        knn_fit =
KNeighborsClassifier(n_neighbors=k_vals[i],p=2,metric='minkowski')
...        knn_fit.fit(x_train,y_train)

...        print ("\nK-value",k_vals[i])
...        tr_accscore =
round(accuracy_score(y_train,knn_fit.predict(x_train)),3)
...        print ("\nK-Nearest Neighbors - Train Confusion
Matrix\n\n",pd.crosstab( y_train, knn_fit.predict(x_train),rownames =
["Actuall"],colnames = ["Predicted"]) )
...        print ("\nK-Nearest Neighbors - Train accuracy:",tr_accscore)
...        print ("\nK-Nearest Neighbors - Train Classification Report\n",
classification_report(y_train,knn_fit.predict(x_train)))

...        ts_accscore =
```

```
round(accuracy_score(y_test,knn_fit.predict(x_test)),3)
...      print ("\n\nK-Nearest Neighbors - Test Confusion
Matrix\n\n",pd.crosstab( y_test,knn_fit.predict(x_test),rownames =
["Actuall"],colnames = ["Predicted"]))
...      print ("\nK-Nearest Neighbors - Test accuracy:",ts_accscore)
...      print ("\nK-Nearest Neighbors - Test Classification
Report\n",classification_report(y_test,knn_fit.predict(x_test)))
...      k_valchart.loc[i, 'K_value'] = k_vals[i]
...      k_valchart.loc[i, 'Train_acc'] = tr_accscore
...      k_valchart.loc[i, 'Test_acc'] = ts_accscore


# Ploting accuracies over varied K-values
>>> import matplotlib.pyplot as plt
>>> plt.figure()
>>> plt.xlabel('K-value')
>>> plt.ylabel('Accuracy')
>>> plt.plot(k_valchart["K_value"],k_valchart["Train_acc"])
>>> plt.plot(k_valchart["K_value"],k_valchart["Test_acc"])

>>> plt.axis([0.9,5, 0.92, 1.005])
>>> plt.xticks([1,2,3,4,5])

>>> for a,b in zip(k_valchart["K_value"],k_valchart["Train_acc"]):
...      plt.text(a, b, str(b),fontsize=10)

>>> for a,b in zip(k_valchart["K_value"],k_valchart["Test_acc"]):
...      plt.text(a, b, str(b),fontsize=10)
>>> plt.legend(loc='upper right')
>>> plt.show()
```

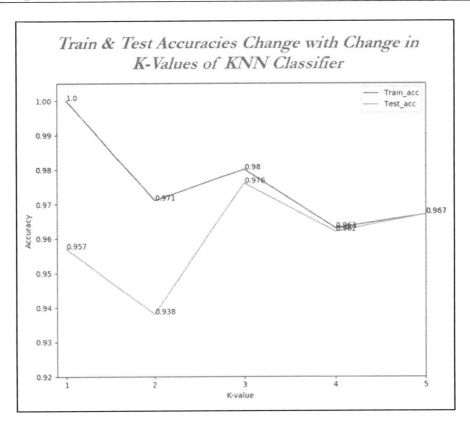

It appears that with less value of k-value, it has more overfitting problems due to the very high value of accuracy on train data and less on test data, with the increase in k-value more the train and test accuracies are converging and becoming more robust. This phenomenon illustrates the typical machine learning phenomenon. As for further analysis, readers are encouraged to try k-values higher than five and see how train and test accuracies are changing. The R code for tuning of k-value in KNN classifier is as follows:

```
# Tuning of K-value on Train & Test Data
k_valchart = data.frame(matrix( nrow=5, ncol=3))
colnames(k_valchart) = c("K_value","Train_acc","Test_acc")
k_vals = c(1,2,3,4,5)

i = 1
for (kv in k_vals) {
  tr_y_pred = knn(train_data,train_data,train_data$Cancer_Ind,k=kv)
  ts_y_pred = knn(train_data,test_data,train_data$Cancer_Ind,k=kv)
  tr_y_act = train_data$Cancer_Ind;ts_y_act = test_data$Cancer_Ind
  tr_tble = table(tr_y_act,tr_y_pred)
  print(paste("Train Confusion Matrix"))
```

```
  print(tr_tble)
  tr_acc = accrcy(tr_y_act,tr_y_pred)
  trprec_zero = prec_zero(tr_y_act,tr_y_pred); trrecl_zero =
recl_zero(tr_y_act, tr_y_pred)
  trprec_one = prec_one(tr_y_act,tr_y_pred); trrecl_one =
recl_one(tr_y_act,tr_y_pred)
  trprec_ovll = trprec_zero *frac_trzero + trprec_one*frac_trone
  trrecl_ovll = trrecl_zero *frac_trzero + trrecl_one*frac_trone
  print(paste("KNN Train accuracy:",tr_acc))
  print(paste("KNN - Train Classification Report"))

print(paste("Zero_Precision",trprec_zero,"Zero_Recall",trrecl_zero))
print(paste("One_Precision",trprec_one,"One_Recall",trrecl_one))
print(paste("Overall_Precision",round(trprec_ovll,4),"Overall_Recall",round
(trrecl_ovll,4)))
  ts_tble = table(ts_y_act,ts_y_pred)
  print(paste("Test Confusion Matrix"))
  print(ts_tble)
  ts_acc = accrcy(ts_y_act,ts_y_pred)
  tsprec_zero = prec_zero(ts_y_act,ts_y_pred); tsrecl_zero =
recl_zero(ts_y_act,ts_y_pred)
  tsprec_one = prec_one(ts_y_act,ts_y_pred); tsrecl_one =
recl_one(ts_y_act,ts_y_pred)
  tsprec_ovll = tsprec_zero *frac_tszero + tsprec_one*frac_tsone
  tsrecl_ovll = tsrecl_zero *frac_tszero + tsrecl_one*frac_tsone

  print(paste("KNN Test accuracy:",ts_acc))
  print(paste("KNN - Test Classification Report"))

print(paste("Zero_Precision",tsprec_zero,"Zero_Recall",tsrecl_zero))
print(paste("One_Precision",tsprec_one,"One_Recall",tsrecl_one))
print(paste("Overall_Precision",round(tsprec_ovll,4),"Overall_Recall",round
(tsrecl_ovll,4)))

  k_valchart[i,1] =kv
  k_valchart[i,2] =tr_acc
  k_valchart[i,3] =ts_acc i = i+1 }
# Plotting the graph
library(ggplot2)
library(grid)
ggplot(k_valchart, aes(K_value))
+ geom_line(aes(y = Train_acc, colour = "Train_Acc")) +
geom_line(aes(y = Test_acc, colour = "Test_Acc"))+
labs(x="K_value",y="Accuracy") +
geom_text(aes(label = Train_acc, y = Train_acc), size = 3)+
geom_text(aes(label = Test_acc, y = Test_acc), size = 3)
```

Naive Bayes

Bayes algorithm concept is quite old and exists from the 18th century since Thomas Bayes. Thomas developed the foundational mathematical principles for determining the probability of unknown events from the known events. For example, if all apples are red in color and average diameter would be about 4 inches then, if at random one fruit is selected from the basket with red color and diameter of 3.7 inch, what is the probability that the particular fruit would be an apple? Naive term does assume independence of particular features in a class with respect to others. In this case, there would be no dependency between color and diameter. This independence assumption makes the Naive Bayes classifier most effective in terms of computational ease for particular tasks such as email classification based on words in which high dimensions of vocab do exist, even after assuming independence between features. Naive Bayes classifier performs surprisingly really well in practical applications.

Bayesian classifiers are best applied to problems in which information from a very high number of attributes should be considered simultaneously to estimate the probability of final outcome. Bayesian methods utilize all available evidence to consider for prediction even features have weak effects on the final outcome to predict. However, we should not ignore the fact that a large number of features with relatively minor effects, taken together its combined impact would form strong classifiers.

Probability fundamentals

Before diving into Naive Bayes, it would be good to reiterate the fundamentals. Probability of an event can be estimated from observed data by dividing the number of trails in which an event occurred with total number of trails. For instance, if a bag contains red and blue balls and randomly picked *10* balls one by one with replacement and out of *10*, 3 red balls appeared in trails we can say that probability of red is *0.3*, $p_{red} = 3/10 = 0.3$. Total probability of all possible outcomes must be 100 percent.

If a trail has two outcomes such as email classification either it is spam or ham and both cannot occur simultaneously, these events are considered as mutually exclusive with each other. In addition, if those outcomes cover all possible events, it would be called as **exhaustive events**. For example, in email classification if *P (spam) = 0.1*, we will be able to calculate *P (ham) = 1- 0.1 = 0.9*, these two events are mutually exclusive. In the following Venn diagram, all the email possible classes are represented (the entire universe) with type of outcomes:

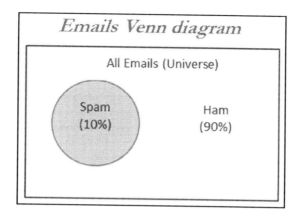

Joint probability

Though mutually exclusive cases are simple to work upon, most of the actual problems do fall under the category of non-mutually exclusive events. By using the joint appearance, we can predict the event outcome. For example, if emails messages present the word like *lottery*, which is very highly likely of being spam rather than ham. The following Venn diagram indicates the joint probability of spam with *lottery*. However, if you notice in detail, lottery circle is not contained completely within the spam circle. This implies that not all spam messages contain the word *lottery* and not every email with the word *lottery* is spam.

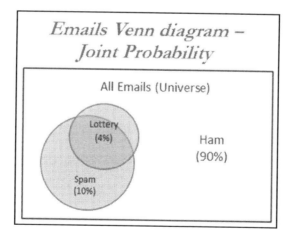

In the following diagram, we have expanded the spam and ham category in addition to the *lottery* word in Venn diagram representation:

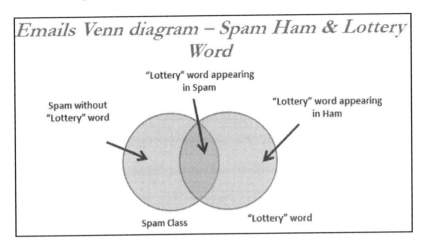

We have seen that 10 percent of all the emails are spam and 4 percent of emails have the word *lottery* and our task is to quantify the degree of overlap between these two proportions. In other words, we need to identify the joint probability of both *p(spam)* and *p(lottery)* occurring, which can be written as *p(spam ∩ lottery)*. In case if both the events are totally unrelated, they are called **independent events** and their respective value is *p(spam ∩ lottery) = p(spam) * p(lottery) = 0.1 * 0.04 = 0.004*, which is 0.4 percent of all messages are spam containing the word Lottery. In general, for independent events *P(A∩ B) = P(A) * P(B)*.

Understanding Bayes theorem with conditional probability

Conditional probability provides a way of calculating relationships between dependent events using Bayes theorem. For example, *A* and *B* are two events and we would like to calculate *P(A \ B)* can be read as the probability of event occurring *A* given the fact that event *B* already occurred, in fact this is known as **conditional probability**, the equation can be written as follows:

$$P(A \backslash B) = \frac{P(B \backslash A) * P(A)}{P(B)} = \frac{P(A \cap B)}{P(B)}$$

To understand better, we will now talk about the email classification example. Our objective is to predict whether email is spam given the word lottery and some other clues. In this case we already knew the overall probability of spam, which is 10 percent also known as **prior probability**. Now suppose you have obtained an additional piece of information that probability of word lottery in all messages, which is 4 percent, also known as **marginal likelihood**. Now, we know the probability that *lottery* was used in previous spam messages and is called the **likelihood**.

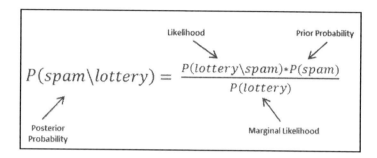

By applying the Bayes theorem to the evidence, we can calculate the posterior probability that calculates the probability that the message is how likely being a spam; given the fact that lottery was appearing in message. On average if the probability is greater than 50 percent it indicates that the message is spam rather than ham.

Word Frequency & Likelihood of Lottery with Spam & Ham

Frequency	Lottery yes	Lottery no	Total
spam	3	19	22
ham	2	76	78
Total	5	95	100

Likelihood	Lottery yes	Lottery no	Total
spam	3/22	19/22	22
ham	2/78	76/78	78
Total	5/100	95/100	100

In the previous table, the sample frequency table that records the number of times *Lottery* appeared in spam and ham messages and its respective likelihood has been shown. Likelihood table reveals that *P(Lottery \ Spam)= 3/22 = 0.13*, indicating that probability is 13 percent that a spam message contains the term *Lottery*. Subsequently we can calculate the *P(Spam ∩ Lottery) = P(Lottery \ Spam) * P(Spam) = (3/22) * (22/100) = 0.03*. In order to calculate the posterior probability, we divide *P(Spam ∩ Lottery)* with *P(Lottery)*, which means *(3/22)*(22/100) / (4/100) = 0.75*. Therefore, the probability is 75 percent that a message is spam, given that message contains the word *Lottery*. Hence, don't believe in quick fortune guys!

Naive Bayes classification

In the past example, we have seen with single word called *lottery*, however, in this case we will be discussing with a few more additional words such as *Million* and *Unsubscribe* to show how actual classifiers do work. Let us construct the likelihood table for the appearance of the three words (*W1*, *W2*, and *W3*), as shown in the following table for *100* emails:

Likelihood	Lottery (W1)		Million (W2)		Unsubscribe (W3)		Total
	yes	no	yes	no	yes	no	
spam	3/22	19/22	11/22	11/22	13/22	9/22	22
ham	2/78	76/78	15/78	63/78	21/78	57/78	78
Total	5/100	95/100	26/100	74/100	34/100	66/100	100

When a new message is received, the posterior probability will be calculated to determine that email message is spam or ham. Let us assume that we have an email with terms *Lottery* and *Unsubscribe*, but it does not have word *Million* in it, with this details, what is the probability of spam?

By using Bayes theorem, we can define the problem as *Lottery = Yes*, *Million = No* and *Unsubscribe = Yes*:

$$P(Spam|W_1 \cap \neg W_2 \cap W_3) = \frac{P(W_1 \cap \neg W_2 \cap W_3 \mid Spam) * P(Spam)}{P(W_1 \cap \neg W_2 \cap W_3)}$$

Solving the preceding equations will have high computational complexity due to the dependency of words with each other. As more number of words are added, this will even explode and also huge memory will be needed for processing all possible intersecting events. This finally leads to intuitive turnaround with independence of words (**cross-conditional independence**) for which it got name of the Naive prefix for Bayes classifier. When both events are independent we can write $P(A \cap B) = P(A) * P(B)$. In fact, this equivalence is much easier to compute with less memory requirement:

$$P(Spam \mid W_1 \cap \neg W_2 \cap W_3) = \frac{P(W_1 \mid Spam) * P(\neg W_2 \mid Spam) * P(W_3 \mid Spam) * P(Spam)}{P(W_1) * P(\neg W_2) * P(W_3)}$$

In a similar way, we will calculate the probability for ham messages as well, as follows:

$$P(Ham \mid W_1 \cap \neg W_2 \cap W_3) = \frac{P(W_1 \mid Ham) * P(\neg W_2 \mid Ham) * P(W_3 \mid Ham) * P(Ham)}{P(W_1) * P(\neg W_2) * P(W_3)}$$

By substituting the preceding likelihood table in the equations, due to the ratio of spam/ham we can just simply ignore the denominator terms in both the equations. Overall likelihood of spam is:

$$P(Spam \mid W_1 \cap \neg W_2 \cap W_3) = \left(\frac{3}{22}\right) * \left(\frac{11}{22}\right) * \left(\frac{13}{22}\right) * \left(\frac{22}{100}\right) = 0.008864$$

$$P(Ham \mid W_1 \cap \neg W_2 \cap W_3) = \left(\frac{2}{78}\right) * \left(\frac{63}{78}\right) * \left(\frac{21}{78}\right) * \left(\frac{78}{100}\right) = 0.004349$$

After calculating ratio, *0.008864/0.004349 = 2.03*, which means that this message is two times more likely to be spam than ham. But we can calculate the probabilities as follows:

P(Spam) = 0.008864/(0.008864+0.004349) = 0.67

P(Ham) = 0.004349/(0.008864+0.004349) = 0.33

By converting likelihood values into probabilities, we can show in a presentable way for either to set-off some thresholds, and so on.

Laplace estimator

In the previous calculation, all the values are nonzeros, which makes calculations well. Whereas in practice some words never appear in past for specific category and suddenly appear at later stages, which makes entire calculations as zeros.

For example, in the previous equation W_3 did have a *0* value instead of *13*, and it will convert entire equations to *0* altogether:

$$P(Spam \mid W_1 \cap \neg W_2 \cap W_3) = \left(\frac{3}{22}\right) * \left(\frac{11}{22}\right) * \left(\frac{0}{22}\right) * \left(\frac{22}{100}\right) = 0$$

In order to avoid this situation, Laplace estimator essentially adds a small number to each of the counts in the frequency table, which ensures that each feature has a nonzero probability of occurring with each class. Usually Laplace estimator is set to *1*, which ensures that each class-feature combination is found in the data at least once:

$$P(Spam|W_1 \cap \neg W_2 \cap W_3) = \left(\frac{4}{25}\right) * \left(\frac{12}{25}\right) * \left(\frac{1}{25}\right) * \left(\frac{22}{100}\right) = 0$$

 If you observe the equation carefully, value *1* is added to all three words in numerator and at the same time three has been added to all denominators to provide equivalence.

Naive Bayes SMS spam classification example

Naive Bayes classifier has been developed using the SMS spam collection data available at `http://www.dt.fee.unicamp.br/~tiago/smsspamcollection/`. In this chapter, various techniques available in NLP techniques have been discussed to preprocess prior to build the Naive Bayes model:

```
>>> import csv

>>> smsdata = open('SMSSpamCollection.txt','r')
>>> csv_reader = csv.reader(smsdata,delimiter='\t')
```

The following `sys` package lines code can be used in case of any `utf-8` errors encountered while using older versions of Python, or else does not necessary with latest version of Python 3.6:

```
>>> import sys
>>> reload (sys)
>>> sys.setdefaultendocing('utf-8')
```

Normal coding starts from here as usual:

```
>>> smsdata_data = []
>>> smsdata_labels = []

>>> for line in csv_reader:
...      smsdata_labels.append(line[0])
...      smsdata_data.append(line[1])

>>> smsdata.close()
```

The following code prints the top 5 lines:

```
>>> for i in range(5):
...      print (smsdata_data[i],smsdata_labels[i])
```

```
Go until jurong point, crazy.. Available only in bugis n great world la e buffet... Cine there got amore
wat... ham
Ok lar... Joking wif u oni... ham
Free entry in 2 a wkly comp to win FA Cup final tkts 21st May 2005. Text FA to 87121 to receive entry
question(std txt rate)T&C's apply 08452810075over18's spam
U dun say so early hor... U c already then say... ham
Nah I don't think he goes to usf, he lives around here though ham
```

After getting preceding output run following code:

```
>>> from collections import Counter
>>> c = Counter( smsdata_labels )
>>> print(c)
```

```
Counter({'ham': 4825, 'spam': 747})
```

Out of 5,572 observations, 4,825 are ham messages, which are about 86.5 percent and 747 spam messages are about remaining 13.4 percent.

Using NLP techniques, we have preprocessed the data for obtaining finalized word vectors to map with final outcomes spam or ham. Major preprocessing stages involved are:

- **Removal of punctuations**: Punctuations needs to be removed before applying any further processing. Punctuations from the `string` library are `!"#$%&\'()*+,-./:;<=>?@[\\]^_`{|}~`, which are removed from all the messages.

- **Word tokenization**: Words are chunked from sentences based on white space for further processing.

- **Converting words into lower case**: Converting to all lower case provides removal of duplicates, such as *Run* and *run*, where the first one comes at start of the sentence and the later one comes in the middle of the sentence, and so on, which all needs to be unified to remove duplicates as we are working on bag of words technique.

- **Stop word removal**: Stop words are the words that repeat so many times in literature and yet are not much differentiator in explanatory power of sentences. For example: *I*, *me*, *you*, *this*, *that*, and so on, which needs to be removed before further processing.

- **of length at least three**: Here we have removed words with length less than three.

- Keeping words of length at least three: Here we have removed words with length less than three. Stemming of words: Stemming process stems the words to its respective root words. Example of stemming is bringing down running to run or runs to run. By doing stemming we reduce duplicates and improve the accuracy of the model.

- **Part-of-speech (POS) tagging**: This applies the speech tags to words, such as noun, verb, adjective, and so on. For example, POS tagging for *running* is verb, whereas for *run* is noun. In some situation *running* is noun and lemmatization will not bring down the word to root word *run*, instead it just keeps the *running* as it is. Hence, POS tagging is a very crucial step necessary for performing prior to applying the lemmatization operation to bring down the word to its root word.

- **Lemmatization of words**: Lemmatization is another different process to reduce the dimensionality. In lemmatization process, it brings down the word to root word rather than just truncating the words. For example, bring *ate* to its root word as *eat* when we pass the *ate* word into lemmatizer with the POS tag as verb.

The `nltk` package has been utilized for all the preprocessing steps, as it consists of all the necessary NLP functionality in one single roof:

```
>>> import nltk
>>> from nltk.corpus import stopwords
>>> from nltk.stem import WordNetLemmatizer
>>> import string
>>> import pandas as pd
>>> from nltk import pos_tag
>>> from nltk.stem import PorterStemmer
```

Function has been written (preprocessing) consists of all the steps for convenience. However, we will be explaining all the steps in each section:

```
>>> def preprocessing(text):
```

The following line of the code splits the word and checks each character if it is in standard punctuations, if so it will be replaced with blank and or else it just does not replace with blanks:

```
...     text2 = " ".join("".join([" " if ch in string.punctuation else ch
    for ch in text]).split())
```

The following code tokenizes the sentences into words based on white spaces and put them together as a list for applying further steps:

```
...     tokens = [word for sent in nltk.sent_tokenize(text2) for word in
            nltk.word_tokenize(sent)]
```

Converting all the cases (upper, lower, and proper) into lowercase reduces duplicates in corpus:

```
...     tokens = [word.lower() for word in tokens]
```

As mentioned earlier, stop words are the words that do not carry much weight in understanding the sentence; they are used for connecting words, and so on. We have removed them with the following line of code:

```
...     stopwds = stopwords.words('english')
...     tokens = [token for token in tokens if token not in stopwds]
```

Keeping only the words with length greater than 3 in the following code for removing small words, which hardly consists of much of a meaning to carry:

```
...     tokens = [word for word in tokens if len(word)>=3]
```

Stemming is applied on the words using `PorterStemmer` function, which stems the extra suffixes from the words:

```
...     stemmer = PorterStemmer()
...     tokens = [stemmer.stem(word) for word in tokens]
```

POS tagging is a prerequisite for lemmatization, based on whether the word is noun or verb, and so on, it will reduce it to the root word:

```
...     tagged_corpus = pos_tag(tokens)
```

The `pos_tag` function returns the part of speed in four formats for noun and six formats for verb. NN (noun, common, singular), NNP (noun, proper, singular), NNPS (noun, proper, plural), NNS (noun, common, plural), VB (verb, base form), VBD (verb, past tense), VBG (verb, present participle), VBN (verb, past participle), VBP (verb, present tense, not third person singular), VBZ (verb, present tense, third person singular):

```
...     Noun_tags = ['NN','NNP','NNPS','NNS']
...     Verb_tags = ['VB','VBD','VBG','VBN','VBP','VBZ']
...     lemmatizer = WordNetLemmatizer()
```

The `prat_lemmatize` function has been created only for the reasons of mismatch between the `pos_tag` function and intake values of the lemmatize function. If the tag for any word falls under the respective noun or verb tags category, n or v will be applied accordingly in the lemmatize function:

```
...     def prat_lemmatize(token,tag):
...         if tag in Noun_tags:
...             return lemmatizer.lemmatize(token,'n')
...         elif tag in Verb_tags:
...             return lemmatizer.lemmatize(token,'v')
...         else:
...             return lemmatizer.lemmatize(token,'n')
```

After performing tokenization and applied all the various operations, we need to join it back to form stings and the following function performs the same:

```
...     pre_proc_text =  " ".join([prat_lemmatize(token,tag) for token,tag
in tagged_corpus])
...     return pre_proc_text
```

The following step applies the preprocessing function to the data and generates new corpus:

```
>>> smsdata_data_2 = []
>>> for i in smsdata_data:
...     smsdata_data_2.append(preprocessing(i))
```

Data will be split into train and test based on 70-30 split and converted to the NumPy array for applying machine learning algorithms:

```
>>> import numpy as np
>>> trainset_size = int(round(len(smsdata_data_2)*0.70))
>>> print ('The training set size for this classifier is ' +
str(trainset_size) + '\n')
>>> x_train = np.array([''.join(rec) for rec in
smsdata_data_2[0:trainset_size]])
>>> y_train = np.array([rec for rec in smsdata_labels[0:trainset_size]])
>>> x_test = np.array([''.join(rec) for rec in
smsdata_data_2[trainset_size+1:len( smsdata_data_2)]])
>>> y_test = np.array([rec for rec in smsdata_labels[trainset_size+1:len(
smsdata_labels)]])
```

The following code converts the words into a vectorizer format and applies **term frequency-inverse document frequency** (TF-IDF) weights, which is a way to increase weights to words with high frequency and at the same time penalize the general terms such as *the, him, at,* and so on. In the following code, we have restricted to most frequent 4,000 words in the vocabulary, none the less we can tune this parameter as well for checking where the better accuracies are obtained:

```
# building TFIDF vectorizer
>>> from sklearn.feature_extraction.text import TfidfVectorizer
>>> vectorizer = TfidfVectorizer(min_df=2, ngram_range=(1, 2),
stop_words='english',
    max_features= 4000,strip_accents='unicode',  norm='l2')
```

The TF-IDF transformation has been shown as follows on both train and test data. The `todense` function is used to create the data to visualize the content:

```
>>> x_train_2 = vectorizer.fit_transform(x_train).todense()
>>> x_test_2 = vectorizer.transform(x_test).todense()
```

Multinomial Naive Bayes classifier is suitable for classification with discrete features (example word counts), which normally requires large feature counts. However, in practice, fractional counts such as TF-IDF will also work well. If we do not mention any Laplace estimator, it does take the value of *1.0* means and it will add *1.0* against each term in numerator and total for denominator:

```
>>> from sklearn.naive_bayes import MultinomialNB
>>> clf = MultinomialNB().fit(x_train_2, y_train)

>>> ytrain_nb_predicted = clf.predict(x_train_2)
>>> ytest_nb_predicted = clf.predict(x_test_2)

>>> from sklearn.metrics import classification_report,accuracy_score
```

```
>>> print ("\nNaive Bayes - Train Confusion
Matrix\n\n",pd.crosstab(y_train, ytrain_nb_predicted,rownames =
["Actuall"],colnames = ["Predicted"]))
>>> print ("\nNaive Bayes- Train accuracy",round(accuracy_score(y_train,
ytrain_nb_predicted),3))
>>> print ("\nNaive Bayes  - Train Classification
Report\n",classification_report(y_train, ytrain_nb_predicted))

>>> print ("\nNaive Bayes - Test Confusion Matrix\n\n",pd.crosstab(y_test,
ytest_nb_predicted,rownames = ["Actuall"],colnames = ["Predicted"]))
>>> print ("\nNaive Bayes- Test accuracy",round(accuracy_score(y_test,
ytest_nb_predicted),3))
>>> print ("\nNaive Bayes  - Test Classification
Report\n",classification_report( y_test, ytest_nb_predicted))
```

```
Naive Bayes - Train Confusion Matrix

 Predicted    ham  spam
Actuall
ham          3381    0
spam           78  441

Naive Bayes- Train accuracy 0.98

Naive Bayes   - Train Classification Report
                 precision    recall  f1-score   support

          ham       0.98      1.00      0.99      3381
         spam       1.00      0.85      0.92       519

avg / total         0.98      0.98      0.98      3900


Naive Bayes - Test Confusion Matrix

 Predicted    ham  spam
Actuall
ham          1440    3
spam           54  174

Naive Bayes- Test accuracy 0.966

Naive Bayes   - Test Classification Report
                 precision    recall  f1-score   support

          ham       0.96      1.00      0.98      1443
         spam       0.98      0.76      0.86       228

avg / total         0.97      0.97      0.96      1671
```

From the previous results it is appearing that Naive Bayes has produced excellent results of 96.6 percent test accuracy with significant recall value of 76 percent for spam and almost 100 percent for ham.

However, if we would like to check what are the top 10 features based on their coefficients from Naive Bayes, the following code will be handy for this:

```
# printing top features
>>> feature_names = vectorizer.get_feature_names()
>>> coefs = clf.coef_
>>> intercept = clf.intercept_
>>> coefs_with_fns = sorted(zip(clf.coef_[0], feature_names))

>>> print ("\n\nTop 10 features - both first & last\n")
>>> n=10
>>> top_n_coefs = zip(coefs_with_fns[:n], coefs_with_fns[:-(n + 1):-1])
>>> for (coef_1, fn_1), (coef_2, fn_2) in top_n_coefs:
...     print('\t%.4f\t%-15s\t\t%.4f\t%-15s' % (coef_1, fn_1, coef_2,
fn_2))
```

```
Top 10 features - both first & last

    -8.7128 1hr              -5.5773 free
    -8.7128 1st love         -5.7141 txt
    -8.7128 2go              -5.8715 text
    -8.7128 2morrow          -6.0127 claim
    -8.7128 2mrw             -6.0740 stop
    -8.7128 2nd inning       -6.0809 mobil
    -8.7128 2nd sm           -6.1059 repli
    -8.7128 30ish            -6.1593 prize
    -8.7128 3rd              -6.1994 servic
    -8.7128 3rd natur        -6.2101 tone
```

Though the R language is not a popular choice for NLP processing, here we have presented the code. Readers are encouraged to change the code and see how accuracies are changing for better understanding of concepts. The R code for Naive Bayes classifier on SMS spam/ham data is as follows:

```
# Naive Bayes
smsdata = read.csv("SMSSpamCollection.csv",stringsAsFactors = FALSE)
# Try the following code for reading in case if you have
#issues while reading regularly with above code
#smsdata = read.csv("SMSSpamCollection.csv",
#stringsAsFactors = FALSE,fileEncoding="latin1")
str(smsdata)
```

```
smsdata$Type = as.factor(smsdata$Type)
table(smsdata$Type)

library(tm)
library(SnowballC)
# NLP Processing
sms_corpus <- Corpus(VectorSource(smsdata$SMS_Details))
corpus_clean_v1 <- tm_map(sms_corpus, removePunctuation)
corpus_clean_v2 <- tm_map(corpus_clean_v1, tolower)
corpus_clean_v3 <- tm_map(corpus_clean_v2, stripWhitespace)
corpus_clean_v4 <- tm_map(corpus_clean_v3, removeWords, stopwords())
corpus_clean_v5 <- tm_map(corpus_clean_v4, removeNumbers)
corpus_clean_v6 <- tm_map(corpus_clean_v5, stemDocument)

# Check the change in corpus
inspect(sms_corpus[1:3])
inspect(corpus_clean_v6[1:3])

sms_dtm <- DocumentTermMatrix(corpus_clean_v6)

smsdata_train <- smsdata[1:4169, ]
smsdata_test <- smsdata[4170:5572, ]

sms_dtm_train <- sms_dtm[1:4169, ]
sms_dtm_test <- sms_dtm[4170:5572, ]

sms_corpus_train <- corpus_clean_v6[1:4169]
sms_corpus_test <- corpus_clean_v6[4170:5572]

prop.table(table(smsdata_train$Type))
prop.table(table(smsdata_test$Type))
frac_trzero = (table(smsdata_train$Type)[[1]])/nrow(smsdata_train)
frac_trone = (table(smsdata_train$Type)[[2]])/nrow(smsdata_train)
frac_tszero = (table(smsdata_test$Type)[[1]])/nrow(smsdata_test)
frac_tsone = (table(smsdata_test$Type)[[2]])/nrow(smsdata_test)

Dictionary <- function(x) {
  if( is.character(x) ) {
    return (x)
  }
  stop('x is not a character vector')
}
# Create the dictionary with at least word appears 1 time
sms_dict <- Dictionary(findFreqTerms(sms_dtm_train, 1))
sms_train <- DocumentTermMatrix(sms_corpus_train,list(dictionary =
sms_dict))
sms_test <- DocumentTermMatrix(sms_corpus_test,list(dictionary = sms_dict))
convert_tofactrs <- function(x) {
```

```
  x <- ifelse(x > 0, 1, 0)
  x <- factor(x, levels = c(0, 1), labels = c("No", "Yes"))
  return(x)
}
sms_train <- apply(sms_train, MARGIN = 2, convert_tofactrs)
sms_test <- apply(sms_test, MARGIN = 2, convert_tofactrs)

# Application of Naïve Bayes Classifier with laplace Estimator
library(e1071)
nb_fit <- naiveBayes(sms_train, smsdata_train$Type,laplace = 1.0)

tr_y_pred = predict(nb_fit, sms_train)
ts_y_pred = predict(nb_fit,sms_test)
tr_y_act = smsdata_train$Type;ts_y_act = smsdata_test$Type

tr_tble = table(tr_y_act,tr_y_pred)
print(paste("Train Confusion Matrix"))
print(tr_tble)

tr_acc = accrcy(tr_y_act,tr_y_pred)
trprec_zero = prec_zero(tr_y_act,tr_y_pred);   trrecl_zero =
recl_zero(tr_y_act,tr_y_pred)
trprec_one = prec_one(tr_y_act,tr_y_pred); trrecl_one =
recl_one(tr_y_act,tr_y_pred)
trprec_ovll = trprec_zero *frac_trzero + trprec_one*frac_trone
trrecl_ovll = trrecl_zero *frac_trzero + trrecl_one*frac_trone

print(paste("Naive Bayes Train accuracy:",tr_acc))
print(paste("Naive Bayes - Train Classification Report"))
print(paste("Zero_Precision",trprec_zero,"Zero_Recall",trrecl_zero))
print(paste("One_Precision",trprec_one,"One_Recall",trrecl_one))
print(paste("Overall_Precision",round(trprec_ovll,4),"Overall_Recall",round
(trrecl_ovll,4)))

ts_tble = table(ts_y_act,ts_y_pred)
print(paste("Test Confusion Matrix"))
print(ts_tble)

ts_acc = accrcy(ts_y_act,ts_y_pred)
tsprec_zero = prec_zero(ts_y_act,ts_y_pred); tsrecl_zero =
recl_zero(ts_y_act,ts_y_pred)
tsprec_one = prec_one(ts_y_act,ts_y_pred); tsrecl_one =
recl_one(ts_y_act,ts_y_pred)
tsprec_ovll = tsprec_zero *frac_tszero + tsprec_one*frac_tsone
tsrecl_ovll = tsrecl_zero *frac_tszero + tsrecl_one*frac_tsone

print(paste("Naive Bayes Test accuracy:",ts_acc))
print(paste("Naive Bayes - Test Classification Report"))
```

```
print(paste("Zero_Precision",tsprec_zero,"Zero_Recall",tsrecl_zero))
print(paste("One_Precision",tsprec_one,"One_Recall",tsrecl_one))
print(paste("Overall_Precision",round(tsprec_ovll,4),"Overall_Recall",round
(tsrecl_ovll,4)))
```

Summary

In this chapter, you have learned about KNN and Naive Bayes techniques, which require somewhat a little less computational power. KNN in fact is called a lazy learner, as it does not learn anything apart from comparing with training data points to classify them into class. Also, you have seen how to tune the k-value using grid search technique. Whereas explanation has been provided for Naive Bayes classifier, NLP examples have been provided with all the famous NLP processing techniques to give you flavor of this field in a very crisp manner. Though in text processing, either Naive Bayes or SVM techniques could be used as these two techniques can handle data with high dimensionality, which is very relevant in NLP, as the number of word vectors are relatively high in dimensions and sparse at the same time.

In the next chapter, we will be discussing SVM and neural networks with introduction to deep learning models, as deep learning is becoming the next generation technology in implementing artificial intelligence, which is also receiving a lot of attention by the data science community recently!

6
Support Vector Machines and Neural Networks

In this chapter, we will be covering both support vector machines and neural networks, which are on the higher side of computational complexity and require relatively significant resources for calculations, but do provide significantly better results compared with other machine learning methods in most cases.

A **support vector machine (SVM)** can be imagined as a surface that maximizes the boundaries between various types of points of data that is represent in multidimensional space, also known as a hyperplane, which creates the most homogeneous points in each subregion.

Support vector machines can be used on any type of data, but have special extra advantages for data types with very high dimensions relative to the observations, for example:

- Text classification, in which language has the very dimensions of word vectors
- For the quality control of DNA sequencing by labeling chromatograms correctly

Support vector machines working principles

Support vector machines are mainly classified into three types based on their working principles:

- Maximum margin classifiers
- Support vector classifiers
- Support vector machines

Maximum margin classifier

People usually generalize support vector machines with maximum margin classifiers. However, there is much more to present in SVMs compared to maximum margin classifiers, which we will be covering in this chapter. It is feasible to draw infinite hyperplanes to classify the same set of data upon, but the million dollar question, is which one to consider as an ideal hyperplane? The maximum margin classifier provides an answer to that: the hyperplane with the maximum margin of separation width.

Hyperplanes: Before going forward, let us quickly review what a hyperplane is. In *n-dimensional* space, a hyperplane is a flat affine subspace of dimension n-1. This means, in 2-dimensional space, the hyperplane is a straight line which separates the 2-dimensional space into two halves. The hyperplane is defined by the following equation:

$$\beta_0 + \beta_1 X_1 + \beta_2 X_2 = 0$$

Points which lay on the hyperplane have to follow the above equation. However, there are regions above and below as well. This means observations could fall in either of the regions, also called the region of classes:

$$\beta_0 + \beta_1 X_1 + \beta_2 X_2 > 0$$

$$\beta_0 + \beta_1 X_1 + \beta_2 X_2 < 0$$

The mathematical representation of the maximum margin classifier is as follows, which is an optimization problem:

$$Objective\ function: \quad \underset{\beta_0, \beta_1, \dots, \beta_n}{\text{maximize}}\ M$$

$$Constraint\ 1: \quad subject\ to\ \sum_{j=1}^{n} \beta_j^2 = 1$$

$$Constraint\ 2: \quad y_i(\beta_0 + \beta_1 x_{i1} + \beta_2 x_{i2} + \cdots + \beta_n x_{in}) \geq M\ \forall\ i = 1, \dots, m$$

$$class\ labels: \quad y_1, \dots y_m \in \{-1, 1\}$$

Constraint 2 ensures that observations will be on the correct side of the hyperplane by taking the product of coefficients with x variables and finally, with a class variable indicator.

> In non-separable cases, the maximum margin classifier will not have a separating hyperplane, which is also known as no feasible solution. This issue will be solved with support vector classifiers, which we will be covering in the next section.

In the following diagram, we can draw infinite separate hyperplanes to separate the two classes (blue and red). However, the maximum margin classifier attempts to fit the widest slab (maximize the margin between positive and negative hyperplanes) between two classes and the observations touching both the positive and negative hyperplanes called support vectors:

> Classifier performance purely depends on the support vectors and any changes to observation values which are not support vectors (or observations that do not touch hyperplanes) do not impact any change in the performance of the Maximum Margin Classifier, as only extreme points are considered in the algorithm.

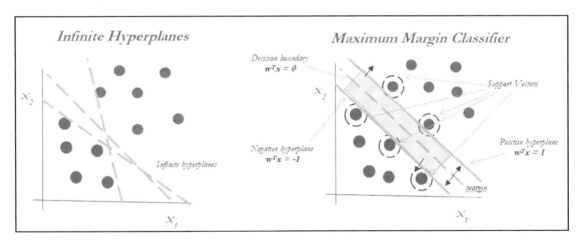

Support vector classifier

Support vector classifiers are an extended version of maximum margin classifiers, in which some violations are tolerated for non-separable cases in order to create the best fit, even with slight errors within the threshold limit. In fact, in real-life scenarios, we hardly find any data with purely separable classes; most classes have a few or more observations in overlapping classes.

The mathematical representation of the support vector classifier is as follows, a slight correction to the constraints to accommodate error terms:

$$Objective\ function: \quad \underset{\beta_0, \beta_1, \dots, \beta_n}{\text{maximize}}\ M$$

$$Constraint\ 1: \quad subject\ to\ \sum_{j=1}^{n} \beta_j^2 = 1$$

$$Constraint\ 2: \quad y_i(\beta_0 + \beta_1 x_{i1} + \beta_2 x_{i2} + \dots + \beta_n x_{in}) \geq M(1 - \varepsilon_i)\ \forall\ i = 1, \dots, m$$

$$Constraint\ 3: \quad \varepsilon_i \geq 0, \sum_{i=1}^{n} \varepsilon_i \leq C$$

$$class\ labels: \quad y_1, \dots y_m \in \{-1, 1\}$$

In constraint 4, the *C* value is a non-negative tuning parameter to either accommodate more or fewer overall errors in the model. Having a high value of *C* will lead to a more robust model, whereas a lower value creates the flexible model due to less violation of error terms. In practice the *C* value would be a tuning parameter as is usual with all machine learning models.

The impact of changing the *C* value on margins is shown in the following diagram; with the high value of *C*, the model would be more tolerating and also have space for violations (errors) in the left diagram, whereas with the lower value of *C*, no scope for accepting violations leads to a reduction in margin width. *C* is a tuning parameter in Support Vector Classifiers:

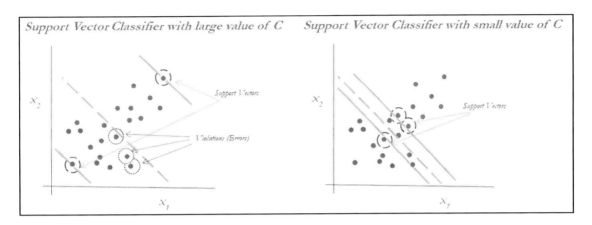

Support vector machines

Support vector machines are used when the decision boundary is non-linear and would not be separable with support vector classifiers whatever the cost function is! The following diagram explains the non-linearly separable cases for both 1-dimension and 2-dimensions:

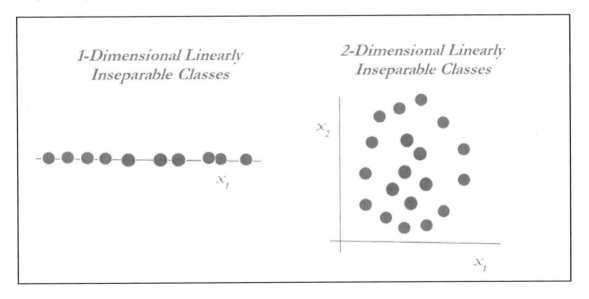

It is apparent that we cannot classify using support vector classifiers whatever the cost value is. Hence, we need to use another way of handling the data, called the kernel trick, using the kernel function to work with non-linearly separable data.

In the following diagram, a polynomial kernel with degree 2 has been applied in transforming the data from 1-dimensional to 2-dimensional data. By doing so, the data becomes linearly separable in higher dimensions. In the left diagram, different classes (red and blue) are plotted on X_1 only, whereas after applying degree 2, we now have 2-dimensions, X_1 and X^2_1 (the original and a new dimension). The degree of the polynomial kernel is a tuning parameter; the practitioner needs to tune them with various values to check where higher accuracies are possible with the model:

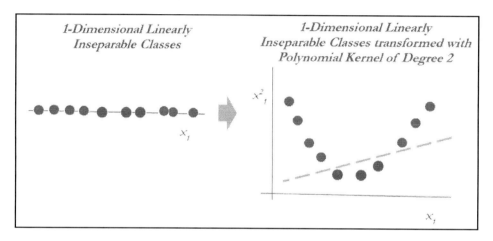

Whereas, in the 2-dimensional case, the kernel trick is applied as below with the polynomial kernel with degree 2. It seems that observations have been classified successfully using a linear plane after projecting the data into higher dimensions:

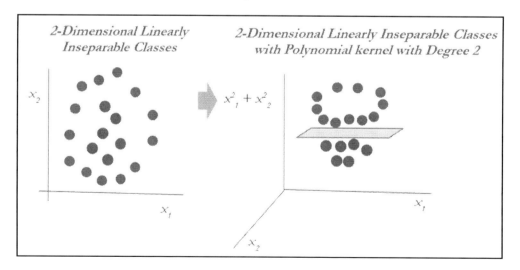

Kernel functions

Kernel functions are the functions that, given the original feature vectors, return the same value as the dot product of its corresponding mapped feature vectors. Kernel functions do not explicitly map the feature vectors to a higher-dimensional space, or calculate the dot product of the mapped vectors. Kernels produce the same value through a different series of operations that can often be computed more efficiently.

The main reason for using kernel functions is to eliminate the computational requirement to derive the higher-dimensional vector space from the given basic vector space, so that observations be separated linearly in higher dimensions. Why someone needs to like this is, derived vector space will grow exponentially with the increase in dimensions and it will become almost too difficult to continue computation, even when you have a variable size of 30 or so. The following example shows how the size of the variables grows.

Example: When we have two variables such as x and y, with a polynomial degree kernel, it needs to compute x^2, y^2, and xy dimensions in addition. Whereas, if we have three variables x, y, and z, then we need to calculate the x^2, y^2, z^2, xy, yz, xz, and xyz vector spaces. You will have realized by this time that the increase of one more dimension creates so many combinations. Hence, care needs to be taken to reduce its computational complexity; this is where kernels do wonders. Kernels are defined more formally in the following equation:

$$K(x,z) = < \Phi(x), \Phi(z) >$$

Polynomial Kernel: Polynomial kernels are popularly used, especially with degree 2. In fact, the inventor of support vector machines, *Vladimir N Vapnik*, developed using a degree 2 kernel for classifying handwritten digits. Polynomial kernels are given by the following equation:

$$K(x,x') = (1 + x * x')^k$$

Radial Basis Function (RBF) / Gaussian Kernel: RBF kernels are a good first choice for problems requiring nonlinear models. A decision boundary that is a hyperplane in the mapped feature space is similar to a decision boundary that is a hypersphere in the original space. The feature space produced by the Gaussian kernel can have an infinite number of dimensions, a feat that would be impossible otherwise. RBF kernels are represented by the following equation:

$$K(x,x') = e(- ||x - x'||^2 / \sigma^2)$$

This is often simplified as the following equation:

$$K(x, x') = e(-\gamma ||x - x'||^2); \quad \gamma = hyperparameter$$

It is advisable to scale the features when using support vector machines, but it is very important when using the RBF kernel. When the value of the gamma γ value is small, it gives you a pointed bump in the higher dimensions; a larger value gives you a softer, broader bump. A small gamma will give you low bias and high variance solutions; on the other hand, a high gamma will give you high bias and low variance solutions and that is how you control the fit of the model using RBF kernels:

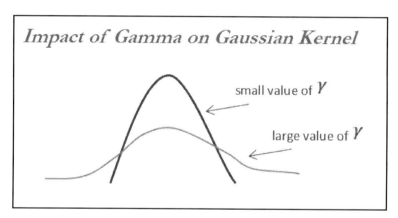

SVM multilabel classifier with letter recognition data example

Letter recognition data has been used from the UCI machine learning repository for illustration purposes using SVM classifiers. The link for downloading the data is here: https://archive.ics.uci.edu/ml/datasets/letter+recognition. The task is to identify each of a large number of black and white rectangular pixel displays as one of the 26 capital letters in the English alphabet (from A to Z; 26 classes altogether) based on a few characteristics in integers, such as x-box (horizontal position of box), y-box (vertical position of box), width of the box, height of the box, and so on:

```
>>> import os
""" First change the following directory link to where all input files do
exist """
>>> os.chdir("D:\\Book writing\\Codes\\Chapter 6")
```

```
>>> import pandas as pd
>>> letterdata = pd.read_csv("letterdata.csv")
>>> print (letterdata.head())
```

letter	xbox	ybox	width	height	onpix	xbar	ybar	x2bar	y2bar	xybar	x2ybar	xy2bar	xedge	xedgey	yedge	yedgex
T	2	8	3	5	1	8	13	0	6	6	10	8	0	8	0	8
I	5	12	3	7	2	10	5	5	4	13	3	9	2	8	4	10
D	4	11	6	8	6	10	6	2	6	10	3	7	3	7	3	9
N	7	11	6	6	3	5	9	4	6	4	4	10	6	10	2	8
G	2	1	3	1	1	8	6	6	6	6	5	9	1	7	5	10

Following code is used to remove the target variable from x variables and at the same time create new y variable for convenience:

```
>>> x_vars = letterdata.drop(['letter'],axis=1)
>>> y_var = letterdata["letter"]
```

As scikit-learn does not directly support characters, we need to convert them into number mappings. Here, we have done so with the dictionary:

```
>>> y_var = y_var.replace({'A':1,'B':2,'C':3,'D':4,'E':5,'F':6,'G':7,
'H':8,'I':9,
'J':10,'K':11,'L':12,'M':13,'N':14,'O':15,'P':16,'Q':17,'R':18,'S':19,'T':2
0,'U':21, 'V':22, 'W':23,'X':24,'Y':25,'Z':26})

>>> from sklearn.metrics import accuracy_score,classification_report
>>> from sklearn.model_selection import train_test_split
>>> x_train,x_test,y_train,y_test =
train_test_split(x_vars,y_var,train_size = 0.7,random_state=42)

# Linear Classifier
>>> from sklearn.svm import SVC
```

Maximum margin classifier - linear kernel

The following code shows a linear classifier (also known as a maximum margin classifier) with cost value as 1.0:

```
>>> svm_fit = SVC(kernel='linear',C=1.0,random_state=43)
>>> svm_fit.fit(x_train,y_train)

>>> print ("\nSVM Linear Classifier - Train Confusion
Matrix\n\n",pd.crosstab(y_train, svm_fit.predict(x_train),rownames =
["Actuall"],colnames = ["Predicted"]) )
>>> print ("\nSVM Linear Classifier - Train
accuracy:",round(accuracy_score(y_train, svm_fit.predict(x_train)),3))
```

```
>>> print ("\nSVM Linear Classifier - Train Classification Report\n",
classification_report(y_train,svm_fit.predict(x_train)))
```

```
SVM Linear Classifier - Train accuracy: 0.876

SVM Linear Classifier - Train Classification Report
             precision    recall  f1-score   support

          1       0.93      0.97      0.95       557
          2       0.82      0.90      0.86       537
          3       0.89      0.91      0.90       535
          4       0.82      0.92      0.87       555
          5       0.81      0.84      0.83       530
          6       0.84      0.89      0.86       564
          7       0.76      0.80      0.78       543
          8       0.75      0.71      0.73       516
          9       0.92      0.88      0.90       534
         10       0.89      0.90      0.90       519
         11       0.84      0.84      0.84       551
         12       0.91      0.89      0.90       530
         13       0.93      0.92      0.93       540
         14       0.94      0.93      0.94       552
         15       0.89      0.78      0.83       535
         16       0.96      0.89      0.92       555
         17       0.88      0.84      0.86       530
         18       0.81      0.85      0.82       524
         19       0.75      0.73      0.74       513
         20       0.92      0.90      0.91       564
         21       0.95      0.94      0.94       552
         22       0.92      0.92      0.92       527
         23       0.93      0.95      0.94       539
         24       0.89      0.89      0.89       542
         25       0.94      0.91      0.92       535
         26       0.90      0.84      0.87       521

avg / total       0.88      0.88      0.88     14000
```

Following code used for printing the test accuracy values:

```
>>> print ("\n\nSVM Linear Classifier - Test Confusion
Matrix\n\n",pd.crosstab(y_test, svm_fit.predict(x_test),rownames =
["Actuall"],colnames = ["Predicted"]))
>>> print ("\nSVM Linear Classifier - Test accuracy:",round(accuracy_score(
y_test,svm_fit.predict(x_test)),3))
>>> print ("\nSVM Linear Classifier - Test Classification Report\n",
classification_report(y_test,svm_fit.predict(x_test)))
```

```
SVM Linear Classifier - Test accuracy: 0.85

SVM Linear Classifier - Test Classification Report
             precision    recall  f1-score   support

          1       0.87      0.94      0.90       232
          2       0.80      0.86      0.83       229
          3       0.86      0.86      0.86       201
          4       0.77      0.89      0.83       250
          5       0.81      0.88      0.84       238
          6       0.81      0.89      0.85       211
          7       0.74      0.75      0.74       230
          8       0.70      0.63      0.67       218
          9       0.89      0.85      0.87       221
         10       0.85      0.85      0.85       228
         11       0.77      0.79      0.78       188
         12       0.93      0.88      0.90       231
         13       0.95      0.93      0.94       252
         14       0.91      0.90      0.91       231
         15       0.86      0.79      0.82       218
         16       0.97      0.83      0.89       248
         17       0.84      0.77      0.81       253
         18       0.74      0.82      0.78       234
         19       0.73      0.72      0.73       235
         20       0.90      0.89      0.89       232
         21       0.94      0.90      0.92       261
         22       0.89      0.93      0.91       237
         23       0.89      0.94      0.91       213
         24       0.91      0.88      0.89       245
         25       0.94      0.88      0.91       251
         26       0.84      0.82      0.83       213

avg / total       0.85      0.85      0.85      6000
```

From the above results, we can see that test accuracy for the linear classifier is 85 percentage, which is a decent value in terms of accuracy. Let us explore the polynomial kernel as well.

Polynomial kernel

A polynomial kernel with degree of 2 has been used in the following code to check whether any improvement in accuracy is possible. The cost value has been kept constant with respect to the linear classifier in order to determine the impact of the non-linear kernel:

```
#Polynomial Kernel
>>> svm_poly_fit = SVC(kernel='poly',C=1.0,degree=2)
>>> svm_poly_fit.fit(x_train,y_train)
>>> print ("\nSVM Polynomial Kernel Classifier - Train Confusion
Matrix\n\n",pd.crosstab(y_train,svm_poly_fit.predict(x_train),rownames =
["Actuall"],colnames = ["Predicted"]) )
>>> print ("\nSVM Polynomial Kernel Classifier - Train
accuracy:",round(accuracy_score( y_train,svm_poly_fit.predict(x_train)),3))
>>> print ("\nSVM Polynomial Kernel Classifier - Train Classification
Report\n", classification_report(y_train,svm_poly_fit.predict(x_train)))
```

```
SVM Polynomial Kernel Classifier - Train accuracy: 0.989

SVM Polynomial Kernel Classifier - Train Classification Report
             precision    recall  f1-score   support

          1       1.00      1.00      1.00       557
          2       0.98      0.98      0.98       537
          3       1.00      0.99      0.99       535
          4       0.97      0.99      0.98       555
          5       0.99      0.98      0.98       530
          6       0.98      0.99      0.98       564
          7       0.98      0.99      0.98       543
          8       0.98      0.95      0.96       516
          9       0.98      0.98      0.98       534
         10       0.99      0.98      0.98       519
         11       0.99      0.98      0.98       551
         12       1.00      0.99      1.00       530
         13       1.00      1.00      1.00       540
         14       1.00      0.99      0.99       552
         15       0.99      1.00      0.99       535
         16       0.99      0.97      0.98       555
         17       1.00      1.00      1.00       530
         18       0.96      0.98      0.97       524
         19       0.99      0.99      0.99       513
         20       1.00      0.99      1.00       564
         21       0.99      1.00      1.00       552
         22       0.99      0.99      0.99       527
         23       1.00      1.00      1.00       539
         24       0.99      1.00      1.00       542
         25       1.00      1.00      1.00       535
         26       1.00      1.00      1.00       521

avg / total       0.99      0.99      0.99     14000
```

```
>>> print ("\n\nSVM Polynomial Kernel Classifier - Test Confusion
Matrix\n\n", pd.crosstab(y_test,svm_poly_fit.predict(x_test),rownames =
["Actual1"],colnames = ["Predicted"]))
>>> print ("\nSVM Polynomial Kernel Classifier - Test
accuracy:",round(accuracy_score( y_test,svm_poly_fit.predict(x_test)),3))
>>> print ("\nSVM Polynomial Kernel Classifier - Test Classification
Report\n", classification_report(y_test,svm_poly_fit.predict(x_test)))
```

```
SVM Polynomial Kernel Classifier - Test accuracy: 0.954

SVM Polynomial Kernel Classifier - Test Classification Report
            precision   recall  f1-score   support

        1      0.98       0.99     0.99       232
        2      0.92       0.96     0.94       229
        3      0.92       0.95     0.93       201
        4      0.91       0.94     0.93       250
        5      0.93       0.96     0.95       238
        6      0.92       0.97     0.94       211
        7      0.94       0.93     0.94       230
        8      0.92       0.87     0.89       218
        9      0.96       0.95     0.96       221
       10      0.96       0.94     0.95       228
       11      0.90       0.93     0.91       188
       12      0.98       0.95     0.97       231
       13      0.98       0.98     0.98       252
       14      0.96       0.94     0.95       231
       15      0.94       0.95     0.94       218
       16      0.99       0.95     0.97       248
       17      0.98       0.93     0.95       253
       18      0.91       0.94     0.92       234
       19      0.98       0.98     0.98       235
       20      0.98       0.97     0.97       232
       21      0.98       0.97     0.98       261
       22      0.98       0.96     0.97       237
       23      0.96       0.97     0.96       213
       24      0.95       0.96     0.96       245
       25      0.97       0.98     0.97       251
       26      0.98       0.98     0.98       213

avg / total    0.95       0.95     0.95      6000
```

The polynomial kernel has produced test accuracy of 95.4 percentage, which is a drastic improvement compared with the test accuracy from the linear classifier, which is 85 percentage. By moving one degree higher, we have achieved a 10 percentage uplift in accuracy.

RBF kernel

In the last experiment, an RBF kernel was used to determine the test accuracy. Here, the cost value is kept constant with respective other kernels but the gamma value has been chosen as 0.1 to fit the model:

```
#RBF Kernel
>>> svm_rbf_fit = SVC(kernel='rbf',C=1.0, gamma=0.1)
>>> svm_rbf_fit.fit(x_train,y_train)
>>> print ("\nSVM RBF Kernel Classifier - Train Confusion
Matrix\n\n",pd.crosstab( y_train,svm_rbf_fit.predict(x_train),rownames =
["Actuall"],colnames = ["Predicted"]))
>>> print ("\nSVM RBF Kernel Classifier - Train
accuracy:",round(accuracy_score( y_train, svm_rbf_fit.predict(x_train)),3))
>>> print ("\nSVM RBF Kernel Classifier - Train Classification Report\n",
classification_report(y_train,svm_rbf_fit.predict(x_train)))
```

```
SVM RBF Kernel Classifier - Train accuracy: 0.998

SVM RBF Kernel Classifier - Train Classification Report
            precision    recall  f1-score    support

         1     1.00       1.00     1.00        557
         2     1.00       1.00     1.00        537
         3     1.00       1.00     1.00        535
         4     1.00       1.00     1.00        555
         5     1.00       0.99     1.00        530
         6     0.99       1.00     0.99        564
         7     0.99       1.00     0.99        543
         8     0.99       0.99     0.99        516
         9     1.00       0.99     0.99        534
        10     0.99       1.00     0.99        519
        11     1.00       1.00     1.00        551
        12     1.00       1.00     1.00        530
        13     1.00       1.00     1.00        540
        14     1.00       1.00     1.00        552
        15     1.00       1.00     1.00        535
        16     1.00       0.99     1.00        555
        17     1.00       1.00     1.00        530
        18     0.99       1.00     1.00        524
        19     1.00       1.00     1.00        513
        20     1.00       1.00     1.00        564
        21     1.00       1.00     1.00        552
        22     0.99       1.00     1.00        527
        23     1.00       1.00     1.00        539
        24     1.00       1.00     1.00        542
        25     1.00       1.00     1.00        535
        26     1.00       1.00     1.00        521

avg / total     1.00       1.00     1.00      14000
```

```
>>> print ("\n\nSVM RBF Kernel Classifier - Test Confusion Matrix\n\n",
pd.crosstab(y_test,svm_rbf_fit.predict(x_test),rownames =
["Actuall"],colnames = ["Predicted"]))
>>> print ("\nSVM RBF Kernel Classifier - Test accuracy:",round(
accuracy_score( y_test,svm_rbf_fit.predict(x_test)),3))
>>> print ("\nSVM RBF Kernel Classifier - Test Classification Report\n",
classification_report(y_test,svm_rbf_fit.predict(x_test)))
```

```
SVM RBF Kernel Classifier - Test accuracy: 0.969

SVM RBF Kernel Classifier - Test Classification Report
              precision    recall  f1-score    support

        1        0.99       1.00      0.99        232
        2        0.93       0.97      0.95        229
        3        0.98       0.93      0.96        201
        4        0.95       0.97      0.96        250
        5        0.98       0.98      0.98        238
        6        0.96       0.98      0.97        211
        7        0.97       0.96      0.96        230
        8        0.94       0.87      0.90        218
        9        0.98       0.95      0.97        221
       10        0.95       0.96      0.96        228
       11        0.93       0.94      0.93        188
       12        0.99       0.98      0.98        231
       13        0.96       1.00      0.98        252
       14        0.99       0.95      0.97        231
       15        0.94       0.97      0.95        218
       16        0.99       0.96      0.97        248
       17        0.99       0.97      0.98        253
       18        0.89       0.96      0.92        234
       19        0.99       0.99      0.99        235
       20        0.98       0.99      0.99        232
       21        1.00       0.99      0.99        261
       22        0.97       0.97      0.97        237
       23        0.99       1.00      0.99        213
       24        0.98       0.96      0.97        245
       25        0.98       0.99      0.99        251
       26        1.00       0.99      0.99        213

avg / total      0.97       0.97      0.97       6000
```

The test accuracy obtained from the RBF kernel is 96.9 percentage, which is slightly better than the polynomial kernel's 95.4 percent. However, by careful tuning of parameters using grid search, test accuracy can be further improved.

Grid search has been performed by changing cost and gamma values using the RBF kernel. The following code describes the details:

```
# Grid Search - RBF Kernel
>>> from sklearn.pipeline import Pipeline
>>> from sklearn.model_selection import train_test_split,GridSearchCV

>>> pipeline = Pipeline([('clf',SVC(kernel='rbf',C=1,gamma=0.1 ))])

>>> parameters = {'clf__C':(0.1,0.3,1,3,10,30),
            'clf__gamma':(0.001,0.01,0.1,0.3,1)}

>>> grid_search_rbf = GridSearchCV(pipeline,parameters,n_jobs=-1,cv=5,
verbose=1, scoring='accuracy')
>>> grid_search_rbf.fit(x_train,y_train)

>>> print ('RBF Kernel Grid Search Best Training score: %0.3f' %
grid_search_rbf.best_score_)
>>> print ('RBF Kernel Grid Search Best parameters set:')
>>> best_parameters = grid_search_rbf.best_estimator_.get_params()

>>> for param_name in sorted(parameters.keys()):
...     print ('\t%s: %r' % (param_name, best_parameters[param_name]))
```

```
RBF Kernel Grid Search Best Training score: 0.968
RBF Kernel Grid Search Best parameters set:
        clf__C: 3
        clf__gamma: 0.1
```

```
>>> predictions = grid_search_rbf.predict(x_test)
>>> print ("RBF Kernel Grid Search - Testing
accuracy:",round(accuracy_score(y_test, predictions),4))
>>> print ("\nRBF Kernel Grid Search - Test Classification
Report",classification_report( y_test, predictions))
>>> print ("\n\nRBF Kernel Grid Search- Test Confusion
Matrix\n\n",pd.crosstab(y_test, predictions,rownames = ["Actuall"],colnames
= ["Predicted"]))
```

```
RBF Kernel Grid Search - Testing accuracy: 0.9715

RBF Kernel Grid Search - Test Classification Report
               precision    recall   f1-score    support

           1      0.99        1.00       0.99        232
           2      0.94        0.98       0.96        229
           3      0.99        0.95       0.97        201
           4      0.97        0.98       0.97        250
           5      0.97        0.97       0.97        238
           6      0.95        0.97       0.96        211
           7      0.97        0.97       0.97        230
           8      0.95        0.89       0.92        218
           9      0.99        0.95       0.97        221
          10      0.95        0.97       0.96        228
          11      0.92        0.95       0.94        188
          12      0.99        0.98       0.98        231
          13      0.96        1.00       0.98        252
          14      0.98        0.95       0.97        231
          15      0.95        0.97       0.96        218
          16      0.98        0.96       0.97        248
          17      0.99        0.97       0.98        253
          18      0.90        0.96       0.93        234
          19      0.99        0.99       0.99        235
          20      0.98        1.00       0.99        232
          21      1.00        0.98       0.99        261
          22      0.98        0.97       0.98        237
          23      0.99        1.00       0.99        213
          24      0.99        0.96       0.98        245
          25      0.99        0.99       0.99        251
          26      1.00        0.98       0.99        213

avg / total       0.97        0.97       0.97       6000
```

By observing the above results, we can conclude that the best test accuracy obtained was 97.15 percentage, which is a higher value than obtained by any other classifiers. Hence, we can conclude that RBF kernels produce the best results possible!

The following R Code for SVM Classifier:

```
# SVM Classifier
# First change the following  directory link to where all the input files
do exist
setwd("D:\\Book  writing\\Codes\\Chapter 6")
letter_data = read.csv("letterdata.csv")
set.seed(123)
numrow = nrow(letter_data)
trnind = sample(1:numrow,size =  as.integer(0.7*numrow))
train_data =  letter_data[trnind,]
test_data = letter_data[-trnind,]
library(e1071)
accrcy <- function(matrx){
  return(  sum(diag(matrx)/sum(matrx)))}
precsn <- function(matrx){
  return(diag(matrx) /  rowSums(matrx)) }
recll <- function(matrx){
  return(diag(matrx) /  colSums(matrx)) }
# SVM - Linear Kernel
svm_fit = svm(letter~.,data = train_data,kernel="linear",cost=1.0,  scale
= TRUE)
tr_y_pred = predict(svm_fit,  train_data)
ts_y_pred =  predict(svm_fit,test_data)
tr_y_act =  train_data$letter;ts_y_act = test_data$letter
tr_tble =  table(tr_y_act,tr_y_pred)
print(paste("Train  Confusion Matrix"))
print(tr_tble)
tr_acc = accrcy(tr_tble)
print(paste("SVM Linear  Kernel Train accuracy:",round(tr_acc,4)))
tr_prec = precsn(tr_tble)
print(paste("SVM Linear  Kernel Train Precision:"))
print(tr_prec)
tr_rcl = recll(tr_tble)
print(paste("SVM Linear Kernel  Train Recall:"))
print(tr_rcl)
ts_tble =  table(ts_y_act,ts_y_pred)
print(paste("Test  Confusion Matrix"))
print(ts_tble)
ts_acc = accrcy(ts_tble)
print(paste("SVM Linear  Kernel Test accuracy:",round(ts_acc,4)))
ts_prec = precsn(ts_tble)
print(paste("SVM Linear  Kernel Test Precision:"))
print(ts_prec)
```

```
ts_rcl = recll(ts_tble)
print(paste("SVM Linear   Kernel Test Recall:"))
print(ts_rcl)
# SVM - Polynomial Kernel
svm_poly_fit =    svm(letter~.,data =
train_data,kernel="poly",cost=1.0,degree = 2     ,scale = TRUE)
tr_y_pred =    predict(svm_poly_fit, train_data)
ts_y_pred =    predict(svm_poly_fit,test_data)
tr_y_act =    train_data$letter;ts_y_act = test_data$letter
tr_tble =    table(tr_y_act,tr_y_pred)
print(paste("Train   Confusion Matrix"))
print(tr_tble)
tr_acc = accrcy(tr_tble)
print(paste("SVM   Polynomial Kernel Train accuracy:",round(tr_acc,4)))
tr_prec = precsn(tr_tble)
print(paste("SVM   Polynomial Kernel Train Precision:"))
print(tr_prec)
tr_rcl = recll(tr_tble)
print(paste("SVM   Polynomial Kernel Train Recall:"))
print(tr_rcl)
ts_tble =    table(ts_y_act,ts_y_pred)
print(paste("Test   Confusion Matrix"))
print(ts_tble)
ts_acc = accrcy(ts_tble)
print(paste("SVM   Polynomial Kernel Test accuracy:",round(ts_acc,4)))
ts_prec = precsn(ts_tble)
print(paste("SVM   Polynomial Kernel Test Precision:"))
print(ts_prec)
ts_rcl = recll(ts_tble)
print(paste("SVM   Polynomial Kernel Test Recall:"))
print(ts_rcl)
# SVM - RBF Kernel
svm_rbf_fit = svm(letter~.,data   =
train_data,kernel="radial",cost=1.0,gamma = 0.2   ,scale = TRUE)
tr_y_pred =    predict(svm_rbf_fit, train_data)
ts_y_pred =    predict(svm_rbf_fit,test_data)
tr_y_act =    train_data$letter;ts_y_act = test_data$letter
tr_tble =    table(tr_y_act,tr_y_pred)
print(paste("Train   Confusion Matrix"))
print(tr_tble)
tr_acc = accrcy(tr_tble)
print(paste("SVM RBF   Kernel Train accuracy:",round(tr_acc,4)))
tr_prec = precsn(tr_tble)
print(paste("SVM RBF   Kernel Train Precision:"))
print(tr_prec)
tr_rcl = recll(tr_tble)
print(paste("SVM RBF   Kernel Train Recall:"))
print(tr_rcl)
```

```
ts_tble =   table(ts_y_act,ts_y_pred)
print(paste("Test   Confusion Matrix"))
print(ts_tble)
ts_acc = accrcy(ts_tble)
print(paste("SVM RBF   Kernel Test accuracy:",round(ts_acc,4)))
ts_prec = precsn(ts_tble)
print(paste("SVM RBF   Kernel Test Precision:"))
print(ts_prec)
ts_rcl = recll(ts_tble)
print(paste("SVM RBF   Kernel Test Recall:"))
print(ts_rcl)
# Grid search - RBF Kernel
library(e1071)
svm_rbf_grid =   tune(svm,letter~.,data =
train_data,kernel="radial",scale=TRUE,ranges   = list(
  cost = c(0.1,0.3,1,3,10,30),
  gamma =   c(0.001,0.01,0.1,0.3,1) ),
  tunecontrol =   tune.control(cross = 5))
print(paste("Best   parameter from Grid Search"))
print(summary(svm_rbf_grid))
best_model =   svm_rbf_grid$best.model
tr_y_pred = predict(best_model,data   = train_data,type = "response")
ts_y_pred =   predict(best_model,newdata = test_data,type = "response")
tr_y_act =   train_data$letter;ts_y_act = test_data$letter
tr_tble =   table(tr_y_act,tr_y_pred)
print(paste("Train   Confusion Matrix"))
print(tr_tble)
tr_acc = accrcy(tr_tble)
print(paste("SVM RBF   Kernel Train accuracy:",round(tr_acc,4)))
tr_prec = precsn(tr_tble)
print(paste("SVM RBF   Kernel Train Precision:"))
print(tr_prec)
tr_rcl = recll(tr_tble)
print(paste("SVM RBF   Kernel Train Recall:"))
print(tr_rcl)
ts_tble =   table(ts_y_act,ts_y_pred)
print(paste("Test   Confusion Matrix"))
print(ts_tble)
ts_acc = accrcy(ts_tble)
print(paste("SVM RBF   Kernel Test accuracy:",round(ts_acc,4)))
ts_prec = precsn(ts_tble)
print(paste("SVM RBF   Kernel Test Precision:"))
print(ts_prec)
ts_rcl = recll(ts_tble)
print(paste("SVM RBF   Kernel Test Recall:"))
print(ts_rcl)
```

Artificial neural networks - ANN

Artificial neural networks (ANNs) model the relationship between a set of input signals and output signals using a model derived from a replica of the biological brain, which responds to stimuli from its sensory inputs. The human brain consists of about 90 billion neurons, with around 1 trillion connections between them; ANN methods try to model problems using interconnected artificial neurons (or nodes) to solve machine learning problems.

As we know, ANNs have taken inspiration from the biological neuron. We will spend some time understanding how biological neurons work. Incoming signals are received by the cell's dendrites through a biochemical process that allows the impulses to be weighted according to their relative importance. As the cell body begins to accumulate the incoming signals, a threshold is reached, at which the cell fires and the output signal is then transmitted via an electrochemical process down the axon. At the axon terminal, an electric signal is again processed as a chemical signal to be passed to its neighboring neurons, which will be dendrites to some other neuron.

A similar working principle is loosely used in building an artificial neural network, in which each neuron has a set of inputs, each of which is given a specific weight. The neuron computes a function on these weighted inputs. A linear neuron takes a linear combination of weighted input and applies an activation function (sigmoid, tanh, relu, and so on) on the aggregated sum. The details are shown in the following diagram.

The network feeds the weighted sum of the input into the logistic function (in case of `sigmoid` function). The logistic function returns a value between 0 and 1 based on the set threshold; for example, here we set the threshold as 0.7. Any accumulated signal greater than 0.7 gives the signal of 1 and vice versa; any accumulated signal less than 0.7 returns the value of 0:

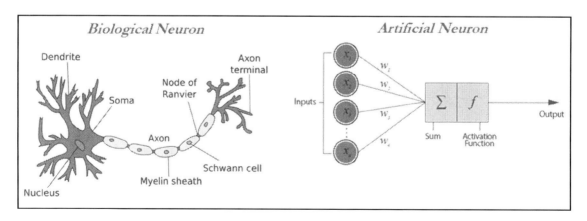

Neural network models are being considered as universal approximators, which means by using a neural network methodology, we can solve any type of problems with the fine-tuned architecture. Hence, studying neural networks is a branch of study and special care is needed. In fact, deep learning is a branch of machine learning, where every problem is being modeled with artificial neural networks.

A typical artificial neuron with n input dendrites can be represented by the following formula. The *w* weights allow each of the *n* inputs of *x* to contribute a greater or lesser amount to the sum of input signals. The accumulated value is passed to the activation function, *f(x)*, and the resulting signal, *y(x)*, is the output axon:

$$y(x) = f(\sum_{i=1}^{n} w_i x_i)$$

The parameters required for choosing for building neural networks are the following:

- **Activation function:** Choosing an activation function plays a major role in aggregating signals into the output signal to be propagated to the other neurons of the network.
- **Network architecture or topology:** This represents the number of layers required and the number of neurons in each layer. More layers and neurons will create a highly non-linear decision boundary, whereas if we reduce the architecture, the model will be less flexible and more robust.
- **Training optimization algorithm:** The selection of an optimization algorithm plays a critical role as well, in order to converge quickly and accurately to the best optimal solutions, which we will be covering in detail in later sections of this chapter.
- **Applications of Neural Networks:** In recent years, neural networks (a branch of deep learning) has gained huge attention in terms of its application in artificial intelligence, in terms of speech, text, vision, and many other areas. We will introduce deep learning in later sections of this chapter. Some of the famous applications are the following:
    - **Images and videos:** To identify an object in an image or to classify whether it is a dog or a cat
    - **Text processing (NLP):** Deep-learning-based chatbot and so on
    - **Speech:** Recognize speech
    - **Structured data processing:** Building highly powerful models to obtain a non-linear decision boundary

Activation functions

Activation functions are the mechanisms by which an artificial neuron processes information and passes it throughout the network. The activation function takes a single number and performs a certain fixed mathematical functional mapping on it. There are many different types of activation functions. The most popular ones are the following:

- Sigmoid
- Tanh
- Relu
- Linear

Sigmoid function: Sigmoid has the mathematical form $\sigma(x) = 1 / (1+e{-x})$. It takes a real-valued number and squashes it into a range between 0 and 1. Sigmoid is a popular choice, which makes calculating derivatives easy and is easy to interpret.

Tanh function: Tanh squashes the real-valued number into the range *[-1, 1]*. The output is zero-centered. In practice, tanh non-linearity is always preferred to sigmoid non-linearity. Also, it can be proved that tanh is scaled sigmoid neuron $tanh(x) = 2\sigma\ (2x) - 1$.

Rectified Linear Unit (ReLU) function: ReLU has become very popular in the last few years. It computes the function $f(x) = max\ (0, x)$. Activation is simply thresholds at zero.

Linear function: The linear activation function is used in linear regression problems, where it always provides a derivative as 1 due to the function used being $f(x) = x$.

Relu is now popularly being used in place of **Sigmoid** or **Tanh** due to its better convergence property.

All the activation functions are described in the following diagram. The linear activation function is used in linear regression cases, whereas all the other activation functions are used for classification problems:

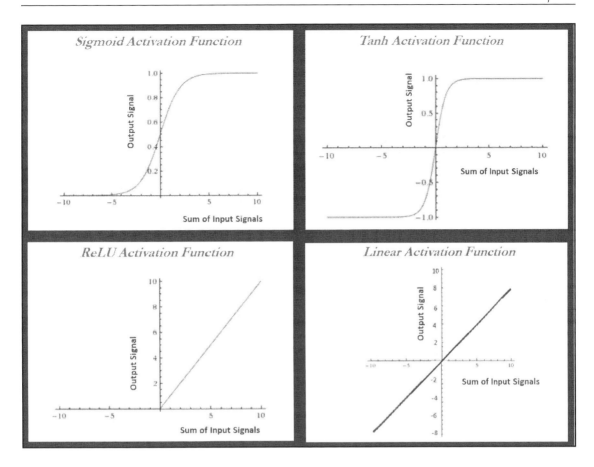

Forward propagation and backpropagation

Forward propagation and backpropagation are illustrated with the two hidden layer deep neural networks in the following example, in which both layers get three neurons each, in addition to input and output layers. The number of neurons in the input layer is based on the number of x (independent) variables, whereas the number of neurons in the output layer is decided by the number of classes the model needs to be predicted.

For ease, we have shown only one neuron in each layer; however, the reader can attempt to create other neurons within the same layer. Weights and biases are initiated from some random numbers, so that in both forward and backward passes, these can be updated in order to minimize the errors altogether.

During forward propagation, features are input to the network and fed through the following layers to produce the output activation. If we see in the hidden layer 1, the activation obtained is the combination of bias weight 1 and weighted combination of input values; if the overall value crosses the threshold, it will trigger to the next layer, else the signal will be 0 to the next layer values. Bias values are necessary to control the trigger points. In some cases, the weighted combination signal is low; in those cases, bias will compensate the extra amount for adjusting the aggregated value, which can trigger for the next level. The complete equation can be seen in the following diagram:

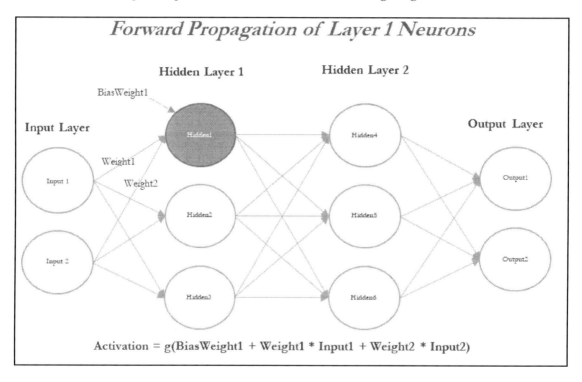

Once all the neurons are calculated in *Hidden Layer 1* (**Hidden1**, **Hidden2**, and **Hidden3** neurons), the next layer of neurons needs to be calculated in a similar way from the output of the hidden neurons from the first layer with the addition of bias (bias weight 4). The following figure describes the hidden neuron 4 shown in *layer 2*:

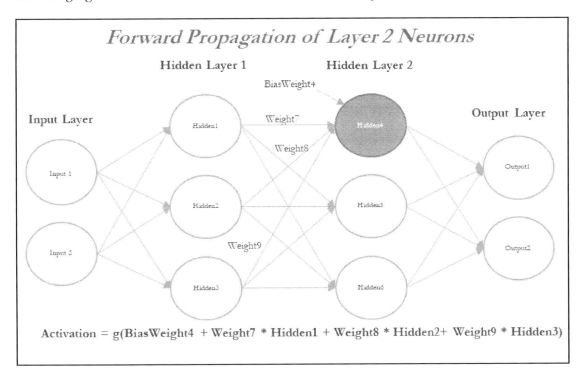

In the last layer (also known as the output layer), outputs are calculated in the same way from the outputs obtained from hidden layer 2 by taking the weighted combination of weights and outputs obtained from hidden layer 2. Once we obtain the output from the model, a comparison needs to be made with the actual value and we need to backpropagate the errors across the net backward in order to correct the weights of the entire neural network:

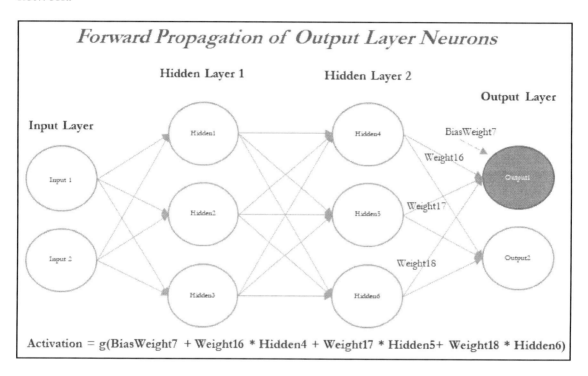

In the following diagram, we have taken the derivative of the output value and multiplied by that much amount to the error component, which was obtained from differencing the actual value with the model output:

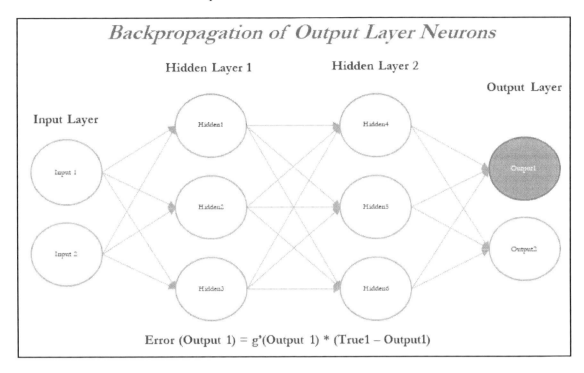

In a similar way, we will backpropagate the error from the second hidden layer as well. In the following diagram, errors are computed from the Hidden 4 neuron in the second hidden layer:

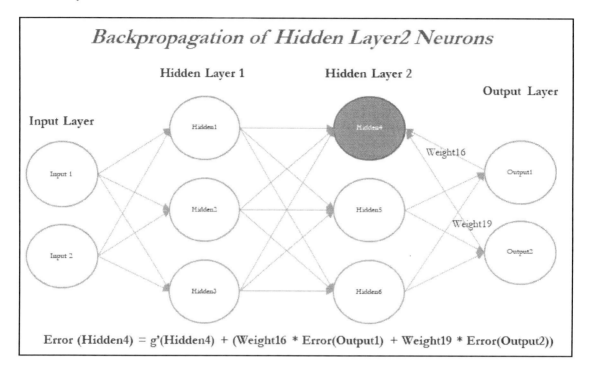

In the following diagram, errors are calculated for the Hidden 1 neuron in layer 1 based on errors obtained from all the neurons in layer 2:

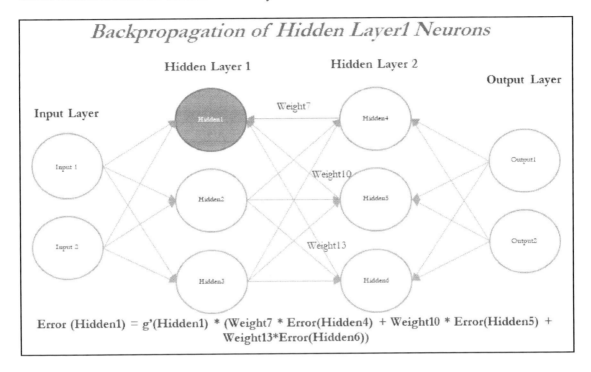

Once all the neurons in hidden layer 1 are updated, weights between inputs and the hidden layer also need to be updated, as we cannot update anything on input variables. In the following diagram, we will be updating the weights of both the inputs and also, at the same time, the neurons in hidden layer 1, as neurons in layer 1 utilize the weights from input only:

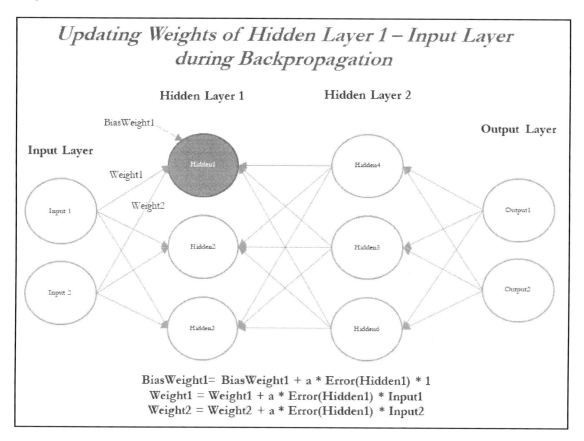

Finally, in the following figure, layer 2 neurons are being updated in the forward propagation pass:

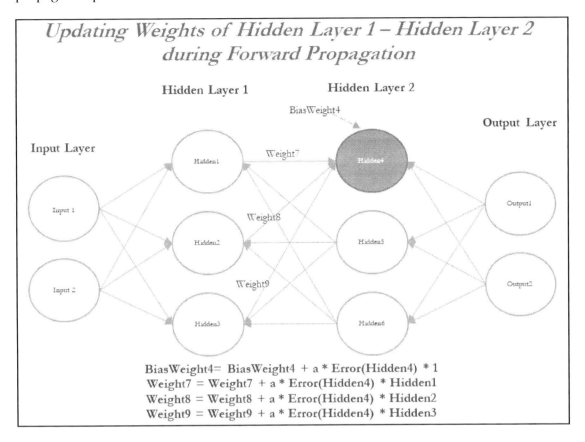

We have not shown the next iteration, in which neurons in the output layer are updated with errors and backpropagation started again. In a similar way, all the weights get updated until a solution converges or the number of iterations is reached.

Optimization of neural networks

Various techniques have been used for optimizing the weights of neural networks:

- **Stochastic gradient descent (SGD)**
- Momentum
- **Nesterov accelerated gradient (NAG)**
- Adaptive gradient (Adagrad)
- Adadelta
- RMSprop
- **Adaptive moment estimation (Adam)**
- **Limited memory Broyden-Fletcher-Goldfarb-Shanno (L-BFGS)**

In practice, **Adam** is a good default choice; we will be covering its working methodology in this section. If you cannot afford full batch updates, then try out L-BFGS:

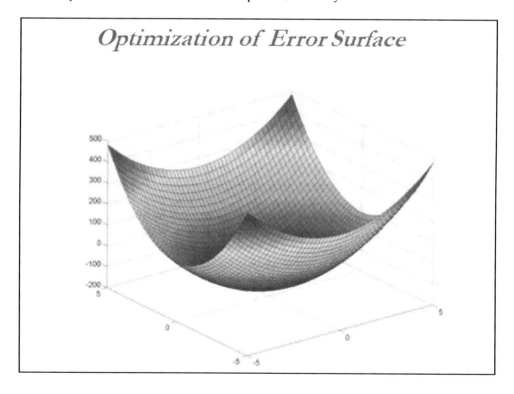

Stochastic gradient descent - SGD

Gradient descent is a way to minimize an objective function $J(\theta)$ parameterized by a model's parameter $\theta \ \varepsilon \ R^d$ by updating the parameters in the opposite direction of the gradient of the objective function with regard to the parameters. The learning rate determines the size of the steps taken to reach the minimum:

- Batch gradient descent (all training observations utilized in each iteration)
- SGD (one observation per iteration)
- Mini batch gradient descent (size of about 50 training observations for each iteration):

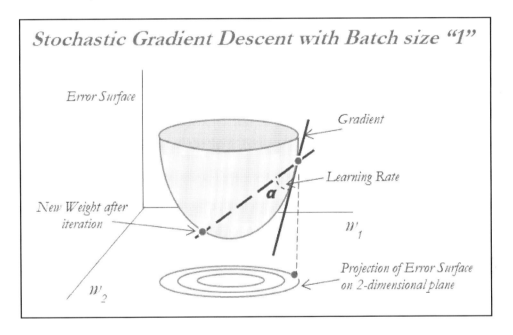

In the following image 2D projection has been observed carefully, in which convergence characteristics of both full batch and stochastic gradient descent with batch size 1 has been compared. If we see, full batch updates, are more smoother due to the consideration of all the observations. Whereas, SGD have wiggly convergence characteristics due to the reason of using 1 observation for each update:

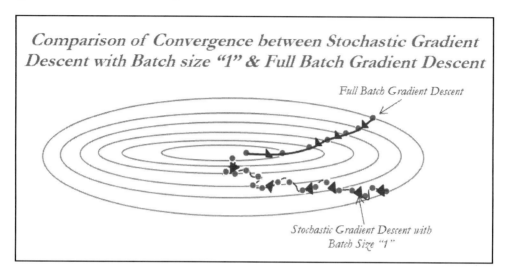

Momentum

SGD has trouble navigating surface curves much more steeply in one dimension than in the other; in these scenarios, SGD oscillates across the slopes of the ravine while only making hesitant progress along the bottom towards the local optimum.

When using momentum, we push a ball down a hill. The ball accumulates momentum as it rolls downhill, becoming faster and faster on the way until it stops (due to air resistance and so on); similarly, the momentum term increases for dimensions whose gradients point in the same direction and reduces updates for dimensions whose gradients change direction. As a result, we gain faster convergence and reduced oscillations:

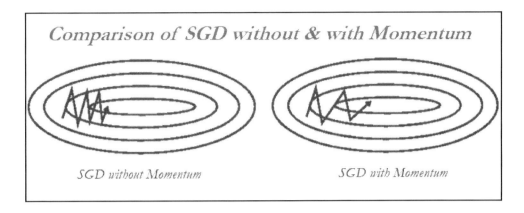

Nesterov accelerated gradient - NAG

If a ball rolls down a hill and blindly follows a slope, it is highly unsatisfactory and it should have a notion of where it is going so that it knows to slow down before the hill slopes up again. NAG is a way to give the momentum term this kind of prescience.

While momentum first computes the current gradient (small blue vector) and then takes a big jump in the direction of the updated accumulated gradient (big blue vector), NAG first makes a big jump in the direction of the previous accumulated gradient (brown vector), measures the gradient, and then makes a correction (green vector). This anticipatory update prevents the ball from going too fast and results in increased responsiveness and performance:

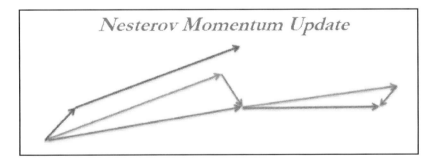

Adagrad

Adagrad is an algorithm for gradient-based optimization that adapts the differential learning rate to parameters, performing larger updates for infrequent parameters and smaller updates for frequent parameters.

Adagrad greatly improves the robustness of SGD and used it to train large-scale neural nets. One of Adagrad's main benefits is that it eliminates the need to manually tune the learning rate. Most implementations use a default value of 0.01 and leave it at that.

Adagrad's main weakness is its accumulation of the squared gradients in the denominator: since every added term is positive, the accumulated sum keeps growing during training. This, in turn, causes the learning rate to shrink and eventually become infinitesimally small, at which point the algorithm is no longer able to acquire additional knowledge. The following algorithms aim to resolve this flaw.

Adadelta

Adadelta is an extension of Adagrad that seeks to reduce its aggressive, monotonically decreasing learning rate. Instead of accumulating all past squared gradients, Adadelta restricts the window of accumulated past gradients to a fixed size w (instead of inefficiently storing w previous squared gradients, the sum of gradients is recursively defined as a decaying average of all past squared gradients).

RMSprop

RMSprop and **Adadelta** were both developed independently around the same time to resolve Adagrad's radically diminishing learning rates (RMSprop also divides the learning rate by an exponentially decaying average of squared gradients).

Adaptive moment estimation - Adam

Adam is another method that computes adaptive learning rates for each parameter. In addition to storing an exponentially decaying average of past squared gradients like Adadelta and RMSprop, Adam also keeps an exponentially decaying average of past gradients, similar to momentum.

When you are in doubt, just use Adam!

Limited-memory broyden-fletcher-goldfarb-shanno - L-BFGS optimization algorithm

L-BFGS is limited memory of BFGS, which is in the family of quasi-Newton methods that approximate the BFGS algorithm, which utilizes a limited amount of computer memory. BFGS is currently considered the most effective, and is by far the most popular, quasi-Newton update formula.

The L-BFGS methodology is best explained with the following diagram, in which iterations start at a random point (xt) and a second derivative, or hessian matrix, is computed at that point, which is a quadratic approximation of the original function; after computing the quadratic function, it computes the minimum in one step, and after calculating the new point ($xt+1$) for which the function value is minimum, that earlier point will become the starting point for the next iteration.

In the second iteration, another quadratic approximation will be taken at a new point (*xt+1*) and another minimum (*xt+2*) calculated in one step. In this way, L-BFGS converges to the solution in a much quicker way and it is effective even on the non-convex functions (in R code, we have used the nnet package, in which L-BFGS has been utilized for optimization purposes):

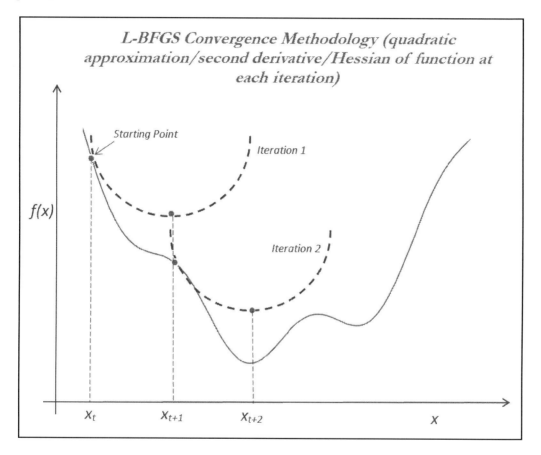

Dropout in neural networks

Dropout is regularization in neural networks to avoid overfitting of the data. Typically, dropout is 0.2 (80 percentage of neurons present randomly all the time) in initial layers and 0.5 in middle layers. One intuitive way to understand the dropout concept would be with the office team, in which a few team members are good with communication with clients though they are not good with technical details, whereas a few are good with technical knowledge but do not have good enough communication skills. Let's say some of the members take leave from the office, and then other members try to fill the shoes of others for the completion of work. In this way, team members who are good with communication will also learn technical details similarly; a few other team members who are good with technical knowledge also learn communication with clients. In this way, all team members will become independent and robust enough to perform all types of work, which is good for the office (given the condition that the manager of the team will give enough leave for all team members in the office!):

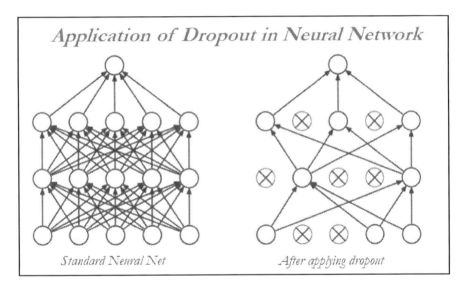

ANN classifier applied on handwritten digits using scikit-learn

An ANN classifier example has been illustrated with the handwritten digits example from the scikit-learn datasets, in which handwritten digits are created from 0 to 9 and their respective 64 features (8 x 8 matrix) of pixel intensities between 0 and 255, as any black and white (or grayscale) image can be represented. In the case of color images, RGB (red, green, and blue) channels will be used to represent all the colors:

```
# Neural Networks - Classifying hand-written digits
>>> import pandas as pd
>>> from sklearn.datasets import load_digits
>>> from sklearn.cross_validation import train_test_split
>>> from sklearn.pipeline import Pipeline
>>> from sklearn.preprocessing import StandardScaler

>>> from sklearn.neural_network import MLPClassifier
>>> digits = load_digits()
>>> X = digits.data
>>> y = digits.target

# Checking dimensions
>>> print (X.shape)
>>> print (y.shape)

# Plotting first digit
>>> import matplotlib.pyplot as plt
>>> plt.matshow(digits.images[0])
>>> plt.show()
```

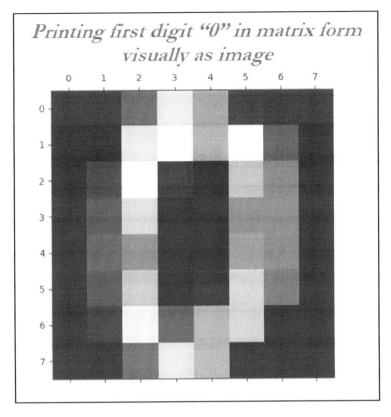

```
>>> from sklearn.model_selection import train_test_split
>>> x_vars_stdscle = StandardScaler().fit_transform(X)
>>> x_train,x_test,y_train,y_test =
train_test_split(x_vars_stdscle,y,train_size = 0.7,random_state=42)

# Grid Search - Neural Network
>>> from sklearn.pipeline import Pipeline
>>> from sklearn.model_selection import train_test_split,GridSearchCV
>>> from sklearn.metrics import accuracy_score,classification_report
```

An MLP classifier has been used with hidden layers of 100 and 50 in the first and second hidden layers consecutively. An Adam optimizer has been used for reduction of errors. A Relu activation function has been used for all the neurons with learning rate as 0.0001. Finally, the total number of iterations as 300 at initiation:

```
>>> pipeline = Pipeline([('mlp',MLPClassifier(hidden_layer_sizes=
(100,50,), activation='relu',solver='adam',alpha=0.0001,max_iter=300 ))])
```

The above parameters are used only for the initiation of the classifier, whereas the following code describes grid search using the pipeline function. The learning rate and maximum number of iterations are used to find the best combinations. However, readers are encouraged to add other features and test where even better results can be obtained:

```
>>> parameters = {'mlp__alpha':(0.001,0.01,0.1,0.3,0.5,1.0),
'mlp__max_iter':(100,200,300)}
```

Grid search with five-fold cross-validation has been used with default number of cores with scoring as accuracy used. Nonetheless, you can change it to 10-fold cross-validation and so on, to see how accuracy changes with a change in the cross-validation metrics:

```
>>> grid_search_nn =
GridSearchCV(pipeline,parameters,n_jobs=-1,cv=5,verbose=1,
scoring='accuracy')
>>> grid_search_nn.fit(x_train,y_train)

>>> print ('\n\nNeural Network Best Training score: %0.3f' %
grid_search_nn.best_score_)
>>> print ('\nNeural Network Best parameters set:')
best_parameters = grid_search_nn.best_estimator_.get_params()
>>> for param_name in sorted(parameters.keys()):
...        print ('\t%s: %r' % (param_name, best_parameters[param_name]))
```

Best parameters at which maximum accuracy value obtained is 96.3 percentage with alpha as 0.001 and maximum iterations as 200:

```
Neural Network Best Training score: 0.963

Neural Network Best parameters set:
        mlp__alpha: 0.001
        mlp__max_iter: 200
```

```
>>> predictions_train = grid_search_nn.predict(x_train)
>>> predictions_test = grid_search_nn.predict(x_test)
>>> print ("\nNeural Network Training
accuracy:",round(accuracy_score(y_train, predictions_train),4))
>>> print ("\nNeural Network Complete report of Training
data\n",classification_report(y_train, predictions_train))
>>> print ("\n\nNeural Network Grid Search- Train Confusion
Matrix\n\n",pd.crosstab(y_train, predictions_train,rownames =
["Actuall"],colnames = ["Predicted"]))
```

```
Neural Network Training accuracy: 1.0

Neural Network Complete report of Training data
             precision    recall  f1-score   support

          0       1.00      1.00      1.00       125
          1       1.00      1.00      1.00       132
          2       1.00      1.00      1.00       130
          3       1.00      1.00      1.00       129
          4       1.00      1.00      1.00       121
          5       1.00      1.00      1.00       116
          6       1.00      1.00      1.00       128
          7       1.00      1.00      1.00       124
          8       1.00      1.00      1.00       131
          9       1.00      1.00      1.00       121

avg / total       1.00      1.00      1.00      1257


Neural Network Grid Search- Train Confusion Matrix

 Predicted    0    1    2    3    4    5    6    7    8    9
Actuall
0           125    0    0    0    0    0    0    0    0    0
1             0  132    0    0    0    0    0    0    0    0
2             0    0  130    0    0    0    0    0    0    0
3             0    0    0  129    0    0    0    0    0    0
4             0    0    0    0  121    0    0    0    0    0
5             0    0    0    0    0  116    0    0    0    0
6             0    0    0    0    0    0  128    0    0    0
7             0    0    0    0    0    0    0  124    0    0
8             0    0    0    0    0    0    0    0  131    0
9             0    0    0    0    0    0    0    0    0  121
```

```
>>> print ("\n\nNeural Network Testing
accuracy:",round(accuracy_score(y_test, predictions_test),4))
>>> print ("\nNeural Network Complete report of Testing
data\n",classification_report( y_test, predictions_test))
>>> print ("\n\nNeural Network Grid Search- Test Confusion
Matrix\n\n",pd.crosstab(y_test, predictions_test,rownames =
["Actuall"],colnames = ["Predicted"]))
```

```
Neural Network Testing accuracy: 0.9759

Neural Network Complete report of Testing data
            precision    recall  f1-score   support

          0       1.00      1.00      1.00        53
          1       1.00      0.98      0.99        50
          2       0.96      0.98      0.97        47
          3       0.98      0.94      0.96        54
          4       0.98      1.00      0.99        60
          5       0.97      0.97      0.97        66
          6       0.98      0.98      0.98        53
          7       0.98      0.98      0.98        55
          8       0.91      0.95      0.93        43
          9       0.98      0.97      0.97        59

avg / total       0.98      0.98      0.98       540



Neural Network Grid Search- Test Confusion Matrix

 Predicted   0   1   2   3   4   5   6   7   8   9
Actuall
0           53   0   0   0   0   0   0   0   0   0
1            0  49   0   0   1   0   0   0   0   0
2            0   0  46   0   0   0   0   0   1   0
3            0   0   1  51   0   1   0   0   1   0
4            0   0   0   0  60   0   0   0   0   0
5            0   0   0   0   0  64   1   1   0   0
6            0   0   0   0   0   1  52   0   0   0
7            0   0   0   0   0   0   0  54   0   1
8            0   0   1   1   0   0   0   0  41   0
9            0   0   0   0   0   0   0   0   2  57
```

The previous figure illustrates that the best test accuracy obtained is 97.59 percentage, which is predicting digits with exceptionally good accuracy.

In the following R code, the `nnet` package has been used, in which L-BFGS has been used as an optimizer. There is a constraint on the number of neurons in the `nnet` package of a maximum value of 13. Hence, we could not check the results with number of neurons more than 13:

Example of R Code for ANN Classifier:

```
# Artificial Neural Networks
setwd("D:\\Book   writing\\Codes\\Chapter 6")
digits_data = read.csv("digitsdata.csv")
remove_cols = c("target")
x_data =   digits_data[,!(names(digits_data) %in% remove_cols)]
y_data = digits_data[,c("target")]
normalize <- function(x)   {return((x - min(x)) / (max(x) - min(x)))}
data_norm <-    as.data.frame(lapply(x_data, normalize))
data_norm <-    replace(data_norm, is.na(data_norm), 0.0)
data_norm_v2 =    data.frame(as.factor(y_data),data_norm)
names(data_norm_v2)[1] = "target"
set.seed(123)
numrow = nrow(data_norm_v2)
trnind = sample(1:numrow,size =   as.integer(0.7*numrow))
train_data =    data_norm_v2[trnind,]
test_data = data_norm_v2[-trnind,]
f <- as.formula(paste("target    ~",
paste(names(train_data)[!names(train_data)   %in% "target"], collapse = " +
")))
library(nnet)
accuracy <-    function(mat){return(sum(diag(mat)) / sum(mat))}
nnet_fit =    nnet(f,train_data,size=c(9),maxit=200)
y_pred =    predict(nnet_fit,newdata = test_data,type = "class")
tble =    table(test_data$target,y_pred)
print(accuracy(tble))
#Plotting nnet from the github   packages
require(RCurl)
root.url<-'https://gist.githubusercontent.com/fawda123'
raw.fun<-paste(root.url,
'5086859/raw/cc1544804d5027d82b70e74b83b3941cd2184354/nnet_plot_fun.r',
  sep='/')
script<-getURL(raw.fun,   ssl.verifypeer = FALSE)
eval(parse(text = script))
rm('script','raw.fun')
# Ploting the neural net
plot(nnet_fit)
# Grid Search - ANN
```

```
neurons =    c(1,2,3,4,5,6,7,8,9,10,11,12,13)
iters =    c(200,300,400,500,600,700,800,900)
initacc = 0
for(itr in iters){
  for(nd in neurons){
    nnet_fit =    nnet(f,train_data,size=c(nd),maxit=itr,trace=FALSE)
    y_pred =    predict(nnet_fit,newdata = test_data,type = "class")
    tble =    table(test_data$target,y_pred)
    acc = accuracy(tble)
    if (acc>initacc){
      print(paste("Neurons",nd,"Iterations",itr,"Test    accuracy",acc))
      initacc = acc
    }
  }
}
```

Introduction to deep learning

Deep learning is a class of machine learning algorithms which utilizes neural networks for building models to solve both supervised and unsupervised problems on structured and unstructured datasets such as images, videos, NLP, voice processing, and so on:

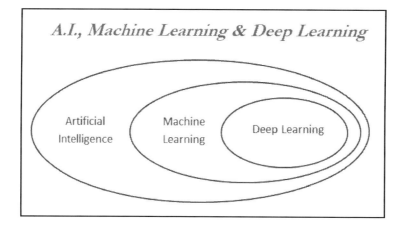

Deep neural network/deep architecture consists of multiple hidden layers of units between input and output layers. Each layer is fully connected with the subsequent layer. The output of each artificial neuron in a layer is an input to every artificial neuron in the next layer towards the output:

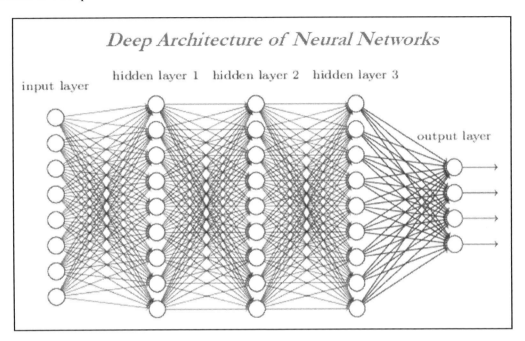

With the more number of hidden layers are being added to the neural network, more complex decision boundaries are being created to classify different categories. Example of complex decision boundary can be seen in the following graph:

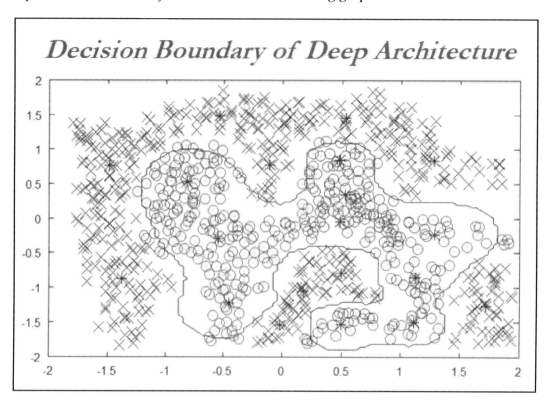

Solving methodology

Backpropagation is used to solve deep layers by calculating the error of the network at output units and propagate back through layers to update the weights to reduce error terms.

Thumb rules in designing deep neural networks: Though there is no hard and fast rule for designing neural networks, the following rules will provide some guidelines:

- All hidden layers should have the same number of neurons per layer
- Typically, two hidden layers are good enough to solve the majority of problems
- Using scaling/batch normalization (mean 0, variance 1) for all input variables after each layer improves convergence effectiveness
- Reduction in step size after each iteration improves convergence, in addition to the use of momentum and dropout

Deep learning software

Deep learning software has evolved multi-fold in recent times. In this chapter, we are using Keras to develop a model, as Keras models are easy to understand and prototype new concepts for newbies. However, lots of other software also exists and is used by many practitioners across the world:

- **Theano:** Python-based deep learning library developed by the University of Montreal
- **TensorFlow:** Google's deep learning library runs on top of Python/C++
- **Keras / Lasagne:** Lightweight wrapper which sits on top of Theano/TensorFlow and enables faster model prototyping
- **Torch:** Lua-based deep learning library with wide support for machine learning algorithms
- **Caffe:** deep learning library primarily used for processing pictures

TensorFlow is recently picking up momentum among the deep learning community, as it is being backed up by Google and also has good visualization capabilities using TensorBoard:

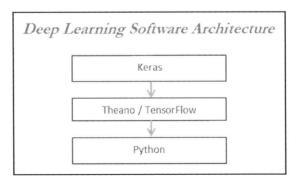

Deep neural network classifier applied on handwritten digits using Keras

We are using the same data as we trained the model on previously using scikit-learn in order to perform apple-to-apple comparison between scikit-learn and the deep learning software Keras. Hence, the data loading steps remain the same:

```
>>> import numpy as np
>> import pandas as pd
>>> import matplotlib.pyplot as plt
>>> from sklearn.datasets import load_digits
>>> from sklearn.model_selection import train_test_split
>>> from sklearn.preprocessing import StandardScaler
>>> from sklearn.metrics import accuracy_score,classification_report
```

From here onward, we will be using the Keras library modules. Various optimizers are selected though; we will be using Adam in our model. Readers are encouraged to try other optimizers as well:

```
>>> from keras.models import Sequential
>>> from keras.layers.core import Dense, Dropout, Activation
>>> from keras.optimizers import Adadelta,Adam,RMSprop
>>> from keras.utils import np_utils
```

By running the previous code, we will get the following message if we are running Keras on a CPU:

```
Using Theano backend.
```

However, if we run it on a GPU, the following code appears. In fact, I have a GPU (model: *NVIDIA GTX 1060*) installed on my personal computer with a memory capacity of 6 GB RAM. For most applications, 6 GB is good enough for starters and enthusiasts, whereas for deep learning researchers, 12 GB might be needed; of course depending upon the nature of the work:

```
Using Theano backend.
WARNING (theano.sandbox.cuda): The cuda backend is deprecated and will be removed in the next release (v0.10).
  Please switch to the gpuarray backend. You can get more information about how to switch at this URL:
  https://github.com/Theano/Theano/wiki/Converting-to-the-new-gpu-back-end%28gpuarray%29

Using gpu device 0: GeForce GTX 1060 6GB (CNMeM is enabled with initial size: 80.0% of memory, cuDNN 5105)
```

In order to change the mode from CPU to GPU and vice versa from GPU to CPU, one needs to update the Theano.rc text file saved in the user folder. The following figure provides the various values to be configured if we are using GPU in the Theano.rc file. For CPU, only the [global] option is needed. Replace the device with CPU in it and delete the rest ([nvcc] and [lib]), as the latter is used for GPU settings only!

```
[global]
floatX = float32
device = gpu

[nvcc]
flags=-LC:\Users\prata\Anaconda2\libs
compiler_bindir=C:\Program Files (x86)\Microsoft Visual Studio 12.0\VC\bin

[lib]
cnmem = 0.8
```

The following code loads the digit data from scikit-learn datasets. A quick piece of code to check the shape of the data, as data embedded in numpy arrays itself, hence we do not need to change it into any other format, as deep learning models get trained on numpy arrays:

```
>>> digits = load_digits()
>>> X = digits.data
>>> y = digits.target
>>> print (X.shape)
>>> print (y.shape)
>>> print ("\nPrinting first digit")
>>> plt.matshow(digits.images[0])
>>> plt.show()
```

The previous code prints the first digit in matrix form. It appears that the following digit looks like a *0*:

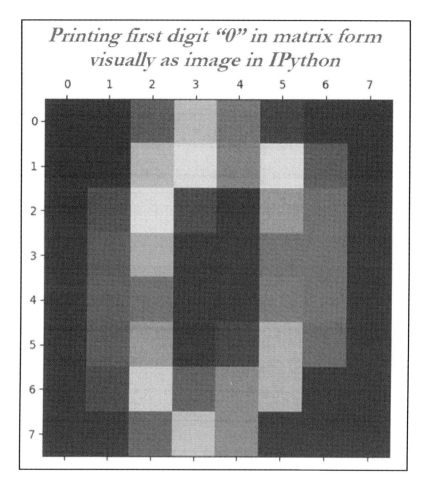

We are performing the standardizing of data with the following code to demean the series, followed by standard deviation to put all the 64 dimensions in a similar scale. Though, in this case, it is not very stringent, as all the values lie between 0 and 255, but by doing so we reduce the computational requirement a little bit:

```
>>> x_vars_stdscle = StandardScaler().fit_transform(X)
```

The following section of the code splits the data into train and test based on a 70-30 split:

```
>>> x_train,x_test,y_train,y_test =
train_test_split(x_vars_stdscle,y,train_size = 0.7,random_state=42)
```

Tuning the hyperparameters plays a crucial role in tuning a deep learning model (of course, this is applicable to any of the machine learning models too!). We have used nb_classes as 10, due to the reason that the digits range from 0-9; batch_size as 128, which means for each batch, we utilize 128 observations to update the weights; and finally, we have used nb_epochs as 200, which means the number of epochs the model needs to be trained is 200 (also, we can imagine that the model will be updated 200 times from start to end):

```
# Defining hyper parameters
>>> np.random.seed(1337)
>>> nb_classes = 10
>>> batch_size = 128
>>> nb_epochs = 200
```

The following code actually creates the n-dimensional vector for multiclass values based on the nb_classes value. Here, we will get the dimension as 10 for all train observations for training using the softmax classifier:

```
>>> Y_train = np_utils.to_categorical(y_train, nb_classes)
```

The core model building code, which looks like Lego blocks, is shown as follows. Here we, initiate the model as sequential rather than parallel and so on:

```
#Deep Layer Model building in Keras
>>> model = Sequential()
```

In the first layer, we are using 100 neurons with input shape as 64 columns (as the number of columns in X is 64), followed by relu activation functions with dropout value as 0.5 (we have chosen dropout randomly; readers are encouraged to try different values and see how the results vary):

```
>>> model.add(Dense(100,input_shape= (64,)))
>>> model.add(Activation('relu'))
>>> model.add(Dropout(0.5))
```

In the second layer, we are using 50 neurons (to compare the results obtained using the scikit-learn methodology, we have used a similar architecture):

```
>>> model.add(Dense(50))
>>> model.add(Activation('relu'))
>>> model.add(Dropout(0.5))
```

In the output layer, the number of classes needs to be used with the softmax classifier:

```
>>> model.add(Dense(nb_classes))
>>> model.add(Activation('softmax'))
```

Here, we are compiling with `categorical_crossentropy`, as the output is multiclass; whereas, if we want to use binary class, we need to use `binary_crossentropy` instead:

```
>>> model.compile(loss='categorical_crossentropy', optimizer='adam')
```

The model is being trained in the following step with all the given batch sizes and number of epochs:

```
#Model training
>>> model.fit(x_train, Y_train, batch_size=batch_size,
nb_epoch=nb_epochs,verbose=1)
```

Here, we just present the starting and ending phase of epochs with loss values. If we observe, loss values have been minimized from 2.6925 to 0.0611 across 200 iterations:

```
Epoch 1/200
1257/1257 [==============================] - 0s - loss: 2.6925
Epoch 2/200
1257/1257 [==============================] - 0s - loss: 2.3545
Epoch 3/200
1257/1257 [==============================] - 0s - loss: 2.1078
Epoch 4/200
1257/1257 [==============================] - 0s - loss: 1.9244
Epoch 5/200
1257/1257 [==============================] - 0s - loss: 1.7515
Epoch 6/200
1257/1257 [==============================] - 0s - loss: 1.6710
Epoch 7/200
1257/1257 [==============================] - 0s - loss: 1.5014
Epoch 8/200
1257/1257 [==============================] - 0s - loss: 1.3561
Epoch 9/200
1257/1257 [==============================] - 0s - loss: 1.2837
Epoch 10/200
1257/1257 [==============================] - 0s - loss: 1.2166
Epoch 11/200
1257/1257 [==============================] - 0s - loss: 1.0852

1257/1257 [==============================] - 0s - loss: 0.0678
Epoch 191/200
1257/1257 [==============================] - 0s - loss: 0.0624
Epoch 192/200
1257/1257 [==============================] - 0s - loss: 0.0694
Epoch 193/200
1257/1257 [==============================] - 0s - loss: 0.0691
Epoch 194/200
1257/1257 [==============================] - 0s - loss: 0.0631
Epoch 195/200
1257/1257 [==============================] - 0s - loss: 0.0770
Epoch 196/200
1257/1257 [==============================] - 0s - loss: 0.0544
Epoch 197/200
1257/1257 [==============================] - 0s - loss: 0.0647
Epoch 198/200
1257/1257 [==============================] - 0s - loss: 0.0665
Epoch 199/200
1257/1257 [==============================] - 0s - loss: 0.0615
Epoch 200/200
1257/1257 [==============================] - 0s - loss: 0.0611
         <keras.callbacks.History at 0x173e37240>
```

```
#Model Prediction
>>> y_train_predclass =
model.predict_classes(x_train,batch_size=batch_size)
>>> y_test_predclass = model.predict_classes(x_test,batch_size=batch_size)
>>> print ("\n\nDeep Neural Network - Train accuracy:"),
(round(accuracy_score(y_train,y_train_predclass),3))
>>> print ("\nDeep Neural Network - Train Classification Report")
>>> print classification_report(y_train,y_train_predclass)
>>> print ("\nDeep Neural Network - Train Confusion Matrix\n")
>>> print (pd.crosstab(y_train,y_train_predclass,rownames =
["Actuall"],colnames = ["Predicted"]) )
```

```
Deep Neural Network  - Train accuracy: 1.0

Deep Neural Network  - Train Classification Report
            precision      recall   f1-score      support

         0       1.00        1.00       1.00          125
         1       1.00        1.00       1.00          132
         2       1.00        1.00       1.00          130
         3       1.00        1.00       1.00          129
         4       1.00        1.00       1.00          121
         5       1.00        1.00       1.00          116
         6       1.00        1.00       1.00          128
         7       1.00        1.00       1.00          124
         8       1.00        1.00       1.00          131
         9       1.00        1.00       1.00          121

avg / total      1.00        1.00       1.00         1257


Deep Neural Network - Train Confusion Matrix

Predicted    0    1    2    3    4    5    6    7    8    9
Actuall
0          125    0    0    0    0    0    0    0    0    0
1            0  132    0    0    0    0    0    0    0    0
2            0    0  130    0    0    0    0    0    0    0
3            0    0    0  129    0    0    0    0    0    0
4            0    0    0    0  121    0    0    0    0    0
5            0    0    0    0    0  116    0    0    0    0
6            0    0    0    0    0    0  128    0    0    0
7            0    0    0    0    0    0    0  124    0    0
8            0    0    0    0    0    0    0    0  131    0
9            0    0    0    0    0    0    0    0    0  121
```

From the previous training results, we have got 100 percentage accuracy on the training data:

```
>>> print ("\nDeep Neural Network - Test
accuracy:"),(round(accuracy_score(y_test, y_test_predclass),3))
>>> print ("\nDeep Neural Network - Test Classification Report")
>>> print (classification_report(y_test,y_test_predclass))
>>> print ("\nDeep Neural Network - Test Confusion Matrix\n")
>>> print (pd.crosstab(y_test,y_test_predclass,rownames =
["Actuall"],colnames = ["Predicted"]) )
```

```
Deep Neural Network - Test accuracy: 0.976

Deep Neural Network - Test Classification Report
             precision    recall  f1-score   support

          0       1.00      1.00      1.00        53
          1       0.98      0.98      0.98        50
          2       0.94      0.98      0.96        47
          3       0.98      0.94      0.96        54
          4       0.98      1.00      0.99        60
          5       0.97      0.97      0.97        66
          6       0.98      0.98      0.98        53
          7       0.98      0.98      0.98        55
          8       0.98      0.95      0.96        43
          9       0.97      0.97      0.97        59

avg / total       0.98      0.98      0.98       540


Deep Neural Network - Test Confusion Matrix

Predicted  0   1   2   3   4   5   6   7   8   9
Actuall
0         53   0   0   0   0   0   0   0   0   0
1          0  49   1   0   0   0   0   0   0   0
2          0   0  46   1   0   0   0   0   0   0
3          0   0   2  51   0   1   0   0   0   0
4          0   0   0   0  60   0   0   0   0   0
5          0   0   0   0   0  64   1   0   0   1
6          0   0   0   0   1   0  52   0   0   0
7          0   0   0   0   0   0   0  54   0   1
8          0   1   0   0   0   1   0   0  41   0
9          0   0   0   0   0   0   0   1   1  57
```

However, the true evaluation is performed on the test data instead. Here, we have got 97.6 percentage accuracy, which is similar to the scikit-learn accuracy of 97.78 percentage. Hence, it has been proved that we have successfully replicated the results in the deep learning software; however, in Keras, we can do much better things than in scikit-learn (such as convolutional neural networks, recurrent neural networks, auto encoders, and so on, which are very advanced in nature).

Summary

In this chapter, you have learned about the most computationally intensive methods, SVMs and neural networks. Support vector machines perform really well on data in which the number of dimensions is very high, where other methods fail to work. By utilizing kernels, SVMs can reach very high test accuracies; we have covered how kernels actually work in detail in this chapter. Neural networks have become very popular in recent times for solving various problems; here, we covered all the deep learning fundamentals required for building a neural network model using both scikit-learn and Keras. In addition, results were compared between scikit-learn and Keras models to show apple-to-apple comparison. By utilizing deep learning, many new-generation artificial intelligence problems can be solved, whether it is text, voice, images, videos, and so on. In fact, deep learning itself has become a separate domain altogether.

In the next chapter, we will be looking at recommendation engines using both content-based and collaborative filtering methods, which is the first classical machine learning example explained to any newbie who would like to understand machine learning.

7
Recommendation Engines

Recommendation engines (REs) are most famously used for explaining what machine learning is to any unknown person or a newbie who wants to understand the field of machine learning. A classic example could be how Amazon recommends books similar to the ones you have bought, which you may also like very much! Also, empirically, the recommender engine seems to be an example of large-scale machine learning that everyone understands, or perhaps already understood. But, nonetheless, recommendation engines are being used everywhere. For example, the people you may know feature in Facebook or LinkedIn, which recommends by showing the most probable people you might like to befriend or professionals in your network who you might be interested in connecting with. Of course, these features drive their businesses big time and it is at the heart of the company's driving force.

The idea behind an RE is to predict what people might like and to uncover relationships between items/products to aid in the discovery process; in this way, it is similar to a search engine. But a major difference is, search engine works in a reactive manner; they show results only when the user requests something—but a recommendation engine is proactive—it tries to present people with relevant content that they did not necessarily search for or that they might not have heard of in the past.

Content-based filtering

Content-based methods try to use the content or attributes of the item, together with some notion of similarity between two pieces of content, to generate similar items with respect to the given item. In this case, cosine similarity is used to determine the nearest user or item to provide recommendations.

Example: If you buy a book, then there is a high chance you'll buy related books which have frequently gone together with all the other customers, and so on.

Cosine similarity

As we will be working on this concept, it would be nice to reiterate the basics. Cosine similarity is a measure of similarity between two nonzero vectors of an inner product space that measures the cosine of the angle between them. Cosine of 0^0 is 1 and it is less than 1 for any other angle:

$$\cos(\theta) = \frac{\sum_{i=1}^{n} A_i B_i}{\sqrt{\sum_{i=1}^{n} A_i^2} \sqrt{\sum_{i=1}^{n} B_i^2}}$$

Here, A_i and B_i are components of vector A and B respectively:

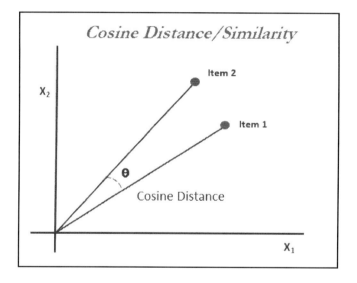

Example: Let us assume $A = [2, 1, 0, 2, 0, 1, 1, 1]$, $B = [2, 1, 1, 1, 1, 0, 1, 1]$ are the two vectors and we would like to calculate the cosine similarity:

$$\sum_{i=1}^{n} A_i B_i = \big((2*2) + (1*1) + (0*1) + (2*1) + (0*1) + (1*0) + (1*1)$$
$$+ (1*1)\big) = 9$$

$$\sqrt{\sum_{i=1}^{n} A_i^2} = \sqrt{(2^2 + 1^2 + 0^2 + 2^2 + 0^2 + 1^2 + 1^2 + 1^2)} = \sqrt{12} = 12 = 3.46$$

$$\sqrt{\sum_{i=1}^{n} B_i^2} = \sqrt{(2^2 + 1^2 + 1^2 + 1^2 + 1^2 + 0^2 + 1^2 + 1^2)} = \sqrt{10} = 3.16$$

$$\cos(\theta) = \frac{9}{3.46 * 3.16} = 0.823$$

A value of *0.823* indicates very high similarity between the two vectors, as the highest possible is *1*. While calculating similar items or users, we will apply cosine similarity on their rating vector and put them in descending order based on cosine similarity, which will sort all the other items based on similarity score, close to the vector we are comparing. We will see this in detail in the example that we will be discussing in a later section of this chapter.

Collaborative filtering

Collaborative filtering is a form of wisdom-of-the-crowd approach, where the set of preferences of many users with respect to items is used to generate estimated preferences of users for items with which they have not yet rated/reviewed. It works on the notion of similarity. Collaborative filtering is a methodology in which similar users and their ratings are determined not by similar age and so on, but by similar preferences exhibited by users, such as similar movies watched, rated, and so on.

Advantages of collaborative filtering over content-based filtering

Collaborative filtering provides many advantages over content-based filtering. A few of them are as follows:

- **Not required to understand item content**: The content of the items does not necessarily tell the whole story, such as movie type/genre, and so on.
- **No item cold-start problem**: Even when no information on an item is available, we still can predict the item rating without waiting for a user to purchase it.
- **Captures the change in user interests over time**: Focusing solely on content does not provide any flexibility on the user's perspective and their preferences.
- **Captures inherent subtle characteristics**: This is very true for latent factor models. If most users buy two unrelated items, then it is likely that another user who shares similar interests with other users is highly likely to buy that unrelated item.

Matrix factorization using the alternating least squares algorithm for collaborative filtering

Alternating least squares (**ALS**) is an optimization technique to solve the matrix factorization problem. This technique achieves good performance and has proven relatively easy to implement. These algorithms are members of a broad class of latent-factor models and they try to explain observed interactions between a large number of users and items/movies through a relatively small number of unobserved, underlying reasons/factors. The matrix factorization algorithm treats the user-item data (matrix dimensions m x n) as a sparse matrix and tries to reconstruct with two lower-dimensional dense matrices (X and Y, where X has dimensions m x k and Y has dimensions k x n, in which k is the number of latent factors).

Latent factors can be interpreted as some explanatory variables which try to explain the reasons behind the behavior of users, as collaborative filtering is all about trying to predict based on the behavior of users, rather than attributes of movies or users, and so on:

$$A_{(m \, x \, n)} \approx X_{(m \, x \, k)} \times Y_{(k \, x \, n)}$$

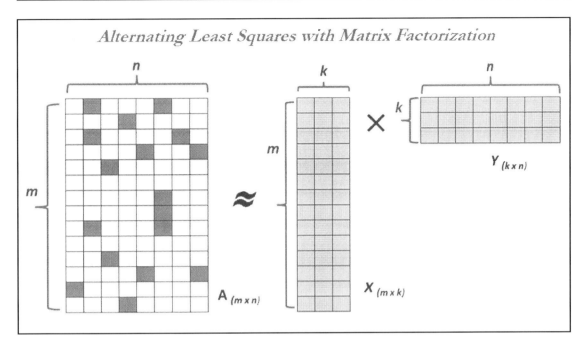

By multiplying X and Y matrices, we try to reconstruct the original matrix A, by reducing the root mean squared errors between original available ratings from sparse matrix A (m x n dimensions) and constructed dense matrix by multiplying X (m x k dimensions) and Y (k x n dimensions) matrices. However, the matrix obtained from multiplying X and Y fills all the slots in m x n dimensions, but we will reduce the errors between only available ratings in A. By doing so, all the other values in blank slots will produce reasonably sensible ratings.

However, in this scenario, there are too many unknown values. Unknown values are nothing but the values that need to be filled in X and Y matrices so that it will try to approximate the original ratings in matrix A as closely as possible. To solve this problem, initially, random values are generated between 0 to 1 from uniform distribution and multiplied by 5 to generate the values between 0 to 5 for both X and Y matrices. In the next step, the ALS methodology is actually applied; the following two steps are applied iteratively until the threshold number of iterations is reached:

1. X values are updated by utilizing Y values, learning rate (λ), and original sparse matrix (A)
2. Y values are updated by utilizing X values, learning rate (λ), and original sparse matrix (A)

The learning rate (λ) is used to control the rate of convergence; a high value leads to rapid change in values (similar to optimization problems) and sometimes will lead to overshoot from the optimum value. In a similar way, a low value requires many iterations to converge the solution.

The mathematical representation of ALS is provided here:

$$A = X \times Y$$

$$X = A \times Y^{-1}$$

$$X = A \times (Y^T \times Y^{T^{-1}}) \times Y^{-1}$$

$$X = A \times Y^T \times (Y\,Y^T)^{-1}$$

$$minimize\ error = \ minimize\ |\,X - A \times Y^T \times (Y\,Y^T)^{-1}\,|$$

The goal is to minimize the error or squared differences between the two. Hence, it has been called the least squares technique. In simple machine learning terminology, we can call this a regression problem, as the error between actual and predicted is being minimized. Practically, this equation was never solved by computing inverses. However, equivalence has been achieved by computing Y from X and again computing X from Y and, this way, it will continue until all iterations are reached and this is where the alternating part came actually. At the start, Y was artificially generated and X will be optimized based on Y, and later by optimizing Y based on X; by doing so, eventually the solution starts to converge towards the optimum over the number of iterations. Basic Python syntax has been provided next; we will be using the same in the following example also, in order to illustrate the movie lens example:

```
X = np.linalg.solve(np.dot(Y,Y.T)+ lmbda * np.eye(n_factors),np.dot(Y,A.T)).T
Y = np.linalg.solve(np.dot(X.T,X)+ lmbda * np.eye(n_factors),np.dot(X.T,A))
```

Evaluation of recommendation engine model

Evaluation of any model needs to be calculated in order to determine how good the model is with respect to the actual data so that its performance can be improved by tuning hyperparameters and so on. In fact, the entire machine learning algorithm's accuracy is measured based on its type of problem. In the case of classification problems, confusion matrix, whereas in regression problems, mean squared error or adjusted R-squared values need to be computed.

Mean squared error is a direct measure of the reconstruction error of the original sparse user-item matrix (also called *A*) with two low-dimensional dense matrices (*X* and *Y*). It is also the objective function which is being minimized across the iterations:

$$Mean\ Squared\ Error = \frac{Sum\ of\ Squared\ Errors}{Number\ of\ Observations}$$

$$RMSE\ (Root\ Mean\ Squared\ Error) = \sqrt{Mean\ Squared\ Error}$$

Root mean squared errors provide the dimension equivalent to the original dimension of the variable measure, hence we can analyze how much magnitude the error component has with the original value. In our example, we have computed the **root mean square error (RMSE)** for the movie lens data.

Hyperparameter selection in recommendation engines using grid search

In any machine learning algorithm, the selection of hyperparameter plays a critical role in how well the model generalizes the underlying data. In a similar way, in recommendation engines, we have the following hyperparameter to play with:

- **Number of iterations**: The higher the number of iterations, the better the algorithm converges. In practice, it has been proven that ALS converges within 10 iterations, but readers are recommended to try various values and see how the algorithm works.

- **Number of latent factors**: These are the explanatory variables which try to provide reasons behind crowd behavior patterns. The higher the latent factors, the better the model, but too high a value may not provide significant lift.
- **Learning rate**: The learning rate is a tunable knob to change the rate of convergence of the algorithm. Too high a value may shoot out rather than converge due to high oscillations, and too low a value may let the algorithm take too many steps to converge.

Readers are encouraged to try various combinations and see how the accuracy value and recommendation results change. In later sections, we have tried with various values to provide illustrations.

Recommendation engine application on movie lens data

The famous movie lens data has been used from the link https://grouplens.org/datasets/movielens/ under the **recommended for education and development** section with the filename displayed as ml-latest-small.zip, in which all the required files are saved in .csv format (ratings.csv, movies.csv, links.csv, and tags.csv). The files that we have used in the following example are ratings and movies only for the sake of simplicity. Nonetheless, readers are encouraged to combine other files to improve accuracy further!

```
>>> import os
""" First change the following directory link to where all input files do
exist """
>>> os.chdir("D:\\Book writing\\Codes\\Chapter 7\\ml-latest-small\\ml-
latest-small")

>>> import pandas as pd
>>> import numpy as np
>>> import matplotlib.pyplot as plt
```

In the following code, the ratings data provides the details of user ID, movie ID, and rating value, which mean each unique user, how many movies he/she has given, and what the ratings are!

```
>>> ratings = pd.read_csv("ratings.csv")
>>> print (ratings.head())
```

userId	movieId	rating	timestamp
1	31	2.5	1260759144
1	1029	3	1260759179
1	1061	3	1260759182
1	1129	2	1260759185
1	1172	4	1260759205

In the movies data, details are stored for each movie with unique movie ID, movie title, and its genre. We have not utilized genre in this chapter; however, you can try adding genre to the data by splitting and converting the text into one hot encoding vector (mapping of categories into numeric space) to enhance the model's accuracy:

```
>>> movies = pd.read_csv("movies.csv")
>>> print (movies.head())
```

movieId	title	genres
1	Toy Story (1995)	Adventure|Animation|Children|Comedy|Fantasy
2	Jumanji (1995)	Adventure|Children|Fantasy
3	Grumpier Old Men (1995)	Comedy|Romance
4	Waiting to Exhale (1995)	Comedy|Drama|Romance
5	Father of the Bride Part II (1995)	Comedy

In the following code, we have combined the ratings and movies data so that titles can be easily retrieved for display:

```
#Combining movie ratings & movie names
>>> ratings = pd.merge(ratings[['userId','movieId','rating']],
movies[['movieId', 'title']],how='left',left_on ='movieId' ,right_on =
'movieId')
```

The following code converts the data into a matrix form where rows are unique user IDs and columns are unique movie IDs, and the values in the matrix are ratings provided by users. This matrix is majorly sparse in nature, hence we are replacing NAN values with zeros to enable calculations. The entire computation in later sections of the code is based on this matrix:

```
>>> rp = ratings.pivot_table(columns = ['movieId'],index =
['userId'],values = 'rating')
>>> rp = rp.fillna(0)
```

A pandas DataFrame is built on top of a NumPy array, hence it would be advisable to use a NumPy array instead of a pandas DataFrame; a little conversion like this saves huge computational overheads while calculating a user-user similarity matrix or item-item similarity matrix.

```
# Converting pandas DataFrame to NumPy for faster execution in loops etc.
>>> rp_mat = rp.as_matrix()
```

 The main reason behind the improved computational performance of NumPy array compared with pandas is due to the homogeneity of elements in NumPy array. At the same time, this feature does not allow NumPy arrays to carry heterogeneous elements (for example, character, numeric, float, and so on.). Also, if someone is writing `for loops` on NumPy arrays means, they might be doing something wrong, as NumPy is built for manipulating all the elements in a shot, rather than hovering around each element.

Sample cosine similarity is illustrated with the following code for dummy values. But, the methodology remains the same for content-based filtering:

```
>>> from scipy.spatial.distance import cosine
#The cosine of the angle between them is about 0.822.
>>> a= np.asarray( [2, 1, 0, 2, 0, 1, 1, 1])
>>> b = np.asarray( [2, 1, 1, 1, 1, 0, 1, 1])
>>> print (1-cosine(a,b))
```

```
Cosine similarity between A and B is 0.8216
```

In the subsequent section, we have covered the following subsections:

- User-user similarity matrix
- Movie-movie (item-item) similarity matrix
- Collaborative filtering using ALS
- Grid search on collaborative filtering

User-user similarity matrix

The following code illustrates user-user similarity matrix computation based on complete brute force calculations (using a for loop inside another for loop with time complexity of On^2). There are many other efficient methods to compute the same, but for ease of understanding for readers, here we have provided one that is as simple as possible:

```
>>> m, n = rp.shape
# User similarity matrix
>>> mat_users = np.zeros((m, m))

>>> for i in range(m):
...        for j in range(m):
...             if i != j:
...                  mat_users[i][j] = (1- cosine(rp_mat[i,:], rp_mat[j,:]))
...             else:
...                  mat_users[i][j] = 0.
>>> pd_users = pd.DataFrame(mat_users,index =rp.index ,columns= rp.index )
```

The following custom function takes any user ID and the number of similar users to be displayed as an input and returns the similar users according to their relevant cosine similarity score:

```
# Finding similar users
>>> def topn_simusers(uid = 16,n=5):
...     users = pd_users.loc[uid,:].sort_values(ascending = False)
...     topn_users = users.iloc[:n,]
...     topn_users = topn_users.rename('score')
...     print ("Similar users as user:",uid)
...     return pd.DataFrame(topn_users)
>>> print (topn_simusers(uid=17,n=10))
```

```
Similar users as user: 17
                score
userId
596          0.379128
23           0.374641
355          0.329605
430          0.328872
608          0.319770
509          0.319313
105          0.309477
457          0.308201
15           0.307179
461          0.299035
```

Our task is not complete by just looking into the similar users themselves; rather, we would like to see what the most highly rated movies of any particular user are too. The following function provides that information for any given user and their most preferred movies:

```
# Finding most rated movies of a user
>>> def topn_movieratings(uid = 355,n_ratings=10):
...     uid_ratings = ratings.loc[ratings['userId']==uid]
...     uid_ratings = uid_ratings.sort_values(by='rating',ascending =
[False])
...     print ("Top",n_ratings ,"movie ratings of user:",uid)
...     return uid_ratings.iloc[:n_ratings,]
>>> print (topn_movieratings(uid=596,n_ratings=10))
```

The following screenshot displays the most rated movies of user 596 and their titles so that we will get an idea which movies that particular user rated most highly:

```
Top 10 movie ratings of user: 596
        userId  movieId  rating                                         title
89645      596     4262     5.0                                Scarface (1983)
89732      596     6874     5.0                        Kill Bill: Vol. 1 (2003)
89353      596      194     5.0                                   Smoke (1995)
89546      596     2329     5.0                     American History X (1998)
89453      596     1193     5.0    One Flew Over the Cuckoo's Nest (1975)
89751      596     8132     5.0                                Gladiator (1992)
89579      596     2858     5.0                       American Beauty (1999)
89365      596      296     5.0                             Pulp Fiction (1994)
89587      596     2959     5.0                               Fight Club (1999)
89368      596      318     5.0            Shawshank Redemption, The (1994)
```

Movie-movie similarity matrix

Previous sections of the code discussed content-based user-user similarity, whereas in the following section, we will be talking about a pure movie-movie similarity relation matrix, so that we will mine a bit deeper into how close each movie is to other movies.

In the following code, time functions are utilized for computing the movie-movie similarity matrix. It took a good 30 minutes on my i7 computer. It may take even more time on moderate computers, hence I have stored the output result and read back for convenience; readers are encouraged to run it and check for themselves though:

```
# Movie similarity matrix
>>> import time
>>> start_time = time.time()
>>> mat_movies = np.zeros((n, n))

>>> for i in range(n):
...     for j in range(n):
...         if i!=j:
...             mat_movies[i,j] = (1- cosine(rp_mat[:,i], rp_mat[:,j]))
...         else:
...             mat_movies[i,j] = 0.
>>> print("--- %s seconds ---" % (time.time() - start_time))

>>> pd_movies = pd.DataFrame(mat_movies,index =rp.columns ,columns=
rp.columns )
```

The following two lines of code are optional; I prefer to read it back from the disk rather than rerunning the code and waiting for 30 minutes:

```
>>> pd_movies.to_csv('pd_movies.csv',sep=',')
>>> pd_movies = pd.read_csv("pd_movies.csv",index_col='movieId')
```

 Readers are encouraged to apply `scipy.spatial.distance.cdist` function with `cosine`, as the parameter can speed up the runtime.

The following code is used to retrieve the most similar n number of top movies based on a user's preference ratings. This analysis is very important to see what other movies are similar to the movies you actually like:

```
# Finding similar movies
>>> def topn_simovies(mid = 588,n=15):
...     mid_ratings = pd_movies.loc[mid,:].sort_values(ascending = False)
...     topn_movies = pd.DataFrame(mid_ratings.iloc[:n,])
...     topn_movies['index1'] = topn_movies.index
...     topn_movies['index1'] = topn_movies['index1'].astype('int64')
...     topn_movies = pd.merge(topn_movies,movies[['movieId','title']],how
= 'left', left_on ='index1' ,right_on = 'movieId')
...     print ("Movies similar to movie
id:",mid,",",movies['title'][movies['movieId'] ==
mid].to_string(index=False),",are")
...     del topn_movies['index1']
...     return topn_movies

>>> print (topn_simovies(mid=589,n=15))
```

After carefully examining the following results, the movies which are similar to `Terminator 2` are `Jurassic Park`, `Terminator`, `The`, `Braveheart`, `Forrest Gump`, `Speed`, and so on; all these movies fall under the action category actually. The results seem to be sound enough for me to select my next movie to watch from this analysis! Content-based filtering seems to be working!

```
Movies similar to movie id: 589 , Terminator 2: Judgment Day (1991) ,are
          589  movieId                                                title
0   0.702256      480                                       Jurassic Park (1993)
1   0.636392     1240                                      Terminator, The (1984)
2   0.633428      110                                          Braveheart (1995)
3   0.619415      356                                        Forrest Gump (1994)
4   0.614814      377                                               Speed (1994)
5   0.605887      380                                           True Lies (1994)
6   0.604555      457                                        Fugitive, The (1993)
7   0.591071      593                              Silence of the Lambs, The (1991)
8   0.579325      367                                            Mask, The (1994)
9   0.577299     1036                                           Die Hard (1988)
10  0.576275      592                                             Batman (1989)
11  0.568341      296                                        Pulp Fiction (1994)
12  0.564779     1196  Star Wars: Episode V - The Empire Strikes Back...
13  0.562415      260            Star Wars: Episode IV - A New Hope (1977)
14  0.553626       47                               Seven (a.k.a. Se7en) (1995)
```

Collaborative filtering using ALS

We have finished content-based filtering and, from the following section onward, we will be discussing collaborative filtering using the ALS method:

```
# Collaborative filtering
>>> import os
""" First change the following directory link to where all input files do
exist """
>>> os.chdir("D:\\Book writing\\Codes\\Chapter 7\\ml-latest-small\\ml-
latest-small")

>>> import pandas as pd
>>> import numpy as np
>>> import matplotlib.pyplot as plt

>>> ratings = pd.read_csv("ratings.csv")
>>> print (ratings.head())

>>> movies = pd.read_csv("movies.csv")
>>> print (movies.head())

>>> rp = ratings.pivot_table(columns = ['movieId'],index =
['userId'],values = 'rating')
>>> rp = rp.fillna(0)
```

```
>>> A = rp.values
>>> print ("\nShape of Original Sparse Matrix",A.shape)
```

```
Shape of Original Sparse Matrix (671, 9066)
```

The initial data processing steps remain the same when compared with content-based filtering. Here, the main file we will be working with is the sparse ratings matrix.

The following `W` matrix actually has the same dimension as the original ratings matrix (matrix `A`) but only has values of 0 or 1 whenever a user provided a rating to any movie (minimum valid rating for any movie is 0.5, with the maximum rating as 5); we needed this type of matrix in calculating errors and so on (we will see its application in a later section of the code) as this way is more convenient to minimize the errors:

```
>>> W = A>0.5
>>> W[W==True]=1
>>> W[W==False]=0
>>> W = W.astype(np.float64,copy=False)
```

Similarly, another matrix, `W_pred`, is also needed to provide recommendations. The `W_pred` matrix has values of 0 or 1, exactly opposite to the `W` matrix. The reason for this is, if we multiply the predicted rating matrix with this `W_pred` matrix, this will make all values 0 for already provided ratings, so that other non-reviewed/non-rated values can be easily put in descending order and suggest the top 5 or 10 movies to the user who has never rated/seen those movies. If you observe carefully, here we are assigned zeros to all diagonal elements too, as we should not recommend the same movie as the most probable movie to users, which is sensible:

```
>>> W_pred = A<0.5
>>> W_pred[W_pred==True]=1
>>> W_pred[W_pred==False]=0
>>> W_pred = W_pred.astype(np.float64,copy=False)
>>> np.fill_diagonal(W_pred,val=0)
```

Hyperparameters are initiated in the following code with sample values, the number of iterations is set to 200, the number of latent factors is set to 100 with learning rate as 0.1:

```
# Parameters
>>> m,n = A.shape
>>> n_iterations = 200
>>> n_factors = 100
>>> lmbda = 0.1
```

The X and Y values are initiated with random numbers from uniform distribution [0-1] and multiplied by 5 for converting between 0 and 5. The number of dimensions for X and Y is (*m* x *k*) and (*k* x *n*) respectively, as we will start with a random value and optimize step by step for each iteration:

```
>>> X = 5 * np.random.rand(m,n_factors)
>>> Y = 5* np.random.rand(n_factors,n)
```

RMSE values are calculated with the following formulas. Here, we are multiplying with the W matrix to consider only the ratings metric in the error calculations; though matrix np.dot(X, Y) has values across the matrix, we should not consider them due to the fact that the error metric needs to be calculated only for the available ratings:

```
>>> def get_error(A, X, Y, W):
...     return np.sqrt(np.sum((W * (A - np.dot(X, Y)))**2)/np.sum(W))
```

The following step is the most critical part of the entire ALS methodology. Initially, here, we are optimizing X based on the given Y, followed by optimizing Y based on the given X; we will repeat this process until we finish all the number of iterations. After every 10 iterations, we print to see how the RMSE value changes with respective to change in number of iterations:

```
>>> errors = []
>>> for itr in range(n_iterations):
...     X = np.linalg.solve(np.dot(Y,Y.T)+ lmbda *
np.eye(n_factors),np.dot(Y,A.T)).T
...     Y = np.linalg.solve(np.dot(X.T,X)+ lmbda *
np.eye(n_factors),np.dot(X.T,A))
...     if itr%10 == 0:
...         print(itr," iterations completed","RMSError value
is:",get_error(A,X,Y,W))
...     errors.append(get_error(A,X,Y,W))
```

```
0   iterations completed RMSError value is: 3.19676116246
10  iterations completed RMSError value is: 1.71706768957
20  iterations completed RMSError value is: 1.70744048332
30  iterations completed RMSError value is: 1.70365296088
40  iterations completed RMSError value is: 1.70162269357
50  iterations completed RMSError value is: 1.70036790059
60  iterations completed RMSError value is: 1.69950635555
70  iterations completed RMSError value is: 1.69886916828
80  iterations completed RMSError value is: 1.69837366251
90  iterations completed RMSError value is: 1.69797493129
100 iterations completed RMSError value is: 1.6976462491
110 iterations completed RMSError value is: 1.6973704614
120 iterations completed RMSError value is: 1.69713586747
130 iterations completed RMSError value is: 1.69693409985
140 iterations completed RMSError value is: 1.69675895539
150 iterations completed RMSError value is: 1.69660570828
160 iterations completed RMSError value is: 1.69647068198
170 iterations completed RMSError value is: 1.69635096853
180 iterations completed RMSError value is: 1.6962442366
190 iterations completed RMSError value is: 1.69614859573
```

From the preceding results, it is apparent that the error values in fact decrease with the number of iterations, which is in fact the algorithm performing as expected. The following code is for plotting the same errors on the graph:

```
>>> print ("RMSError of rated movies: ",get_error(A,X,Y,W))
>>> plt.plot(errors);
>>> plt.ylim([0, 3.5]);
>>> plt.xlabel("Number of Iterations");plt.ylabel("RMSE")
>>> plt.title("No.of Iterations vs. RMSE")
>>> plt.show()
```

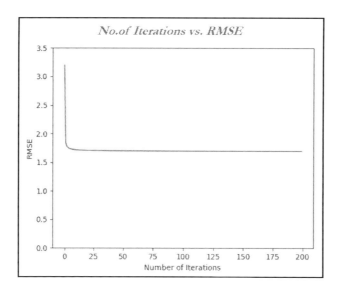

Once the number of iterations has finished, we will get updated *X* and *Y* matrices, which will be utilized to create the entire predicted ratings matrix, which can be obtained from a simple dot product, as follows:

```
>>> A_hat = np.dot(X,Y)
```

After calculating the predicted matrix (`A_hat`), the next and final task is to utilize it to recommend the most relevant movies to users. In the following code, we recommend movies to any particular user based on their movie review patterns or ratings provided:

```
>>> def print_recommovies(uid=315,n_movies=15,pred_mat = A_hat,wpred_mat =
W_pred ):
...      pred_recos = pred_mat*wpred_mat
...      pd_predrecos = pd.DataFrame(pred_recos,index =rp.index ,columns=
rp.columns )
...      pred_ratings = pd_predrecos.loc[uid,:].sort_values(ascending =
False)
...      pred_topratings = pred_ratings[:n_movies,]
...      pred_topratings = pred_topratings.rename('pred_ratings')
...      pred_topratings = pd.DataFrame(pred_topratings)
...      pred_topratings['index1'] = pred_topratings.index
...      pred_topratings['index1'] =
pred_topratings['index1'].astype('int64')
...      pred_topratings =
pd.merge(pred_topratings,movies[['movieId','title']],how = 'left',left_on
='index1' ,right_on = 'movieId')
...      del pred_topratings['index1']
...      print ("\nTop",n_movies,"movies predicted for the user:",uid,"
based on collaborative filtering\n")
...      return pred_topratings

>>> predmtrx =
print_recommovies(uid=355,n_movies=10,pred_mat=A_hat,wpred_mat=W_pred)
>>> print (predmtrx)
```

```
Top 10 movies predicted for the user: 355  based on collaborative filtering

   pred_ratings  movieId                                  title
0      2.739938     1213                        Goodfellas (1990)
1      2.441184     1197                 Princess Bride, The (1987)
2      2.315458     1923  There's Something About Mary (1998)
3      2.153286     2987         Who Framed Roger Rabbit? (1988)
4      2.075566     5010                   Black Hawk Down (2001)
5      2.051015     5903                       Equilibrium (2002)
6      1.960500     8798                        Collateral (2004)
7      1.910131     8622                  Fahrenheit 9/11 (2004)
8      1.831957     1298            Pink Floyd: The Wall (1982)
9      1.806256     8957                              Saw (2004)
```

From the previous recommendations, we can see that the movie user 355 might like most is `Goodfellas`, followed by `Princess Bride`, `There's Something About Mary`, and so on. Well, these recommendations need to be judged by the user himself!

Grid search on collaborative filtering

As we mentioned earlier, we need to tune the parameters in order to see where we will get the best possible machine learning model. Tuning the parameters is a kind of de-facto standard in any machine learning model. In the following code, we have tried various combinations for number of iterations, latent factors, and learning rate. The entire code will remain more or less the same, but we always keep a tab on the least minimum errors we have seen; if any new errors comes up as less than the existing errors, we print the combinations accordingly:

```python
# Grid Search on Collaborative Filtering
>>> niters = [20,50,100,200]
>>> factors = [30,50,70,100]
>>> lambdas = [0.001,0.01,0.05,0.1]

>>> init_error = float("inf")

>>> print("\n\nGrid Search results of ALS Matrix Factorization:\n")
>>> for niter in niters:
...     for facts in factors:
...         for lmbd in lambdas:
...             X = 5 * np.random.rand(m,facts)
...             Y = 5* np.random.rand(facts,n)
...             for itr in range(niter):
...                 X = np.linalg.solve(np.dot(Y,Y.T)+ lmbd *
np.eye(facts), np.dot(Y,A.T)).T
...                 Y = np.linalg.solve(np.dot(X.T,X)+ lmbd *
np.eye(facts), np.dot(X.T,A))
...             error = get_error(A,X,Y,W)
...             if error<init_error:
...                 print ("No.of iters",niter,"No.of
Factors",facts,"Lambda",lmbd, "RMSE",error)
...                 init_error = error
```

```
Grid Search results of ALS Matrix Factorization:

No.of iters 20 No.of Factors 30 Lambda 0.001 RMSE 2.31865832925
No.of iters 20 No.of Factors 50 Lambda 0.001 RMSE 2.10419912052
No.of iters 20 No.of Factors 70 Lambda 0.001 RMSE 1.92914027529
No.of iters 20 No.of Factors 100 Lambda 0.001 RMSE 1.70778244481
No.of iters 50 No.of Factors 100 Lambda 0.001 RMSE 1.69999934341
No.of iters 100 No.of Factors 100 Lambda 0.001 RMSE 1.69728358653
No.of iters 200 No.of Factors 100 Lambda 0.001 RMSE 1.69534546465
```

The best possible RMSE value obtained from the grid search is 1.695345, which is less than the RMSE value from the basic method, which is 1.6961. Hence, it is always advisable to perform grid search before implementing any algorithm.

In R code, the `recommenderlab` package has been used for solving the collaborative filtering problem, as this package has many features and functionalities to be played around with. But basic content-based filtering algorithms have been built from first principles:

The following R code may take about 30 minutes to run (of course runtime depends on the system configuration though!).

The R code for the recommendation engine (both content-based and collaborative filtering) is as follows:

```
setwd("D:\\Book writing\\Codes\\Chapter 7\\ml-latest-small\\ml-latest-
small")
ratings = read.csv("ratings.csv")
movies = read.csv("movies.csv")

ratings = ratings[,!names(ratings) %in% c("timestamp")]

library(reshape2)

# Creating Pivot table
ratings_mat = acast(ratings,userId~movieId)
ratings_mat[is.na(ratings_mat)] =0

# Content-based filtering
library(lsa)
a = c(2, 1, 0, 2, 0, 1, 1, 1)
b = c(2, 1, 1, 1, 1, 0, 1, 1)
print (paste("Cosine similarity between A and B is",round(cosine(a,b), 4)))

m = nrow(ratings_mat);n = ncol(ratings_mat)
```

```
# User similarity
matrix mat_users = matrix(nrow = m, ncol = m)
for (i in 1:m){
  for (j in 1:m){
    if (i != j){
      mat_users[i,j] = cosine(ratings_mat[i,],ratings_mat[j,])
    } else {
      mat_users[i,j] = 0.0
    }
  }
}
colnames(mat_users) = rownames(ratings_mat);
rownames(mat_users) = rownames(ratings_mat)
df_users = as.data.frame(mat_users)

# Finding similar users
topn_simusers <- function(uid=16,n=5){
  sorted_df = sort(df_users[uid,],decreasing = TRUE)[1:n]
  print(paste("Similar users as user:",uid))
  return(sorted_df)
}
print(topn_simusers(uid = 17,n=10))

# Finding most rated movies of a user
library(sqldf)

ratings_withmovie = sqldf(" select a.*,b.title from ratings as a left join
movies as b on a.movieId = b.movieId")

# Finding most rated movies of a user
topn_movieratings <- function(uid=355,n_ratings=10){
  uid_ratings = ratings_withmovie[ratings_withmovie$userId==uid,]
  sorted_uidrtng = uid_ratings[order(-uid_ratings$rating),]
  return(head(sorted_uidrtng,n_ratings))
}
print( topn_movieratings(uid = 596,n=10))

# Movies similarity matrix
mat_movies = matrix(nrow = n, ncol = n)
for (i in 1:n){
  for (j in 1:n){
    if (i != j){
      mat_movies[i,j] = cosine(ratings_mat[,i],ratings_mat[,j])
    } else {
      mat_movies[i,j] = 0.0
    }
  }
}
```

```
colnames(mat_movies) = colnames(ratings_mat);
rownames(mat_movies) = colnames(ratings_mat)
df_movies = as.data.frame(mat_movies)

write.csv(df_movies,"df_movies.csv")

df_movies = read.csv("df_movies.csv")
rownames(df_movies) = df_movies$X
colnames(df_movies) = c("aaa",df_movies$X)
df_movies = subset(df_movies, select=-c(aaa))

# Finding similar movies
topn_simovies <- function(mid=588,n_movies=5){
  sorted_df = sort(df_movies[mid,],decreasing = TRUE)[1:n_movies]
  sorted_df_t = as.data.frame(t(sorted_df))
  colnames(sorted_df_t) = c("score")
  sorted_df_t$movieId = rownames(sorted_df_t)

  print(paste("Similar",n_movies, "movies as compared to the
movie",mid,"are :"))
  sorted_df_t_wmovie = sqldf(" select a.*,b.title from sorted_df_t as a
left join movies as b on a.movieId = b.movieId")
  return(sorted_df_t_wmovie)
}
print(topn_simovies(mid = 589,n_movies=15))

# Collaborative filtering
ratings = read.csv("ratings.csv")
movies = read.csv("movies.csv")

library(sqldf)
library(reshape2)
library(recommenderlab)

ratings_v2 = ratings[,-c(4)]
ratings_mat = acast(ratings_v2,userId~movieId)
ratings_mat2 = as(ratings_mat, "realRatingMatrix")

getRatingMatrix(ratings_mat2)

#Plotting user-item complete matrix
image(ratings_mat2, main = "Raw Ratings")

# Fitting ALS method on Data
rec=Recommender(ratings_mat2[1:nrow(ratings_mat2)],method="UBCF",
param=list(normalize = "Z-score",method="Cosine",nn=5, minRating=1))
rec_2=Recommender(ratings_mat2[1:nrow(ratings_mat2)],method="POPULAR")
```

```
print(rec)
print(rec_2)

names(getModel(rec))
getModel(rec)$nn

# Create predictions for all the users
recom_pred = predict(rec,ratings_mat2[1:nrow(ratings_mat2)],
type="ratings")

# Putting predictions into list
rec_list<-as(recom_pred,"list")
head(summary(rec_list))

print_recommendations <- function(uid=586,top_nmovies=10){
   recoms_list = rec_list[[uid]]
   sorted_df = as.data.frame(sort(recoms_list,decreasing =
TRUE)[1:top_nmovies])
   colnames(sorted_df) = c("score")
   sorted_df$movieId = rownames(sorted_df)
   print(paste("Movies recommended for the user",uid,"are follows:"))
   sorted_df_t_wmovie = sqldf(" select a.*,b.title from sorted_df as a left
join movies as b on a.movieId = b.movieId")
   return(sorted_df_t_wmovie)
}
print(print_recommendations(uid = 580,top_nmovies = 15))
```

Summary

In this chapter, you have learned about content-based and collaborative filtering techniques for recommending movies to users, either by considering the other users using cosine similarity, or matrix factorization to calculate by considering movie ratings. Computationally, content-based filtering is quicker to compute, but considers only one dimension, either other users or other similar movies. Whereas, in collaborative filtering, recommendations are provided by considering both the user and movie dimensions. All the Python implementation has been done from the first principles, as we do not have a good enough package for the same, and also, it is nice to know the basics. In R programming, we used the recommenderlab package to apply collaborative filtering. At the end, a grid search example was shown on how to tune the hyperparameter in recommendation engines.

In the next chapter, we will be covering the details of unsupervised learning, more precisely, clustering and principal component analysis models.

8
Unsupervised Learning

The goal of unsupervised learning is to discover the hidden patterns or structures of the data in which no target variable exists to perform either classification or regression methods. Unsupervised learning methods are often more challenging, as the outcomes are subjective and there is no simple goal for the analysis, such as predicting the class or continuous variable. These methods are performed as part of exploratory data analysis. On top of that, it can be hard to assess the results obtained from unsupervised learning methods, since there is no universally accepted mechanism for performing the validation of results.

Nonetheless, unsupervised learning methods have growing importance in various fields as a trending topic nowadays, and many researchers are actively working on them at the moment to explore this new horizon. A few good applications are:

- **Genomics**: Unsupervised learning applied to understanding genomic-wide biological insights from DNA to better understand diseases and peoples. These types of tasks are more exploratory in nature.
- **Search engine**: Search engines might choose which search results to display to a particular individual based on the click histories of other similar users.
- **Knowledge extraction**: To extract the taxonomies of concepts from raw text to generate the knowledge graph to create the semantic structures in the field of NLP.
- **Segmentation of customers**: In the banking industry, unsupervised learning like clustering is applied to group similar customers, and based on those segments, marketing departments design their contact strategies. For example, older, low-risk customers will be targeted with fixed deposit products and high-risk, younger customers will be targeted with credit cards or mutual funds, and so on.
- **Social network analysis**: To identify the cohesive groups of people in social networks who are more connected with each other and have similar characteristics in common.

In this chapter, we will be covering the following techniques to perform unsupervised learning with data which is openly available:

- K-means clustering
- Principal component analysis
- Singular value decomposition
- Deep auto encoders

K-means clustering

Clustering is the task of grouping observations in such a way that members of the same cluster are more similar to each other and members of different clusters are very different from each other.

Clustering is commonly used to explore a dataset to either identify the underlying patterns in it or to create a group of characteristics. In the case of social networks, they can be clustered to identify communities and to suggest missing connections between people. Here are a few examples:

- In anti-money laundering measures, suspicious activities and individuals can be identified using anomaly detection
- In biology, clustering is used to find groups of genes with similar expression patterns
- In marketing analytics, clustering is used to find segments of similar customers so that different marketing strategies can be applied to different customer segments accordingly

The k-means clustering algorithm is an iterative process of moving the centers of clusters or centroids to the mean position of their constituent points, and reassigning instances to their closest clusters iteratively until there is no significant change in the number of cluster centers possible or number of iterations reached.

The cost function of k-means is determined by the Euclidean distance (square-norm) between the observations belonging to that cluster with its respective centroid value. An intuitive way to understand the equation is, if there is only one cluster ($k=1$), then the distances between all the observations are compared with its single mean. Whereas, if, number of clusters increases to 2 ($k= 2$), then two-means are calculated and a few of the observations are assigned to cluster *1* and other observations are assigned to cluster two-based on proximity. Subsequently, distances are calculated in cost functions by applying the same distance measure, but separately to their cluster centers:

$$J = \sum_{k=1}^{K} \sum_{i \in C_k} \| x_i - \mu_k \|^2$$

K-means working methodology from first principles

The k-means working methodology is illustrated in the following example in which 12 instances are considered with their X and Y values. The task is to determine the optimal clusters out of the data.

Instance	X	Y
1	7	8
2	2	4
3	6	4
4	3	2
5	6	5
6	5	7
7	3	3
8	1	4
9	5	4
10	7	7
11	7	6
12	2	1

After plotting the data points on a 2D chart, we can see that roughly two clusters are possible, where below-left is the first cluster and the top-right is another cluster, but in many practical cases there would be so many variables (or dimensions) that, we cannot simply visualize them. Hence, we need a mathematical and algorithmic way to solve these types of problems.

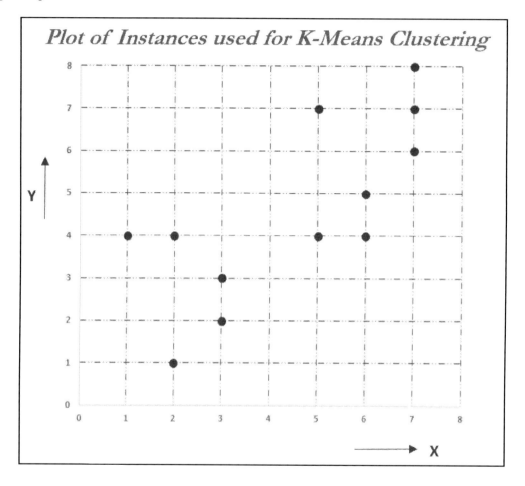

Iteration 1: Let us assume two centers from two instances out of all the *12* instances. Here, we have chosen instance *1 (X = 7, Y = 8)* and instance *8 (X = 1, Y = 4)*, as they seem to be at both extremes. For each instance, we will calculate its Euclidean distances with respect to both centroids and assign it to the nearest cluster center.

Instance	X	Y	Centroid 1 distance	Centroid 2 distance	Assigned cluster
1	7	8	7.21	0.00	C2
2	2	4	1.00	6.40	C1
3	6	4	5.00	4.12	C2
4	3	2	2.83	7.21	C1
5	6	5	5.10	3.16	C2
6	5	7	5.00	2.24	C2
7	3	3	2.24	6.40	C1
8	1	4	0.00	7.21	C1
9	5	4	4.00	4.47	C1
10	7	7	6.71	1.00	C2
11	7	6	6.32	2.00	C2
12	2	1	3.16	8.60	C1
Centroid 1	1	4			
Centroid 2	7	8			

The Euclidean distance between two points *A (X1, Y1)* and *B (X2, Y2)* is shown as follows:

$$Euclidean\ Distance\ between\ A\ \&\ B = \sqrt{(X2 - X1)^2 + (Y2 - Y1)^2}$$

Centroid distance calculations are performed by taking Euclidean distances. A sample calculation has been shown as follows. For instance, six with respect to both centroids (centroid 1 and centroid 2).

$$Distance\ w.r.to\ Centroid\ 1\ for\ Instance\ 6 = \sqrt{(5 - 1)^2 + (7 - 4)^2} = 5.00$$

$$Distance\ w.r.to\ Centroid\ 2\ for\ Instance\ 6 = \sqrt{(5 - 7)^2 + (7 - 8)^2} = 2.24$$

The following chart describes the assignment of instances to both centroids, which was shown in the preceding table format:

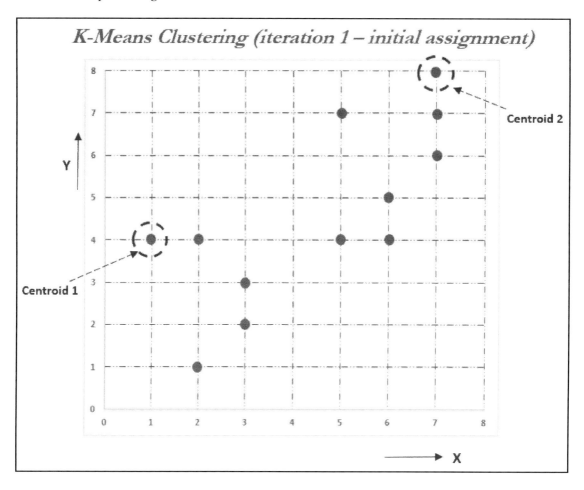

If we carefully observe the preceding chart, we realize that all the instances seem to be assigned appropriately apart from instance *9 (X = 5, Y = 4)*. However, in later stages, it should be assigned appropriately. Let us see in the below steps how the assignments evolve.

Iteration 2: In this iteration, new centroids are calculated from the assigned instances for that cluster or centroid. New centroids are calculated based on the simple average of the assigned points.

Instance	X	Y	Assigned cluster
1	7	8	C2
2	2	4	C1
3	6	4	C2
4	3	2	C1
5	6	5	C2
6	5	7	C2
7	3	3	C1
8	1	4	C1
9	5	4	C1
10	7	7	C2
11	7	6	C2
12	2	1	C1
Centroid 1	2.67	3	
Centroid 2	6.33	6.17	

Sample calculations for centroids 1 and 2 are shown as follows. A similar methodology will be applied on all subsequent iterations as well:

$$Centroid\ 1\ coordinates = Average\ coordinates\ (Instance\ 2, 4, 7, 8, 9, \& 12)$$

$$Centroid\ 2\ coordinates = Average\ coordinates\ (Instance\ 1, 3, 5, 6, 10\ \& 11)$$

$$Centroid\ 1\ X = \frac{(2 + 3 + 3 + 1 + 5 + 2)}{6} = 2.67$$

$$Centroid\ 1\ Y = \frac{(4 + 2 + 3 + 4 + 4 + 1)}{6} = 3.0$$

$$Centroid\ 2\ X = \frac{(7 + 6 + 6 + 5 + 7 + 7)}{6} = 6.33$$

$$Centroid\ 2\ Y = \frac{(8 + 4 + 5 + 7 + 7 + 6)}{6} = 6.17$$

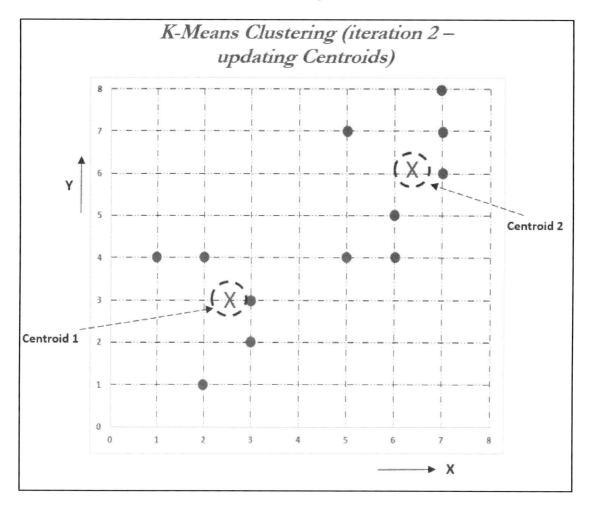

After updating the centroids, we need to reassign the instances to the nearest centroids, which we will be performing in iteration 3.

Iteration 3: In this iteration, new assignments are calculated based on the Euclidean distance between instances and new centroids. In the event of any changes, new centroids will be calculated iteratively until no changes in assignments are possible or the number of iterations is reached. The following table describes the distance measures between new centroids and all the instances:

Instance	X	Y	Centroid 1 distance	Centroid 2 distance	Previously assigned cluster	Newly assigned cluster	Changed?
1	7	8	6.61	1.95	C2	C2	No
2	2	4	1.20	4.84	C1	C1	No
3	6	4	3.48	2.19	C2	C2	No
4	3	2	1.05	5.34	C1	C1	No
5	6	5	3.88	1.22	C2	C2	No
6	5	7	4.63	1.57	C2	C2	No
7	3	3	0.33	4.60	C1	C1	No
8	1	4	1.95	5.75	C1	C1	No
9	5	4	2.54	2.55	C1	C1	No
10	7	7	5.89	1.07	C2	C2	No
11	7	6	5.27	0.69	C2	C2	No
12	2	1	2.11	6.74	C1	C1	No
Centroid 1	2.67	3					
Centroid 2	6.33	6.17					

It seems that there are no changes registered. Hence, we can say that the solution is converged. One important thing to note here is that all the instances are very clearly classified well, apart from instance 9 (X = 5, Y = 4). Based on instinct, it seems like it should be assigned to centroid 2, but after careful calculation, that instance is more proximate to cluster 1 than cluster 2. However, the difference in distance is low (2.54 with centroid 1 and 2.55 with centroid 2).

Optimal number of clusters and cluster evaluation

Though selecting number of clusters is more of an art than science, optimal number of clusters are chosen where, there will not be much marginal increase in explanation ability by increasing number of clusters are possible. In practical applications, usually business should be able to provide what would be approximate number of clusters they are looking for.

The elbow method

The elbow method is used to determine the optimal number of clusters in k-means clustering. The elbow method plots the value of the cost function produced by different values of k. As you know, if k increases, average distortion will decrease, each cluster will have fewer constituent instances, and the instances will be closer to their respective centroids. However, the improvements in average distortion will decline as k increases. The value of k at which improvement in distortion declines the most is called the elbow, at which we should stop dividing the data into further clusters.

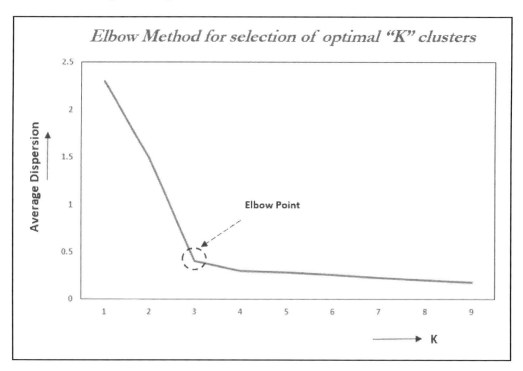

Evaluation of clusters with silhouette coefficient: the silhouette coefficient is a measure of the compactness and separation of the clusters. Higher values represent a better quality of cluster. The silhouette coefficient is higher for compact clusters that are well separated and lower for overlapping clusters. Silhouette coefficient values do change from -1 to +1, and the higher the value is, the better.

The silhouette coefficient is calculated per instance. For a set of instances, it is calculated as the mean of the individual sample's scores.

$$s = \frac{ba}{\max(a, b)}$$

a is the mean distance between the instances in the cluster, *b* is the mean distance between the instance and the instances in the next closest cluster.

K-means clustering with the iris data example

The famous iris data has been used from the UCI machine learning repository for illustration purposes using k-means clustering. The link for downloading the data is here: `http://archive.ics.uci.edu/ml/datasets/Iris`. The iris data has three types of flowers: setosa, versicolor, and virginica and their respective measurements of sepal length, sepal width, petal length, and petal width. Our task is to group the flowers based on their measurements. The code is as follows:

```
>>> import os
""" First change the following directory link to where all input files do
exist """
>>> os.chdir("D:\\Book writing\\Codes\\Chapter 8")

K-means algorithm from scikit-learn has been utilized in the following
example

# K-means clustering
>>> import numpy as np
>>> import pandas as pd
>>> import matplotlib.pyplot as plt
>>> from scipy.spatial.distance import cdist, pdist

>>> from sklearn.cluster import KMeans
>>> from sklearn.metrics import silhouette_score

>>> iris = pd.read_csv("iris.csv")
```

```
>>> print (iris.head())
```

sepal_length	sepal_width	petal_length	petal_width	class
5.1	3.5	1.4	0.2	Iris-setosa
4.9	3	1.4	0.2	Iris-setosa
4.7	3.2	1.3	0.2	Iris-setosa
4.6	3.1	1.5	0.2	Iris-setosa
5	3.6	1.4	0.2	Iris-setosa

Following code is used to separate `class` variable as dependent variable for creating colors in plot and unsupervised learning algorithm applied on given x variables without any target variable does present:

```
>>> x_iris = iris.drop(['class'],axis=1)
>>> y_iris = iris["class"]
```

As sample metrics, three clusters have been used, but in real life we do not know how many clusters data will fall under in advance, hence we need to test the results by trial and error. The maximum number of iterations chosen here is 300 in the following, however, this value can also be changed and the results checked accordingly:

```
>>> k_means_fit = KMeans(n_clusters=3,max_iter=300)
>>> k_means_fit.fit(x_iris)

>>> print ("\nK-Means Clustering - Confusion
Matrix\n\n",pd.crosstab(y_iris, k_means_fit.labels_,rownames =
["Actuall"],colnames = ["Predicted"]) )
>>> print ("\nSilhouette-score: %0.3f" % silhouette_score(x_iris,
k_means_fit.labels_, metric='euclidean'))
```

```
K-Means Clustering - Confusion Matrix

 Predicted         0   1   2
Actuall
Iris-setosa       50   0   0
Iris-versicolor    0  48   2
Iris-virginica     0  14  36

Silhouette-score: 0.553
```

From the previous confusion matrix, we can see that all the setosa flowers are clustered correctly, whereas 2 out of 50 versicolor, and 14 out of 50 virginica flowers are incorrectly classified.

 Again, to reiterate, in real-life examples we do not have the category names in advance, so we cannot measure accuracy, and so on.

Following code is used to perform sensitivity analysis to check how many number of clusters does actually provide better explanation of segments:

```
>>> for k in range(2,10):
...     k_means_fitk = KMeans(n_clusters=k,max_iter=300)
...     k_means_fitk.fit(x_iris)
...     print ("For K value",k,",Silhouette-score: %0.3f" %
silhouette_score(x_iris, k_means_fitk.labels_, metric='euclidean'))
```

```
For K value 2 ,Silhouette-score: 0.681
For K value 3 ,Silhouette-score: 0.553
For K value 4 ,Silhouette-score: 0.498
For K value 5 ,Silhouette-score: 0.489
For K value 6 ,Silhouette-score: 0.368
For K value 7 ,Silhouette-score: 0.360
For K value 8 ,Silhouette-score: 0.363
For K value 9 ,Silhouette-score: 0.339
```

The silhouette coefficient values in the preceding results shows that K value 2 and K value 3 have better scores than all the other values. As a thumb rule, we need to take the next K value of the highest silhouette coefficient. Here, we can say that K value 3 is better. In addition, we also need to see the average within cluster variation value and elbow plot before concluding the optimal K value.

```
# Avg. within-cluster sum of squares
>>> K = range(1,10)

>>> KM = [KMeans(n_clusters=k).fit(x_iris) for k in K]
>>> centroids = [k.cluster_centers_ for k in KM]

>>> D_k = [cdist(x_iris, centrds, 'euclidean') for centrds in centroids]

>>> cIdx = [np.argmin(D,axis=1) for D in D_k]
>>> dist = [np.min(D,axis=1) for D in D_k]
>>> avgWithinSS = [sum(d)/x_iris.shape[0] for d in dist]
```

```
# Total with-in sum of square
>>> wcss = [sum(d**2) for d in dist]
>>> tss = sum(pdist(x_iris)**2)/x_iris.shape[0]
>>> bss = tss-wcss

# elbow curve - Avg. within-cluster sum of squares
>>> fig = plt.figure()
>>> ax = fig.add_subplot(111)
>>> ax.plot(K, avgWithinSS, 'b*-')
>>> plt.grid(True)
>>> plt.xlabel('Number of clusters')
>>> plt.ylabel('Average within-cluster sum of squares')
```

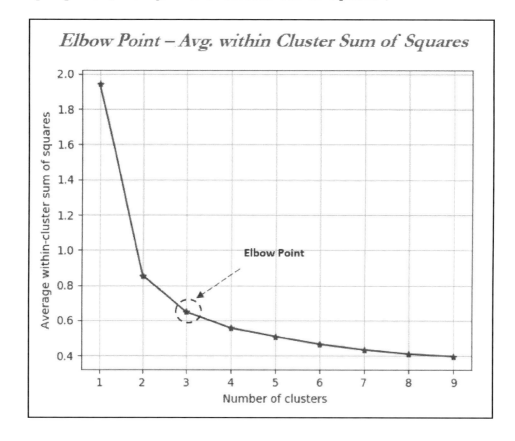

From the elbow plot, it seems that at the value of three, the slope changes drastically. Here, we can select the optimal k-value as three.

```
# elbow curve - percentage of variance explained
>>> fig = plt.figure()
>>> ax = fig.add_subplot(111)
>>> ax.plot(K, bss/tss*100, 'b*-')
>>> plt.grid(True)
>>> plt.xlabel('Number of clusters')
>>> plt.ylabel('Percentage of variance explained')
>>> plt.show()
```

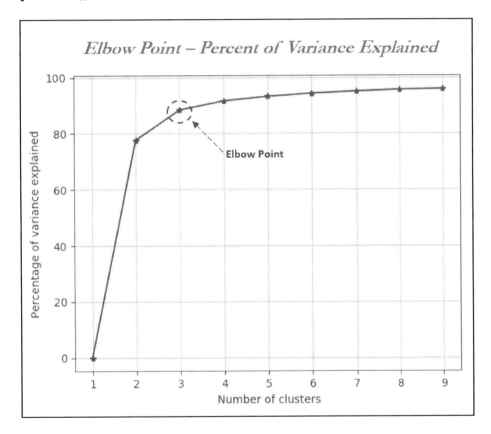

Last but not least, the total percentage of variance explained value should be greater than 80 percent to decide the optimal number of clusters. Even here, a k-value of three seems to give a decent value of total variance explained. Hence, we can conclude from all the preceding metrics (silhouette, average within cluster variance, and total variance explained), that three clusters are ideal.

The R code for k-means clustering using iris data is as follows:

```
setwd("D:\\Book   writing\\Codes\\Chapter 8")
iris_data = read.csv("iris.csv")
x_iris =   iris_data[,!names(iris_data) %in% c("class")]
y_iris = iris_data$class
km_fit = kmeans(x_iris,centers   = 3,iter.max = 300 )
print(paste("K-Means   Clustering- Confusion matrix"))
table(y_iris,km_fit$cluster)
mat_avgss = matrix(nrow = 10,   ncol = 2)
# Average within the cluster   sum of square
print(paste("Avg. Within   sum of squares"))
for (i in (1:10)){
  km_fit =   kmeans(x_iris,centers = i,iter.max = 300 )
  mean_km =   mean(km_fit$withinss)
  print(paste("K-Value",i,",Avg.within   sum of squares",round(mean_km,
2)))
  mat_avgss[i,1] = i
  mat_avgss[i,2] = mean_km
}
plot(mat_avgss[,1],mat_avgss[,2],type   = 'o',xlab = "K_Value",ylab = "Avg.
within sum of square")
title("Avg. within sum of   squares vs. K-value")
mat_varexp = matrix(nrow = 10,   ncol = 2)
# Percentage of Variance   explained
print(paste("Percent.   variance explained"))
for (i in (1:10)){
  km_fit =   kmeans(x_iris,centers = i,iter.max = 300 )
  var_exp =   km_fit$betweenss/km_fit$totss
  print(paste("K-Value",i,",Percent   var explained",round(var_exp,4)))
  mat_varexp[i,1]=i
  mat_varexp[i,2]=var_exp
}
plot(mat_varexp[,1],mat_varexp[,2],type   = 'o',xlab = "K_Value",ylab =
"Percent Var explained")
title("Avg. within sum of   squares vs. K-value")
```

Principal component analysis - PCA

Principal component analysis (PCA) is the dimensionality reduction technique which has so many utilities. PCA reduces the dimensions of a dataset by projecting the data onto a lower-dimensional subspace. For example, a 2D dataset could be reduced by projecting the points onto a line. Each instance in the dataset would then be represented by a single value, rather than a pair of values. In a similar way, a 3D dataset could be reduced to two dimensions by projecting variables onto a plane. PCA has the following utilities:

- Mitigate the course of dimensionality
- Compress the data while minimizing the information lost at the same time
- Principal components will be further utilized in the next stage of supervised learning, in random forest, boosting, and so on
- Understanding the structure of data with hundreds of dimensions can be difficult, hence, by reducing the dimensions to 2D or 3D, observations can be visualized easily

PCA can easily be explained with the following diagram of a mechanical bracket which has been drawn in the machine drawing module of a mechanical engineering course. The left-hand side of the diagram depicts the top view, front view, and side view of the component. However, on the right-hand side, an isometric view has been drawn, in which one single image has been used to visualize how the component looks. So, one can imagine that the left-hand images are the actual variables and the right-hand side is the first principal component, in which most variance has been captured.

Finally, three images have been replaced by a single image by rotating the axis of direction. In fact, we replicate the same technique in PCA analysis.

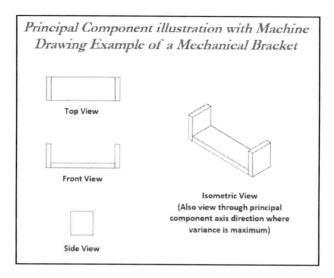

Principal component working methodology is explained in the following sample example, in which actual data has been shown in a 2D space, in which *X* and *Y* axis are used to plot the data. Principal components are the ones in which maximum variation of the data is captured.

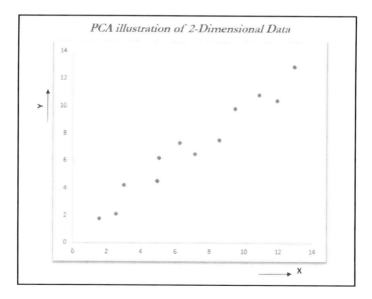

The following diagram illustrates how it looks after fitting the principal components. The first principal component covers the maximum variance in the data and the second principal component is orthogonal to the first principal component, as we know all principal components are orthogonal to each other. We can represent whole data with the first principal component itself. In fact, that is how it is advantageous to represent the data with fewer dimensions, to save space and also to grab maximum variance in the data, which can be utilized for supervised learning in the next stage. This is the core advantage of computing principal components.

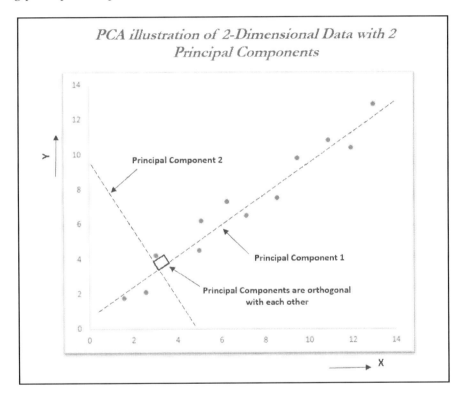

Eigenvectors and eigenvalues have significant importance in the field of linear algebra, physics, mechanics, and so on. Refreshing, basics on eigenvectors and eigenvalues is necessary when studying PCAs. Eigenvectors are the axes (directions) along which a linear transformation acts simply by *stretching/compressing* and/or *flipping*; whereas, eigenvalues give you the factors by which the compression occurs. In another way, an eigenvector of a linear transformation is a nonzero vector whose direction does not change when that linear transformation is applied to it.

More formally, A is a linear transformation from a vector space and $\vec{v}$ is a nonzero vector, then eigen vector of A if $\vec{Av}$ is a scalar multiple of $\vec{v}$. The condition can be written as the following equation:

$$A\vec{v} = \lambda \vec{v}$$

In the preceding equation, $\vec{v}$ is an eigenvector, A is a square matrix, and λ is a scalar called an eigenvalue. The direction of an eigenvector remains the same after it has been transformed by A; only its magnitude has changed, as indicated by the eigenvalue, That is, multiplying a matrix by one of its eigenvectors is equal to scaling the eigenvector, which is a compact representation of the original matrix. The following graph describes eigenvectors and eigenvalues in a graphical representation in a 2D space:

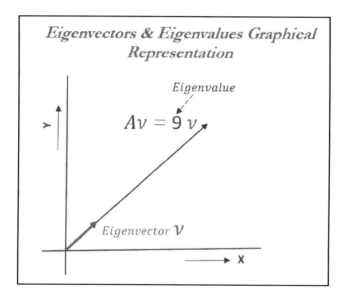

The following example describes how to calculate eigenvectors and eigenvalues from the square matrix and its understanding. Note that eigenvectors and eigenvalues can be calculated only for square matrices (those with the same dimensions of rows and columns).

$$A = \begin{bmatrix} 2 & -4 \\ 4 & -6 \end{bmatrix}$$

Recall the equation that the product of A and any eigenvector of A must be equal to the eigenvector multiplied by the magnitude of eigenvalue:

$$(A - \lambda I)\vec{v} = 0$$

$$|A - \lambda * I| = \left| \begin{bmatrix} 2 & -4 \\ 4 & -6 \end{bmatrix} - \begin{bmatrix} \lambda & 0 \\ 0 & \lambda \end{bmatrix} \right| = 0$$

A characteristic equation states that the determinant of the matrix, that is the difference between the data matrix and the product of the identity matrix and an eigenvalue is 0.

$$\left| \begin{bmatrix} 2 - \lambda & -4 \\ 4 & -6 - \lambda \end{bmatrix} \right| = (\lambda + 2)(\lambda + 2) = 0$$

Both eigenvalues for the preceding matrix are equal to -2. We can use eigenvalues to substitute for eigenvectors in an equation:

$$A\vec{v} = \lambda \vec{v}$$

$$(A - \lambda I)\vec{v} = 0$$

$$\left(\begin{bmatrix} 2 & -4 \\ 4 & -6 \end{bmatrix} - \begin{bmatrix} \lambda & 0 \\ 0 & \lambda \end{bmatrix} \right)\vec{v} = \begin{bmatrix} 2 - \lambda & -4 \\ 4 & -6 - \lambda \end{bmatrix} \vec{v} =$$

$$\begin{bmatrix} 2 - \lambda & -4 \\ 4 & -6 - \lambda \end{bmatrix} \begin{bmatrix} v_{1,1} \\ v_{1,2} \end{bmatrix} = 0$$

Substituting the value of eigenvalue in the preceding equation, we will obtain the following formula:

$$\begin{bmatrix} 2 - (-2) & -4 \\ 4 & -6 - (-2) \end{bmatrix} \begin{bmatrix} v_{1,1} \\ v_{1,2} \end{bmatrix} = \begin{bmatrix} 4 & -4 \\ 4 & -4 \end{bmatrix} \begin{bmatrix} v_{1,1} \\ v_{1,2} \end{bmatrix} = 0$$

The preceding equation can be rewritten as a system of equations, as follows:

$$4 * v_{1,1} - 4 * v_{1,2} = 0$$

$$4 * v_{1,1} - 4 * v_{1,2} = 0$$

This equation indicates it can have multiple solutions of eigenvectors we can substitute with any values which hold the preceding equation for verification of equation. Here, we have used the vector *[1 1]* for verification, which seems to be proved.

$$\begin{bmatrix} 2 & -4 \\ 4 & -6 \end{bmatrix} \begin{bmatrix} 1 \\ 1 \end{bmatrix} = -2 \begin{bmatrix} 1 \\ 1 \end{bmatrix} = \begin{bmatrix} -2 \\ -2 \end{bmatrix}$$

PCA needs unit eigenvectors to be used in calculations, hence we need to divide the same with the norm or we need to normalize the eigenvector. The 2-norm equation is shown as follows:

$$\|x\| = \sqrt{x_1^2 + x_2^2 + \cdots + x_n^2}$$

The norm of the output vector is calculated as follows:

$$\left\| \begin{bmatrix} 1 \\ 1 \end{bmatrix} \right\| = \sqrt{1^2 + 1^2} = \sqrt{2}$$

The unit eigenvector is shown as follows:

$$\begin{bmatrix} 1 \\ 1 \end{bmatrix} / \sqrt{2} = \begin{bmatrix} 0.7071 \\ 0.7071 \end{bmatrix}$$

PCA working methodology from first principles

PCA working methodology is described in the following sample data, which has two dimensions for each instance or data point. The objective here is to reduce the 2D data into one dimension (also known as the **principal component**):

Instance	X	Y
1	0.72	0.13
2	0.18	0.23
3	2.50	2.30
4	0.45	0.16
5	0.04	0.44

6	0.13	0.24
7	0.30	0.03
8	2.65	2.10
9	0.91	0.91
10	0.46	0.32
Column mean	0.83	0.69

The first step, prior to proceeding with any analysis, is to subtract the mean from all the observations, which removes the scale factor of variables and makes them more uniform across dimensions.

X	Y
0.72 - 0.83 = -0.12	0.13 - 0.69 = - 0.55
0.18 - 0.83 = -0.65	0.23 - 0.69 = - 0.46
2.50 - 0.83 = 1.67	2.30 - 0.69 = 1.61
0.45 - 0.83 = -0.38	0.16 - 0.69 = - 0.52
0.04 - 0.83 = -0.80	0.44 - 0.69 = - 0.25
0.13 - 0.83 = -0.71	0.24 - 0.69 = - 0.45
0.30 - 0.83 = -0.53	0.03 - 0.69 = - 0.66
2.65 - 0.83 = 1.82	2.10 - 0.69 = 1.41
0.91 - 0.83 = 0.07	0.91 - 0.69 = 0.23
0.46 - 0.83 = -0.37	0.32 - 0.69 = -0.36

Principal components are calculated using two different techniques:

- Covariance matrix of the data
- Singular value decomposition

We will be covering the singular value decomposition technique in the next section. In this section, we will solve eigenvectors and eigenvalues using covariance matrix methodology.

Covariance is a measure of how much two variables change together and it is a measure of the strength of the correlation between two sets of variables. If the covariance of two variables is zero, we can conclude that there will not be any correlation between two sets of the variables. The formula for covariance is as follows:

$$cov\ (x, y) = \frac{\sum_{i=1}^{n}(X_i - \bar{X})(Y_i - \bar{Y})}{n - 1}$$

A sample covariance calculation is shown for X and Y variables in the following formulas. However, it is a 2 x 2 matrix of an entire covariance matrix (also, it is a square matrix).

$$cov\ (Y, Y) =$$

$$\frac{((-0.55)^2 + (-0.46)^2 + (1.61)^2 + (-0.52)^2 + (-0.25)^2 + (-0.45)^2 + (-0.66)^2 + (1.41)^2 + (0.23)^2 + (-0.36)^2)}{10 - 1}$$

$$cov\ (Y, Y) = 0.697029$$

$$Covariance\ matrix = C = \begin{bmatrix} 0.91335 & 0.75969 \\ 0.75969 & 0.69702 \end{bmatrix}$$

Since the covariance matrix is square, we can calculate eigenvectors and eigenvalues from it. You can refer to the methodology explained in an earlier section.

$$|A - \lambda * I| = \left| \begin{bmatrix} 0.91335 & 0.75969 \\ 0.75969 & 0.69702 \end{bmatrix} - \begin{bmatrix} \lambda & 0 \\ 0 & \lambda \end{bmatrix} \right| = 0$$

By solving the preceding equation, we can obtain eigenvectors and eigenvalues, as follows:

$$Eigenvalues = \begin{bmatrix} 1.5725 & 0.0378 \end{bmatrix}$$

$$Unit\ Eigenvectors = \begin{bmatrix} 0.7553 & -0.6553 \\ 0.6553 & 0.7553 \end{bmatrix}$$

The preceding mentioned results can be obtained with the following Python syntax:

```
>>> import numpy as np
>>> w, v = np.linalg.eig(np.array([[ 0.91335 ,0.75969 ],[ 0.75969,0.69702]]))
\>>> print ("\nEigen Values\n", w)
>>> print ("\nEigen Vectors\n", v)
```

```
Eigen Values
 [ 1.57253666  0.03783334]

Eigen Vectors
 [[ 0.75530088 -0.6553782 ]
 [ 0.6553782   0.75530088]]
```

Once we obtain the eigenvectors and eigenvalues, we can project data into principal components. The first eigenvector has the greatest eigenvalue and is the first principal component, as we would like to reduce the original 2D data into 1D data.

$$
\begin{bmatrix}
-0.12 & -0.55 \\
-0.65 & -0.46 \\
1.67 & 1.61 \\
-0.38 & -0.52 \\
-0.80 & -0.25 \\
-0.71 & -0.45 \\
-0.53 & -0.66 \\
1.82 & 1.41 \\
0.07 & 0.23 \\
-0.37 & -0.36
\end{bmatrix}
\begin{bmatrix}
0.7553 \\
0.6553
\end{bmatrix}
=
\begin{bmatrix}
-0.45 \\
-0.79 \\
2.31 \\
-0.63 \\
-0.76 \\
-0.82 \\
-0.83 \\
2.29 \\
0.20 \\
-0.51
\end{bmatrix}
$$

From the preceding result, we can see the 1D projection of the first principal component from the original 2D data. Also, the eigenvalue of 1.5725 explains the fact that the principal component explains variance of 57 percent more than the original variables. In the case of multi-dimensional data, the thumb rule is to select the eigenvalues or principal components with a value greater than what should be considered for projection.

PCA applied on handwritten digits using scikit-learn

The PCA example has been illustrated with the handwritten digits example from scikit-learn datasets, in which handwritten digits are created from 0-9 and its respective 64 features (8 x 8 matrix) of pixel intensities. Here, the idea is to represent the original features of 64 dimensions into as few as possible:

```
# PCA - Principal Component Analysis
>>> import matplotlib.pyplot as plt
```

```
>>> from sklearn.decomposition import PCA
>>> from sklearn.datasets import load_digits

>>> digits = load_digits()
>>> X = digits.data
>>> y = digits.target


>>> print (digits.data[0].reshape(8,8))
```

```
[[  0.   0.   5.  13.   9.   1.   0.   0.]
 [  0.   0.  13.  15.  10.  15.   5.   0.]
 [  0.   3.  15.   2.   0.  11.   8.   0.]
 [  0.   4.  12.   0.   0.   8.   8.   0.]
 [  0.   5.   8.   0.   0.   9.   8.   0.]
 [  0.   4.  11.   0.   1.  12.   7.   0.]
 [  0.   2.  14.   5.  10.  12.   0.   0.]
 [  0.   0.   6.  13.  10.   0.   0.   0.]]
```

Plot the graph using the `plt.show` function:

```
>>> plt.matshow(digits.images[0])
>>> plt.show()
```

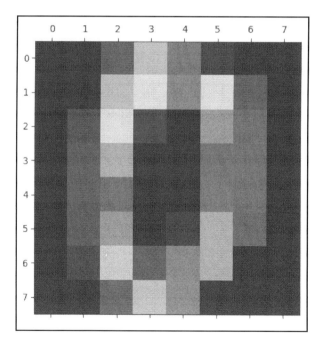

Before performing PCA, it is advisable to perform scaling of input data to eliminate any issues due to different dimensions of the data. For example, while applying PCA on customer data, their salary has larger dimensions than the customer's age. Hence, if we do not put all the variables in a similar dimension, one variable will explain the entire variation rather than its actual impact. In the following code, we have applied scaling on all the columns separately:

```
>>> from sklearn.preprocessing import scale
>>> X_scale = scale(X,axis=0)
```

In the following, we have used two principal components, so that we can represent the performance on a 2D graph. In later sections, we have applied 3D as well.

```
>>> pca = PCA(n_components=2)
>>> reduced_X = pca.fit_transform(X_scale)

>>> zero_x, zero_y = [],[] ; one_x, one_y = [],[]
>>> two_x,two_y = [],[]; three_x, three_y = [],[]
>>> four_x,four_y = [],[]; five_x,five_y = [],[]
>>> six_x,six_y = [],[]; seven_x,seven_y = [],[]
>>> eight_x,eight_y = [],[]; nine_x,nine_y = [],[]
```

In the following section of code, we are appending the relevant principal components to each digit separately so that we can create a scatter plot of all 10 digits:

```
>>> for i in range(len(reduced_X)):
...     if y[i] == 0:
...         zero_x.append(reduced_X[i][0])
...         zero_y.append(reduced_X[i][1])
...     elif y[i] == 1:
...         one_x.append(reduced_X[i][0])
...         one_y.append(reduced_X[i][1])

...     elif y[i] == 2:
...         two_x.append(reduced_X[i][0])
...         two_y.append(reduced_X[i][1])

...     elif y[i] == 3:
...         three_x.append(reduced_X[i][0])
...         three_y.append(reduced_X[i][1])

...     elif y[i] == 4:
...         four_x.append(reduced_X[i][0])
...         four_y.append(reduced_X[i][1])

...     elif y[i] == 5:
...         five_x.append(reduced_X[i][0])
```

```
...            five_y.append(reduced_X[i][1])

...        elif y[i] == 6:
...            six_x.append(reduced_X[i][0])
...            six_y.append(reduced_X[i][1])

...        elif y[i] == 7:
...            seven_x.append(reduced_X[i][0])
...            seven_y.append(reduced_X[i][1])

...        elif y[i] == 8:
...            eight_x.append(reduced_X[i][0])
...            eight_y.append(reduced_X[i][1])
...        elif y[i] == 9:
...            nine_x.append(reduced_X[i][0])
...            nine_y.append(reduced_X[i][1])

>>> zero = plt.scatter(zero_x, zero_y, c='r', marker='x',label='zero')
>>> one = plt.scatter(one_x, one_y, c='g', marker='+')
>>> two = plt.scatter(two_x, two_y, c='b', marker='s')

>>> three = plt.scatter(three_x, three_y, c='m', marker='*')
>>> four = plt.scatter(four_x, four_y, c='c', marker='h')
>>> five = plt.scatter(five_x, five_y, c='r', marker='D')

>>> six = plt.scatter(six_x, six_y, c='y', marker='8')
>>> seven = plt.scatter(seven_x, seven_y, c='k', marker='*')
>>> eight = plt.scatter(eight_x, eight_y, c='r', marker='x')

>>> nine = plt.scatter(nine_x, nine_y, c='b', marker='D')


>>> plt.legend((zero,one,two,three,four,five,six,seven,eight,nine),
...            ('zero','one','two','three','four','five','six',
'seven','eight','nine'),
...            scatterpoints=1,
...            loc='lower left',
...            ncol=3,
...            fontsize=10)

>>> plt.xlabel('PC 1')
>>> plt.ylabel('PC 2')

>>> plt.show()
```

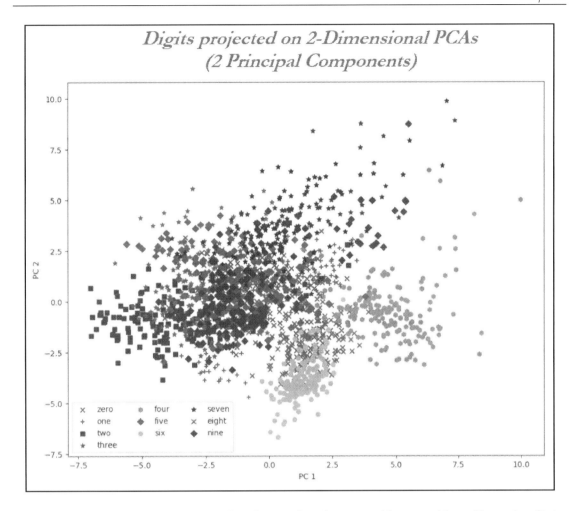

Though the preceding plot seems a bit cluttered, it does provide some idea of how the digits are close to and distant from each other. We get the idea that digits *6* and *8* are very similar and digits *4* and *7* are very distant from the center group, and so on. However, we should also try with a higher number of PCAs, as, sometimes, we might not be able to represent every variation in two dimensions itself.

In the following code, we have applied three PCAs so that we can get a better view of the data in a 3D space. The procedure is very much similar as with two PCAs, except for creating one extra dimension for each digit (*X*, *Y*, and *Z*).

```
# 3-Dimensional data
>>> pca_3d = PCA(n_components=3)
>>> reduced_X3D = pca_3d.fit_transform(X_scale)

>>> zero_x, zero_y,zero_z = [],[],[] ; one_x, one_y,one_z = [],[],[]
>>> two_x,two_y,two_z = [],[],[]; three_x, three_y,three_z = [],[],[]
>>> four_x,four_y,four_z = [],[],[]; five_x,five_y,five_z = [],[],[]
>>> six_x,six_y,six_z = [],[],[]; seven_x,seven_y,seven_z = [],[],[]
>>> eight_x,eight_y,eight_z = [],[],[]; nine_x,nine_y,nine_z = [],[],[]


>>> for i in range(len(reduced_X3D)):
...      if y[i]==10:
...           continue
...      elif y[i] == 0:
...           zero_x.append(reduced_X3D[i][0])
...           zero_y.append(reduced_X3D[i][1])
...           zero_z.append(reduced_X3D[i][2])
...      elif y[i] == 1:
...           one_x.append(reduced_X3D[i][0])
...           one_y.append(reduced_X3D[i][1])
...           one_z.append(reduced_X3D[i][2])

...      elif y[i] == 2:
...           two_x.append(reduced_X3D[i][0])
...           two_y.append(reduced_X3D[i][1])
...           two_z.append(reduced_X3D[i][2])

...      elif y[i] == 3:
...           three_x.append(reduced_X3D[i][0])
...           three_y.append(reduced_X3D[i][1])
...           three_z.append(reduced_X3D[i][2])

...      elif y[i] == 4:
...           four_x.append(reduced_X3D[i][0])
...           four_y.append(reduced_X3D[i][1])
...           four_z.append(reduced_X3D[i][2])

...      elif y[i] == 5:
...           five_x.append(reduced_X3D[i][0])
...           five_y.append(reduced_X3D[i][1])
...           five_z.append(reduced_X3D[i][2])

...      elif y[i] == 6:
```

```
...                six_x.append(reduced_X3D[i][0])
...                six_y.append(reduced_X3D[i][1])
...                six_z.append(reduced_X3D[i][2])

...        elif y[i] == 7:
...                seven_x.append(reduced_X3D[i][0])
...                seven_y.append(reduced_X3D[i][1])
...                seven_z.append(reduced_X3D[i][2])

...        elif y[i] == 8:
...                eight_x.append(reduced_X3D[i][0])
...                eight_y.append(reduced_X3D[i][1])
...                eight_z.append(reduced_X3D[i][2])
...        elif y[i] == 9:
...                nine_x.append(reduced_X3D[i][0])
...                nine_y.append(reduced_X3D[i][1])
...                nine_z.append(reduced_X3D[i][2])


# 3- Dimensional plot
>>> from mpl_toolkits.mplot3d import Axes3D
>>> fig = plt.figure()
>>> ax = fig.add_subplot(111, projection='3d')

>>> ax.scatter(zero_x, zero_y,zero_z, c='r', marker='x',label='zero')
>>> ax.scatter(one_x, one_y,one_z, c='g', marker='+',label='one')
>>> ax.scatter(two_x, two_y,two_z, c='b', marker='s',label='two')

>>> ax.scatter(three_x, three_y,three_z, c='m', marker='*',label='three')
>>> ax.scatter(four_x, four_y,four_z, c='c', marker='h',label='four')
>>> ax.scatter(five_x, five_y,five_z, c='r', marker='D',label='five')

>>> ax.scatter(six_x, six_y,six_z, c='y', marker='8',label='six')
>>> ax.scatter(seven_x, seven_y,seven_z, c='k', marker='*',label='seven')
>>> ax.scatter(eight_x, eight_y,eight_z, c='r', marker='x',label='eight')

>>> ax.scatter(nine_x, nine_y,nine_z, c='b', marker='D',label='nine')

>>> ax.set_xlabel('PC 1')
>>> ax.set_ylabel('PC 2')
>>> ax.set_zlabel('PC 3')

>>> plt.legend(loc='upper left', numpoints=1, ncol=3, fontsize=10,
bbox_to_anchor=(0, 0))

>>> plt.show()
```

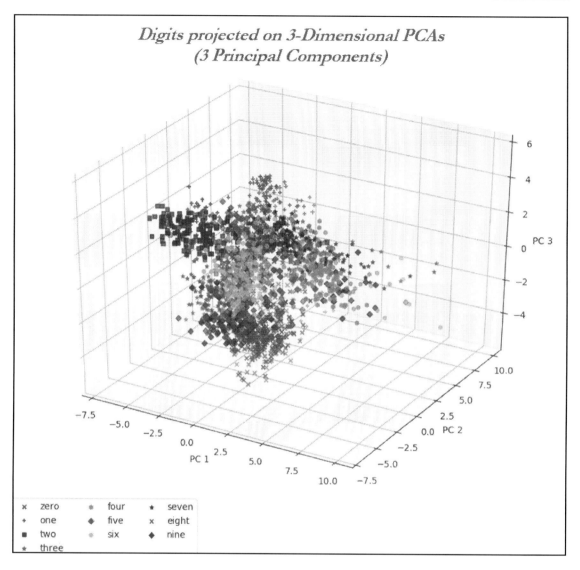

matplotlib plots have one great advantage over other software plots such as R plot, and so on. They are interactive, which means that we can rotate them and see how they looks from various directions. We encourage the reader to observe the plot by rotating and exploring. In a 3D plot, we can see a similar story with more explanation. Digit 2 is at the extreme left and digit 0 is at the lower part of the plot. Whereas, digit 4 is at the top-right end, digit 6 seems to be more towards the *PC 1* axis. In this way, we can visualize and see how digits are distributed. In the case of 4 PCAs, we need to go for subplots and visualize them separately.

Choosing the number of PCAs to be extracted is an open-ended question in unsupervised learning, but there are some turnarounds to get an approximated view. There are two ways we can determine the number of clusters:

- Check where the total variance explained is diminishing marginally
- Total variance explained greater than 80 percent

The following code does provide the total variance explained with the change in number of principal components. With the more number of PCs, more variance will be explained. But however, the challenge is to restrict it as less PCs possible, this will be achieved by restricting where the marginal increase in variance explained start diminishes.

```
# Choosing number of Principal Components
>>> max_pc = 30

>>> pcs = []
>>> totexp_var = []

>>> for i in range(max_pc):
...        pca = PCA(n_components=i+1)
...        reduced_X = pca.fit_transform(X_scale)
...        tot_var = pca.explained_variance_ratio_.sum()
...        pcs.append(i+1)
...        totexp_var.append(tot_var)

>>> plt.plot(pcs,totexp_var,'r')
>>> plt.plot(pcs,totexp_var,'bs')
>>> plt.xlabel('No. of PCs',fontsize = 13)
>>> plt.ylabel('Total variance explained',fontsize = 13)

>>> plt.xticks(pcs,fontsize=13)
>>> plt.yticks(fontsize=13)
>>> plt.show()
```

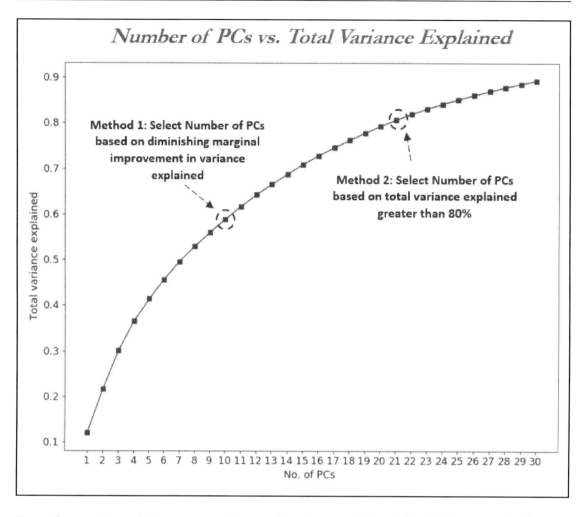

From the previous plot, we can see that total variance explained diminishes marginally at 10 PCAs; whereas, total variance explained greater than 80 percent is given at 21 PCAs. It is up to the business and user which value to choose.

The R code for PCA applied on handwritten digits data is as follows:

```
# PCA
digits_data = read.csv("digitsdata.csv")
remove_cols = c("target")
x_data =  digits_data[,!(names(digits_data) %in% remove_cols)]
y_data = digits_data[,c("target")]
# Normalizing the data
normalize <- function(x)   {return((x - min(x)) / (max(x) - min(x)))}
```

```
data_norm <-   as.data.frame(lapply(x_data, normalize))
data_norm <-   replace(data_norm, is.na(data_norm), 0.0)
# Extracting Principal   Components
pr_out =prcomp(data_norm)
pr_components_all = pr_out$x
# 2- Dimensional PCA
K_prcomps = 2
pr_components =   pr_components_all[,1:K_prcomps]
pr_components_df =   data.frame(pr_components)
pr_components_df =   cbind(pr_components_df,digits_data$target)
names(pr_components_df)[K_prcomps+1]   = "target"
out <- split(   pr_components_df , f = pr_components_df$target )
zero_df = out$`0`;one_df =   out$`1`;two_df = out$`2`; three_df = out$`3`;
four_df = out$`4`
five_df = out$`5`;six_df =   out$`6`;seven_df = out$`7`;eight_df =
out$`8`;nine_df = out$`9`
library(ggplot2)
# Plotting 2-dimensional PCA
ggplot(pr_components_df, aes(x   = PC1, y = PC2, color =
factor(target,labels = c("zero","one","two",   "three","four",
"five","six","seven","eight","nine"))))   +
geom_point()+ggtitle("2-D   PCA on Digits Data") +
labs(color = "Digtis")
# 3- Dimensional PCA
# Plotting 3-dimensional PCA
K_prcomps = 3
pr_components =   pr_components_all[,1:K_prcomps]
pr_components_df =   data.frame(pr_components)
pr_components_df =   cbind(pr_components_df,digits_data$target)
names(pr_components_df)[K_prcomps+1]   = "target"
pr_components_df$target =   as.factor(pr_components_df$target)
out <- split(   pr_components_df , f = pr_components_df$target )
zero_df = out$`0`;one_df =   out$`1`;two_df = out$`2`; three_df = out$`3`;
four_df = out$`4`
five_df = out$`5`;six_df =   out$`6`;seven_df = out$`7`;eight_df =
out$`8`;nine_df = out$`9`
library(scatterplot3d)
colors <- c("darkred",   "darkseagreen4", "deeppink4", "greenyellow",
"orange",   "navyblue", "red", "tan3", "steelblue1",   "slateblue")
colors <- colors[as.numeric(pr_components_df$target)]
s3d =   scatterplot3d(pr_components_df[,1:3], pch = 16, color=colors,
xlab = "PC1",ylab = "PC2",zlab   = "PC3",col.grid="lightblue",main = "3-D
PCA on   Digits Data")
legend(s3d$xyz.convert(3.1,   0.1, -3.5), pch = 16, yjust=0,
       legend =   levels(pr_components_df$target),col =colors,cex =
1.1,xjust = 0)
# Choosing number of Principal   Components
pr_var =pr_out$sdev ^2
```

```
pr_totvar = pr_var/sum(pr_var)
plot(cumsum(pr_totvar), xlab="Principal   Component", ylab ="Cumilative
Prop. of Var.",   ylim=c(0,1),type="b",main = "PCAs vs. Cum prop of Var
Explained")
```

Singular value decomposition - SVD

Many implementations of PCA use singular value decomposition to calculate eigenvectors and eigenvalues. SVD is given by the following equation:

$$X = U \, \Sigma \, V^T$$

Operations performed on data = (rotate) (stretch) (rotate)

Columns of U are called left singular vectors of the data matrix, the columns of V are its right singular vectors, and the diagonal entries of Σ are its singular values. Left singular vectors are the eigenvectors of the covariance matrix and the diagonal element of Σ are the square roots of the eigenvalues of the covariance matrix.

Before proceeding with SVD, it would be advisable to understand a few advantages and important points about SVD:

- SVD can be applied even on rectangular matrices; whereas, eigenvalues are defined only for square matrices. The equivalent of eigenvalues obtained through the SVD method are called singular values, and vectors obtained equivalent to eigenvectors are known as singular vectors. However, as they are rectangular in nature, we need to have left singular vectors and right singular vectors respectively for their dimensions.

- If a matrix A has a matrix of eigenvectors P that is not invertible, then A does not have an eigen decomposition. However, if A is $m \times n$ real matrix with $m > n$, then A can be written using a singular value decomposition.

- Both U and V are orthogonal matrices, which means $U^T U = I$ (I with $m \times m$ dimension) or $V^T V = I$ (here I with $n \times n$ dimension), where two identity matrices may have different dimensions.

- Σ is a non-negative diagonal matrix with $m \times n$ dimensions.

Then computation of singular values and singular vectors is done with the following set of equations:

$$X^T X = V \Sigma^T \Sigma V^T$$

In the first stage, singular values/eigenvalues are calculated with the equation. Once we obtain the singular/eigenvalues, we will substitute to determine the *V* or right singular/eigen vectors:

$$\det(X^T X - \lambda * I) = 0$$

Once we obtain the right singular vectors and diagonal values, we will substitute to obtain the left singular vectors *U* using the equation mentioned as follows:

$$X V = U \Sigma$$

In this way, we will calculate the singular value decompositions of the original system of equations matrix.

SVD applied on handwritten digits using scikit-learn

SVD can be applied on the same handwritten digits data to perform an apple-to-apple comparison of techniques.

```
# SVD
>>> import matplotlib.pyplot as plt
>>> from sklearn.datasets import load_digits

>>> digits = load_digits()
>>> X = digits.data
>>> y = digits.target
```

In the following code, 15 singular vectors with 300 iterations are used, but we encourage the reader to change the values and check the performance of SVD. We have used two types of SVD functions, as a function `randomized_svd` provide the decomposition of the original matrix and a `TruncatedSVD` can provide total variance explained ratio. In practice, uses may not need to view all the decompositions and they can just use the `TruncatedSVD` function for their practical purposes.

```
>>> from sklearn.utils.extmath import randomized_svd
>>> U,Sigma,VT =
randomized_svd(X,n_components=15,n_iter=300,random_state=42)

>>> import pandas as pd
>>> VT_df = pd.DataFrame(VT)

>>> print ("\nShape of Original Matrix:",X.shape)
>>> print ("\nShape of Left Singular vector:",U.shape)
>>> print ("Shape of Singular value:",Sigma.shape)
>>> print ("Shape of Right Singular vector",VT.shape)
```

```
Shape of Original Matrix: (1797, 64)

Shape of Left Singular vector: (1797, 15)
Shape of Singular value: (15,)
Shape of Right Singular vector (15, 64)
```

By looking at the previous screenshot, we can see that the original matrix of dimension (1797 x 64) has been decomposed into a left singular vector (1797 x 15), singular value (diagonal matrix of 15), and right singular vector (15 x 64). We can obtain the original matrix by multiplying all three matrices in order.

```
>>> n_comps = 15
>>> from sklearn.decomposition import TruncatedSVD
>>> svd = TruncatedSVD(n_components=n_comps, n_iter=300, random_state=42)
>>> reduced_X = svd.fit_transform(X)

>>> print("\nTotal Variance explained for %d singular features are
%0.3f"%(n_comps, svd.explained_variance_ratio_.sum()))
```

```
Total Variance explained for 15 singular features is 0.834
```

The total variance explained for 15 singular value features is 83.4 percent. But the reader needs to change the different values to decide the optimum value.

The following code illustrates the change in total variance explained with respective to change in number of singular values:

```
# Choosing number of Singular Values
>>> max_singfeat = 30
>>> singfeats = []
>>> totexp_var = []

>>> for i in range(max_singfeat):
...        svd = TruncatedSVD(n_components=i+1, n_iter=300, random_state=42)
...        reduced_X = svd.fit_transform(X)
...        tot_var = svd.explained_variance_ratio_.sum()
...        singfeats.append(i+1)
...        totexp_var.append(tot_var)

>>> plt.plot(singfeats,totexp_var,'r')
>>> plt.plot(singfeats,totexp_var,'bs')
>>> plt.xlabel('No. of Features',fontsize = 13)
>>> plt.ylabel('Total variance explained',fontsize = 13)

>>> plt.xticks(pcs,fontsize=13)
>>> plt.yticks(fontsize=13)
>>> plt.show()
```

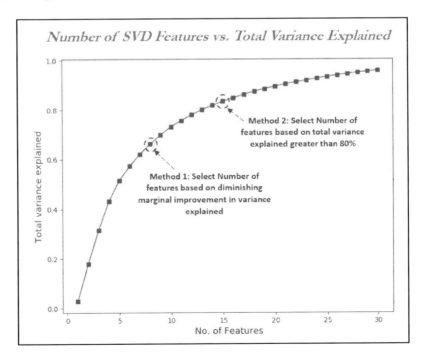

From the previous plot, we can choose either 8 or 15 singular vectors based on the requirement.

The R code for SVD applied on handwritten digits data is as follows:

```
#SVD
library(svd)
digits_data = read.csv("digitsdata.csv")
remove_cols = c("target")
x_data =   digits_data[,!(names(digits_data) %in% remove_cols)]
y_data = digits_data[,c("target")]
sv2 <- svd(x_data,nu=15)
# Computing the square of the   singular values, which can be thought of as
the vector of matrix energy
# in order to pick top singular   values which preserve at least 80% of
variance explained
energy <- sv2$d ^ 2
tot_varexp = data.frame(cumsum(energy)   / sum(energy))
names(tot_varexp) = "cum_var_explained"
tot_varexp$K_value =   1:nrow(tot_varexp)
plot(tot_varexp[,2],tot_varexp[,1],type   = 'o',xlab = "K_Value",ylab =
"Prop. of Var Explained")
title("SVD - Prop. of Var   explained with K-value")
```

Deep auto encoders

The auto encoder neural network is an unsupervised learning algorithm that applies backpropagation setting the target values to be equal to the inputs $y^{(i)} = x^{(i)}$. Auto encoder tries to learn a function $h_{w,b}(x) \approx x$, means it tries to learn an approximation to the identity function, so that output $\hat{x}$ that is similar to x.

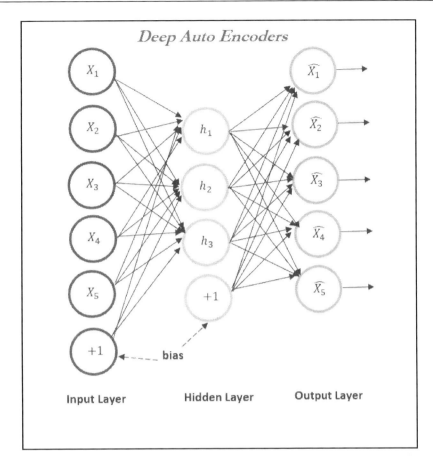

Though trying to replicate the identity function seems trivial function to learn, by placing the constraints on the network, such as by limiting number of hidden units, we can discover interesting structures about the data. Let's say input picture of size 10 x 10 pixels has intensity values which have, altogether, 100 input values, the number of neurons in the second layer (hidden layer) is 50 units, and the output layer, finally, has 100 units of neurons as we need to pass the image to map it to itself and while achieving this representation in the process we would force the network to learn a compressed representation of the input, which is hidden unit activations $a^{(2)} \varepsilon R^{100}$, with which we must try to reconstruct the 100 pixel input x. If the input data is completely random without any correlations, and so on. it would be very difficult to compress, whereas if the underlying data have some correlations or detectable structures, then this algorithm will be able to discover the correlations and represent them compactly. In fact, auto encoder often ends up learning a low-dimensional representation very similar to PCAs.

Model building technique using encoder-decoder architecture

Training the auto encoder model is a bit tricky, hence a detailed illustration has been provided for better understanding for readers. During the training phase, the whole encoder-decoder section is trained against the same input as an output of decoder. In order to achieve the desired output, features will be compressed during the middle layer, as we are passing through the convergent and divergent layers. Once enough training has been done by reducing the error values over the number of iterations, we will use the trained encoder section to create the latent features for next stage of modeling, or for visualization, and so on.

In the following diagram, a sample has been shown. The input and output layers have five neurons, whereas the number of neurons has been gradually decreased in the middle sections. The compressed layer has only two neurons, which is the number of latent dimensions we would like to extract from the data.

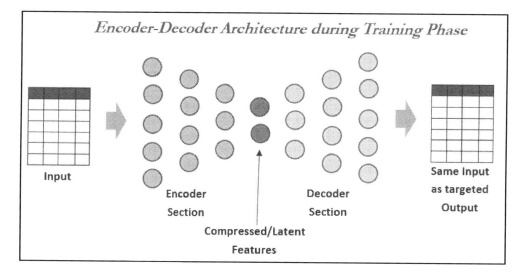

The following diagram depicts using the trained encoder section to create latent features from the new input data, which will be utilized for visualization or for utilizing in the next stage of the model:

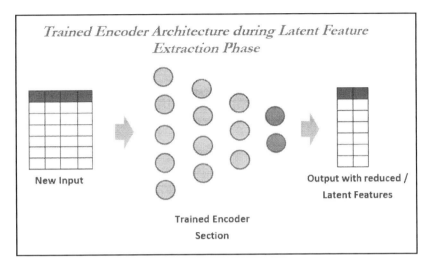

Deep auto encoders applied on handwritten digits using Keras

Deep auto encoders are explained with same handwritten digits data to show the comparison of how this non-linear method differs to linear methods like PCA and SVD. Non-linear methods generally perform much better, but these methods are kind of black-box models and we cannot determine the explanation behind that. Keras software has been utilized to build the deep auto encoders here, as they work like Lego blocks, which makes it easy for users to play around with different architectures and parameters of the model for better understanding:

```
# Deep Auto Encoders
>>> import matplotlib.pyplot as plt
>>> from sklearn.preprocessing import StandardScaler
>>> from sklearn.datasets import load_digits

>>> digits = load_digits()
>>> X = digits.data
>>> y = digits.target

>>> print (X.shape)
```

```
>>> print (y.shape)
>>> x_vars_stdscle = StandardScaler().fit_transform(X)
>>> print (x_vars_stdscle.shape)
```

```
(1797L, 64L)
(1797L,)
(1797L, 64L)
```

Dense neuron modules from Keras used for constructing encoder-decoder architecture:

```
>>> from keras.layers import Input,Dense
>>> from keras.models import Model
```

```
Using Theano backend.
WARNING (theano.sandbox.cuda): The cuda backend is deprecated and will be removed in the next release (v0.10).
Please switch to the gpuarray backend. You can get more information about how to switch at this URL:
 https://github.com/Theano/Theano/wiki/Converting-to-the-new-gpu-back-end%23gpuarray%29

Using gpu device 0: GeForce GTX 1060 6GB (CNMeM is enabled with initial size: 80.0% of memory, cuDNN 5105)
```

GPU of NVIDIA GTX 1060 has been used here, also cuDNN and CNMeM libraries are installed for further enhancement of speed up to 4x-5x on the top of regular GPU performance. These libraries utilize 20 percent of GPU memory, which left the 80 percent of memory for working on the data. The user needs to be careful, if they have low memory GPUs like 3 GB to 4 GB, they may not be able to utilize these libraries.

 The reader needs to consider one important point that, syntax of Keras code, will remain same in both CPU and GPU mode.

The following few lines of codes are the heart of the model. Input data have 64 columns. We need to take those columns into the input of the layers, hence we have given the shape of 64. Also, names have been assigned to each layer of the neural network, which we will explain the reason for in an upcoming section of the code. In the first hidden layer, 32 dense neurons are utilized, which means all the 64 inputs from the input layer are connected to 32 neurons in first hidden layer. The entire flow of dimensions are like *64, 32, 16, 2, 16, 32, 64*. We have compressed input to two neurons, in order to plot the components on a 2D plot, whereas, if we need to plot a 3D data (which we will be covering in the next section), we need to change the hidden three-layer number to three instead of two. After training is complete, we need to use encoder section and predict the output.

```
# 2-Dimensional Architecture

>>> input_layer = Input(shape=(64,),name="input")

>>> encoded = Dense(32, activation='relu',name="h1encode")(input_layer)
>>> encoded = Dense(16, activation='relu',name="h2encode")(encoded)
>>> encoded = Dense(2, activation='relu',name="h3latent_layer")(encoded)

>>> decoded = Dense(16, activation='relu',name="h4decode")(encoded)
>>> decoded = Dense(32, activation='relu',name="h5decode")(decoded)
>>> decoded = Dense(64, activation='sigmoid',name="h6decode")(decoded)
```

To train the model, we need to pass the starting and ending point of the architecture. In the following code, we have provided input as `input_layer` and output as `decoded`, which is the last layer (the name is `h6decode`):

```
>>> autoencoder = Model(input_layer, decoded)
```

Adam optimization has been used to optimize the mean square error, as we wanted to reproduce the original input at the end of the output layer of the network:

```
>>> autoencoder.compile(optimizer="adam", loss="mse")
```

The network is trained with 100 epochs and a batch size of 256 observations per each batch. Validation split of 20 percent is used to check the accuracy on randomly selected validation data in order to ensure robustness, as if we just train only on the train data may create the overfitting problem, which is very common with highly non-linear models:

```
# Fitting Encoder-Decoder model
>>> autoencoder.fit(x_vars_stdscle, x_vars_stdscle,
epochs=100,batch_size=256, shuffle=True,validation_split= 0.2 )
```

```
Train on 1437 samples, validate on 360 samples
Epoch 1/100
1437/1437 [==============================] - 0s - loss: 1.2314 - val_loss: 1.0451
Epoch 2/100
1437/1437 [==============================] - 0s - loss: 1.2164 - val_loss: 1.0279
Epoch 3/100
1437/1437 [==============================] - 0s - loss: 1.1970 - val_loss: 1.0047
Epoch 4/100
1437/1437 [==============================] - 0s - loss: 1.1722 - val_loss: 0.9756
Epoch 5/100
1437/1437 [==============================] - 0s - loss: 1.1430 - val_loss: 0.9419
Epoch 95/100
1437/1437 [==============================] - 0s - loss: 0.9084 - val_loss: 0.7339
Epoch 96/100
1437/1437 [==============================] - 0s - loss: 0.9079 - val_loss: 0.7341
Epoch 97/100
1437/1437 [==============================] - 0s - loss: 0.9075 - val_loss: 0.7334
Epoch 98/100
1437/1437 [==============================] - 0s - loss: 0.9073 - val_loss: 0.7331
Epoch 99/100
1437/1437 [==============================] - 0s - loss: 0.9067 - val_loss: 0.7330
Epoch 100/100
1437/1437 [==============================] - 0s - loss: 0.9061 - val_loss: 0.7326
        <keras.callbacks.History at 0x6985c978>
```

From the previous results, we can see that the model has been trained on 1,437 train examples and validation on 360 examples. By looking into the loss value, both train and validation losses have decreased from 1.2314 to 0.9361 and 1.0451 to 0.7326 respectively. Hence, we are moving in the right direction. However, readers are encouraged to try various architectures and number of iterations, batch sizes, and so on to see how much the accuracies can be further improved.

Once the encoder-decoder section has been trained, we need to take only the encoder section to compress the input features in order to obtain the compressed latent features, which is the core idea of dimensionality reduction altogether! In the following code, we have constructed another model with a trained input layer and a middle hidden layer (h3latent_layer). This is the reason behind assigning names for each layer of the network.

```
# Extracting Encoder section of the Model for prediction of latent
variables
>>> encoder =
Model(autoencoder.input,autoencoder.get_layer("h3latent_layer").output)

Extracted encoder section of the whole model used for prediction of input
variables to generate sparse 2-dimensional representation, which is being
performed with the following code
# Predicting latent variables with extracted Encoder model
>>> reduced_X = encoder.predict(x_vars_stdscle)
```

Just to check the dimensions of the reduced input variables and we can see that for all observations, we can see two dimensions or two column vector:

```
>>> print (reduced_X.shape)
```

```
(1797L, 2L)
```

The following section of the code is very much similar to 2D PCA:

```
>>> zero_x, zero_y = [],[] ; one_x, one_y = [],[]
>>> two_x,two_y = [],[]; three_x, three_y = [],[]
>>> four_x,four_y = [],[]; five_x,five_y = [],[]
>>> six_x,six_y = [],[]; seven_x,seven_y = [],[]
>>> eight_x,eight_y = [],[]; nine_x,nine_y = [],[]

# For 2-Dimensional data
>>> for i in range(len(reduced_X)):
...        if y[i] == 0:
...            zero_x.append(reduced_X[i][0])
...            zero_y.append(reduced_X[i][1])
...        elif y[i] == 1:
...            one_x.append(reduced_X[i][0])
...            one_y.append(reduced_X[i][1])

...        elif y[i] == 2:
...            two_x.append(reduced_X[i][0])
...            two_y.append(reduced_X[i][1])
```

```
...        elif y[i] == 3:
...            three_x.append(reduced_X[i][0])
...            three_y.append(reduced_X[i][1])

...        elif y[i] == 4:
...            four_x.append(reduced_X[i][0])
...            four_y.append(reduced_X[i][1])

...        elif y[i] == 5:
...            five_x.append(reduced_X[i][0])
...            five_y.append(reduced_X[i][1])

...        elif y[i] == 6:
...            six_x.append(reduced_X[i][0])
...            six_y.append(reduced_X[i][1])

...        elif y[i] == 7:
...            seven_x.append(reduced_X[i][0])
...            seven_y.append(reduced_X[i][1])

...        elif y[i] == 8:
...            eight_x.append(reduced_X[i][0])
...            eight_y.append(reduced_X[i][1])
...        elif y[i] == 9:
...            nine_x.append(reduced_X[i][0])
...            nine_y.append(reduced_X[i][1])


>>> zero = plt.scatter(zero_x, zero_y, c='r', marker='x',label='zero')
>>> one = plt.scatter(one_x, one_y, c='g', marker='+')
>>> two = plt.scatter(two_x, two_y, c='b', marker='s')

>>> three = plt.scatter(three_x, three_y, c='m', marker='*')
>>> four = plt.scatter(four_x, four_y, c='c', marker='h')
>>> five = plt.scatter(five_x, five_y, c='r', marker='D')

>>> six = plt.scatter(six_x, six_y, c='y', marker='8')
>>> seven = plt.scatter(seven_x, seven_y, c='k', marker='*')
>>> eight = plt.scatter(eight_x, eight_y, c='r', marker='x')

>>> nine = plt.scatter(nine_x, nine_y, c='b', marker='D')


>>> plt.legend((zero,one,two,three,four,five,six,seven,eight,nine),
...
('zero','one','two','three','four','five','six','seven','eight','nine'),
...             scatterpoints=1,loc='lower right',ncol=3,fontsize=10)
```

```
>>> plt.xlabel('Latent Feature 1',fontsize = 13)
>>> plt.ylabel('Latent Feature 2',fontsize = 13)

>>> plt.show()
```

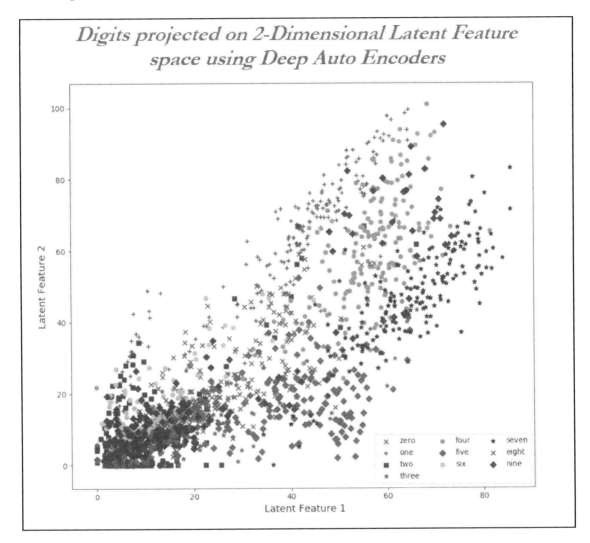

From the previous plot we can see that data points are well separated, but the issue is the direction of view, as these features does not vary as per the dimensions perpendicular to each other, similar to principal components, which are orthogonal to each other. In the case of deep auto encoders, we need to change the view of direction from the *(0, 0)* to visualize this non-linear classification, which we will see in detail in the following 3D case.

The following is the code for 3D latent features. All the code remains the same apart from the `h3latent_layer`, in which we have to replace the value from 2 to 3, as this is the end of encoder section and we will utilize it in creating the latent features and, eventually, it will be used for plotting purposes.

```
# 3-Dimensional architecture
>>> input_layer = Input(shape=(64,),name="input")

>>> encoded = Dense(32, activation='relu',name="h1encode")(input_layer)
>>> encoded = Dense(16, activation='relu',name="h2encode")(encoded)
>>> encoded = Dense(3, activation='relu',name="h3latent_layer")(encoded)

>>> decoded = Dense(16, activation='relu',name="h4decode")(encoded)
>>> decoded = Dense(32, activation='relu',name="h5decode")(decoded)
>>> decoded = Dense(64, activation='sigmoid',name="h6decode")(decoded)

>>> autoencoder = Model(input_layer, decoded)
autoencoder.compile(optimizer="adam", loss="mse")

# Fitting Encoder-Decoder model
>>> autoencoder.fit(x_vars_stdscle, x_vars_stdscle,
epochs=100,batch_size=256, shuffle=True,validation_split= 0.2)
```

```
Train on 1437 samples, validate on 360 samples
Epoch 1/100
1437/1437 [==============================] - 0s - loss: 1.2355 - val_loss: 1.0553
Epoch 2/100
1437/1437 [==============================] - 0s - loss: 1.2274 - val_loss: 1.0466
Epoch 3/100
1437/1437 [==============================] - 0s - loss: 1.2167 - val_loss: 1.0340
Epoch 4/100
1437/1437 [==============================] - 0s - loss: 1.2010 - val_loss: 1.0156
Epoch 5/100
1437/1437 [==============================] - 0s - loss: 1.1786 - val_loss: 0.9891
Epoch 95/100
1437/1437 [==============================] - 0s - loss: 0.8047 - val_loss: 0.6486
Epoch 96/100
1437/1437 [==============================] - 0s - loss: 0.8044 - val_loss: 0.6477
Epoch 97/100
1437/1437 [==============================] - 0s - loss: 0.8041 - val_loss: 0.6472
Epoch 98/100
1437/1437 [==============================] - 0s - loss: 0.8037 - val_loss: 0.6467
Epoch 99/100
1437/1437 [==============================] - 0s - loss: 0.8033 - val_loss: 0.6466
Epoch 100/100
1437/1437 [==============================] - 0s - loss: 0.8032 - val_loss: 0.6464
```

From the previous results we can see that, with the inclusion of three dimensions instead of two, loss values obtained are less than in the 2D use case. Train and validation losses for two latent factors after 100 epochs are 0.9061 and 0.7326, and for three latent factors after 100 epochs, are 0.8032 and 0.6464. This signifies that, with the inclusion of one more dimension, we can reduce the errors significantly. This way, the reader can change various parameters to determine the ideal architecture for dimensionality reduction:

```
# Extracting Encoder section of the Model for prediction of latent
variables
>>> encoder =
Model(autoencoder.input,autoencoder.get_layer("h3latent_layer").output)

# Predicting latent variables with extracted Encoder model
>>> reduced_X3D = encoder.predict(x_vars_stdscle)

>>> zero_x, zero_y,zero_z = [],[],[] ; one_x, one_y,one_z = [],[],[]
>>> two_x,two_y,two_z = [],[],[]; three_x, three_y,three_z = [],[],[]
>>> four_x,four_y,four_z = [],[],[]; five_x,five_y,five_z = [],[],[]
>>> six_x,six_y,six_z = [],[],[]; seven_x,seven_y,seven_z = [],[],[]
>>> eight_x,eight_y,eight_z = [],[],[]; nine_x,nine_y,nine_z = [],[],[]

>>> for i in range(len(reduced_X3D)):
...         if y[i]==10:
...             continue
...         elif y[i] == 0:
...             zero_x.append(reduced_X3D[i][0])
...             zero_y.append(reduced_X3D[i][1])
...             zero_z.append(reduced_X3D[i][2])
...         elif y[i] == 1:
...             one_x.append(reduced_X3D[i][0])
...             one_y.append(reduced_X3D[i][1])
...             one_z.append(reduced_X3D[i][2])

...         elif y[i] == 2:
...             two_x.append(reduced_X3D[i][0])
...             two_y.append(reduced_X3D[i][1])
...             two_z.append(reduced_X3D[i][2])

...         elif y[i] == 3:
...             three_x.append(reduced_X3D[i][0])
...             three_y.append(reduced_X3D[i][1])
...             three_z.append(reduced_X3D[i][2])

...         elif y[i] == 4:
...             four_x.append(reduced_X3D[i][0])
...             four_y.append(reduced_X3D[i][1])
...             four_z.append(reduced_X3D[i][2])
```

```
...        elif y[i] == 5:
...            five_x.append(reduced_X3D[i][0])
...            five_y.append(reduced_X3D[i][1])
...            five_z.append(reduced_X3D[i][2])

...        elif y[i] == 6:
...            six_x.append(reduced_X3D[i][0])
...            six_y.append(reduced_X3D[i][1])
...            six_z.append(reduced_X3D[i][2])

...        elif y[i] == 7:
...            seven_x.append(reduced_X3D[i][0])
...            seven_y.append(reduced_X3D[i][1])
...            seven_z.append(reduced_X3D[i][2])

...        elif y[i] == 8:
...            eight_x.append(reduced_X3D[i][0])
...            eight_y.append(reduced_X3D[i][1])
...            eight_z.append(reduced_X3D[i][2])
...        elif y[i] == 9:
...            nine_x.append(reduced_X3D[i][0])
...            nine_y.append(reduced_X3D[i][1])
...            nine_z.append(reduced_X3D[i][2])



# 3- Dimensional plot
>>> from mpl_toolkits.mplot3d import Axes3D
>>> fig = plt.figure()
>>> ax = fig.add_subplot(111, projection='3d')

>>> ax.scatter(zero_x, zero_y,zero_z, c='r', marker='x',label='zero')
>>> ax.scatter(one_x, one_y,one_z, c='g', marker='+',label='one')
>>> ax.scatter(two_x, two_y,two_z, c='b', marker='s',label='two')

>>> ax.scatter(three_x, three_y,three_z, c='m', marker='*',label='three')
>>> ax.scatter(four_x, four_y,four_z, c='c', marker='h',label='four')
>>> ax.scatter(five_x, five_y,five_z, c='r', marker='D',label='five')

>>> ax.scatter(six_x, six_y,six_z, c='y', marker='8',label='six')
>>> ax.scatter(seven_x, seven_y,seven_z, c='k', marker='*',label='seven')
>>> ax.scatter(eight_x, eight_y,eight_z, c='r', marker='x',label='eight')

>>> ax.scatter(nine_x, nine_y,nine_z, c='b', marker='D',label='nine')

>>> ax.set_xlabel('Latent Feature 1',fontsize = 13)
>>> ax.set_ylabel('Latent Feature 2',fontsize = 13)
>>> ax.set_zlabel('Latent Feature 3',fontsize = 13)
```

```
>>> ax.set_xlim3d(0,60)

>>> plt.legend(loc='upper left', numpoints=1, ncol=3, fontsize=10,
bbox_to_anchor=(0, 0))

>>> plt.show()
```

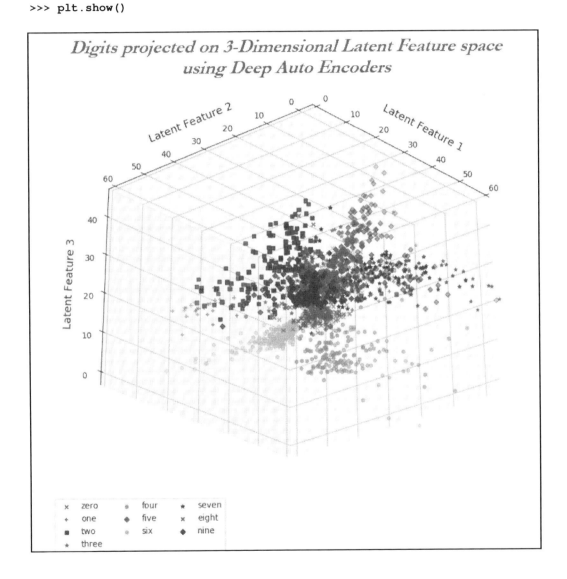

3D plots from deep auto encoders do provide well separated classification compared with three PCAs. Here we have got better separation of the digits. One important point the reader should consider here is that the above plot is the rotated view from *(0, 0, 0)*, as data separation does not happen across orthogonal planes (like PCAs), hence we need to see the view from origin in order to see this non-linear classification.

Summary

In this chapter, you have learned about various unsupervised learning methods to identify the structures and patterns within the data using k-mean clustering, PCA, SVD and deep auto encoders. Also, the k-means clustering algorithm explained with iris data. Methods were shown on how to choose the optimal k-value based on various performance metrics. Handwritten data from scikit-learn was been utilized to compare the differences between linear methods like PCA and SVD with non-linear techniques and deep auto encoders. The differences between PCA and SVD were given in detail, so that the reader can understand SVD, which can be applied even on rectangular matrices where the number of users and number of products are not necessarily equal. At the end, through visualization, it has been proven that deep auto encoders are better at separating digits than linear unsupervised learning methods like PCA and SVD.

In the next chapter, we will be discussing various reinforcement learning methods and their utilities in artificial intelligence and so on.

9
Reinforcement Learning

Reinforcement learning (**RL**) is the third major section of machine learning after supervised and unsupervised learning. These techniques have gained a lot of traction in recent years in the application of artificial intelligence. In reinforcement learning, sequential decisions are to be made rather than one shot decision making, which makes it difficult to train the models in few cases. In this chapter, we would be covering various techniques used in reinforcement learning with practical examples to support with. Though covering all topics are beyond the scope of this book, but we did cover most important fundamentals here for a reader to create enough enthusiasm on this subject. Topics discussed in this chapter are:

- Markov decision process
- Bellman equations
- Dynamic programming
- Monte Carlo methods
- Temporal difference learning
- Recent trends in artificial intelligence with the integrated application of reinforcement learning and machine learning

Introduction to reinforcement learning

Reinforcement learning mimics how humans learn: by interacting with environment, repeating actions for which the reward that is received is higher, and avoiding risky moves for which there is a low or negative reward as an outcome of their actions.

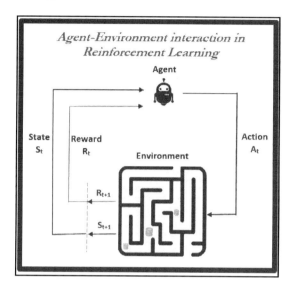

Comparing supervised, unsupervised, and reinforcement learning in detail

As machine learning has three major sections, let's take a high level look at the major differences and similarities:

- **Supervised learning:** In supervised learning, we have a training set for which we have given right answer for every training algorithm. The training example contains all the right answers, and the job of the training algorithm is to replicate the right answers.
- **Unsupervised learning:** In unsupervised learning, we have a set of unlabeled data and a learning algorithm. The job of the learning algorithm is to find the structure in the data with algorithms like k-means, PCA, and so on.
- **Reinforcement learning:** In reinforcement learning, we do not have a target variable. Instead we have reward signals, and the agent needs to plan the path on its own to reach the goal where the reward exists.

Characteristics of reinforcement learning

- The feedback of a reward signal is not instantaneous. It is delayed by many timesteps
- Sequential decision making is needed to reach a goal, so time plays an important role in reinforcement problems (no IID assumption of the data holds good here)
- The agent's action affects the subsequent data it receives

In reinforcement learning, a little bit of supervision is needed, but much less supervision compared to supervised learning.

The following are a few actual live examples of reinforcement learning problems:

- **Autonomous helicopter:** The objective of autonomous helicopter is to change its roll, pitch and yaw to control its position by controlling the joystick, pedals, and so on. Sensors send inputs 10 times a second which provide an accurate estimate of position and orientation of the helicopter. The helicopter's job is to receive this input and to control the stick to move accordingly. It is very hard to provide information on what the helicopter needs to do next when the helicopter is in this position and orientation, and no training sets are available to control actions. Instead, RL algorithms gives different types of feedback: it will give a reward signal when the helicopter is doing well, and negative rewards when the helicopter is doing the wrong thing. Based on these signals, the helicopter controls the journey. The job of the learning algorithms is to provide the reward functions and train the path on its own.
- **Computer chess:** A computer playing a game of chess is another example in which, at any stage in the game, we won't know in advance what the optimal move would be; so it is very hard to play chess using a supervised learning algorithm. It is hard to say X's is board position and Y is the optimal moves for this particular board position. Instead, whenever it wins a game, we provide a reward (+1), and whenever it loses a game, we give a negative reward (-1), and we let the algorithm figure out the necessary moves to win the game over a period of time.
- **Training a cat:** We give a cat a reward when it does a good thing, and every time it does a bad thing, we make it clear that this is bad behavior. Over a period of time, the cat learns to do more of the good things and less of the bad.

Reasons why reinforced learning is more difficult than supervised learning include:

- This is not a one-shot decision-making problem. So, in supervised learning, an algorithm predicts whether someone has cancer or not based on given attributes; whereas in RL, you have to keep taking actions over a period of time. We call this sequential decision making.

- In a game of chess, we made 60 moves before winning/losing. We are not sure which ones were right moves, and which ones were wrong moves. At move 25, we made a wrong move, which ultimately led us to lose the game at move 60.

- Credit assignment problem: (positive or negative reward) to do more of a good thing and less of a bad thing.

- In an example of a car crash, at some point before the crash, the driver might brake. However, it's not the braking that caused the crash, but something happened before the braking, which ultimately caused the crash. RL learns the patterns over a period of time, which might include driving too fast just before, not observing other road traffic, ignoring warning signs, and so on.

- RL is applied to different applications, and used for sequential decision making when there are long term consequences.

Reinforcement learning basics

Before we deep dive into the details of reinforcement learning, I would like to cover some of the basics necessary for understanding the various nuts and bolts of RL methodologies. These basics appear across various sections of this chapter, which we will explain in detail whenever required:

- **Environment:** This is any system that has states, and mechanisms to transition between states. For example, the environment for a robot is the landscape or facility it operates.

- **Agent:** This is an automated system that interacts with the environment.

- **State:** The state of the environment or system is the set of variables or features that fully describe the environment.

- **Goal or absorbing state or terminal state:** This is the state that provides a higher discounted cumulative reward than any other state. A high cumulative reward prevents the best policy from being dependent on the initial state during training. Whenever an agent reaches its goal, we will finish one episode.

- **Action:** This defines the transition between states. The agent is responsible for performing, or at least recommending, an action. Upon execution of the action, the agent collects a reward (or punishment) from the environment.

- **Policy:** This defines the action to be selected and executed for any state of the environment. In other words, policy is the agent's behavior; it is a map from state to action. Policies could be either deterministic or stochastic.
- **Best policy:** This is the policy generated through training. It defines the model in Q-learning and is constantly updated with any new episode.
- **Rewards**: This quantifies the positive or negative interaction of the agent with the environment. Rewards are usually immediate earnings made by the agent reaching each state.
- **Returns or value function**: A value function (also called returns) is a prediction of future rewards of each state. These are used to evaluate the goodness/badness of the states, based on which, the agent will choose/act on for selecting the next best state:

$$V_\pi(S) = E_\pi[\, R_t + \gamma\, R_{t+1} + \gamma^2\, R_{t+2} + \cdots \setminus S_t = s\,]$$

- **Episode:** This defines the number of steps necessary to reach the goal state from an initial state. Episodes are also known as trials.
- **Horizon:** This is the number of future steps or actions used in the maximization of the reward. The horizon can be infinite, in which case, the future rewards are discounted in order for the value of the policy to converge.
- **Exploration versus Exploitation:** RL is a type of trial and error learning. The goal is to find the best policy; and at the same time, remain alert to explore some unknown policies. A classic example would be treasure hunting: if we just go to the locations greedily (expoitation), we fail to look for other places where hidden treasure might also exist (exploration). By exploring the unknown states, and by taking chances, even when the immediate rewards are low and without losing the maximum rewards, we might achieve greater goals. In other words, we are escaping the local optimum in order to achieve a global optimum (which is exploration), rather than just a short-term focus purely on the immediate rewards (which is exploitation). Here are a couple of examples to explain the difference:
    - **Restaurant selection**: By exploring unknown restaurants once in a while, we might find a much better one than our regular favorite restaurant:
        - **Exploitation**: Going to your favorite restaurant
        - **Exploration**: Trying a new restaurant
    - **Oil drilling example:** By exploring new untapped locations, we may get newer insights that are more beneficial that just exploring the same place:
        - **Exploitation**: Drill for oil at best known location

- **Exploration**: Drill at a new location
- **State-Value versus State-Action Function:** In action-value, Q represents the expected return (cumulative discounted reward) an agent is to receive when taking Action A in State S, and behaving according to a certain policy $\pi(a|s)$ afterwards (which is the probability of taking an action in a given state).

  In state-value, the value is the expected return an agent is to receive from being in state s behaving under a policy $\pi(a|s)$. More specifically, the state-value is an expectation over the action-values under a policy:

$$V(S) = \sum_a \pi(a\backslash s)\, Q(s,a)$$

- **On-policy versus off-policy TD control:** An off-policy learner learns the value of the optimal policy independently of the agent's actions. Q-learning is an off-policy learner. An on-policy learner learns the value of the policy being carried out by the agent, including the exploration steps.
- **Prediction and control problems:** Prediction talks about how well I do, based on the given policy: meaning, if someone has given me a policy and I implement it, how much reward I will get get for that. Whereas, in control, the problem is to find the best policy so that I can maximize the reward.
- **Prediction:** Evaluation of the values of states for a given policy.

  For the uniform random policy, what is the value function for all states?

- **Control:** Optimize the future by finding the best policy.

  What is the optimal value function over all possible policies, and what is the optimal policy?

  Usually in reinforcement learning, we need to solve the prediction problem first, in order to solve the control problem after, as we need to figure out all the policies to figure out the best or optimal one.

- **RL Agent Taxonomy:** An RL agent includes one or more of the following components:
    - **Policy:** Agent's behavior function (map from state to action); Policies can be either deterministic or stochastic
    - **Value function:** How good is each state (or) prediction of expected future reward for each state

- **Model:** Agent's representation of the environment. A model predicts what the environment will do next:
    - **Transitions:** p predicts the next state (that is, dynamics):

$$P_{s,a}(S') = \mathbb{P}[S' = s' \mid S = s, A = a]$$

    - **Rewards:** R predicts the next (immediate) reward

$$R_a(S) = \mathbb{E}[R \mid S = s, A = a]$$

Let us explain the various categories possible in RL agent taxonomy, based on combinations of policy and value, and model individual components with the following maze example. In the following maze, you have both the start and the goal; the agent needs to reach the goal as quickly as possible, taking a path to gain the total maximum reward and the minimum total negative reward. Majorly five categorical way this problem can be solved:

- Value based
- Policy based
- Actor critic
- Model free
- Model based

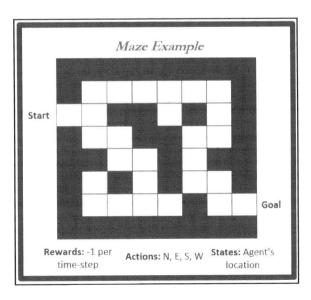

Category 1 - value based

Value function does look like the right-hand side of the image (the sum of discounted future rewards) where every state has some value. Let's say, the state one step away from the goal has a value of -1; and two steps away from the goal has a value of -2. In a similar way, the starting point has a value of -16. If the agent gets stuck at the wrong place, the value could be as much as -24. In fact, the agent does move across the grid based on the best possible values to reach its goal. For example, the agent is at a state with a value of -15. Here, it can choose to move either north or south, so it chooses to move north due to the high reward, which is -14 rather, than moving south, which has a value of -16. In this way, the agent chooses its path across the grid until it reaches the goal.

- **Value Function**: Only values are defined at all states
- **No Policy (Implicit)**: No exclusive policy is present; policies are chosen based on the values at each state

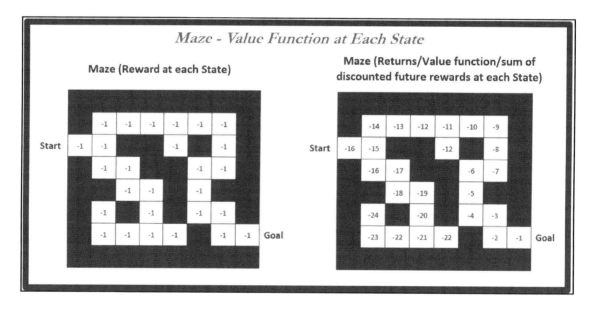

Category 2 - policy based

The arrows in the following image represent what an agent chooses as the direction of the next move while in any of these states. For example, the agent first moves east and then north, following all the arrows until the goal has been reached. This is also known as mapping from states to actions. Once we have this mapping, an agent just needs to read it and behave accordingly.

- **Policy**: Policies or arrows that get adjusted to reach the maximum possible future rewards. As the name suggests, only policies are stored and optimized to maximize rewards.
- **No value function**: No values exist for the states.

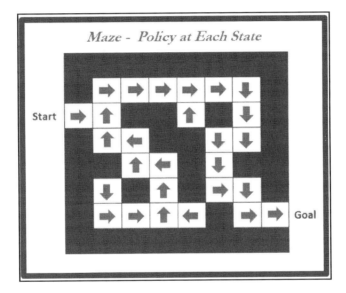

Category 3 - actor-critic

In Actor-Critic, we have both policy and value functions (or a combination of value-based and policy-based). This method is the best of both worlds:

- Policy
- Value Function

Category 4 - model-free

In RL, a fundamental distinction is if it is model-based or model-free. In model-free, we do not explicitly model the environment, or we do not know the entire dynamics of a complete environment. Instead, we just go directly to the policy or value function to gain the experience and figure out how the policy affects the reward:

- Policy and/or value function
    - No model

Category 5 - model-based

In model-based RL, we first build the entire dynamics of the environment:

- Policy and/or value function
- Model

After going through all the above categories, the following Venn diagram shows the entire landscape of the taxonomy of an RL agent at one single place. If you pick up any paper related to reinforcement learning, those methods can fit in within any section of this landscape.

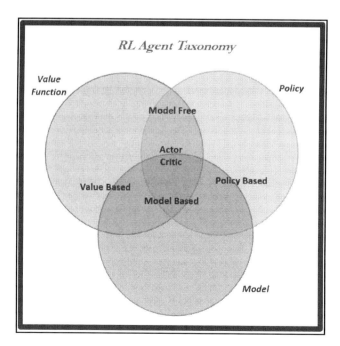

Fundamental categories in sequential decision making

There are two fundamental types of problems in sequential decision making:

- **Reinforcement learning** (for example, autonomous helicopter, and so on):
    - Environment is initially unknown
    - Agent interacts with the environment and obtain policies, rewards, values from the environment
    - Agent improves its policy
- **Planning** (for example, chess, Atari games, and so on):
    - Model of environment or complete dynamics of environment is known
    - Agent performs computation with its model (without any external interaction)
    - Agent improves its policy
    - These are the type of problems also known as reasoning, searching, introspection, and so on

Though the preceding two categories can be linked together as per the given problem, but this is basically a broad view of the two types of setups.

Markov decision processes and Bellman equations

Markov decision process (**MDP**) formally describes an environment for reinforcement learning. Where:

- Environment is fully observable
- Current state completely characterizes the process (which means the future state is entirely dependent on the current state rather than historic states or values)
- Almost all RL problems can be formalized as MDPs (for example, optimal control primarily deals with continuous MDPs)

Central idea of MDP: MDP works on the simple Markovian property of a state; for example, S_{t+1} is entirely dependent on latest state S_t rather than any historic dependencies. In the following equation, the current state captures all the relevant information from the history, which means the current state is a sufficient statistic of the future:

$$\mathbb{P}\left[S_{t+1} \mid S_t\right] = \mathbb{P}\left[S_{t+1} \mid S_1, S_2, \ldots \ldots, S_t\right]$$

An intuitive sense of this property can be explained with the autonomous helicopter example: the next step is for the helicopter to move either to the right, left, to pitch, or to roll, and so on, entirely dependent on the current position of the helicopter, rather than where it was five minutes before.

Modeling of MDP: RL problems models the world using MDP formulation as a five tuple $(S, A, \{P_{sa}\}, y, R)$

- S - Set of States (set of possible orientations of the helicopter)
- A - Set of Actions (set of all possible positions that can pull the control stick)
- P_{sa} - State transition distributions (or state transition probability distributions) provide transitions from one state to another and the respective probabilities needed for the Markov process:

$$\sum_{s'} P_{s,a}(s') = 1 \ ; \ P_{s,a}(s') \geq 0$$

$$State\,Transition\,Probabilities = from\,state(s) \overset{to\,state\,(s')}{\begin{bmatrix} p_{11} & \cdots & p_{1n} \\ \vdots & \ddots & \vdots \\ p_{m1} & \cdots & p_{mn} \end{bmatrix}}$$

- γ - Discount factor:

$$0 \leq \gamma < 1$$

- R - Reward function (maps set of states to real numbers, either positive or negative):

$$R : S \rightarrow \mathbb{R}$$

Returns are calculated by discounting the future rewards until terminal state is reached.

Bellman Equations for MDP: Bellman equations are utilized for the mathematical formulation of MDP, which will be solved to obtain the optimal policies of the environment. Bellman equations are also known as dynamic programming equations, and are a necessary condition for the optimality associated with the mathematical optimization method that is known as dynamic programming. Bellman equations are linear equations which can be solvable for the entire environment. However, the time complexity for solving these equations is $O(n^3)$, which becomes computationally very expensive when the number of states in an environment is large; and sometimes, it is not feasible to explore all the states because the environment itself is very large. In those scenarios, we need to look at other ways of solving problems.

In Bellman equations, value function can be decomposed into two parts:

- Immediate reward R_{t+1}, from the successor state you will end up with
- Discounted value of successor states $\gamma v(S_{t+1})$ you will get from that timestep onwards:

$$v(s) = \mathbb{E}\left[G_t \mid S_t = s\right]$$

$$= \mathbb{E}\left[R_{t+1} + \gamma R_{t+2} + \gamma^2 R_{t+3} + \cdots \mid S_t = s\right]$$

$$= \mathbb{E}\left[R_{t+1} + \gamma(R_{t+2} + \gamma R_{t+3} + \cdots) \mid S_t = s\right]$$

$$= \mathbb{E}\left[R_{t+1} + \gamma(G_{t+1}) \mid S_t = s\right]$$

$$= \mathbb{E}\left[R_{t+1} + \gamma(G_{t+1}) \mid S_t = s\right]$$

$$= \mathbb{E}\left[R_{t+1} + \gamma v(S_{t+1}) \mid S_t = s\right]$$

Grid world example of MDP: Robot navigation tasks live in the following type of grid world. An obstacle is shown the cell (2,2), through which the robot can't navigate. We would like the robot to move to the upper-right cell (4,3) and when it reaches that position, the robot will get a reward of +1. The robot should avoid the cell (4,2), as, if it moved in to that cell, it would receive a-1 reward.

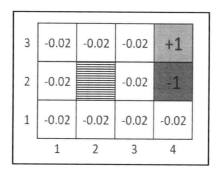

Robot can be in any of the following positions:

- *11 States* - (except cell (2,2), in which we have got an obstacle for the robot)
- A = {N-north, S-south, E-east, W-west}

In the real world, robot movements are noisy, and a robot may not be able to move exactly where it has been asked to. Examples might include that some of its wheels slipped, its parts were loosely connected, it had incorrect actuators, and so on. When asked to move by 1 meter, it may not be able to move exactly 1 meter; instead it may move 90-105 centimeters, and so on.

In a simplified grid world, stochastic dynamics of a robot can be modeled as follows. If we command the robot to go north, there is a 10% chance that the robot could drag towards the left and a 10 % chance that it could drag towards the right. Only 80 percent of the time it may actually go north. When a robot bounces off the wall (including obstacles) and just stays at the same position, nothing happens:

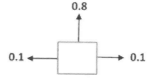

Every state in this grid world example is represented by (x, y) co-ordinates. Let's say it is at state (3,1) and we asked the robot to move north, then the state transition probability matrices are as follows:

$$State\ transisition\ probabilites = \ P_{s,a}(s')$$

$$P_{(3,1),N}((3,2)) = 0.8$$

$$P_{(3,1),N}((4,1)) = 0.1$$

$$P_{(3,1),N}((4,1)) = 0.1$$

$$P_{(3,1),N}((3,3)) = 0$$

The probability of staying in the same position is 0 for the robot.

As we know, that sum of all the state transition probabilities sums up to 1:

$$\sum_{s'} P_{s,a}(s') = 1$$

Reward function:

$$R((4,3)) = +1$$

$$R((4,2)) = -1$$

$$For\ all\ other\ states, R(S) = -0.02$$

For all the other states, there are small negative reward values, which means it charges the robot for battery or fuel consumption when running around the grid, which creates solutions that do not waste moves or time while reaching the goal of reward +1, which encourages the robot to reach the goal as quickly as possible with as little fuel used as possible.

World ends, when the robot reaches either +1 or -1 states. No more rewards are possible after reaching any of these states; these can be called absorbing states. These are zero-cost absorbing states and the robot stays there forever.

MDP working model:

- At state S_0
- Choose a_0
- Get to $S_1 \sim P_{s0,\,a0}$
- Choose a_1
- Get to $S_2 \sim P_{s1,\,a1}$
- and so on ....

After a while, it takes all the rewards and sums up to obtain:

$$Total\ Payoff = R(S_0) + \gamma\,R(S_1) + \gamma^2 R(S_2) + \cdots$$

$$where\ 0 \leq \gamma < 1$$

Discount factor models an economic application, in which one dollar earned today is more valuable than one dollar earned tomorrow.

Robot needs to choose actions over time (a_0, a_1, a_2, ...) to maximize the expected payoff:

$$E\ [\ R(S_0) + \gamma\,R(S_1) + \gamma^2 R(S_2) + \cdots\ ]$$

Over the period, a reinforcement learning algorithm learns a policy which is a mapping of actions for each states, which means it is a recommended action, which the robot needs to take based on the state in which it exists:.

$$Policy\ \Pi : S \rightarrow A$$

Optimal Policy for Grid World: Policy maps from states to actions, which means that, if you are in a particular state, you need to take this particular action. The following policy is the optimal policy which maximizes the expected value of the total payoff or sum of discounted rewards. Policy always looks into the current state rather than previous states, which is the Markovian property:

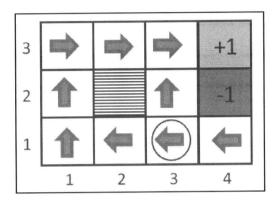

One tricky thing to look at is at the position (3,1): optimal policy shows to go left (West) rather than going (north), which may have a fewer number of states; however, we have an even riskier state that we may step into. So, going left may take longer, but it safely arrives at the destination without getting into negative traps. These types of things can be obtained from computing, which do not look obvious to humans, but a computer is very good at coming up with these policies:

Define: V^π, V^*, π^*

V^π = For any given policy π, value function is $V^\pi : S \rightarrow R$ such that V^π (S) is expected total payoff starting in state S, and execute π

$$V^\Pi(S) = E\left[R(S_0) + \gamma R(S_1) + \gamma^2 R(S_2) + \cdots \setminus \pi, S_0 = s \right]$$

Random policy for grid world: The following is an example of a random policy and its value functions. This policy is a rather bad policy with negative values. For any policy, we can write down the value function for that particular policy:

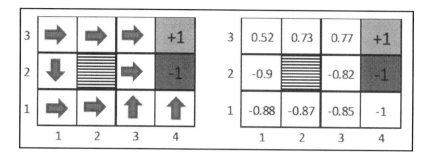

$$V^{\Pi}(S) = E\,[\,R(S_0) + \gamma\,(\,R(S_1) + \gamma\,R(S_2) + \cdots)\,\backslash\,\pi, S_0 = s\,]$$

$$V^{\Pi}(S) = E\,[\,R(S_0) + V^{\Pi}(S_1)\,\backslash\,\pi, S_0 = s\,]$$

$$S_0 \to s\,;\ \ S_1 \to\ s'$$

$$P_{S\,\pi(S)} = probability\ of\ taking\ action\ from\ state\ s$$

$$Bellman\ Equations:\quad V^{\Pi}(S) =\ R(S) + \gamma \sum_{S'} P_{S\,\pi(S)}\,(S')\,V^{\pi}(S')$$

In simple English, Bellman equations illustrate that the value of the current state is equal to the immediate reward and discount factor applied to the expected total payoff of new states (S') multiplied by their probability to take action (policy) into those states.

Bellman equations are used to solve value functions for a policy in close form, given fixed policy, how to solve the value function equations.

Bellman equations impose a set of linear constraints on value functions. It turns out that we solve the value function at the any state S by solving a set of linear equations.

Example of Bellman equations with a grid world problem:

The chosen policy for cell *(3,1)* is to move north. However, we have stochasticity in the system that about 80 percent of the time it moves in the said direction, and *20%* of the time it drifts sideways, either left (10 percent) or right (10 percent).

$$\pi\left(\,(3,1)\,\right) = North$$

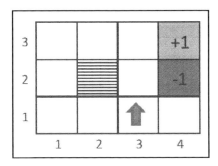

$$V^{\Pi}\big((3,1)\big) = R\big((3,1)\big) + \gamma\,[0.8 * V^{\Pi}\big((3,2)\big) + 0.1 * V^{\Pi}\big((4,1)\big) + 0.1 * V^{\Pi}\big((2,1)\big)]$$

Similar equations can be written for all the 11 states of the MDPs within the grid. We can obtain the following metrics, from which we will solve all the unknown values, using a system of linear equation methods:

- 11 equations
- 11 unknown value function variables
- 11 constraints

This is solving an n variables with n equations problem, for which we can find the exact form of solution using a system of equations easily to get an exact solution for V (π) for the entire closed form of the grid, which consists of all the states.

Dynamic programming

Dynamic programming is a sequential way of solving complex problems by breaking them down into sub-problems and solving each of them. Once it solves the sub-problems, then it puts those subproblem solutions together to solve the original complex problem. In the reinforcement learning world, Dynamic Programming is a solution methodology to compute optimal policies given a perfect model of the environment as a Markov Decision Process (MDP).

Dynamic programming holds good for problems which have the following two properties. MDPs in fact satisfy both properties, which makes DP a good fit for solving them by solving Bellman Equations:

- Optimal substructure
    - Principle of optimality applies
    - Optimal solution can be decomposed into sub-problems
- Overlapping sub-problems
    - Sub-problems recur many times
    - Solutions can be cached and reused
- MDP satisfies both the properties - luckily!
    - Bellman equations have recursive decomposition of state-values
    - Value function stores and reuses solutions

Though, classical DP algorithms are of limited utility in reinforcement learning, both because of their assumptions of a perfect model and high computational expense. However, it is still important, as they provide an essential foundation for understanding all the methods in the RL domain.

Algorithms to compute optimal policy using dynamic programming

Standard algorithms to compute optimal policies for MDP utilizing Dynamic Programming are as follows, and we will be covering both in detail in later sections of this chapter:

- **Value Iteration algorithm:** An iterative algorithm, in which state values are iterated until it reaches optimal values; and, subsequently, optimum values are utilized to determine the optimal policy
- **Policy Iteration algorithm:** An iterative algorithm, in which policy evaluation and policy improvements are utilized alternatively to reach optimal policy

Value Iteration algorithm: Value Iteration algorithms are easy to compute for the very reason of applying iteratively on only state values. First, we will compute the optimal value function V^*, then plug those values into the optimal policy equation to determine the optimal policy. Just to give the size of the problem, for 11 possible states, each state can have four policies (N-north, S-south, E-east, W-west), which gives an overall 11^4 possible policies. The value iteration algorithm consists of the following steps:

1. Initialize $V(S) = 0$ for all states S
2. For every S, update:

$$V(S) = R(S) + \max_{a} \gamma \sum_{s'} P_{s,a}(S') V(S')$$

3. By repeatedly computing step 2, we will eventually converge to optimal values for all the states:

$$V(S) \rightarrow V^*(S)$$

There are two ways of updating the values in step 2 of the algorithm

- **Synchronous update** - By performing synchronous update (or Bellman backup operator) we will perform RHS computing and substitute LHS of the equation represented as follows:

    Synchronous update or Bellman backup operator $=>$ $V := B(V)$

- **Asynchronous update** - Update the values of the states one at a time rather than updating all the states at the same time, in which states will be updated in a fixed order (update state number 1, followed by 2, and so on.). During convergence, asynchronous updates are a little faster than synchronous updates.

Illustration of value iteration on grid world example: The application of the Value iteration on a grid world is explained in the following image, and the complete code for solving a real problem is provided at the end of this section. After applying the previous value iteration algorithm on MDP using Bellman equations, we've obtained the following optimal values V* for all the states (Gamma value chosen as *0.99*):

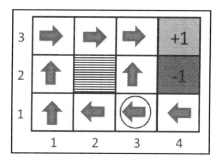

When we plug these values in to our policy equation, we obtain the following policy grid:

$$Optimal\ Policy\ Equation = \ \Pi^*(S) = \underset{a}{\mathrm{argmax}} \sum_{s'} P_{s,a}(S')\,V^*(S')$$

Here, at position (3,1) we would like to prove mathematically why an optimal policy suggests taking going left (west) rather than moving up (north):

$$West\ Direction = \sum_{s'} P_{s,a}(S')\,V^*(S')$$

$$= 0.8 * 0.75 + 0.1 * 0.69 + 0.1 * 0.71 = 0.740$$

Due to the wall, whenever the robot tries to move towards South (downwards side), it will remain in the same place, hence we assigned the value of the current position 0.71 for probability of 0.1.

Similarly, for north, we calculated the total payoff as follows:

$$North\ Direction = \sum_{s'} P_{s,a}(S')\, V^*(S')$$

$$= 0.8 * 0.69 + 0.1 * 0.75 + 0.1 * 0.49 \quad = 0.676$$

So, it would be optimal to move towards the west rather than north, and therefore the optimal policy is chosen to do so.

Policy Iteration Algorithm: Policy iterations are another way of obtaining optimal policies for MDP in which policy evaluation and policy improvement algorithms are applied iteratively until the solution converges to the optimal policy. Policy Iteration Algorithm consists of the following steps:

1. Initialize random policy π
2. Repeatedly do the following until convergence happens
   - Solve Bellman equations for the current policy for obtaining V^π for using system of linear equations:

$$Solve\ Bellman\ Equations\ for\ a\ given\ policy => \quad V := V^\Pi$$

   - Update the policy as per the new value function to improve the policy by pretending the new value is an optimal value using argmax formulae:

$$Calculate\ optimal\ policy\ for\ a\ given\ value\ function => \quad \Pi(S)$$
$$= \operatorname*{argmax}_{a} \sum_{s'} P_{s,a}(S')\, V(S')$$

3. By repeating these steps, both value and policy will converge to optimal values:

$$V \rightarrow V^*$$

$$\Pi \rightarrow \Pi^*$$

Policy iterations tend to do well with smaller problems. If an MDP has an enormous number of states, policy iterations will be computationally expensive. As a result, large MDPs tend to use value iterations rather than policy iterations.

What if we don't know exact state transition probabilities in real life examples $P_{s,a}$?

We need to estimate the probabilities from the data by using the following simple formulae:

$$P_{s,a}(S') = \frac{Number\ of\ times\ took\ action\ "a"\ in\ state\ "s"\ got\ to\ "s'\ "}{Number\ of\ times\ took\ action\ "a"\ in\ "s"}$$

$$or = \frac{1}{|S|}\ if\ we\ do\ not\ have\ data\ for\ some\ states$$

If for some states no data is available, which leads to 0/0 problem, we can take a default probability from uniform distributions.

Grid world example using value and policy iteration algorithms with basic Python

The classic grid world example has been used to illustrate value and policy iterations with Dynamic Programming to solve MDP's Bellman equations. In the following grid, the agent will start at the south-west corner of the grid in (1,1) position and the goal is to move towards the north-east corner, to position (4,3). Once it reaches the goal, the agent will get a reward of +1. During the journey, it should avoid the danger zone (4,2), because this will give out a negative penalty of reward -1. The agent cannot get into the position where the obstacle (2,2) is present from any direction. Goal and danger zones are the terminal states, which means the agent continues to move around until it reaches one of these two states. The reward for all the other states would be -0.02. Here, the task is to determine the optimal policy (direction to move) for the agent at every state (11 states altogether), so that the agent's total reward is the maximum, or so that the agent can reach the goal as quickly as possible. The agent can move in 4 directions: north, south, east and west.

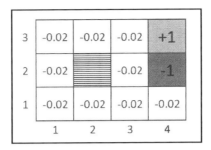

The complete code was written in the Python programming language with class implementation. For further reading, please refer to object oriented programming in Python to understand class, objects, constructors, and so on.

Import the `random` package for generating moves in any of the N, E, S, W directions:

```
>>> import random, operator
```

The following `argmax` function calculated the maximum state among the given states, based on the value for each state:

```
>>> def argmax(seq, fn):
...     best = seq[0]; best_score = fn(best)
...     for x in seq:
...         x_score = fn(x)
...     if x_score > best_score:
...         best, best_score = x, x_score
...     return best
```

To add two vectors at component level, the following code has been utilized for:

```
>>> def vector_add(a, b):
...     return tuple(map(operator.add, a, b))
```

Orientations provide what the increment value would be, which needs to be added to the existing position of the agent; orientations can be applied on the *x*-axis or *y*-axis:

```
>>> orientations = [(1,0), (0, 1), (-1, 0), (0, -1)]
```

The following function is used to turn the agent in the right direction, as we know at every command the agent moves in that direction about 80% of the time, whilst 10% of the time it would move right, and 10% it would move left.:

```
>>> def turn_right(orientation):
...     return orientations[orientations.index(orientation)-1]
>>> def turn_left(orientation):
...     return orientations[(orientations.index(orientation)+1) %
```

```
len(orientations)]
>>> def isnumber(x):
...     return hasattr(x, '__int__')
```

The Markov decision process is defined as a class here. Every MDP is defined by an initial position, state, transition model, reward function, and gamma values.

```
>>> class MDP:
... def __init__(self, init_pos, actlist, terminals, transitions={},
states=None, gamma=0.99):
...     if not (0 < gamma <= 1):
...         raise ValueError("MDP should have 0 < gamma <= 1 values")
...     if states:
...         self.states = states
...     else:
...         self.states = set()
...     self.init_pos = init_pos
...     self.actlist = actlist
...     self.terminals = terminals
...     self.transitions = transitions
...     self.gamma = gamma
...     self.reward = {}
```

Returns a numeric reward for the state:

```
... def R(self, state):
...     return self.reward[state]
```

Transition model with from a state and an action, returns a list of (probability, result-state) pairs for each state:

```
... def T(self, state, action):
...     if(self.transitions == {}):
...         raise ValueError("Transition model is missing")
...     else:
...         return self.transitions[state][action]
```

Set of actions that can be performed at a particular state:

```
... def actions(self, state):
...     if state in self.terminals:
...         return [None]
...     else:
...         return self.actlist
```

Class `GridMDP` is created for modeling a 2D grid world with grid values at each state, terminal positions, initial position, and gamma value (discount):

```
>>> class GridMDP(MDP):
... def __init__(self, grid, terminals, init_pos=(0, 0), gamma=0.99):
```

The following code is used for reversing the grid, as we would like to see *row 0* at the bottom instead of at the top:

```
... grid.reverse()
```

The following __init__ command is a constructor used within the grid class for initializing parameters:

```
... MDP.__init__(self, init_pos, actlist=orientations,
terminals=terminals, gamma=gamma)
... self.grid = grid
... self.rows = len(grid)
... self.cols = len(grid[0])
... for x in range(self.cols):
...     for y in range(self.rows):
...         self.reward[x, y] = grid[y][x]
...         if grid[y][x] is not None:
...             self.states.add((x, y))
```

State transitions provide randomly 80% toward the desired direction and 10% for left and right. This is to model the randomness in a robot which might slip on the floor, and so on:

```
... def T(self, state, action):
...     if action is None:
...         return [(0.0, state)]
...     else:
...         return [(0.8, self.go(state, action)),
...                 (0.1, self.go(state, turn_right(action))),
...                 (0.1, self.go(state, turn_left(action)))]
```

Returns the state that results from going in the direction, subject to where that state is in the list of valid states. If the next state is not in the list, like hitting the wall, then the agent should remain in the same state:

```
... def go(self, state, direction):
...     state1 = vector_add(state, direction)
...     return state1 if state1 in self.states else state
```

Convert a mapping from (x, y) to v into [[..., v, ...]] grid:

```
... def to_grid(self, mapping):
...     return list(reversed([[mapping.get((x, y), None)
...                            for x in range(self.cols)]
...                            for y in range(self.rows)]))
```

Convert orientations into arrows for better graphical representations:

```
... def to_arrows(self, policy):
...     chars = {(1, 0): '>', (0, 1): '^', (-1, 0): '<', (0, -1):
...     'v', None: '.'}
...     return self.to_grid({s: chars[a] for (s, a) in policy.items()})
```

The following code is used for solving an MDP, using value iterations, and returns optimum state values:

```
>>> def value_iteration(mdp, epsilon=0.001):
...     STSN = {s: 0 for s in mdp.states}
...     R, T, gamma = mdp.R, mdp.T, mdp.gamma
...     while True:
...         STS = STSN.copy()
...         delta = 0
...         for s in mdp.states:
...             STSN[s] = R(s) + gamma * max([sum([p * STS[s1] for
...             (p, s1) in T(s,a)]) for a in mdp.actions(s)])
...             delta = max(delta, abs(STSN[s] - STS[s]))
...         if delta < epsilon * (1 - gamma) / gamma:
...             return STS
```

Given an MDP and a utility function STS, determine the best policy, as a mapping from state to action:

```
>>> def best_policy(mdp, STS):
...     pi = {}
...     for s in mdp.states:
...         pi[s] = argmax(mdp.actions(s), lambda a: expected_utility(a, s,
STS, mdp))
...     return pi
```

The expected utility of doing a in state s, according to the MDP and STS:

```
>>> def expected_utility(a, s, STS, mdp):
...     return sum([p * STS[s1] for (p, s1) in mdp.T(s, a)])
```

The following code is used to solve an MDP using policy iterations by alternatively performing policy evaluation and policy improvement steps:

```
>>> def policy_iteration(mdp):
...     STS = {s: 0 for s in mdp.states}
...     pi = {s: random.choice(mdp.actions(s)) for s in mdp.states}
...     while True:
...         STS = policy_evaluation(pi, STS, mdp)
...         unchanged = True
...         for s in mdp.states:
...             a = argmax(mdp.actions(s),lambda a: expected_utility(a, s,
STS, mdp))
...             if a != pi[s]:
...                 pi[s] = a
...                 unchanged = False
...         if unchanged:
...             return pi
```

The following code is used to return an updated utility mapping U from each state in the MDP to its utility, using an approximation (modified policy iteration):

```
>>> def policy_evaluation(pi, STS, mdp, k=20):
...     R, T, gamma = mdp.R, mdp.T, mdp.gamma
..      for i in range(k):
...         for s in mdp.states:
...             STS[s] = R(s) + gamma * sum([p * STS[s1] for (p, s1) in T(s,
pi[s])])
...     return STS

>>> def print_table(table, header=None, sep=' ', numfmt='{}'):
...     justs = ['rjust' if isnumber(x) else 'ljust' for x in table[0]]
...     if header:
...         table.insert(0, header)
...     table = [[numfmt.format(x) if isnumber(x) else x for x in row]
...             for row in table]
...     sizes = list(map(lambda seq: max(map(len, seq)),
...                 list(zip(*[map(str, row) for row in table]))))
...     for row in table:
...         print(sep.join(getattr(str(x), j)(size) for (j, size, x)
...             in zip(justs, sizes, row)))
```

The following is the input grid of a 4 x 3 grid environment that presents the agent with a sequential decision-making problem:

```
>>> sequential_decision_environment = GridMDP([[-0.02, -0.02, -0.02, +1],
...                                            [-0.02, None, -0.02, -1],
...                                            [-0.02, -0.02, -0.02,
-0.02]],
...                                            terminals=[(3, 2), (3, 1)])
```

The following code is for performing a value iteration on the given sequential decision-making environment:

```
>>> value_iter =
best_policy(sequential_decision_environment,value_iteration
(sequential_decision_environment, .01))
>>> print("\n Optimal Policy based on Value Iteration\n")
>>> print_table(sequential_decision_environment.to_arrows(value_iter))
```

The code for policy iteration is:

```
>>> policy_iter = policy_iteration(sequential_decision_environment)
>>> print("\n Optimal Policy based on Policy Iteration & Evaluation\n")
>>> print_table(sequential_decision_environment.to_arrows(policy_iter))
```

From the preceding output with two results, we can conclude that both value and policy iterations provide the same optimal policy for an agent to move across the grid to reach the goal state in the quickest way possible. When the problem size is large enough, it is computationally advisable to go for value iteration rather than policy iteration, as in policy iterations, we need to perform two steps at every iteration of the policy evaluation and policy improvement.

Monte Carlo methods

Using **Monte Carlo (MC)** methods, we will compute the value functions first and determine the optimal policies. In this method, we do not assume complete knowledge of the environment. MC require only experience, which consists of sample sequences of states, actions, and rewards from actual or simulated interactions with the environment. Learning from actual experiences is striking because it requires no prior knowledge of the environment's dynamics, but still attains optimal behavior. This is very similar to how humans or animals learn from actual experience rather than any mathematical model. Surprisingly, in many cases it is easy to generate experience sampled according to the desired probability distributions, but infeasible to obtain the distributions in explicit form.

Monte Carlo methods solve the reinforcement learning problem based on averaging the sample returns over each episode. This means that we assume experience is divided into episodes, and that all episodes eventually terminate, no matter what actions are selected. Values are estimated and policies are changed only after the completion of each episode. MC methods are incremental in an episode-by-episode sense, but not in a step-by-step (which is an online learning, and which we will cover the same in Temporal Difference learning section) sense.

Monte Carlo methods sample and average returns for each state-action pair over the episode. However, within the same episode, the return after taking an action in one stage depends on the actions taken in later states. Because all the action selections are undergoing learning, the problem becomes non-stationary from the point of view of the earlier state. In order to handle this non-stationarity, we adapt the idea of policy iteration from dynamic programming, in which, first, we compute the value function for a fixed arbitrary policy; and, later, we improve the policy.

Comparison between dynamic programming and Monte Carlo methods

Dynamic programming requires a complete knowledge of the environment or all possible transitions, whereas Monte Carlo methods work on a sampled state-action trajectory on one episode. DP includes only one-step transition, whereas MC goes all the way to the end of the episode to the terminal node. One important fact about the MC method is that the estimates for each state are independent, which means the estimate for one state does not build upon the estimate of any other state, as in the case of DP.

Key advantages of MC over DP methods

The following are the key advantages of MC over DP methods:

- In terms of computational expense, MC methods are more attractive due to the advantage of estimating the value of single state independent of the number of states
- Many sample episodes can be generated, starting from the state of interest, averaging returns from only these states and ignoring all the other states
- MC methods have the ability to learn from actual experience or simulated experience

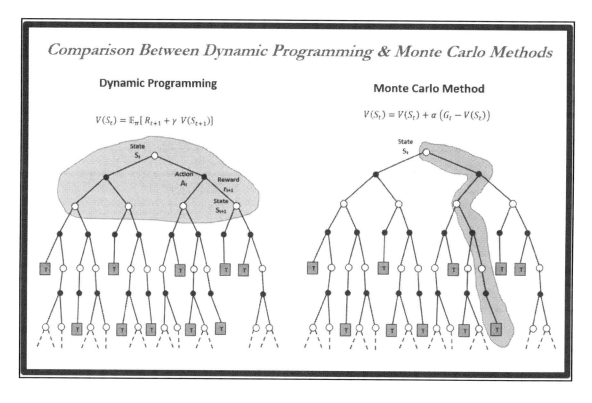

Monte Carlo prediction

As we know, Monte Carlo methods predict the state-value function for a given policy. The value of any state is the expected return or expected cumulative future discounted rewards starting from that state. These values are estimated in MC methods simply to average the returns observed after visits to that state. As more and more values are observed, the average should converge to the expected value based on the law of large numbers. In fact, this is the principle applicable in all Monte Carlo methods. The Monte Carlo Policy Evaluation Algorithm consist of the following steps:

1. Initialize:

$$\pi \leftarrow policy\ to\ be\ evaluated$$
$$V \leftarrow arbitrary\ state - value\ function$$
$$Returns(s) \leftarrow an\ empty\ list, for\ all\ s \in S$$

2. Repeat forever:
   - Generate an episode using π
   - For each state s appearing in the episode:
       - G return following the first occurrence of s
       - Append G to Returns(s)
       - V(s) average(Returns(s))

The suitability of Monte Carlo prediction on grid-world problems

The following diagram has been plotted for illustration purposes. However, practically, Monte Carlo methods cannot be easily used for solving grid-world type problems, due to the fact that termination is not guaranteed for all the policies. If a policy was ever found that caused the agent to stay in the same state, then the next episode would never end. Step-by-step learning methods like (**State-Action-Reward-State-Action** (**SARSA**), which we will be covering in a later part of this chapter in TD Learning Control) do not have this problem because they quickly learn during the episode that such policies are poor, and switch to something else.

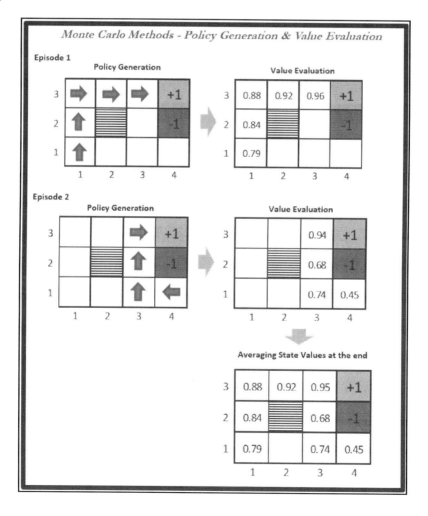

Modeling Blackjack example of Monte Carlo methods using Python

The objective of the popular casino card game Blackjack is to obtain cards, the sum of whose numerical values is as great as possible, without exceeding the value of 21. All face cards (king, queen, and jack) count as 10, and an ace can count as either 1 or as 11, depending upon the way the player wants to use it. Only the ace has this flexibility option. All the other cards are valued at face value. The game begins with two cards dealt to both dealer and players. One of the dealer's cards is face up and the other is face down. If the player has a 'Natural 21' from these first two cards (an ace and a 10-card), the player wins unless the dealer also has a Natural, in which case the game is a draw. If the player does not have a natural, then he can ask for additional cards, one by one (hits), until he either stops (sticks) or exceeds 21 (goes bust). If the player goes bust, he loses; if the player sticks, then it's the dealer's turn. The dealer hits or sticks according to a fixed strategy without choice: the dealer usually sticks on any sum of 17 or greater, and hits otherwise. If the dealer goes bust, then the player automatically wins. If he sticks, the outcome would be either win, lose, or draw, determined by whether the dealer or the player's sum total is closer to 21.

The Blackjack problem can be formulated as an episodic finite MDP, in which each game of Blackjack is an episode. Rewards of +1, -1, and 0 are given for winning, losing, and drawing for each episode respectively at the terminal state and the remaining rewards within the state of game are given the value as 0 with no discount (gamma = 1). Therefore, the terminal rewards are also the returns for this game. We draw the cards from an infinite deck so that no traceable pattern exists. The entire game is modeled in Python in the following code.

The following snippets of code have taken inspiration from *Shangtong Zhang*'s Python codes for RL, and are published in this book with permission from the student of *Richard S. Sutton*, the famous author of *Reinforcement : Learning: An Introduction* (details provided in the *Further reading* section).

The following package is imported for array manipulation and visualization:

```
>>> from __future__ import print_function
>>> import numpy as np
>>> import matplotlib.pyplot as plt
>>> from mpl_toolkits.mplot3d import Axes3D
```

At each turn, the player or dealer can take one of the actions possible: either to hit or to stand. These are the only two states possible :

```
>>> ACTION_HIT = 0
>>> ACTION_STAND = 1
>>> actions = [ACTION_HIT, ACTION_STAND]
```

The policy for player is modeled with 21 arrays of values, as the player will get bust after going over the value of 21:

```
>>> policyPlayer = np.zeros(22)

>>> for i in range(12, 20):
...         policyPlayer[i] = ACTION_HIT
```

The player has taken the policy of stick if he gets a value of either 20 or 21, or else he will keep hitting the deck to draw a new card:

```
>>> policyPlayer[20] = ACTION_STAND
>>> policyPlayer[21] = ACTION_STAND
```

Function form of target policy of a player:

```
>>> def targetPolicyPlayer(usableAcePlayer, playerSum, dealerCard):
...         return policyPlayer[playerSum]
```

Function form of behavior policy of a player:

```
>>> def behaviorPolicyPlayer(usableAcePlayer, playerSum, dealerCard):
...         if np.random.binomial(1, 0.5) == 1:
...             return ACTION_STAND
...         return ACTION_HIT
```

Fixed policy for the dealer is to keep hitting the deck until value is 17 and then stick between 17 to 21:

```
>>> policyDealer = np.zeros(22)
>>> for i in range(12, 17):
...         policyDealer[i] = ACTION_HIT
>>> for i in range(17, 22):
...         policyDealer[i] = ACTION_STAND
```

The following function is used for drawing a new card from the deck with replacement:

```
>>> def getCard():
...     card = np.random.randint(1, 14)
...     card = min(card, 10)
...     return card
```

Let's play the game!

```
>>> def play(policyPlayerFn, initialState=None, initialAction=None):
```

1. Sum of the player, player's trajectory and whether player uses ace as 11:

```
...         playerSum = 0
...         playerTrajectory = []
...         usableAcePlayer = False
```

2. Dealer status of drawing cards:

```
...         dealerCard1 = 0
...         dealerCard2 = 0
...         usableAceDealer = False

...         if initialState is None:
```

3. Generate a random initial state:

```
...             numOfAce = 0
```

4. Initializing the player's cards:

```
...             while playerSum < 12:
```

5. If the sum of a player's cards is less than 12, always hit the deck for drawing card:

```
...                 card = getCard()
...                 if card == 1:
...                     numOfAce += 1
...                     card = 11
...                     usableAcePlayer = True
...                 playerSum += card
```

6. If the player's sum is larger than 21, he must hold at least one ace, but two aces is also possible. In that case, he will use ace as 1 rather than 11. If the player has only one ace, then he does not have a usable ace any more:

```
...            if playerSum > 21:
...                playerSum -= 10
...                if numOfAce == 1:
...                    usableAcePlayer = False
```

7. Initializing the dealer cards:

```
...            dealerCard1 = getCard()
...            dealerCard2 = getCard()

...        else:
...            usableAcePlayer = initialState[0]
...            playerSum = initialState[1]
...            dealerCard1 = initialState[2]
...            dealerCard2 = getCard()
```

8. Initialize the game state:

```
...        state = [usableAcePlayer, playerSum, dealerCard1]
```

9. Initializing the dealer's sum:

```
...        dealerSum = 0
...        if dealerCard1 == 1 and dealerCard2 != 1:
...            dealerSum += 11 + dealerCard2
...            usableAceDealer = True
...        elif dealerCard1 != 1 and dealerCard2 == 1:
...            dealerSum += dealerCard1 + 11
...            usableAceDealer = True
...        elif dealerCard1 == 1 and dealerCard2 == 1:
...            dealerSum += 1 + 11
...            usableAceDealer = True
...        else:
...            dealerSum += dealerCard1 + dealerCard2
```

10. The game starts from here, as the player needs to draw extra cards from here onwards:

```
...         while True:
...             if initialAction is not None:
...                 action = initialAction
...                 initialAction = None
...             else:
```

11. Get action based on the current sum of a player:

```
...                 action = policyPlayerFn(usableAcePlayer, playerSum,
dealerCard1)
```

12. Tracking the player's trajectory for importance sampling:

```
...                 playerTrajectory.append([action, (usableAcePlayer,
playerSum, dealerCard1)])

...                 if action == ACTION_STAND:
...                     break
```

13. Get new a card if the action is to hit the deck:

```
...                 playerSum += getCard()
```

14. Player busts here if the total sum is greater than 21, the game ends, and he gets a reward of -1. However, if he has an ace at his disposable, he can use it to save the game, or else he will lose.

```
...                 if playerSum > 21:
...                     if usableAcePlayer == True:
...                         playerSum -= 10
...                         usableAcePlayer = False
...                     else:
...                         return state, -1, playerTrajectory
```

15. Now it's the dealer's turn. He will draw cards based on a sum: if he reaches 17, he will stop, otherwise keep on drawing cards. If the dealer also has ace, he can use it to achieve the bust situation, otherwise he goes bust:

```
...         while True:
...             action = policyDealer[dealerSum]
...             if action == ACTION_STAND:
...                 break
...             dealerSum += getCard()
...             if dealerSum > 21:
```

```
...                          if usableAceDealer == True:
...                              dealerSum -= 10
...                              usableAceDealer = False
...                          else:
...                              return state, 1, playerTrajectory
```

16. Now we compare the player's sum with the dealer's sum to decide who wins without going bust:

```
...          if playerSum > dealerSum:
...              return state, 1, playerTrajectory
...          elif playerSum == dealerSum:
...              return state, 0, playerTrajectory
...          else:
...              return state, -1, playerTrajectory
```

The following code illustrates the Monte Carlo sample with *On-Policy*:

```
>>> def monteCarloOnPolicy(nEpisodes):
...         statesUsableAce = np.zeros((10, 10))
...         statesUsableAceCount = np.ones((10, 10))
...         statesNoUsableAce = np.zeros((10, 10))
...         statesNoUsableAceCount = np.ones((10, 10))
...         for i in range(0, nEpisodes):
...             state, reward, _ = play(targetPolicyPlayer)
...             state[1] -= 12
...             state[2] -= 1
...             if state[0]:
...                 statesUsableAceCount[state[1], state[2]] += 1
...                 statesUsableAce[state[1], state[2]] += reward
...             else:
...                 statesNoUsableAceCount[state[1], state[2]] += 1
...                 statesNoUsableAce[state[1], state[2]] += reward
...         return statesUsableAce / statesUsableAceCount, statesNoUsableAce /
statesNoUsableAceCount
```

The following code discusses Monte Carlo with Exploring Starts, in which all the returns for each state-action pair are accumulated and averaged, irrespective of what policy was in force when they were observed:

```
>>> def monteCarloES(nEpisodes):
...         stateActionValues = np.zeros((10, 10, 2, 2))
...         stateActionPairCount = np.ones((10, 10, 2, 2))
```

Behavior policy is greedy, which gets `argmax` of the average returns (s, a):

```
...         def behaviorPolicy(usableAce, playerSum, dealerCard):
...             usableAce = int(usableAce)
...             playerSum -= 12
...             dealerCard -= 1
...             return np.argmax(stateActionValues[playerSum, dealerCard,
usableAce, :]
                        / stateActionPairCount[playerSum, dealerCard,
usableAce, :])
```

Play continues for several episodes and, at each episode, randomly initialized state, action, and update values of state-action pairs:

```
...         for episode in range(nEpisodes):
...             if episode % 1000 == 0:
...                 print('episode:', episode)
...             initialState = [bool(np.random.choice([0, 1])),
                            np.random.choice(range(12, 22)),
                            np.random.choice(range(1, 11))]
...             initialAction = np.random.choice(actions)
...             _, reward, trajectory = play(behaviorPolicy, initialState,
initialAction)
...             for action, (usableAce, playerSum, dealerCard) in trajectory:
...                 usableAce = int(usableAce)
...                 playerSum -= 12
...                 dealerCard -= 1
```

Update values of state-action pairs:

```
...                 stateActionValues[playerSum, dealerCard, usableAce, action]
+= reward
...                 stateActionPairCount[playerSum, dealerCard, usableAce,
action] += 1
...         return stateActionValues / stateActionPairCount
```

Print the state value:

```
>>> figureIndex = 0
>>> def prettyPrint(data, tile, zlabel='reward'):
...     global figureIndex
...     fig = plt.figure(figureIndex)
...     figureIndex += 1
...     fig.suptitle(tile)
...     ax = fig.add_subplot(111, projection='3d')
...     x_axis = []
...     y_axis = []
...     z_axis = []
```

```
...        for i in range(12, 22):
...            for j in range(1, 11):
...                x_axis.append(i)
...                y_axis.append(j)
...                z_axis.append(data[i - 12, j - 1])
...        ax.scatter(x_axis, y_axis, z_axis,c='red')
...        ax.set_xlabel('player sum')
...        ax.set_ylabel('dealer showing')
...        ax.set_zlabel(zlabel)
```

On-Policy results with or without a usable ace for 10,000 and 500,000 iterations:

```
>>> def onPolicy():
...        statesUsableAce1, statesNoUsableAce1 = monteCarloOnPolicy(10000)
...        statesUsableAce2, statesNoUsableAce2 = monteCarloOnPolicy(500000)
...        prettyPrint(statesUsableAce1, 'Usable Ace & 10000 Episodes')
...        prettyPrint(statesNoUsableAce1, 'No Usable Ace & 10000 Episodes')
...        prettyPrint(statesUsableAce2, 'Usable Ace & 500000 Episodes')
...        prettyPrint(statesNoUsableAce2, 'No Usable Ace & 500000 Episodes')
...        plt.show()
```

Optimized or Monte Carlo control of policy iterations:

```
>>> def MC_ES_optimalPolicy():
...        stateActionValues = monteCarloES(500000)
...        stateValueUsableAce = np.zeros((10, 10))
...        stateValueNoUsableAce = np.zeros((10, 10))
    # get the optimal policy
...        actionUsableAce = np.zeros((10, 10), dtype='int')
...        actionNoUsableAce = np.zeros((10, 10), dtype='int')
...        for i in range(10):
...            for j in range(10):
...                stateValueNoUsableAce[i, j] = np.max(stateActionValues[i,
j, 0, :])
...                stateValueUsableAce[i, j] = np.max(stateActionValues[i, j,
1, :])
...                actionNoUsableAce[i, j] = np.argmax(stateActionValues[i, j,
0, :])
...                actionUsableAce[i, j] = np.argmax(stateActionValues[i, j,
1, :])
...        prettyPrint(stateValueUsableAce, 'Optimal state value with usable
Ace')
...        prettyPrint(stateValueNoUsableAce, 'Optimal state value with no
usable Ace')
...        prettyPrint(actionUsableAce, 'Optimal policy with usable Ace',
'Action (0 Hit, 1 Stick)')
...        prettyPrint(actionNoUsableAce, 'Optimal policy with no usable Ace',
'Action (0 Hit, 1 Stick)')
```

```
...        plt.show()

# Run on-policy function
>>> onPolicy()
```

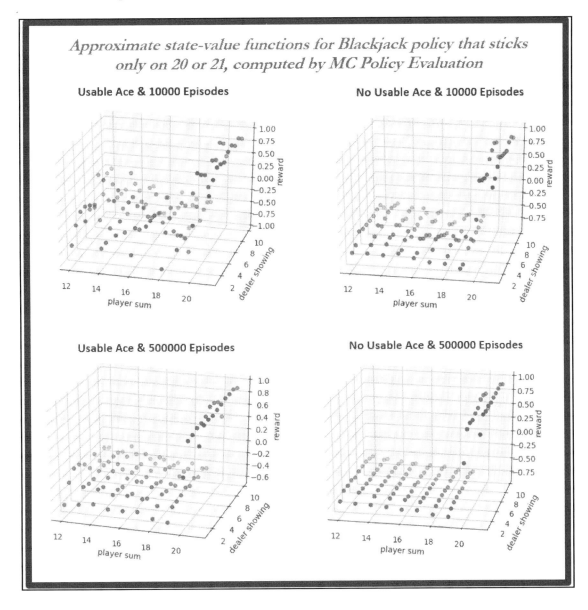

From the previous diagram, we can conclude that a usable ace in a hand gives much higher rewards even at the low player sum combinations, whereas for a player without a usable ace, values are pretty distinguished in terms of earned reward if those values are less than 20.

```
# Run Monte Carlo Control or Explored starts
>>> MC_ES_optimalPolicy()
```

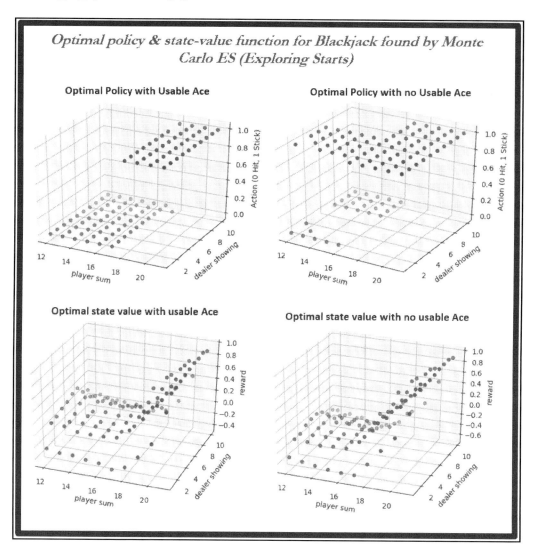

From the optimum policies and state values, we can conclude that, with a usable ace at our disposal, we can hit more than stick, and also that the state values for rewards are much higher compared with when there is no ace in a hand. Though the results we are talking about are obvious, we can see the magnitude of the impact of holding an ace in a hand.

Temporal difference learning

Temporal Difference (TD) learning is the central and novel theme of reinforcement learning. TD learning is the combination of both **Monte Carlo (MC)** and **Dynamic Programming (DP)** ideas. Like Monte Carlo methods, TD methods can learn directly from the experiences without the model of environment. Similar to Dynamic Programming, TD methods update estimates based in part on other learned estimates, without waiting for a final outcome, unlike MC methods, in which estimates are updated after reaching the final outcome only.

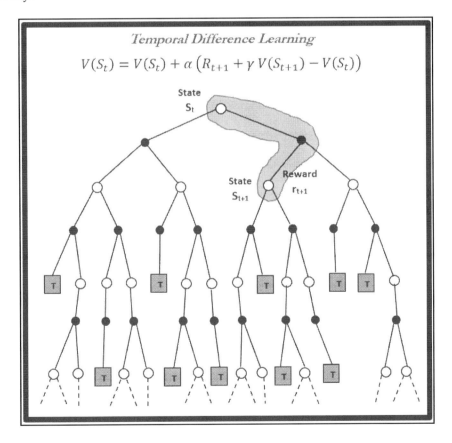

Comparison between Monte Carlo methods and temporal difference learning

Though Monte-Carlo methods and Temporal Difference learning have similarities, there are inherent advantages of TD-learning over Monte Carlo methods.

Monte Carlo methods	Temporal Difference learning
MC must wait until the end of the episode before the return is known.	TD can learn online after every step and does not need to wait until the end of episode.
MC has high variance and low bias.	TD has low variance and some decent bias.
MC does not exploit the Markov property.	TD exploits the Markov property.

TD prediction

Both TD and MC use experience to solve z prediction problem. Given some policy π, both methods update their estimate v of v_π for the non-terminal states S_t occurring in that experience. Monte Carlo methods wait until the return following the visit is known, then use that return as a target for $V(S_t)$.

$$V(S_t) \leftarrow V(S_t) + \alpha \left[G_t - V(S_t) \right]$$
$G_t - actual\ return\ following\ time\ t\ ;\ \alpha - constant\ step\ size\ parameter$

The preceding method can be called as a constant - α MC, where MC must wait until the end of the episode to determine the increment to $V(S_t)$ (only then is G_t known).

TD methods need to wait only until the next timestep. At time $t+1$, they immediately form a target and make a useful update using the observed reward R_{t+1} and the estimate $V(S_{t+1})$. The simplest TD method, known as *TD(0)*, is:

$$V(S_t) \leftarrow V(S_t) + \alpha \left[R_{t+1} + \gamma\, V(S_{t+1}) - V(S_t) \right]$$

Target for MC update is G_t, whereas the target for the TD update is $R_{t+1} + y\, V(S_{t+1})$.

In the following diagram, a comparison has been made between TD with MC methods. As we've written in equation TD(0), we use one step of real data and then use the estimated value of the value function of next state. In a similar way, we can also use two steps of real data to get a better picture of the reality and estimate value function of the third stage.

However, as we increase the steps, which eventually need more and more data to perform parameter updates, the more time it will cost. When we take infinite steps until it touches the terminal point for updating parameters in each episode, TD becomes the Monte Carlo method.

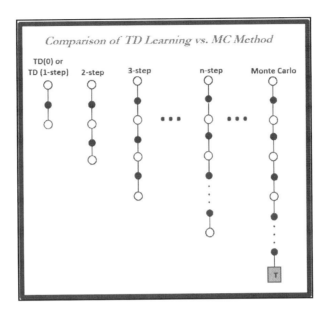

TD (0) for estimating v algorithm consists of the following steps:

1. Initialize:

   Input policy to be evaluated $\rightarrow \pi$
   Initialize arbitrary state $-$ value function $\rightarrow V(s)$ *(e.g:* $V(s) = 0, \forall s \in S^+$)

2. Repeat (for each episode):
   - Initialize S
   - Repeat (for each step of episode):
     - A <- action given by π for S
     - Take action A, observe R,S'
     - $V(S) \leftarrow V(S) + \alpha\,[R + \gamma\,V(S') - V(S)]$
     - $S \leftarrow S'$

3. Until S is terminal.

Driving office example for TD learning

In this simple example, you travel from home to the office every day and you try to predict how long it will take to get to the office in the morning. When you leave your home, you note that time, the day of the week, the weather (whether it is rainy, windy, and so on) any other parameter which you feel is relevant. For example, on Monday morning you leave at exactly 8 a.m. and you estimate it takes 40 minutes to reach the office. At 8:10 a.m., and you notice that a VIP is passing, and you need to wait until the complete convoy has moved out, so you re-estimate that it will take 45 minutes from then, or a total of 55 minutes. Fifteen minutes later you have completed the highway portion of your journey in good time. Now you enter a bypass road and you now reduce your estimate of total travel time to 50 minutes. Unfortunately, at this point, you get stuck behind a bunch of bullock carts and the road is too narrow to pass. You end up having to follow those bullock carts until you turn onto the side street where your office is located at 8:50. Seven minutes later, you reach your office parking. The sequence of states, times, and predictions are as follows:

State	Elapsed Time (minutes)	Predicted Time to Go	Predicted Total Time
leaving home, Monday at 8 a.m.	0	40	40
reaching car, minister convoy passes by	10	45	55
exiting highway	25	25	50
by pass road, behind bullockcarts	30	20	50
entering office street	50	7	57
arrive office parking space	57	0	57

Rewards in this example are the elapsed time at each leg of the journey and we are using a discount factor (gamma, $v = 1$), so the return for each state is the actual time to go from that state to the destination (office). The value of each state is the predicted time to go, which is the second column in the preceding table, also known the current estimated value for each state encountered.

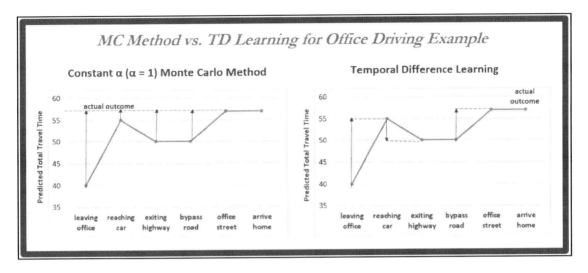

In the previous diagram, Monte Carlo is used to plot the predicted total time over the sequence of events. Arrows always show the change in predictions recommended by the constant-α MC method. These are errors between the estimated value in each stage and the actual return (57 minutes). In the MC method, learning happens only after finishing, for which it needs to wait until 57 minutes passed. However, in reality, you can estimate before reaching the final outcome and correct your estimates accordingly. TD works on the same principle, at every stage it tries to predict and correct the estimates accordingly. So, TD methods learn immediately and do not need to wait until the final outcome. In fact, that is how humans predict in real life. Because of these many positive properties, TD learning is considered as novel in reinforcement learning.

SARSA on-policy TD control

State-action-reward-state-action (SARSA) is an on-policy TD control problem, in which policy will be optimized using policy iteration (GPI), only time TD methods used for evaluation of predicted policy. In the first step, the algorithm learns an SARSA function. In particular, for an on-policy method we estimate $q_\pi\ (s, a)$ for the current behavior policy π and for all states (s) and actions (a), using the TD method for learning v_π. Now, we consider transitions from state-action pair to state-action pair, and learn the values of state-action pairs:

$$Q(S, A) \leftarrow Q(S, A) + \alpha\ [R + \gamma\ Q(S', A) - Q(S, A)]$$

This update is done after every transition from a non-terminal state S_t. If S_{t+1} is terminal, then $Q\ (S_{t+1},\ A_{t+1})$ is defined as zero. This rule uses every element of the quintuple of events $(S_t,\ A_t,\ Rt,\ St_{+1},\ A_{t+1})$, which make up a transition from one state-action pair to the next. This quintuple gives rise to the name SARSA for the algorithm.

As in all on-policy methods, we continually estimate q_π for the behavior policy π, and at the same time change π toward greediness with respect to q_π. The algorithm for computation of SARSA is given as follows:

1. Initialize:

$$Q(s, a), \forall\ s \in S, a \in A(s),\ arbitrarily, and\ Q(terminal - state, .) = 0$$

2. Repeat (for each episode):
   - Initialize S
   - Choose A from S using policy derived from Q (for example, ε- greedy)
   - Repeat (for each step of episode):
     - Take action A, observe R,S'
     - Choose A' from using S' policy derived from Q (for example, ε - greedy)
     - $Q(S, A) \leftarrow Q(S, A)\ + \alpha\ [R\ + \gamma\ Q(S', A)\ - Q(S, A)]$
     - $S \leftarrow\ S'; A \leftarrow\ A'$

3. Until S is terminal

Q-learning - off-policy TD control

Q-learning is the most popular method used in practical applications for many reinforcement learning problems. The off-policy TD control algorithm is known as Q-learning. In this case, the learned action-value function, Q directly approximates q_*, the optimal action-value function, independent of the policy being followed. This approximation simplifies the analysis of the algorithm and enables early convergence proofs. The policy still has an effect, in that it determines which state-action pairs are visited and updated. However, all that is required for correct convergence is that all pairs continue to be updated. As we know, this is a minimal requirement in the sense that any method guaranteed to find optimal behavior in the general case must require it. An algorithm of convergence is shown in the following steps:

1. Initialize:

$$Q(s,a), \forall s \in S, a \in A(s), \; arbitrarily, and \; Q(terminal - state, .) = 0$$

2. Repeat (for each episode):
     - Initialize S
     - Repeat (for each step of episode):
          - Choose A from S using policy derived from Q (for example, ε - greedy)
          - Take action A, observe R,S'
          - $Q(S,A) \leftarrow Q(S,A) + \alpha [R + \gamma Q(S',A) - Q(S,A)]$
          - $S \leftarrow S'; A \leftarrow A'$

3. Until S is terminal

Cliff walking example of on-policy and off-policy of TD control

A cliff walking grid-world example is used to compare SARSA and Q-learning, to highlight the differences between on-policy (SARSA) and off-policy (Q-learning) methods. This is a standard undiscounted, episodic task with start and end goal states, and with permitted movements in four directions (north, west, east and south). The reward of -1 is used for all transitions except the regions marked *The Cliff*, stepping on this region will penalize the agent with reward of -100 and sends the agent instantly back to the start position.

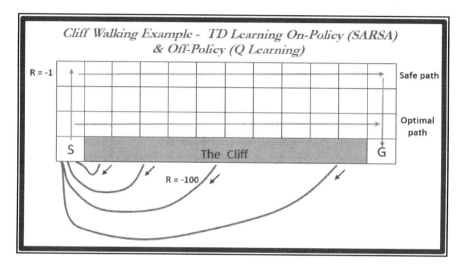

The following snippets of code have taken inspiration from Shangtong Zhang's Python codes for RL and are published in this book with permission from the student of *Richard S. Sutton*, the famous author of *Reinforcement Learning: An Introduction* (details provided in the *Further reading* section):

```
# Cliff-Walking - TD learning - SARSA & Q-learning
>>> from __future__ import print_function
>>> import numpy as np
>>> import matplotlib.pyplot as plt

# Grid dimensions
>>> GRID_HEIGHT = 4
>>> GRID_WIDTH = 12

# probability for exploration, step size,gamma
>>> EPSILON = 0.1
>>> ALPHA = 0.5
```

```
>>> GAMMA = 1

# all possible actions
>>> ACTION_UP = 0; ACTION_DOWN = 1;ACTION_LEFT = 2;ACTION_RIGHT = 3
>>> actions = [ACTION_UP, ACTION_DOWN, ACTION_LEFT, ACTION_RIGHT]

# initial state action pair values
>>> stateActionValues = np.zeros((GRID_HEIGHT, GRID_WIDTH, 4))
>>> startState = [3, 0]
>>> goalState = [3, 11]

# reward for each action in each state
>>> actionRewards = np.zeros((GRID_HEIGHT, GRID_WIDTH, 4))
>>> actionRewards[:, :, :] = -1.0
>>> actionRewards[2, 1:11, ACTION_DOWN] = -100.0
>>> actionRewards[3, 0, ACTION_RIGHT] = -100.0

# set up destinations for each action in each state
>>> actionDestination = []
>>> for i in range(0, GRID_HEIGHT):
...     actionDestination.append([])
...     for j in range(0, GRID_WIDTH):
...         destinaion = dict()
...         destinaion[ACTION_UP] = [max(i - 1, 0), j]
...         destinaion[ACTION_LEFT] = [i, max(j - 1, 0)]
...         destinaion[ACTION_RIGHT] = [i, min(j + 1, GRID_WIDTH - 1)]
...         if i == 2 and 1 <= j <= 10:
...             destinaion[ACTION_DOWN] = startState
...         else:
...             destinaion[ACTION_DOWN] = [min(i + 1, GRID_HEIGHT - 1), j]
...         actionDestination[-1].append(destinaion)
>>> actionDestination[3][0][ACTION_RIGHT] = startState

# choose an action based on epsilon greedy algorithm
>>> def chooseAction(state, stateActionValues):
...     if np.random.binomial(1, EPSILON) == 1:
...         return np.random.choice(actions)
...     else:
...         return np.argmax(stateActionValues[state[0], state[1], :])


# SARSA update

>>> def sarsa(stateActionValues, expected=False, stepSize=ALPHA):
...     currentState = startState
...     currentAction = chooseAction(currentState, stateActionValues)
...     rewards = 0.0
...     while currentState != goalState:
```

```
...              newState = actionDestination[currentState[0]][currentState[1]]
[currentAction]

...              newAction = chooseAction(newState, stateActionValues)
...              reward = actionRewards[currentState[0], currentState[1],
currentAction]
...          rewards += reward
...          if not expected:
...              valueTarget = stateActionValues[newState[0], newState[1],
newAction]
...          else:
...              valueTarget = 0.0
...              actionValues = stateActionValues[newState[0], newState[1],
:]
...              bestActions = np.argwhere(actionValues ==
np.max(actionValues))
...              for action in actions:
...                  if action in bestActions:

...                      valueTarget += ((1.0 - EPSILON) / len(bestActions)
+ EPSILON / len(actions)) * stateActionValues[newState[0], newState[1],
action]

...                  else:
...                      valueTarget += EPSILON / len(actions) *
stateActionValues[newState[0], newState[1], action]
...              valueTarget *= GAMMA
...          stateActionValues[currentState[0], currentState[1],
currentAction] += stepSize * (reward+ valueTarget -
stateActionValues[currentState[0], currentState[1], currentAction])
...          currentState = newState
...          currentAction = newAction
...      return rewards


# Q-learning update
>>> def qlearning(stateActionValues, stepSize=ALPHA):
...      currentState = startState
...      rewards = 0.0
...      while currentState != goalState:
...          currentAction = chooseAction(currentState, stateActionValues)
...          reward = actionRewards[currentState[0], currentState[1],
currentAction]
...          rewards += reward
...          newState = actionDestination[currentState[0]][currentState[1]]
[currentAction]
...          stateActionValues[currentState[0], currentState[1],
currentAction] += stepSize * (reward + GAMMA *
np.max(stateActionValues[newState[0], newState[1], :]) -
```

```
...                    stateActionValues[currentState[0], currentState[1],
currentAction])
...             currentState = newState
...         return rewards


# print optimal policy
>>> def printOptimalPolicy(stateActionValues):
...         optimalPolicy = []
...         for i in range(0, GRID_HEIGHT):
...             optimalPolicy.append([])
...             for j in range(0, GRID_WIDTH):
...                 if [i, j] == goalState:
...                     optimalPolicy[-1].append('G')
...                     continue
...                 bestAction = np.argmax(stateActionValues[i, j, :])
...                 if bestAction == ACTION_UP:
...                     optimalPolicy[-1].append('U')
...                 elif bestAction == ACTION_DOWN:
...                     optimalPolicy[-1].append('D')
...                 elif bestAction == ACTION_LEFT:
...                     optimalPolicy[-1].append('L')
...                 elif bestAction == ACTION_RIGHT:
...                     optimalPolicy[-1].append('R')
...         for row in optimalPolicy:
...             print(row)


>>> def SARSAnQLPlot():
    # averaging the reward sums from 10 successive episodes
...         averageRange = 10

    # episodes of each run
...         nEpisodes = 500

    # perform 20 independent runs
...         runs = 20

...         rewardsSarsa = np.zeros(nEpisodes)
...         rewardsQlearning = np.zeros(nEpisodes)
...         for run in range(0, runs):
...             stateActionValuesSarsa = np.copy(stateActionValues)
...             stateActionValuesQlearning = np.copy(stateActionValues)
...             for i in range(0, nEpisodes):
                # cut off the value by -100 to draw the figure more elegantly
...                 rewardsSarsa[i] += max(sarsa(stateActionValuesSarsa), -100)
...                 rewardsQlearning[i] +=
max(qlearning(stateActionValuesQlearning), -100)
```

```
    # averaging over independent runs
...     rewardsSarsa /= runs
...     rewardsQlearning /= runs

    # averaging over successive episodes
...     smoothedRewardsSarsa = np.copy(rewardsSarsa)
...     smoothedRewardsQlearning = np.copy(rewardsQlearning)
...     for i in range(averageRange, nEpisodes):
...         smoothedRewardsSarsa[i] = np.mean(rewardsSarsa[i -
averageRange: i + 1])
...         smoothedRewardsQlearning[i] = np.mean(rewardsQlearning[i -
averageRange: i + 1])

    # display optimal policy
...     print('Sarsa Optimal Policy:')
...     printOptimalPolicy(stateActionValuesSarsa)
...     print('Q-learning Optimal Policy:')
...     printOptimalPolicy(stateActionValuesQlearning)

    # draw reward curves
...     plt.figure(1)
...     plt.plot(smoothedRewardsSarsa, label='Sarsa')
...     plt.plot(smoothedRewardsQlearning, label='Q-learning')
...     plt.xlabel('Episodes')
...     plt.ylabel('Sum of rewards during episode')
...     plt.legend()


# Sum of Rewards for SARSA versus Qlearning
>>> SARSAnQLPlot()
```

```
Sarsa Optimal Policy:
['R', 'R', 'R', 'R', 'R', 'R', 'R', 'R', 'D', 'R', 'R', 'D']
['U', 'U', 'U', 'U', 'R', 'U', 'U', 'R', 'D', 'R', 'U', 'D']
['R', 'R', 'R', 'U', 'U', 'R', 'U', 'U', 'R', 'R', 'R', 'D']
['U', 'U', 'U', 'U', 'U', 'U', 'U', 'U', 'U', 'U', 'U', 'G']
Q-Learning Optimal Policy:
['D', 'R', 'D', 'R', 'R', 'D', 'R', 'D', 'D', 'D', 'D', 'D']
['R', 'R', 'R', 'R', 'R', 'D', 'D', 'D', 'R', 'D', 'D', 'D']
['R', 'R', 'R', 'R', 'R', 'R', 'R', 'R', 'R', 'R', 'R', 'D']
['U', 'U', 'U', 'U', 'U', 'U', 'U', 'U', 'U', 'U', 'U', 'G']
```

After an initial transient, Q-learning learns the value of optimal policy to walk along the optimal path, in which the agent travels right along the edge of the cliff. Unfortunately, this will result in occasionally falling off the cliff because of ε-greedy action selection. Whereas SARSA, on the other hand, takes the action selection into account and learns the longer and safer path through the upper part of the grid. Although Q-learning learns the value of the optimal policy, its online performance is worse than that of the SARSA, which learns the roundabout and safest policy. Even if we observe the following sum of rewards displayed in the following diagram, SARSA has a less negative sum of rewards during the episode than Q-learning.

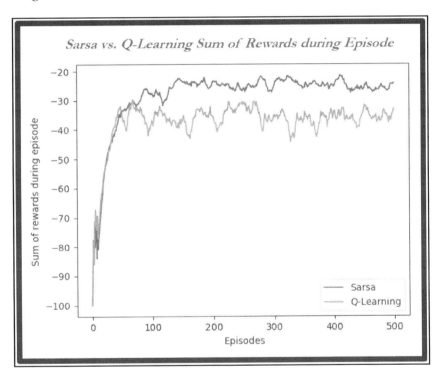

Applications of reinforcement learning with integration of machine learning and deep learning

Reinforcement learning combined with machine learning, or deep learning, has created state-of-the-art artificial intelligence solutions for various cutting-edge problems in recent times. A complete explanation with code examples is beyond the scope of this book, but we will give you a high-level view of what is inside these technologies. The following are the most popular and known recent trends in this field, but the applications are not just restricted to these:

- Automotive vehicle control (self-driving cars)
- Google DeepMind AlphaGo for playing Go games
- Robotics (with a soccer example)

Automotive vehicle control - self-driving cars

Self-driving cars are the new trend in the industry and many tech giants are working in this area now. Deep learning technologies, like convolutional neural networks, are used to learn Q-functions which control the actions, like moving forward, backward, taking left and right turns, and so on, by mixing and matching from the available action space. The entire algorithm is called a **DQN (DeepQ Network)**. This approach can be used in playing games like Atari, racing, and so on. For complete details, please refer to the paper *Deep Reinforcement Learning for Simulated Autonomous Vehicle Control* by *April Yu, Raphael Palesfky-Smith*, and *Rishi Bedi* from Stanford University.

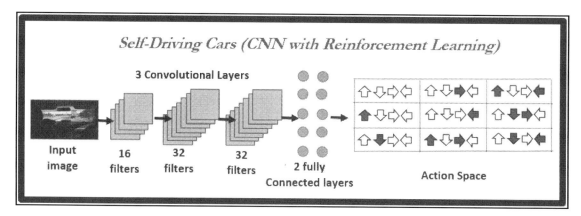

Google DeepMind's AlphaGo

Google DeepMind's AlphaGo is a new sensation in the field of artificial intelligence, as many industry experts had predicted that it would take about 10 years to beat human players but AlphaGo's victory against humans has proved them wrong. The main complexity of Go is due to its exhaustive search space: let's say b is game's breadth, and d is its depth, which means the combinations to explore for Go are ($b{\sim}250$, $d{\sim}150$), whereas for chess they are ($b{\sim}35$, $d{\sim}80$). This makes clear the difference in complexity of Go over chess. In fact, IBM Deep Blue beat Garry Kasparov in 1997 using a brute force or exhaustive search technique, which is not possible with the a game of Go.

AlphaGo uses value networks to evaluate the board positions and policy networks to select moves. Neural networks play Go at the level of state-of-the-art Monte-Carlo tree search programs used to simulate and estimate the value of each state in a search tree. For further reading, please refer to the paper *Mastering the Game of Go with Deep Neural Networks and Tree Search*, by *David Silver et al*, from *Google DeepMind*.

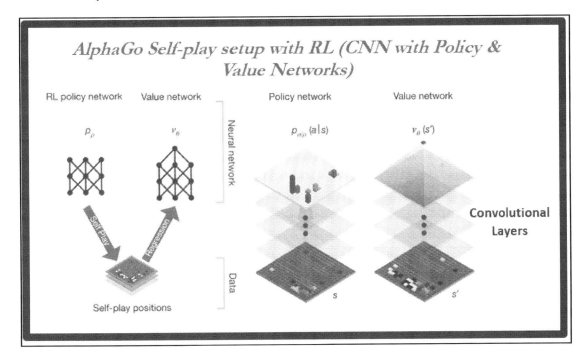

Robo soccer

Robotics as a reinforcement learning domain differs considerably from most well-studied reinforcement learning standard problems. Problems in robotics are often best represented with high-dimensional, continuous states and actions. 10-30 dimensional continuous actions common in robot reinforcement learning are considered large. The application of reinforcement learning on robotics involves so many sets of challenges, including a noise-free environment, taking into consideration real physical systems, and learning by real-world experience could be costly. As a result, algorithms or processes needs to be robust enough to do what is necessary. In addition, the generation of reward values and reward functions for the environments that guide the learning system would be difficult.

Though there are multiple ways to model robotic reinforcement learning, one applied value function approximation method used multi-layer perceptrons to learn various sub-tasks, such as learning defenses, interception, position control, kicking, motor speed control, dribbling, and penalty shots. For further details, refer to the paper *Reinforcement Learning in Robotics: A Survey*, by *Jens Kober*, *Andrew Bagnell*, and *Jan Peters*.

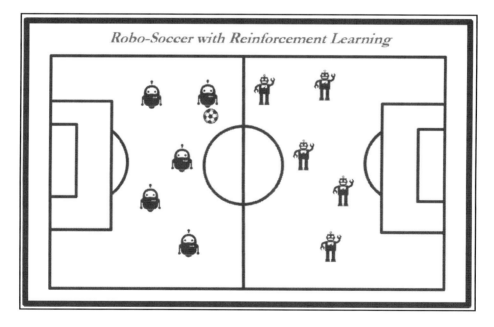

There is much to cover, and this book serves as an introduction to reinforcement learning rather than an exhaustive discussion. For interested readers, please look through the resources in the *Further reading* section. We hope you will enjoy it!

Further reading

There are many classic resources available for reinforcement learning, and we encourage the reader to go through them:

- R.S. Sutton and A.G. Barto, *Reinforcement Learning: An Introduction. MIT Press,* Cambridge, MA, USA, 1998
- *RL Course* by *David Silver* from YouTube: `https://www.youtube.com/watch?v=2pWv7GOvuf0&list=PL7-jPKtc4r78-wCZcQn5IqyuWhBZ8fOxT`
- *Machine Learning* (Stanford) by *Andrew NG* form YouTube (Lectures 16- 20): `https://www.youtube.com/watch?v=UzxYlbK2c7E&list=PLA89DCFA6ADACE599`
- *Algorithms for reinforcement learning* by *Csaba* from *Morgan & Claypool* Publishers
- *Artificial Intelligence: A Modern Approach* 3rd Edition, by *Stuart Russell* and *Peter Norvig, Prentice Hall*

Summary

In this chapter, you've learned various reinforcement learning techniques, like Markov decision process, Bellman equations, dynamic programming, Monte Carlo methods, Temporal Difference learning, including both on-policy (SARSA) and off-policy (Q-learning), with Python examples to understand its implementation in a practical way. You also learned how Q-learning is being used in many practical applications nowadays, as this method learns from trial and error by interacting with environments.

Next, we looked at some other practical applications for reinforcement learning with machine learning, and deep learning utilized to solve state-of-the-art problems.

Finally, *Further reading* has been provided for you if you would like to pursue reinforcement learning full-time. We wish you all the best!

Index

Printed in Great Britain
by Amazon